In the Kingdom of Shadows

In the Kingdom of Shadows

A Companion to Early Cinema

Colin Harding and Simon Popple

cygnus arts

London Cygnus Arts
Madison & Teaneck Fairleigh Dickinson University Press

Published in the United Kingdom by
Cygnus Arts (a division of Golden Cockerel Press)
16 Barter Street, London WC1A 2AH

Published in the United States of America by
Fairleigh Dickinson University Press,
440 Forsgate Drive, Cranbury, NJ 08512

First published 1996

ISBN 1 900541 05 X

Library of Congress Cataloguing-in-Publication Data

In the kingdom of shadows : a companion to early cinema / [edited by] Colin Harding
and Simon Popple.
    p.   cm.
    Includes bibliographical references.
    ISBN 0–8386–3274–8 (alk. paper)
    1. Motion pictures—Great Britain—History. 2. Silent films—Great Britain—
History and criticism.
I. Harding, Colin. II. Popple, Simon.
PN1993.5.G7I5 1996
791.43'0841—dc20   98–25744
                                     CIP

British Library Cataloguing-in-Publication Data

Harding, Colin
In the kingdom of shadows : a companion to early cinema
1.Motion pictures—Great Britain—History 2.Motion picture industry—Great Britain
—History 3.Motion pictures—Social aspects—Great Britain
I.Title II.Popple, Simon
791.4'3'0941

Published with the co-operation of

**The National Museum of Photography, Film & Television
is a part of the National Museum of Science and Industry**

Printed and bound in Slovenia by Gorenjski Tisk

CONTENTS

A WONDERFUL INVENTION
THE CINÉMATOGRAPHE OF M. LUMIÈRE

. . . M. Lumière's five-syllabled invention is yet in its infancy; its possibilities are almost awe-inspiring. At present the photographs are no bigger than postage stamps, and thrown life-size on to the screen, they inevitably lose certain details. When practice has brought about perfection, where will the invention stop? Imagine it worked in connection with the phonograph. The past will become annihilated; our great parliamentary debates, our monster meetings, our operatic and theatrical performances, will remain forever, or even longer. I do not dare to think of the scientific and medical possibilities, but am content to dwell on the more popular ones.

The Sketch, 18 March 1896

Foreword

by Rachael Low

A HUNDRED YEARS AGO THE WORK OF INVENTORS in the two fields of photography and of optical toys exploiting the persistence of vision came together. The first performance of 'animated photographs' projected onto a screen before an audience which had paid to see them took place in 1895. In other words, the cinema industry was born.

Fifty years later, when the pioneers of this new industry were old men, we began to ask them for their reminiscences and records, their catalogues and diaries, newspaper cuttings and photographs, to establish before they were too old who they were, what had happened and what it had been like at the time. The writing of film history began.

It is interesting to see how things have moved on since then in this business of film history. Experts argue solemnly over minutiae. The archaeologists of cinema piece together their shards of evidence, discuss the exact length of minutes-long films, whether a few frames here or there have been lost, who first used a big close-up, a scene change, a reaction shot or an inter-title. The search for firsts is intense. The extent to which exhibitors used 'lecturers' or narrators is one contentious point on which there is still very little contemporary evidence.

The Kingdom of Shadows puts flesh on the bare bones of the industry as it developed in Britain between 1895 and 1915. Drawing mainly on a number of periodicals, the authors have selected texts and illustrations to evoke the period. The pompous and flowery style of many of the excerpts, and indeed their naivety, suggest the more innocent world of a hundred years ago and the lack of sophistication of many of the people involved. We have, of course, that old cliché of the cheating husband whose wife discovers his secret when she sees him on a news film with his girlfriend. This was a favourite horror story of the time. There are the fulminations of those who saw the cinema as a source of corruption, introducing the young to crime. There are curiosities. *The Kinora*, a primitive hand-held home movie of 1910, came to nothing. More interesting is a piece about the practical difficulties of filming in very cold temperatures by H. G. Ponting (the cameraman who accompanied Captain Scott on the early stages of his final expedition to the South Pole in 1912) and the thoughts of stage celebrities like Sarah Bernhardt on the special problems of acting for the camera in 1915. Scenes of war, real or faked, were popular with the public from the beginning.

There is a detailed account of how to make trick films taken from a classic book on cinematography written by Frederick Talbot in 1912, although these were already rather old fashioned by then. And there is friendly advice for would-be script writers. There were always people, it seems, who believed they could make pin money by writing in their spare time if only someone would tell them how to write.

It is interesting to see the contrast between the attitudes of film inventor Birt Acres and the early Brighton film maker G. A. Smith. Acres was one of the first to succeed in projecting moving pictures on a screen and in 1897 he gave a thoughtful lecture to a camera club in which he explained some of the technology of film and expressed his belief that it would be more than a "nine-days wonder" and indeed would prove to have artistic value. This can be set against an interview in 1900 with the busy and buoyant film maker Smith, fascinated with technical trickery and the creation of illusion but with no apparent interest in future possibilities such as narrative. It throws a curious light on the learned film historians of today, pouring over the significance of his tiny films. *Grandma's Reading Glass* of 1900, for example, was a 100-foot long big close-up which he himself regarded as an amusing trick but which is now taken rather seriously as a step in the development of film technique. When I interviewed Smith some fifty years later he was, naturally, happy to be lionised in his old age but clearly puzzled by all the fuss, believing his early work on colour cinematography to be much more important.

The book includes rich material on the travelling showmen who set up their grand gilded frontages at annual charter fairs all over the country, as well as a detailed account of the finances of established cinemas just before the 1914 war and a survey of jobs in the exhibition industry. Early contacts of royalty with the cinema are traced and there was some anxiety at the time, apparently, as to whether it was quite proper to show the heir to the throne in an unguarded moment scratching his head. Reactions to the new art form include passages by Maxim Gorky, Luis Buñuel and Jean Renoir. A writer in 1896 looks down on the realism of the film, feeling that something which merely records what is in front of it lacks the element of selection which is the essence of art. The "paltry assemblage of facts" has, he considers, no artistic future. However, even at this early date, a more far-seeing writer in *The Sketch* realises that there is more to it than that and shows greater awareness of the enormous possibilities of the new medium.

This anthology shows us society coming to terms with the new phenomenon, just as later generations had to encompass first television and later still the whole spectrum of information technology. The authors' introductions to each topic suggest interesting and stimulating insights, but they modestly present the results of their digging as a 'companion' to assist other serious students of the history of cinema.

Preface

IN THE KINGDOM OF SHADOWS stems from our shared love of early cinema. It is the result of several years spent reading and collecting literature associated with this period. We were conscious of the growing interest in the cinema's formative years, prompted not only by its impending centenary but also in the burgeoning academic activity centred on early cinema. Rather than add to the ever-growing number of interpretive and analytical texts relating to early cinema, we felt that there was also a need for a collection of contemporary, contextual material which might prompt new areas of study and investigation. We have selected material which, from our own perspective, provides fresh insights into just how cinema impacted on society during its first twenty years. Again, aware of a tradition of using contemporary, nearly always technical, sources in the construction of histories about early cinema, we consciously sought to use those sources frequently overlooked by historians. What we have gathered is, we hope, a selection of material which gives a fascinating, enlightening and, above all else, entertaining glimpse into this vibrant period at the beginning of cinema's history.

The National Museum of Photography, Film & Television has one of the world's most important collections relating to the early history of cinematography. We are extremely grateful to the Museum for giving us permission to reproduce many items from its collection in this book.

The extract from *My Life and My Films* by Jean Renoir has been reprinted by permission of the Peters Fraser & Dunlop Group Ltd. The extract from *My Last Breath* by Luis Buñuel, published by Jonathan Cape and Alfred A. Knopf Inc., has been reprinted by permission of the Estate of the author. Every effort has been made, where necessary, to contact copyright holders. The authors and publisher will be pleased to make good any errors or omissions in future editions and apologise to those concerned.

This book was made possible only with the assistance of many people. We should like to thank sincerely all those who helped with this project.

The support and encouragement of our colleagues at the National Museum of Photography, Film & Television and the Department of the History of Art and Design at the Manchester Metropolitan University has been indispensable. Without them, this book would never have appeared. In particular, we should like to thank Mary Murphy, Michael Harvey, Bob Cox, Paul Thompson and Barbara Binder.

Much of the initial research for this book was undertaken at Bradford Central Library. We should like to express our thanks to Bob Duckett and the staff of Bradford Central Libraries for all their help.

Invaluable assistance was also given by staff at the British Film Institute, the National Film and Television Archive and the Scottish Film Archive. We should also like to show out gratitude to Gordon Taylor of The Salvation Army Archive, Pamela Clark at The Royal Archives, Windsor Castle, Robert Sharp of the Science Museum Library, Michael Pritchard of Christie's South Kensington, Stephen Herbert and Jimmy Offer.

Special thanks, of course, to Rachael Low, Richard Brown, Stephen Bottomore and Vanessa Toulmin for their contributions.

Lastly, we should like to thank both Judiths for their tolerance and understanding.

Colin Harding and Simon Popple, 1996

1 The First Sight

OUR FIRST VISIT TO THE CINEMA is, perhaps, one of the few indelible memories we all share. That voyage into the dark and the sense of escape that cinema engenders was by no means a totally new experience for the first generation of cinema goers in the 1890s. It was, rather, an extension of much older forms of entertainment such as the magic lantern show, the showman's tent and the music hall and theatre, all of which were to become the early home of the cinema. However, whilst the environments in which these various entertainments thrived may have been familiar, the cinema was regarded as a wholly new addition to the panoply of visual delights offered to audiences a hundred years ago.

The moving image itself is a far older phenomenon than one might at first imagine. Natural philosophers and entertainers alike had long sought to imbue static images with a lifelike quality only realisable through the imitation of movement. The mimesis of motion was possible through a number of approaches—the physical manipulation of objects (as in puppetry and shadow play), static images (as in the lantern slide), the use of optical trickery (as in the popular spectacle of Pepper's Ghost) and, lastly, the demonstration of the principle of the persistence of vision through a series of weird and wonderful optical toys with names like the Thaumatrope, Phenakistoscope and the familiar Zoetrope. What the theory of the persistence of vision demonstrated, although the Victorian conception is flawed, was that repeated exposure to static sequential images at a high frequency was registered by the brain as a continuous moving image. What these early experimenters with optical toys, such as Michael Faraday, Joseph Plateau and Simon Stampfer were demonstrating in the early part of the nineteenth century was that this particular capacity of the human brain opened up the

potential to replicate and reconstitute images of objects in movement. Their serious attempts, which were commercially available as popular parlour toys, were hindered in one major respect. The images they used to represent sequences of movement were hand drawn, little more than primitive cartoons.

The other side to this equation was the almost simultaneous announcement of a commercially viable method of photography in 1839 by two men, the Englishman, Henry William Fox Talbot and the Frenchman, Louis-Jaques Mandé Daguerre. It was the marriage of these two scientific principles that was eventually to result in the cinema.

As a result of these pre-cinematic technologies and patterns of popular entertainment, the arrival of the commercial cinema on December 28, 1895 at the Salon Indien, Grande Café, Paris was not entirely unexpected.

Thomas Edison's Kinetoscope, launched to the public in New York on April 14, 1894, employed exactly the same principles as the Lumière's Cinématographe. However, since it did not project its images on to a screen, it failed to provide for a truly mass audience. Even projection itself was a well-established art, with its own conventions and patterns of practice, such as the use of music and narration as an accompaniment to images, which influenced strongly the ways in which early cinema was presented to its audiences. Indeed, for a while, the magic lantern and the cinema, existed side by side, sharing the same exhibition sites and much of the same technology. The earliest exhibitors of cinema were often lanternists in their own right.

Given these historical antecedents, the variety of responses to the cinema was broad and almost always conditioned by schools of critical thought relating to existing entertainments and technologies. The most popular, almost mythologised, image of the effects of cinema on early audiences is that of spectators at the Lumière film shows fleeing an oncoming train, seemingly emerging from the screen onto their laps. This was, however, by no means the only response.

Early responses to the cinema came from three broad areas: firstly, the photographic and scientific community; secondly, the entertainment sector; thirdly, and most vividly, the general press and general public. Science and technology played an overwhelming part in the everyday lives of British citizens in the nineteenth century. Scientists and industrialists became the celebrities of their day, their works celebrated on a national scale. The Great Exhibition of 1851 was the first public expression of the new found fascination with science and technology, and since the first great wave of industrialisation Britain was increasingly engulfed in a mass of changes which were to alter the very nature of society irrevocably.

It was through these new, accelerated technologies that the mechanical means of recording these changes appeared, through photography, the phonograph, and latterly cinema. This period was also characterised by the growth of mass literacy and the great democratising influence of a fledgling mass print media. The growth of publishing as an industry spawned an explosion in the number of journals and ushered in the age of the magazine.

As a consequence a contemporary record of the development and emergence of cinema was transmitted through a myriad of scientific and photographic journals such as *The British Journal of Photography*. These contain not only a scientific record of the development of cinema, but an equally important philosophical and often moralising snapshot of the responses to the new media.

If we consider the coverage these journals provided of the first year of the commercial cinema in Great Britain in 1896 what is immediately apparent is an uncertainty as to just how to treat cinema, or, as they commonly termed it, kinematography. In nearly all of these examples cinema as both a technological and aesthetic medium was aligned with photography. Indeed it was treated as the logical extension of the photographic medium.

The language used to describe early cinema often betrays such a comparison and is interesting since it concerns itself primarily with the veracity and consistency of the images produced. The commentators themselves refer to the "lifelike", "living" or "moving" nature of these images. Above all, they attested to the "realism" with which the images had been rendered. In many respects the images themselves are regarded as almost identical to the technology which has produced them. They are treated, by and large, as a qualitative testimony to the standard of the apparatus in use. This was also a common feature of the early reviews of photographic experimentation in 1839 and underlines some of the difficulties in articulating a debate about the nature of what was essentially a wholly new art form. The first reports of the daguerreotype in early 1839 expressed the same concerns over the realism of the images—their "clarity", "verisimilitude" and "faithfulness"—but seemed less concerned with the wider aesthetic possibilities offered by photography. These early scientific and photographic writers borrowed a language which, in its turn, was largely adapted from a set of descriptive European art terms. Daguerre's images were often referred to as "drawings" and Talbot described his own experimental images as "photogenic drawings". It was only later that Sir John Herschel popularised the term 'photography'. Cinema itself enjoyed a rapidly expanding nomenclature but the images were initially treated as photographic rather than cinematic. There is a real sense of cinema's growing independence through reading such reviews.

Contemporary accounts of the arrival and growth of the cinema were not limited to the scientific and photographic press but were greeted with a mixture of excitement and trepidation in the entertainment world because of the obvious financial and competitive implications. The magic lantern establishment seemed to have the most to fear from the cinema, although ultimately cinema was also instrumental in the decline of the music hall. *The Optical Magic Lantern Journal and Photographic Enlarger* in 1896 initially reported the benefits of the cinema:

> The latest lantern for projecting scenes in which motion is seen is that of the well-known plate makers and chemists, A. and L. Lumière. The apparatus—or Kinematograph as it is called is

capable of use either for taking photographs or projecting positive pictures on the screen, and thus serves two purposes.[1]

Yet that same month 'The Magic Lantern Record' of *The British Journal of Photography* was rather more forthright in its appraisal:

> My advice to all lanternists is this, take the first opportunity of going to the Marlborough Hall, to see the "living photographs" I have described, and country readers up for the day should time themselves to be in Regent Street (Oxford Street end) five or ten minutes before any of the hours between two and ten p.m. As this may sound something of an advertisement, I may add I have no interest whatever in this invention, but simply a desire to inform the lantern world of a novelty they ought not to miss, and to set manufacturers thinking, so that they can produce apparatus to give as good, if not better results; for the lantern industry, without doubt, wants "waking up".[2]

The cinema also found a welcoming home within the other main entertainment institutions, the Theatre and Music hall, appearing not only as an item on variety bills but as an integral part of other artists' performances. The famous illusionist and magician David Devant was one of the first to use the cinema as a part of his act and many famous stars of stage and music hall made films. Beerbohm Tree appeared in the first Shakespeare film, a version of his popular production of *King John* and popular stars such as Dan Leno and George Robey made a quick transition from stage to screen, to be followed later by Charlie Chaplin and Fred Emney.

But perhaps the most interesting and broad responses came from the general press and directly from cinema's first audiences. The writer Maxim Gorky provides us with perhaps the most lyrical and prophetic of these early reviews, fearing the uses to which the medium would be put by unscrupulous entrepreneurs. But what above all characterises these responses to the first sight of the cinema, whether favourable or not, is a sense that something irrevocable has come to pass.

1. *The Optical Magic Lantern Journal and Photographic Enlarger*, March 1896.
2. *The Magic Lantern Record* [supplement to *The British Journal of Photography*], March 1896.

Frames from the Lumière film *Workers Leaving the Factory*, **c. 1895.**

Maxim Gorky
newspaper review of the
Lumière programme at the
Nizhni-Novgorod fair
Nizhegorodski listok
4 July 1896

LAST NIGHT I WAS IN THE KINGDOM OF SHADOWS.

If you only knew how strange it is to be there. It is a world without sound, without colour. Everything there—the earth, the trees, the people, the water and the air—is dipped in monotonous grey. Grey rays of the sun across the grey sky, grey eyes in grey faces, and the leaves of the trees are ashen grey. It is not life but its shadow, it is not motion but its soundless spectre.

Here I shall try to explain myself, lest I be suspected of madness or indulgence in symbolism. I was at Aumont's and saw Lumière's cinématograph—moving photography. The extraordinary impression it creates is so unique and complex that I doubt my ability to describe it with all its nuances. However, I shall try to convey its fundamentals.

When the lights go out in the room in which Lumière's invention is shown, there suddenly appears on the screen a large grey picture, 'A Street in Paris'—shadows of a bad engraving. As you gaze at it, you see carriages, buildings and people in various poses, all frozen into immobility. All this is in grey, and the sky above is also grey—you anticipate nothing new in this all too familiar scene, for you have seen pictures of Paris streets more than once. But suddenly a strange flicker passes through the screen and the picture stirs to life. Carriages coming from somewhere in the perspective of the picture are moving straight at you, into the darkness in which you sit; somewhere from afar people appear and loom larger as they come closer to you; in the foreground children are playing with a dog, bicyclists tear along, and pedestrians cross the street picking their way among the carriages. All this moves, teems with life and, upon approaching the edge of the screen, vanishes somewhere beyond it.

And all this in strange silence where no rumble of the wheels is heard, no sound of footsteps or of speech. Nothing. Not a single note of the intricate symphony that always accompanies the movements of people. Noiselessly, the ashen-grey foliage of the trees sways in the wind, and the grey silhouettes of the people, as though condemned to eternal silence and cruelly punished by being deprived of all the colours of life, glide noiselessly along the grey ground.

Their smiles are lifeless, even though their movements are full of living energy and are so swift as to be almost imperceptible. Their laughter is soundless, although you see the muscles contracting in their grey faces. Before you a life is surging, a life deprived of words and shorn of the living spectrum of colours—the grey, the soundless, the bleak and dismal life.

It is terrifying to see, but it is the movement of shadows, only of shadows. Curses and ghosts, the evil spirits that have cast entire cities into eternal sleep, come to mind and you feel as though Merlin's vicious trick is being enacted before you. As though he had bewitched the entire street, he compressed its many-storied buildings from roof-tops to foundations to yard-like size. He dwarfed the people in corresponding proportion, robbing them of the power of speech and scraping together all the pigment of earth and sky into a monotonous grey colour.

Under this guise he showed his grotesque creation into a niche in the dark room of a restaurant. Suddenly something clicks, everything vanishes and a train appears on the screen. It speeds straight at you—watch out! It seems as though it will plunge into the darkness in which you sit, turning you into a ripped sack full of lacerated flesh and splintered bones, and crushing into dust and into broken fragments this hall and this building, so full of wine, music and vice.

But this, too, is but a train of shadows.

Noiselessly, the locomotive disappears beyond the edge of the screen. The train comes to a stop, and grey figures silently emerge from the cars, soundlessly greet their friends, laugh, walk, run, bustle, and . . . are gone. And here is another picture. Three men seated at the table, playing cards. Their faces are tense, their hands move swiftly. The cupidity of the players is betrayed by the trembling fingers and by the twitching of their facial muscles. They play . . . Suddenly, they break into laughter, and the waiter who has stopped at their table with beer, laughs too. They laugh until their sides split but not a sound is heard. It seems as if these people have died and their shadows have been condemned to play cards in silence unto eternity. Another picture. A gardener watering flowers. The light grey stream of water, issuing from a hose, breaks into a fine spray. It falls upon the flowerbeds and upon the grass blades weighted down by the water. A boy enters, steps on the hose, whereupon the boy steps back and a stream of water hits the gardener in the face. You imagine the spray will reach you, and you want to shield yourself. But on the screen the gardener has already begun to chase the rascal all over the garden and having caught him, gives him a beating. But the beating is soundless, nor can you hear the gurgle of the water as it gushes from the hose left lying on the ground.

This mute, grey life finally begins to disturb and distress you. It seems as though it carries a warning, fraught with a vague but sinister meaning that makes your heart grow faint. You are forgetting where you are. Strange imaginings invade your mind and your consciousness begins to wane and grow dim . . .

But suddenly, alongside of you, a gay chatter and a provoking laughter of a woman is heard

Frames from R. W. Paul's *The Soldier's Courtship*, 1896.

. . . and you remember that you are at Aumont's, Charles Aumont's . . . But why of all places should this remarkable invention of Lumière find its way and be demonstrated here, this invention which affirms once again the energy and the curiosity of the human mind, forever striving to solve and grasp all and . . . while on the way to the solution of the mystery of life, incidentally builds Aumont's fortune? I do not yet see the scientific importance of Lumière's invention but, no doubt, it is there, and it could probably be applied to the general ends of science, that is, of bettering man's life and the developing of his mind. This is not to be found at Aumont's where vice alone is being encouraged and popularised. Why then at Aumont's, among the 'victims of social needs' and among the loafers who here buy their kisses? Why here, of all places, are they showing this latest achievement of science? And soon probably Lumières invention will be perfected, but in the spirit of Aumont-Toulon and Company.

Besides those pictures I have already mentioned, is featured *The Family Breakfast*, an idyll of three. A young couple with its chubby first-born is seated at the breakfast table. The two are so much in love, and are so charming, gay and happy, and the baby is so amusing. The picture creates a fine, felicitous impression. Has this family scene a place at Aumont's?

And here is still another. Women workers, in a thick, gay and laughing crowd, rush out of the factory gates into the street. This too is out of place at Aumont's. Why remind here of the possibility of a clean, toiling life? This reminder is useless. Under the best of circumstances this picture will only painfully sting the woman who sells her kisses.

I am convinced that these pictures will soon be replaced by others of a genre more suited to the general tone of the *Concert Parisien*. For example, they will show a picture entitled: *As She Undresses, or Madam at Her Bath*, or *A Woman in Stockings*. They could also depict a sordid squabble between a husband and wife and serve it to the public under the heading of *The Blessings of Family Life*.

Yes, no doubt, this is how it will be done. The bucolic and the idyll could not possibly find their place in Russia's markets thirsting for the piquant and the extravagant. I also could suggest a few themes for development by means of a cinematograph and for the amusement of the market place. For instance: to impale a fashionable parasite upon a picket fence, as is the way of the Turks, photograph him, then show it.

It is not exactly piquant but quite edifying.

'THE PEOPLE'S PALACE'

Bradford Telegraph and Argus
7 April 1896

DESPITE THE MANY COUNTER-ATTRACTIONS which the holiday season offered, a very large number of persons were attracted to the Bradford People's Palace last night by the excellent company which Mr. Andrew Roberton has provided for this week. The principal novelty which his programme includes is a visit of the invention known as the Cinématographe. This somewhat ponderous word is used to indicate an adaptation of the principle of the recently much improved Kinetoscope to magic-lantern purposes. It is hardly necessary to explain that the principle of the instrument, with the improvement of which Edison's name is associated, is the continuity of impression as of a continuous motion which is produced on the eye when a series of photographic pictures taken at intervals of a few seconds only are exhibited consecutively and rapidly. The exhibition given last night shows that the technical difficulties in the application of this principle to the extingencies of the lantern have been carefully thought out, and in great measure overcome. A considerable number of series of pictures were shown, among them a series representing a barber's shop, a dentist's operating-room, and a blacksmith's forge, in all of which the movements were of the most lively character.

Perhaps, however, the most original success was achieved in regard to some pictures representing the postures of dancers, which were not only vividly represented, but very pretty as well. Beside this attraction the programme is a strong one. The sisters Phillips and the brothers Lorenzi needed no introduction to the patrons of the People's Palace, and their humorous and clever entertainment produced much merriment. Mr. T. H. Fayme, an eccentric character comedian of considerable ability, also secured a very favourable reception from a section of the house, and might, no doubt, have made a larger number of friends by a little more taste in the choice of his songs. The two Brewers, eccentric comedians and dancers, gave a very funny turn, and Mr. F. W. Malburn showed some clever musical feats. The programme is also contributed to by Miss Winifred Yates and Mr. Robert Emslie, Miss Nora Gordon, Miss Nellie Melrose, Messrs. Kennedy and Allen, and others.

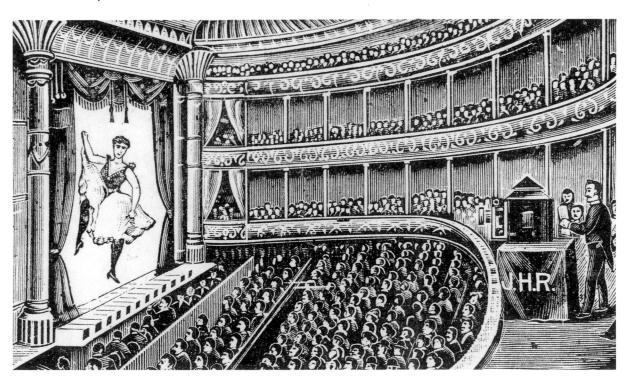

From an advertisement for J. H. Rigg, Leeds, 1896.

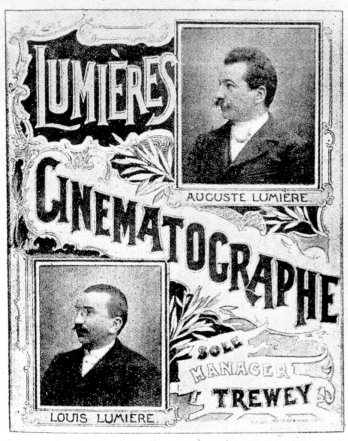

MARLBOROUGH HALL
REGENT STREET.

LUMIÈRES CINÉMATOGRAPHE

AUGUSTE LUMIÈRE

LOUIS LUMIÈRE

SOLE MANAGER TREWEY

Edited by HERBERT NORTH.

PUBLISHED BY
W. CONSTABLE, Advertising Agent, Bradford.

Anonymous poem
The British Journal of Photography,
4 December 1896

Such a bustle and a hurry
O'er the "living picture" craze
Rivals rushing full of worry
In these advertising days.
Each the first and each the only
Each the others widely chaff
All of them proclaiming boldly
Their's the first A-Kind-O-Graph.
But its a wonder really
How the constant flood of life
O'er the screen keeps moving freely
Full of action- stir and strife.
There the waves are wildly breaking
There the swimmer stems the tide.
The cyclist his record making,
With the countless varied scenes beside.
'Tis far from perfect in its movements
'Tis very hard upon the eyes;
The jolty wobble no improvements,
Smooth running films a surprise.
Still successful beyond reason,
Spite of all its erring ways,
Holding first place in the season
Is the "Living Picture" craze.

**Programme for performances of the Lumière Cinémato-
graphe at the Marlborough Hall, February 1896.**
National Museum of Photography, Film & Television.

The Times
22 February 1896

THE CINÉMATOGRAPHE

THE CINÉMATOGRAPHE, which is the invention of MM. A. and L. Lumière, is a contrivance belonging to the same family as Edison's kinetoscope and the old 'Wheel of Life',
but in a rather higher state of development. The spectator no longer gazes through a narrow
aperture at the changing picture, but has it presented to him full size on a large screen. The principle, however, is much the same, consisting simply of passing rapidly before the eye a series of
pictures representing the successive stages of the action or the changing scene that has to be
reproduced. It is stated that in the present case the interval of time between each photograph is
about 1/900th of a minute, or, in other words, that of, say, as a crowd of people are passing
along a street, nine hundred successive photographs are taken in a minute. When these photographs are thrown on a screen by means of the electric light at the same rate and order as they
were taken, an exact reproduction of the moving people is obtained. Another subject that lends
itself very effectively to this treatment is a railway train entering and stopping at a station. The
movements of the people leaving the carriages and the bustle on the platform are reproduced
with lifelike fidelity.

WITH SIXPENCE TO SPEND I had gone to a funny little shop in the Lambeth Walk where Pollock's gory melodramas for his toy Theatres were sold, sheets of characters for a penny plain, twopence coloured. Fourpence went rapturously on "Alone in the Pirates' Lair". With twopence jingling a farewell in my pocket, since the toffee-shop was near, I zig-zagged through the hurlyburly of the busy street, when presto! . . . the great adventure began. It was outside a derelict greengrocer's shop. The hawk-eyed gentleman on a fruit-crate was bewildering a sceptical crowd. In that shuttered shop there was a miracle to be seen for a penny, but only twenty-four could enter at a time, there wasn't room for any more. His peroration was magnificent . . . "You've seen pictures of people in books, all frozen stiff . . . you've never seen pictures with people coming alive, moving about like you and me. Well, go inside and see for yourself, living pictures for a penny, and then tell me if I'm a liar!"

One of my pennies went suddenly; I joined twenty-three other sceptics inside. Stale cabbage leaves and a smell of dry mud gave atmosphere to a scene from Hogarth. A furtive youth did things to a tin oven on iron legs, and a white sheet swung from the ceiling. We grouped round the oven and wondered. Suddenly things happened, someone turned down a gas-jet, the tin apparatus burst into a fearful clatter, and an oblong picture slapped on to the sheet and began a violent dance.

After a while I discerned it was a picture of a house, but a house on fire. Flames and smoke belched from the windows, and miracle of miracles, little human figures darted about below, and then . . . Bang! . . . the show was over. Exactly one minute . . . I had been to the Cinema!

George Pearson,
Flashback: Autobiography of a British Film-maker
1957, p. 14

Advertisement for Lumière's Cinématographe, 1897.

EDISON'S BEAUTIFUL OPTICAL INSTRUMENT, the Kinetoscope, has now become familiar to most people through its exhibition in various large towns. By means of it, a photograph, or rather a series of photographs, constitutes a marvellous living picture, and the only drawback of the effect pictured in the very small scale of the pictures. It has therefore been the endeavour of many inventors to adapt the mechanism of the Kinetoscope to the optical or magic lantern, so that the original pictures, that are not more than one inch in length, can be magnified to several feet. This has been done with more or less success by MM. Lumière of Paris, and the apparatus is now being exhibited in London. What we may call the action of the pictures thus exhibited is most realistic. In one instance, a busy railway station is shown, a train is seen approaching, it draws up at the platform, the carriage doors open, the passengers alight and talk to one another, and the guard steps forward and signals the engine-driver to proceed on his journey. It is evident that this apparatus when perfected will be as much valued by artists as a means of studying motion, as it is by mere amusement seekers; but the assertion that one day we shall be able, by means of these projected pictures in association with the phonograph, to reproduce operas, and other dramatic representations, is at present, to say the least, premature.

'The Month: Science and Arts',
Chambers's Journal
25 April 1896

The Royale Viograph Cinema, France 1899.

Punch, 6 August 1898

AT THE PALACE

THEN COMES 'THE AMERICAN BIOGRAPH'. Wonderful!! But, my eyes! my head!! and the whizzing and whirling and twittering of nerves, and blinkings and winkings that it causes in not a few among the spectators, who could not be content with half the show, or even a third of it. It is a night-mare! There's a rattling, and a shattering, and there are sparks, and there are showers of quivering snow-flakes always falling, and amidst these appear children fighting in bed, a house on fire, with inmates saved by the arrival of fire engines, which, at some interval, are followed by warships pitching about at sea, sailors running up riggings and disappearing into space, trains at full speed coming directly at you, and never getting there, but jumping out of the picture into outer darkness where the audience is, and then, the train having vanished, all the country round takes it into its head to follow as hard as ever it can, rocks, mountains, trees, towns, gateways, castles, rivers, landscapes, bridges, platforms, telegraph-poles, all whirling and squirling and racing against one another, as if to see which will get to the audience first, and then, suddenly . . . all disappear into space!! Phew! We breathe again!! But, O heads! O brandies and sodas! O Whiskies and waters! Restoratives, quick! It is wonderful, most wonderful! Nay, we had almost said, with the learned Dr. Johnson, that we wished 'it were impossible.' But to wish this is to to put the clock back, and the show is over in excellent time to allow of supper and refreshment where you will. Still, just a third of the American Biograph, as invented by Herman Casler, would suffice for this particular deponent, and for not a few others. Anyway, the Palace thoroughly deserves its present most evident popularity.

ALL WENT WELL AT THE BEGINNING of our visit to Dufayel . . . At the entrance to the store a man wearing a braided cap asked us if we wanted to see the 'cinema'. His cap was rather like the uniform cap of the *collège de Saint-croix*, where my brother Pierre, the future actor, had been sent as a boarder . . . A man wearing such a cap could only be safeguarding the small fragment of the world which was the only one I knew. It was therefore in a spirit of comparative confidence that I allowed Bibon to take me into the projection room.

The Grands Magasins Dufayel were in the forefront of progress. They had been the first to sell on credit. The building, with its walls of real stone and large glass windows shedding their light on imitation Henri II sideboards, gave to those privileged to enter that temple of mass-produced goods an impression of solidity capable of withstanding anything. The free cinema was another of their daring innovations. Gabrielle's account of the incident was terse and lacking in detail. Scarcely had we taken our seats than the room was plunged in darkness. A terrifying machine shot out a fearsome beam of light piercing the obscurity, and a series of incomprehensible pictures appeared on the screen, accompanied by the sound of a piano at one end and at the other a sort of hammering that came from the machine. I yelled in my usual fashion and had to be taken out. I never thought that the staccato rhythm of the Maltese cross was later to become for me the sweetest of music. At the time I did not grasp the importance of that basic part of both camera and projector without which the cinema would not exist.

So my first encounter with the idol was a complete failure. Gabrielle was sorry we had not stayed. The film was about a big river and she thought that in a corner of the screen she had glimpsed a crocodile.

Jean Renoir
My Life and My Films
1974, pp. 17–18

I THINK I WAS ABOUT EIGHT YEARS OLD when I discovered the cinema, at a theatre called the Farrucini. There were two doors, one exclusively for exiting, one for entering, set in a beautiful wooden facade. Outside, a cluster of lemonade sellers equipped with a variety of musical instruments hawked their wares to passers-by. In reality, the Farrucini was little more than a shack; it had wooden benches and a tarpaulin roof.

. . . I remember how enthralled I was by my first cartoon; it was about a pig who wore a tricolour sash around his waist and sang. (The sound came from a record player hidden behind the screen.) I'm quite sure that it was a colour film, which at that time meant that each image had been painted by hand.

Movies then were little more than a curiosity, like the sideshow at a country fair. They were simply the primitive products of a newly discovered technique. Apart from trains and streetcars, already habitual parts of our lives, such 'modern' techniques were not much in evidence in Saragossa. In fact in 1908, there was only one automobile in the entire city, an electric one.

Luis Buñuel
My Last Breath
1984, p. 31

THE DIARY OF A DAUGHTER OF EVE

Black and White
4 April 1896

TUESDAY—NO HOUSE IS COMPLETE without a cinematographe. I yearn for one for my private use, and I revelled in the show at the Empire last night. Julia suggests that as I never move I should have small service for such a toy; She even ventured to observe that my tastes were childish, my joy in the performance reminding her of nothing but the enthusiasm I was wont to exhibit at a Punch and Judy show. Julia's stupidity really begins to bore me. the charm of the cinematographe to me is that it showed me life as I know it.

The Scotsman
2 June 1896

THE MANAGEMENT OF THE EMPIRE has made a distinct hit. Last night everything worked with perfect smoothness. The Cinématographe, seen in its full perfection, seemed to come to the audience as something of a revelation. When the first of the series of pictures appeared on the screen they applauded heartily, and as one picture after another was exhibited their enthusiasm grew. The management of the light was perfect; the movement of the figures were wonderfully natural; and the general effect was singularly pleasing. The series opened with a view representing the dinner-hour at a factory gate at Lyons, in which the hurry and bustle of the operatives leaving their work at mid-day were admirably depicted. A most effective view was the arrival of the Paris mail at an intermediate station; in another the troubles of a photographer with a fidgetty patron were admirably hit off. Particularly attractive also, was the representation full of life and movement of the Champs Elysees; and the sea pieces were wonderfully fine. Altogether, the Cinématographe under Mons. Trewey's direction proved one of the greatest attractions which has been seen at the Empire for some time, and the audience were so enthusiastic in their applause that the curtain was raised and a beautiful sea-scape under moonlight the waves dashing upon the rocks was shown.

The Royal Polytechnic Institution, scene of the first public Lumière screening in Britain, 21 February 1896.
The University of Westminster

The Scotsman
14 April 1896

THE GREAT ATTRACTION FOR THE WEEK at the Empire is an exhibition of the 'Cinématographe'—a kind of electric magic lantern by which the instantaneous photographs of Edison's wonderful kinetoscope are thrown upon a screen in the sight of the audience . . . Mr Moss is to be congratulated for his enterprise in securing the first appearance of it in the provinces. Unfortunately in Edinburgh last night the exhibition somehow misfired. In the Cinématographe views the light seemed not to be powerful enough to render the celluloid sufficiently transparent, and a somewhat indistinct picture in consequence appeared upon the screen—such as might have been thrown if the instrument had not been properly focused. Another defect was that the photographs were passed too slowly before the lens, so that while the action was vivid and life-like, it was in the dancing and pugilistic scenes especially, of too funeral a character. It was noticed that the lighter photographs showed best upon the screen. Such, for example, were the shoeblack, the policeman and the sailor which was the first and the best of the ten scenes exhibited. The cockfight was also exceedingly good, the action of the birds flying at each other with outstretched wings being very realistic.

O. Winter
New Review
February 1896

L IFE IS A GAME PLAYED ACCORDING TO A SET OF RULES—physical, moral, artistic—for the moment ironbound in severity, yet ever shifting. The heresy of today is tomorrow's dogma, and many a martyr has won an unwilling crown for the defence of a belief, which his son's bootblack accepts as indisputable. The tyranny of the arts, most masterful of all, seldom outlasts a generation; time brings round an instant revenge for a school's contempt of its predecessor; and all the while science is clamorously breaking the laws, which man, in his diffidence, believes to be irrefragable.

When the first rude photograph was taken, it was already a miracle; but stability was the condition of its being, and the frozen smirk of an impossible tranquillity hindered its perfection. Even the 'snap-shot', which revealed poses indiscoverable to the human eye, was, at best, a mere effect of curiosity, and became, in the hands of Mr. Muybridge and others, the instrument of a pitiless pedantry.

But, meantime, the moving picture was perfected, and, at last, by a skilful adaptation of an ingenious toy, you may contemplate life itself thrown moving and alert upon a screen. Imagine a room or theatre brilliant with electric lights and decorated with an empty back-cloth. Suddenly the lights are extinguished, and to the whirring sound of countless revolutions the back-cloth quivers into being. A moment since it was white and inanimate; now it bustles with the movement and masquerade of tremulous life. Whirr! And a train, running (so to say) out of the cloth, floats upon your vision. It draws up at the platform; guards and porters hustle to their toil; weary passengers lean through the window to unfasten the cumberous door, sentimentalists hasten to intercept their friends; and the whole common drama of luggage and fatigue is enacted before your eyes. The lights leap up, and at their sudden descent you see upon the cloth a factory at noon disgorging its inmates. Men and women jostle and laugh; a swift bicycle seizes the occasion of an empty space; a huge hound crosses the yard in placid content; you can catch the very changing expression of a mob happy in its release; you note the varying speed of the footsteps; not one of the smaller signs of human activity escapes you. And then, again, a sudden light, and recurring darkness.

Then, once more, the sound and flicker of machinery; and you see on the bare cloth a tumbling sea, with a crowd of urchins leaping and scrambling in the waves. The picture varies, but the effect is always the same—the terrifying effect of life, but of life with a difference.

It is life stripped of colour and of sound. Though you are conscious of the sunshine, the picture is subdued to a uniform and baffling grey. Though the waves break upon an imagined shore, they break in a silence which doubles your shrinking from their reality. The boys laugh with eyes and mouth—that you can see at a glance. But they laugh in a stillness which no ripple disturbs.

The figures move after their appointed habit; it is thus and not otherwise that they have behaved yesterday and will behave tomorrow. They are not marionettes, because they are individuals, while a marionette is always generalised into an aspect of pity or ridicule. The disproportion of foreground and background adds to your embarrassment, and although you know that the scene has a mechanical and intimate correspondence with truth, you recognise its inherent falsity. The brain and the eyes understand not the process of the sensitive plate. They are ever composing, eliminating, and selecting, as if by instinct.

"Music-Hall Managers are all eager for the Cinemato-graphe now, and won't be happy till they get it." *L'Entracte,* 1896.

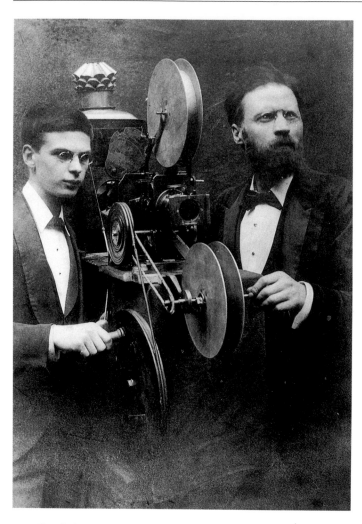

Goodwin Norton & Son,
c. 1898. *National Museum of*
Photography, Film & Television.

They work far more rapidly than the most elaborate mechanism. They discard one impression and take on another before the first has passed the period of its legitimate endurance. They permit no image to touch them without alteration or adaptation.

The dullest eye, the deafest ear, has a personality, generally unconscious, which transforms every scene, and modifies every sound. A railway station, for instance, is a picture with a thousand shifting focuses. The most delicate instrument is forced to render every incident at the same pace and with the same prominence, only reserving to itself the monstrous privilege of enlarging the foreground beyond recognition. If you or I meet an arriving train, we either compose the scattered elements into a simple picture, and with the directness distinguishing the human vision from the photographic lens, reject the countless details which hamper and confuse our composition, or we stand on the platform eager to recognise a familiar face. The rest of the throng, hastily scanned, falls into a shadowy background. Thus in the moving picture, thrown upon the screen, the crowd is severally and unconsciously choosing or rejecting the objects of sight. But we find the task impossible. The grey photograph unfolds at an equal pace and with a sad deliberation. We cannot follow the shadows in their enthusiasm of recognition; the scene is forced to trickle upon our nerves with an equal effect; it is neither so quick nor so changeful as life. From the point of view of display the spectacle fails, because its personages lack the wan quality of entertainment: self-consciousness. The ignorant man falls back upon the ancient wonderment. 'Ain't it lifelike!' He exclaims in all sincerity, though he possesses the faculty of comparison but roughly developed, and is apt to give an interpretation of reality to the most absurd symbols.

Here, then, is life; life it must be because a machine knows not how to invent; but it is life which you may only contemplate through a mechanical medium, life which eludes you in your daily pilgrimage. It is wondrous, even terrific; the smallest whiff of smoke goes upward in the picture; and the house falls to the ground without an echo. It is all true, and it is all false. "Why hath not man a microscopic eye?" asked Pope; and the answer came prosaic as the question: "The reason it is plain, he is not a fly." So you may formulate the demand: Why does not man see with the vision of the Cinématograph? And the explanation is pat: Man cannot see with the mechanical unintelligence of a plate, exposed forty times in a second.

Yet such has ever been the ambition of the British painter. He would go forth into the fields, and adjust his eyes to the scene as though they were a telescope. He would register the far distant background with a monstrous conscientiousness, although he had to travel a mile to discover its qualities. He would exaggerate the foreground with the clumsy vulgarity of a photographic plate, which knows no better cunning, and would reveal to himself, with the unintelligent aid of a magnifying glass, a thousand details which would escape the notice of everything save an inhuman machine. And while he was a far less able register of the facts than the Cinématograph, he was an even worse artist. He aimed at an unattainable and undesirable reality, and he failed. The newest toy attains this false reality without a struggle. Both the Cinématograph and the Pre-Raphaelite suffer from the same vice. The one and the other are incapable of selection; they grasp at every straw that comes in their way; they see the trivial and important, the near and the distant, with the same fecklessly impartial eye. And the Pre-Raphaelite is the worse, because he is not forced into a fatal course by scientific necessity. He is not racked upon a machine that makes two thousand revolutions in a minute, though he deserves to be. No; he pursues his niggled path in the full knowledge of his enormity, and with at least a chance, if ever he opened his eye, of discovering the straight road. The eye of the true impressionist, on the other hand, is the Cinématograph's antithesis. It never permits itself to see everything or to be perplexed by a minute survey of the irrelevant. It picks and chooses from nature as it pleaseth; it is shortsighted, when myopia proves its advantage; it can catch the distant lines, when a reasoned composition demands so far a research. It is artistic, because it is never mechanical, because it expresses a personal bias both in its choice and in its rejection. It looks beyond the foreground and to the larger, more spacious lines of landscape. Nature in its material, whereas Fred Walker and his fellows might have been inspired by a series of photographic plates.

Maguire and Baucus, no date.
*National Museum of Photography,
Film & Television.*

Literature, too, has ever hankered unconsciously after the Cinématograph. Is not Zola the M. Lumière of his art? And might not the sight of the Cinématograph have saved the realist from a wilderness of lost endeavour? As the toy registers every movement without any expressed relation to its fellow, so the old and fearless realist believed in the equal value of all facts. He collected information in the spirit of the swiftly moving camera, or of the statistician. Nothing came amiss to him, because he considered nothing of supreme importance. He emptied his notebooks upon foolscap and believed himself an artist. His work was so faithful in detail that in the bulk it conveyed no meaning whatever. The characters and incidents were as grey and silent as the active shadows of the Cinématograph. M. Zola and M. Huysmans (in his earlier incarnation) posed as the Columbuses of a new art, and all the while they were merely playing the despised part of the newspaper reporter. They fared forth, notebook in hand, and described the most casual accidents as though they were essentials of a rapid life. They made an heroic effort to strip the brain of its power of argument and generalisation. They were as keenly convinced that all phenomena are of equal value as is the impersonal lens, which today is the academician's best friend. But they forget that the human brain is not mechanical: it cannot avoid the tasks of selection and revision, and when it measures itself against a photographic apparatus it fails perforce.

It is the favourite creed of the realists that truth is valuable for its own sake, that the description of a tiresome hat or an infamous pair of trousers has a merit of its own closely allied to accuracy. But life in itself is seldom interesting—so much has been revealed by photography; life, until it be crystallised into an arbitrary mould, is as flat and fatuous as the passing bus. The realist, however, has formulated his ambition: the master of the future, says he, will produce the very gait and accent of the back-parlour. This ambition may already be satisfied by the Cinématograph, with the phonograph to aid, and while the sorriest pedant cannot call the result supremely amusing, so the most sanguine of photographers cannot pronounce it artistic. At least we have been permitted to see the wild hope of the realists accomplished. We may look upon life moving without purpose, without beauty, with no better impulse than a foolish curiosity; and though the spectacle frightens rather than attracts, we owe it a debt of gratitude, because it proves the complete despair of modern realism.

As the realistic painter, with his patient, unspeculative eye bent upon a relentless foreground, produces an ugly, tangled version of nature, so the disciple of Zola perplexes his indomitable industry by the compilation of contradictory facts. Not even M. Zola himself, for all his acute intelligence, discovered that Lourdes, for instance, was a mere flat record. By the force of a painful habit, he differentiated his characters; he did not chose a single hero to be the mule (as it were), who would sustain all the pains and all the sins of the world. No, he bravely labelled his abstractions with names and qualities, but he played the trick with so little conviction, that a plain column and a half of bare fact would have conveyed as much information and more amusement. Now, M. Zola has at last relieved the gloom of ill digested facts by adroitly thrown pétards. When you find his greyness at its greyest, he will flick in a superfluous splash of scarlet, to arouse you from your excusable lethargy. But in America, where even the novel may be 'machine-made', they know far better than to throw pétards. Their whole theory of art is summed up in the Cinématograph, so long as the instrument does its work in such an unexciting atmosphere as the backyard of a Boston villa. Life in the States, they murmur, is not romantic. Therefore the novel has no right to be romantic. Because Boston is hopelessly dull, therefore Balzac is an impostor. For them, the instantaneous photograph, and a shorthand clerk. And, maybe, when the historian of the future has exhausted the advertisement columns of the pompous journals, he may turn (for statistics) to the American novel, first cousin, by a hazard, to the Cinématograph.

The dominant lesson of M. Lumière's invention is this: the one real thing in life, art, or literature, is unreality. It is only by the freest translation of facts into no other medium that you can catch that fleeting impression of reality, which a paltry assemblage of the facts themselves can never impart. The master quality of the world is human invention, whose liberal exercise demonstrates the fatuity of a near approach to 'life'. The man who invents, may invent harmoniously; he may choose his own key, and bend his own creations to his imperious will. And if he be an artist, he will complete his work without hesitancy or contradiction. But he who insists upon a minute and conscientious vision, is forthwith hampered by his own material, and is almost forced to see discordantly. Hence it is that M. Zola is interesting only in isolated pages. His imagination is so hopelessly crippled by sight, that he cannot sustain his eloquence beyond the limit of a single impression. Suppose he does astonish you by a flash of entertainment, he relapses instantly into dullness, since for him, as for the Cinématograph, things are interesting, not because they are beautiful or happily combined, but because they exist, or because they recall, after their clumsy fashion, a familiar experience.

Has, then, the Cinématograph a career? Artistically, no; statistically, a thousand times yes. Its results will be beautiful only by accident, until the casual, unconscious life of the street learns to compose itself into rhythmical pictures. And this lesson will never be learned outside the serene and perfect air of heaven. But if only the invention be widely and properly applied, then history may be written, as it is acted. With the aid of these modern miracles, we may bottle (so to say) the world's acutest situations. They will be poured out to the students of the future without colour and without accent, and though their very impartiality may mislead, at least they will provide the facts for a liberal judgement. At least they will give what an ingenious critic of the drama once described as 'slabs of life'. For the Cinématograph the phrase is well chosen; but for Ibsen, who prompted its invention, no phrase were more ridiculous. For whatever your opinion of Hedda Gabler, at least you must absolve its author from a too eager rivalry with M. Lumière's hastily-revolving toy.

And now, that Science may ever keep abreast of literature, come M. Röntgen's invention to play the part of the psychologist. As M. Bourget (shall we say?) uncovers the secret motives and inclinations of his characters, when all you ask of him is a single action, so M. Röntgen bids photography pierce the husk of flesh and blood and reveal to the world the skeletons of living men. In Science the penetration may be invaluable; in literature it destroys the impression, and substitutes pedantry for intelligence. M. Röntgen, however, would commit no worse an outrage than the cure of the sick and the advancement of knowledge. Wherefore he is absolved from the mere suspicion of an onslaught upon art. But it is not without its comedy, that photography's last inventions are twin echoes of modern literature. The Cinématograph is but realism reduced to other terms, less fallible and more amusing; while M. Röntgen's rays suggest that, though a too intimate discourse may be fatal to romance, the doctor and the curiosity-monger may find it profitable to pierce through our "too, too solid flesh" and count the rattling bones within.

✻

2 The Uses of Cinema

AS WITH THE INTRODUCTION OF any new technology, cinema immediately captured the public imagination. The possibilities for its employment seemed endless, from a base adjunct to music hall and side-show performances to an almost noble aid to the surgeon, scientist and historian alike. There were of course as many prophetic declarations in its favour as there were cautionary and condemnatory warnings. However, once the initial novelty of the first few months of its introduction began to wane, cinematographers faced a dilemma. Could the cinema survive in its present form, or like many entertainments before, would it merely fade from prominence once something more exciting came on the scene? The parallel with the simultaneous introduction of Röntgen Rays or the X-rays in January 1896 as a popular entertainment bears reference. This new 'invisible photography', pioneered by Wilhelm Röntgen, proved a massive draw as a form of entertainment in the early months of 1896, at the exact moment cinema was launched commercially in Britain. The public went wild at demonstrations of this magic art which allowed them to look inside their own bodies and going to the X-rays was as popular as going to the movies.

Yet by the end of the year they had all but disappeared from public exhibition. The same fate had previously befallen Thomas Edison's Kinetoscope. Would cinema be next? Certainly some commentators thought so, including the future film maker Cecil Hepworth:

> There are plenty of wonderful rumours floating about anent the immense fortunes being made over the animated photographs craze. A few lucky ones there were—plucky would perhaps be a better word—who when the tide came were business-like enough to take it at the flood who now find the Shakespearean dictum fully borne out beyond their wildest hopes. But there are many others who are inclined to dub the whole thing a delusion and a snare, men who have laboured—wisely perhaps, but too slowly, and who are already beginning to feel themselves entangled in those side eddies which, so far from leading on to fortune, generally drag their victims into uncomfortably deep water. That the present boom in these animated palsey-scopes cannot last for ever is a fact which the great majority of people seem to be losing sight of altogether, and yet it is only common sense to suppose that it will not be so very long before the great British Public gets tired of the uncomfortably jerky photographs.[1]

Hepworth's pessimism was perhaps motivated by a recognition that increasing competition meant that cinema would become swamped with second-rate practitioners with their "jerky" shows and inferior "pictures". Indeed it is quite striking that the "pictures" themselves did not attract more attention in this early period, as cinema would depend upon them for its future.

Their content, execution and delivery was to alter dramatically over the next twenty years and it was through them that cinema's full potential would be realised. As a form of fictional, narrativised entertainment, the cinema would make great leaps and bounds and these developments are the subject of a later chapter.

The Röntgen Ray may have disappeared from the entertainment arena with an almost indecent haste, but they found their real application in the medical and scientific world. Cinema went one stage further, straddling these two disparate worlds and ensuring a future based on its diversity and adaptability. From the very start cinema demonstrated a massive potential in terms of representation; a facility to document and preserve virtually every facet of daily life and go beyond into worlds both unfamiliar and unimagined. Whilst audiences were initially attracted by the sheer replication of movement, this comprehension was augmented by a transport of delights. Influenced by the new novel by H. G. Wells, *The Time Machine*, the early film pioneer Robert Paul was inspired to employ the new medium of cinema in the creation of a time machine:

> He had been reading the weird romance, *The Time Machine*, and it had suggested an entertainment to him, of which animated photographs formed an essential part. In a room capable of accommodating some hundred people, he would arrange seats to which a slight motion could be given. He would plunge the apartment into Cimmerian darkness, and introduce a wailing wind. Although the audience actually moved but a few inches, the sensation would be of travelling through space. From time to time the journey would be combined with panoramic effects. Fantastic scenes of future ages would first be shown. Then the audience would set forth upon its homeward journey. The conductor would regretfully intimate that he had over-shot the mark, and travelled into the past—cue for another series of pictures. Mr Paul had for a long time been at work on this scheme, and had discussed it here and there. [2]

Although never realised, Paul's scheme demonstrated a desire to take the cinema beyond the immediate bounds of its early exhibition, into new contexts and circumstances. An adaptation of this idea emerged in the guise of Hale's Tours from 1904 onwards. Audiences were placed in a mock train carriage and shown films taken as if the carriage was in motion, accompanied by movement and real smoke! Later that year, in July 1896, Robert Paul was also proposing to the British Museum that they establish a National Film Archive to preserve a record of British society, ostensibly from his own films. Unfortunately for us they declined his kind offer.

Others shared Paul's conviction that there was more to the cinema than vicarious entertainment. In 1898 the Polish Lumière cameraman Boleslaw Matuszewski issued what was effectively the first film manifesto, *Une Nouvelle Source de l'Histoire* in which outlined the possibility of establishing an archive of historical film. He published a further title, *La Photographie Animée* which contained a number of suggestions for the use of the cinema in the service of science and education as well as entertainment. Indeed it was Matuszewski who had pioneered the filming of surgery in Warsaw that very same year. The educational potential of the cinema was to prove a controversial issue in Britain in 1913 when the London County Council proposed a series of experimental screenings of educational films to school children.

These first stirrings developed rapidly during the late 1890s and early 1900s as the number of uses of the cinema increased. The scientific application of the cinema proved extremely popular, as both public and professional audiences were drawn to the subjects of these films. These were further augmented by the pioneering use of microscopic and slow motion time-lapse photography and several firms began to specialise in the production of scientific and natural history films. One in particular, The Charles Urban Trading Company, pioneered the introduction of scientific films with the popular *Unseen World* series in 1903.

Another great use of the cinema was the capturing of what were generally regarded as 'Actualities', or news and documentary subjects, by the camera which covered public and sporting events, wars and civil disturbance, ethnographic, topographic and industrial subjects. In an era when foreign travel was still the privilege of the rich or a necessity of war and when the majority of the population had been no further than the seaside, one can only guess at the impact these images must have had. For the first time cinema-goers had the opportunity to watch people and places they had only seen in static, graphic and photographic representations. People became familiar with royal and state events and subjects like the Derby, the Boat Race, boxing matches and the F.A. Cup proved extremely popular. Initially, these actuality and news films were shown alongside a staple diet of cinema fare, alongside features, comedies and melodramas. It was not long before specialised news cinemas began to appear. The first in Britain, called the Daily Bioscope, opened opposite Liverpool Street Station in London on 23 May 1906. This was closely followed by the birth of the newsreel and the launch of the *Topical Budget* in 1911. Physical horizons were further expanded by films of exploration, mountaineering and big game hunting, such as Cherry Kearton's films of Theodore Roosevelt's African expedition of 1908.

But perhaps more than any other film of this type, Herbert Ponting's films of the ill-fated Scott Antarctic expedition of 1911 produced some of the most stunning and strangely alien images the British public had seen. Whilst exposure to subjects from distant places and remote habitats was making the world a smaller place for cinema's audience, there was also a curious, almost antithetical process taking place.

One of the earliest and most emulated films was the Lumière film of their workers leaving the factory. Auguste Lumière filmed his own workers on many occasions and screened the efforts to his workforce to constant exclamations of delight. Whether these reactions were motivated by delight at the process of the cinema, or more the result of seeing themselves represented is a matter of debate. Film exhibitors often emulated this popular practice whenever they moved to a new town, inviting the locals to be filmed and then to visit a screening to see themselves.

So as well as offering up whole new worlds and experiences cinema was also directly focused on the individual. People saw themselves and the rest of humankind represented on the screen before them. Their own lives, occupations and circumstances were called into question by this new medium and comparisons were not always favourable. Cinema's ability to depict real people and situations had repercussions in its fictional representation. It was characterised as a medium suited for detection and identification. Stories about people recognising missing relatives, or people caught in compromising situations by the camera became the standard plots of fictional stories about the cinema. Rudyard Kipling provided one such example in his 1904 short story 'Mrs Bathurst'.

Like the bugs that the camera exposed to the public through the lens of the microscope, cinema's audience was itself only so many microbes on a rather large piece of rotten cheese.

---

1. 'On the Lantern Screen', *The Amateur Photographer*, 6 November 1896.
2. 'An Interview with Robert William Paul', *The Era*, 25 April 1896.

CERTAINLY FEW PEOPLE, if any, can have foreseen in the invention of the cinematograph that which would to a great extent revolutionise the world of teaching; and yet this is precisely what the instrument promises to do, though originally offered to the public only as a toy, an amusement for an idle hour, in the form of a superior magic-lantern combining motion with pictorial effect.

The cinematograph—with several variations of name, but based on similar principles—has already excited considerable attention and popular favour, by bringing scenes of national and stirring interest before spectators prevented from seeing the actual occurrences, and with a promptitude which made the representation more valuable. Now it appears about to enter on a path of usefulness the extent and value of which it is impossible to estimate; for it has been recognised that as an unrivalled means of demonstration for the use of teachers, and in cases where the eye and hand require to be educated and trained, there is unmistakable evidence that before long its application will be widely established. Every one will understand the enormous advantage, to those engaged in imparting instruction, of a demonstrator which can be called upon to repeat the examples required to explain a lesson whenever and as often as may be required, and can, moreover, be depended upon to reproduce the examples in precisely the same way. The latter attribute makes the cinematograph extremely useful, especially in cases where delicate and exact manipulation is required, and gives the instrument an enormous advantage over a mere flesh-and-blood performer, whose fatigue, state of health, the weather, and numberless other circumstances might cause variations. The use of the cinematograph, by which moving reflections of the subject under consideration will be distinctly seen by all, also enables a much larger number of students to assist at an illustrated lecture, and to derive benefit from the demonstrations. In addition, the lecturer—whether he be the author of the examples or not, and no matter how practiced and expert he may be—might be expected to give a far more clear and lucid interpretation of his subject if freed from the embarrassment of simultaneous performance.

To students unable to attend the lectures of the cleverest and ablest professors, as well as those whom fate compels to reside at some distance from the centres of education, the cinematograph in its new function will come as an incalculable boon; for it will be possible by its aid to repeat the illustrative action of the greatest authority on any given subject, and by means of an accompanying lecture to repeat the lesson not only as many times as may be required, but in as many different places. This will enable the poor as well as the rich, the country as well as the town mouse, to enjoy the same high advantages.

It has always been acknowledged that 'example is better than precept', and a moment's consideration will help any one realise the vast field for instruction thus opened, for there is scarcely any branch of instruction that does not require a certain amount of demonstration; and the pupil can be so thoroughly familiarised with the movements required for any special purpose, through constant repetition by mechanical means, that there will be far less difficulty experienced in practical work than if the ordinary methods of teaching were followed.

**Mrs J. E. Whitby
'The Future of the
Cinematograph'**
Chambers's Journal
19 May 1900

*"Suggestion for the R.A.
A Mutoscope of the Pictures,
for the use of visitors in
hurry. The Royal Academy
"done" in five minutes."
Punch*, 10 May 1899.

"The Home Cinematograph for Sufferers from Insomnia." *Punch,* **9 April 1913.**

That the same illustrations may be given again and again is an economic advantage which will be apparent to all. Thus, the movements required for swimming might be studied, before the pupil entered the water, by means of a representation of a swimmer actually breasting the waves; cooking classes could be held and lessons given without fire; dancing could be taught, and gymnastics imitated; in fact, there is no end to the subjects which could be treated. It would also be possible, and might be advantageous, for pupils to compare the methods of different demonstrators; while the demonstrators themselves might gain by being able to see and judge of themselves and their actions when imparting instruction.

Useful as all of this undoubtedly promises to be, the cinematograph, however, proposes to make its greatest mark in the science of surgery, and by its illustrative power to add immensely to the knowledge of that science, as well as to simplify the means of acquiring it. All centres of medical education possess amphitheatres in which is carried on the practical study of those surgical operations to which poor suffering humanity has to submit.

These studies are usually practiced on corpses; and though this may be highly necessary in the interests of all, and for the promotion of science, it is a gruesome idea, and most people will hail with satisfaction the news that the use of the cinematograph will do away with or at least lessen the necessity for dissection. No demonstration, however clearly given, on a dead body can possibly equal all that may be learnt from studying the same operation performed on a living patient; and it is just this which the cinematograph will ensure. Even when it is possible for students to watch an operation on a patient, a large number of spectators is impossible, while for various reasons those present must keep at a distance, and thus have a difficulty in seeing the operations. All these disadvantages the cinematograph promises to remove; the benefits to be derived from its employment as a demonstrator in surgical lectures being proved on its exhibition before the British Medical Association when in Edinburgh. There seems to be little doubt, therefore, that the cinematograph is destined to become a recognised factor in the course of surgical instruction. Amongst others who will benefit by its introduction may also be reckoned those people—and there are many such nowadays- who, although not actually following the profession of medicine or surgery, interest themselves in assisting the suffering, as they will thus acquire a knowledge of certain facts of immeasurable importance in a moment of urgency.

It has also been suggested that, by familiarising people with the sights the cinematograph might show, much of the terror felt regarding a surgical operation could be dispelled; while the apparent precision and care with which everything is done, as well as the calmness of the surgeon and his assistants, would induce a feeling of confidence.

Enough has, perhaps, been said to prove that the cinematograph has a future of usefulness totally unsuspected by those who first launched it, and of an extent no one in these days of marvellous discoveries can possibly foretell; while, in addition, there is stimulus given to, and the change likely to result in, the art of photography, of which the cinematograph is a part.

THE CINEMATOGRAPH IN EDUCATION

A Striking Experiment

The Times
27 October 1913

S OME MONTHS AGO a proposal to utilise the cinematograph as an adjunct to school work came before the London County Council, but for some reason the project was shelved. Possibly it may be revived now the EVENING NEWS has shown the way by the performance which was given at the West-End Cinema on Saturday morning. The occasion marked the inauguration of a series of special exhibitions of educational pictures which are to be given, for the benefit of children of school age, in all the parts of London during the winter. The presence of the Lord Mayor (Sir David Burnett), the Chairman of the London County Council (Mr. Cyril Cobb), and a host of others interested in the welfare of the child, and the hearty applause which greeted the various pictures, held out high hopes that the cinematograph may soon bear its fair share in the task of education.

The film maker, it should be added, is not to blame for the present position. For some years pictures have been produced which have had a distinct educational value, but as a rule they have been exhibited under unfavourable conditions. A child's mind can hardly be in a fit condition to take in the full significance of a picture of geographical, commercial, or historical interest when he has just witnessed an exciting drama of the 'Wild West' and is waiting eagerly for a farcical episode of the "follow-your-leader" variety. Educationally the isolated picture has, perhaps, little value, but the EVENING NEWS performances obviate this difficulty by presenting a series of pictures, every one of them of some educational significance, which will hold the attention of the scholar from the start and help him in the work which he has on hand. As far as one can see, there is only one real danger which has to be avoided, and that is the possibility of showing a child so much that at the end he retains a jumbled mass of recollections, unless the pictures are explained while the entertainment is in progress, or unless the programme is carefully annotated, as was the case on Saturday. In such an exhibition it is possible to make full use of the value of contrast. Few pictures will appeal more strongly to the child, after the wet and cold of the London streets, than those dealing with the picturesque splendours of Turkestan or Cairo, the various processes of manufacture in a Bombay iron and steel foundry, or the work of picking cocoa pods and preparing them for the market.

Quite the most interesting of the many excellent films displayed on Saturday was that which showed an ascent of the Matterhorn made earlier in the year. The picture, which is the property of Messrs. Jury, has not yet been shown in public, but it is certain to attract a great amount of attention in geographical circles. The film was secured in July by Mr. Frederick Burlington, who, with his guides and his cinematograph apparatus, succeeded in reaching the summit of the Matterhorn. Many thousands of people who have never seen, and are never likely to see, the Alps, will gain some idea of the difficulties that beset the intrepid climber. Every stage of the ascent is shown, though some of the pictures must have been taken at the greatest personal danger, and at the summit the troubles of the party were increased by a gale of wind and snow, which, despite the discomfort, have greatly enhanced the value of the film. For the rest, the pictures shown covered a very wide educational field, from the making of a silk hat in London to the manufacture of a steel rail in Bombay; from studies of fish life to a journey along the Manchester Ship Canal; and from a day in the Paris Zoological Gardens to a remarkable film in which the ants and grasshoppers of Professor Losdki of Moscow, were presented into the service of the cinematograph.

❁

THE KINEMA IN THE CLASS-ROOM
WHERE CHILDREN LEARN THEIR LESSONS FROM MOVING PICTURES

CHOOSING THE DAY'S LESSONS

THE PICTURE PARADE: THE PUPILS OFF TO SEE THE KINEMA

SCHOOL-BOOKS OF THE FUTURE

THE KINEMA CLASS: WAITING TO BEGIN

PEEPING TOM

THE INSTITUTE AND KINEMA-ROOM AT NETTLEBED

QUESTION TIME

THE ART OF DEFENCE — GIRLS FENCING IN THE GYMNASIUM

MEN IN THE SHOOTING GALLERY AT THE VILLAGE INSTITUTE

The pioneer of kinema education is the wonderful village of Nettlebed, in Oxfordshire, where for the past year moving pictures have played a prominent part in the school. The village is fortunate in having Mr. Robert Fleming, a wealthy railway magnate, as a resident, and he has spent large sums in providing the villagers with amusements, and the children with a well-thought-out scheme of education aided by the kinema. Children come to the school from many miles around, and no one is ever absent on the days when the pictures are shown.

THE KINEMATOGRAPH having literally at its birth been dragged into the service of the omnipotent music hall (much in a similar way to that in which the poor x-rays are now being trotted out at every bazaar) as a novel and interesting form of entertainment (which it undoubtedly is), its scientific value is likely to be obscured, if not temporarily lost—a misfortune which every earnest worker in science should, I think, do his utmost to avert. From an educational point of view its value in the future will probably be as much in advance of the ordinary magic lantern as the magic lantern of to-day is in advance of the toy lanterns of our boyhood. In meteorology, isolated photographs of a storm or storm clouds, or the results of a whirlwind, are held in high esteem, but how much more valuable would be a series showing such a storm or whirlwind actually in action?—such a result has now become possible. Photography has already done good service in the detection of crime, and the identification of criminals; the latter result would be much strengthened by a faithful representation of some particular gait, habit or characteristic of the criminal—the Kinematograph will do this for us. Photographs of machinery at rest in all its diversified branches are of the very greatest value both in business and in the education of the student—how much more valuable will be photographs—faithfully representing its wonderful and oftentimes complicated movements?—not only will the poorer educational institutions, which are unable to purchase elaborate models, benefit, but the would-be purchaser, the inventor, and the private student, will also reap their share. In medicine, the peculiar habits and characteristics engendered by obscure diseases can now be faithfully recorded and placed on one side for future comparison, and mutual helpful guidance. I know of recent instance in veterinary science in which the peculiar movements and actions indulged in by a horse suffering from an obscure disease would have been far more easily understood and far more faithfully represented at a certain meeting by the Kineto-scopical principle than by a series of isolated instantaneous pictures, and a not too clear description, as they actually were.

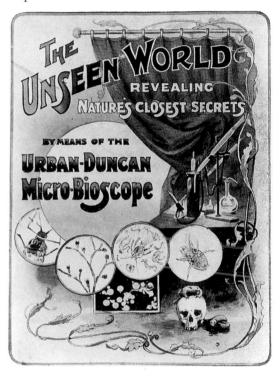

V. E. Johnson, M.A., 'The Kinematograph from a Scientific Point of View' *Photography* 10 December 1896

Medicine in all its branches has, or will very shortly have, three very powerful assistants in the x-rays, the Kinematograph, and the photo-chromoscope, the latter, which—in the course of time—will undoubtedly show in the clearest and most convincing manner possible the exact outward appearance engendered by any particular disease, obscure and much-debated problems re the soaring, sailing and rowing flight of birds, are likely to soon be rendered much clearer, if not completely solved, by the Kinematograph. That vexed question of a cat always alighting on its feet, the surface tension of fluids as exhibited in bursting soap bubbles, the flight of projectiles, and that peculiar and mysterious half twist indulged in by a tennis racket when compelled to turn a somersault in the air, etc. The Kinematograph will have something to reveal in all these instances and many others—in fact, I scarcely know of any problem in science where movement of any kind is concerned in which the Kinematograph will not be helpful and oftentimes a powerful assistant. When king Roderick first visited the necromantic tower of Toledo—or at least so runs legendary history—he beheld on the linen cloth taken by him from the coffer the painted figures of men on horseback of fierce demeanour; anon the picture became animated, and there at length appeared depicted upon its magic surface a great filed of battle with Christians and Moslems engaged in deadly conflict, accompanied with the clash of arms, the braying of trumpets, the neighing of horses. Can the imagination conceive that which the mind of science cannot execute? Of a Truth:

> The Photographic art is ever able
> To endow with truth mere fable.

Advertisement from the Charles Urban Trading Company 1903 catalogue for the 'Unseen World' series of scientific films.

**R. H. Mere,
'The Wonders of the
Biograph'**
Pearson's Magazine
February 1899

POSTERITY WILL HAVE GOOD CAUSE to bless the nineteenth-century geniuses who were responsible for the invention of the Biograph. The Biograph, it may be well to explain at the outset, is an instrument for taking in rapid succession a series of photographs of any living, moving scene, and of bringing these photographs before the eye so quickly that one is enabled to see the entire scene reproduced as in actual life. It is the highest type of countless instruments named with all manner of variations on the words Kinematograph, Kinetoscope and Animatograph.

This new art of animated picture-taking will deserve a high rank among the triumphs of latter-day ingenuity. It brings the past to the present, and it enables the present to be handed down to the future. Already we look back and witness, as they occurred in life, events of the last two or three years which might never have been faithfully preserved without the Biograph's help. For example, we may watch each incident in the Queen's triumphal procession through the streets of London on the day of her Diamond Jubilee. Provided the films are still in existence, our descendants a thousand years hence may do likewise.

All over the world the Biograph operators are busily at work recording scenes for the benefit of the future. They are illustrating the world's history. Pomps and pageants, wars, business and pleasure pastimes, country scenes, town scenes, sea scenes, mountain scenes, the people, the events, the tragedies, and the humours of the day; in short, every phase of present-day life is being faithfully recorded. The purpose of this article is to show how the wonders of the Biograph are brought about.

As the Biograph has become a favourite amusement at public entertainments, an enormous outlay of labour and expense must be incurred in order to secure a constant supply of exciting and topical subjects. Take the last Derby, for instance; it was photographed in the afternoon (the race was run at 3.20), by six o'clock the photographs had been hurried up to London, and at ten o'clock the same evening the audience at the Palace Theatre were watching every detail of the race which had taken place but a few hours before; in fact, before the last stragglers had returned from the Epsom course. On Trafalgar Day a similar feat was performed, and Nelson's monument, with the busy throng gazing at the decorations, was shown to an audience on the same evening; and so with the arrival of the Guards from the Sudan, and their glorious welcome as they passed through London's streets.

A staff of skilled operators is always maintained in readiness for instant dispatch if necessary to the utmost parts of the world.

A striking incident will illustrate the part the Biograph is playing. The Biograph Syndicate photographed the Diamond Jubilee procession and gave an exhibition in London. Ten days later the Jubilee procession was being watched in New York, two days after that in Chicago, and three days later in San Francisco, more than 5,000 miles distant from London. Six weeks after the date of the Jubilee procession it was being exhibited on the Biograph in Australia. Thus in all parts of the world the gorgeous pageant which London had witnessed but a short time before was re-enacted again, and thousands of her majesty's subjects in Britain's far-off colonies were enabled to view her triumph.

**Advertisement for the Charles
Urban Trading Company, 1903.**

More recently, splendid Biograph records have been secured of the coronation of the young Queen of Holland, and also of recent British, French and German military manoeuvres. The home-coming of Lord Kitchener, the Sirdar, was made the occasion of special effort. This event was illustrated with what will probably stand as an unbroken record for some time to come. A series of photographs was taken of the Sirdar boarding the steamer at Calais in the afternoon, and also of his reception at Dover by the mayor and corporation of that town.

These views were reproduced the same evening at the Palace Theatre, London!

In the recent war between Spain and America, the Biograph operators were well to the front. At the outbreak of the hostilities, operators were dispatched to obtain interesting snapshots of camp life, and to secure films of the battle themselves. For the second part of this programme it was necessary to charter a special vessel, and although it carried an American cargo, it had to sail under the British flag to avoid capture and subsequent delay. By way of showing the little excitements these operators experienced, the following account is interesting:-

"Although we sailed under the British flag, we did not always go through unmolested. On one occasion we were fired upon by a Spanish gunboat, and barely escaped capture—a very thrilling experience.

The gunboat in question was lying in shore, but unfortunately happened to catch sight of our dispatch boat, and promptly started in pursuit. We were greatly alarmed, capture meant delay, and we did everything possible to escape. Furnaces were fed with oil and sides of bacon, the stokers were urged on to their work with champagne, and all our lights were 'doused' in order that our boat might be lost in the growing darkness.

The excessive heat caused the stacks to glow red-hot. At one time the gunboat was close enough to fire, and repeated shots were discharged at us, luckily without effect. At last, after the most nerve-trying ordeal I have ever undergone, we reached the neutral harbour of St. Thomas."

This war correspondent is a modest man, and omits to add how he endeavoured to make the captain sally forth again, how the chief engineer, thoroughly frightened with has last experience, refused to re-visit Cuban waters, and finally how, with his health broken by hardships and his spirit crushed with worry, he had to return to New York with his valuable films in a 'tramp' steamer.

Immediately upon his return, however, another man was sent to the scene of operations, and he too, was involved in a number of perilous adventures. That he might obtain a better view of the opposing fleets under fire he desired to be landed from the dispatch boat. For a few hours all went well; then suddenly the dispatch boat found that a Spanish cruiser was coming towards her "full steam ahead." The dispatch boat promptly abandoned the correspondent—and ran away. The operator remained on the beach guarding his apparatus for three days and three nights, and during this time he was without any shelter from the elements and without food or water.

The upshot of all this was that when he eventually reached New York, he sent in his films— and disappeared completely. After weeks of tracking and manhunting, it was found that he had suffered so severely from his exposure that he became delirious, and walked about the street in a semi-conscious manner, finally stumbling into a hospital, where for a long time he lay in a precarious state.

That it may not be thought that only war correspondents meet with dangerous adventures, here is an example of what the home operators have had to undergo.

On one occasion the entire fire department of the Atlantic City, U.S.A., turned out for the benefit of the Biograph representative. The parade was exceptionally large, and the square in which the exhibition took place was crowded with several thousand spectators. The various 'steamers' galloped past at their highest speed, and all went well until the hand engine appeared, with the men dragging it at a trot. At this moment the chemical engine, drawn by a pair of grey horses, came dashing down the street at full gallop until it ran parallel with the men on foot. By this time they were both approaching the camera, which was standing well out in the street, and too late the driver of the engine discovered that there was not room for the engine to pass between the camera and the men who were running on foot.

In this dilemma he had a choice of three evils to decide upon in about two seconds. Firstly to pull to the left and run over the men on foot; secondly, to pull to the right, run into the crowd and probably kill or maim dozens of people; thirdly to drive over the camera, by the side of which were standing the two operators. In these two seconds he chose the last alternative and dashed full speed at the camera. The pole of the engine struck the camera right in the centre, breaking the heavy box, scattering the mechanism far and wide, and flinging the operators back into the crowd. How those men escaped instant death will never be known, and they were lucky indeed to get off with a few bruises apiece.

By another stroke of good look, when the wreckage was collected it was found that the light-tight box containing the exposed films had quite escaped injury; the result being that when the films were developed the full scene was given up to the very moment when the horses, with ears back and heads forward, bore down upon the camera!

Another curious experience occurred when an operator was endeavouring to photograph the 'shooting' of the Falls on the Saint Lawrence River from a moving boat, which was to descend with the instrument aboard. The camera was placed a little further forward than originally planned, and, as a result, on the boat giving a sudden lurch, the camera went overboard and had to be fished up from twenty feet of water. It was some considerable time before it was grappled with and caught, and then a much larger boat had to be obtained to lift the weight—nearly four hundred pounds—from the bottom of the river. There are one two little points about the Biograph worth recording. Forty negatives per second can be taken, the exposure for each film being less than 1:200th of a second. The ordinary length of a film is about 200ft., but on the occasion of a Paris fire about 700ft. were used, representing 3500 separate and distinct pictures. The number of feet of film used by the Company during the year is 750,000ft., or 142 miles. On one film as much as £1200 has been expended.

The most difficult set of films to obtain was series of sittings which have been given by His Holiness Pope Leo XIII.

Appreciating how few have had the opportunity of visiting Rome and seeing the Pope, the Biograph Company determined, if possible, to procure for the world at large a life-like representation of scenes in and about the Vatican, together with the personality of the Pope himself. After nearly a year's patient work, fortified by letters from eminent personages in other countries, together with frequent interviews with Count Soderini, Count Pecci, the Pope's nephew, and His Excellency Monsignor della Volpe, Mr Dickson, the technician of the English Biograph Syndicate, succeeded in securing five separate and distinct sittings, making a total of over 17,000 negatives.

As may be surmised, it was no easy undertaking, objections being raised at every move in the negotiations. The Vatican officials, however, together with the Pope, eventually yielded, in consideration of the many petitions presented setting forth the pleasure such a series of views would give to the people in all countries. One of the most interesting of the series is that in which the Pope is seen giving his benediction to the people of the world through the medium of this apparatus.

"I wished also to take a picture of His Holiness driving through the Vatican gardens," says Mr. Dickson. "The carriage was a opened purposely, and, in spite of the terrific heat of the sun, His Holiness abstained most graciously from raising his parasol. This, I am told, was the first time for twenty years that Pope Leo XIII's carriage had ever been seen open. Proceeding and following the carriage were mounted guards, commanded by Count Camillo Pecci. When the carriage stopped His Excellency Monsignor della Volpe knelt, and kissing the Pope's ring, asked for a special blessing on the purpose of his mission, so that his holiness is seen giving his benediction through the medium of the camera".

The natural question to ask here is, whether such interesting records ought not to be kept among the archives of the country?

The answer is quite satisfactory—it is expressed intention to give copies of all interesting subjects to the British Museum. These will be shown by means of the Mutoscope, so that people of a hundred—aye, even a thousand years hence, may see, by merely turning a handle, as we ourselves have seen, all the stirring events now marking the close of our present century.

Pope Leo XIII filmed by W. K. L. Dickson in 1898.

THE CINEMATOGRAPH IN SURGERY

Chambers's Journal
26 August 1899

THE ANIMATED PHOTOGRAPHS which for some time have been the delight of thousands of sightseers and holiday-makers in all parts of the civilised world have now appeared in a new and, it would seem, a very useful role. A celebrated French surgeon, M. Doyen, has conceived the idea of picturing in this manner the various phases of an operation from the first cut of the knife to the final adjustment of the bandages, each detail of the work being as excellently shown that a mistake could hardly be made by a receptive observer. At a recent demonstration at the University of Kiel, before a select company of doctors and other scientific men, a complete series of these surgical studies were thrown on a screen, and excited great enthusiasm among those present. The only drawback that we can see to this method of demonstration is, that it is only applicable to operations of very short duration, for the cinematograph film of fifty feet in length—the usual size—is complete in less than one minute; while many a surgical operation, and notably those requiring the greatest care and skill, will cover a period of half-an-hour or more.

Above:
"*Inside a cow and other 'hides': strange bird-photography.*
Concealed inside a dummy cow, with his
cinematograph-camera, to make living-pictures of
tropical bird-life: Mr. Frank Newman at work."
The Illustrated London News, 27 June 1914.

Right:
"A cinematographer obtaining scenic views of the
Rockies under thrilling circumstances."
The Sphere, 20 January 1912.

TRAINING OF OMNIBUS DRIVERS:

The Cinematograph and the Prevention of Accidents

The Times
2 May 1913

THE HOUSE OF COMMONS COMMITTEE appointed to inquire into motor-traffic in London heard further evidence yesterday from the London General Omnibus Company. Sir G. Toulmin presided.

Mr. A. H. Stanley, the general manager for the company, said the police regulations required that drivers should be over 21 years of age, hold medical certificates for physical fitness, and certificates of good conduct covering three years. The number of applicants enabled the company to add to these requirements by raising the age, and extending certificates to five years, and also to select married men with experiences of driving in London in preference to others. Since August 13, 1912, up to January 15 this year 30 men of the minimum age had been engaged; 277 between the ages of 22 and 25; 289 between 26 and 30; 165 between 31 and 35; 103 between 36 and 40; and 85 over 40, these being exceptional cases in favour of old employees. Of the total number 55 per cent. were married at the time, and he had little doubt that many others corrected the disability very quickly; and 66 per cent. had had three years' experience of London driving. Tramway car drivers were not apt to accommodate themselves to the more flexible conditions of omnibus travelling and taxi-cab drivers to the reduced speed; carmen or drivers of heavier vehicles were candidates of the most satisfactory type, and from these about 80 per cent. were selected.

Cinematograph demonstrations were used in instructing the staff for showing how common forms of accident might be avoided. The witness explained that for producing films vehicles were arranged to make close resemblance to actual accidents.

❈

A FILM OF THE
DECREPIT HORSE TRAFFIC

The Times
27 February 1914

THE ROYAL SOCIETY FOR THE PREVENTION OF CRUELTY TO ANIMALS has enlisted the cinematograph on behalf of the Bill dealing with the decrepit horse traffic which has been introduced into the House of Commons by Colonel Walker, M.P. The measure provides that it shall be illegal to export alive from this country any horse of the value of £10 or less, and to illustrate the extent to which the trade is carried on the Society have taken a series of pictures from the arrival of the beasts on the Continent to their slaughter in public or private slaughterhouses.

It may be said at once that the pictures as shown privately yesterday are never likely to be displayed before the general public, for, deeply impressive as they are, no censor would pass them for general exhibition, and no cinematograph theatre manager would put them into an ordinary programme. The earlier pictures show the arrival of the animals and their weary progress through the streets, and to these, pathetic as they are, no objection could be taken. But in the closing stages, by way of an argument in favour of a humane killer, the film shows a primitive method of slaughtering the unfortunate beasts by driving a knife into the chest. As the blood surges out the animal's death struggles are seen with repulsive realism. The Society itself admits that these pictures cannot be shown in public, however vividly they prove the need for some improvement of existing conditions.

The Strand Magazine
vol. XII (July–
December, 1896)

THE PRINCE'S DERBY
Shown by Lightning Photography

WE ARE TOLD THAT NOTHING IS NEW. Out of the ancient Zoetrope or wheel of life, was evolved the gyroscope, which was exhibited in a gallery at the Polytechnic more than sixty years ago. This was a wheel of black silhouette figures, revolving before a mirror, and giving the appearance of vitality. Half a century or so later, Mr. Edison produced his kinetoscope—a band of progressive pictures passing before the eye applied to an optical peep-hole, and creating the effects of life and motion.

During the Indian Exhibition last year, Mr. R. W. Paul, a clever electrical engineer, of Hatton Garden, made and exhibited the kinetoscopes there, and noticing the rush for these marvellous machines, he wondered if their fascinating pictures could be reproduced on a screen, so that thousands might see them at one time. This idea has been brought to a triumphantly successful issue, though not without infinite patience and ingenuity on the part of the inventor. In Edison's machine, the photos are magnified six times only, whilst in Mr. Paul's apparatus, prints no bigger than a postage-stamp are projected on a ten-foot screen. Plainly, then, such very high magnification calls for absolute perfection in the tiny originals.

Briefly explained, the whole thing amounts to this: hundreds of photographs are taken with amazing rapidity—say, twenty a second—on an enormous length of transparent celluloid ribbon. These photos are subsequently shown magic-lantern fashion, also with extreme rapidity, the results being "living pictures" which completely baffle description; they must be seen to be appreciated. On this page Mr. Paul is seen with his unique camera; he is looking into the "finder" ready to commence turning the hand-wheel the moment the desired picture comes into the field . . .

"Mr Paul and His Camera."

The sensitive film is fed from a spool and passes an opening in front of the lens. The process of taking one scene is as follows: The film is moved forward exactly three-quarters of an inch (the width of the photo); then it stops for the exposure, and moves on again for the next. While the film is actually moving, the light has to be cut off by the revolving shutter so as to prevent blurring, the exposure occurring only when the film is quite stationary. All these conditions are necessary for every picture; and yet Mr. Paul can take with this camera over 2,000 photos per minute!

. . . The ribbon is made to pass step by step through a kind of magic lantern at precisely the same rate at which the photos were taken. Each picture pauses in front of the lantern aperture just sufficiently long enough to appear momentarily on the screen, before being followed by the next. Thus the eye gets the different phases of the scene presented in rapid order. While one photo, is giving place to the next, the lantern aperture is covered with a movable shutter operating at a speed which deceives the eye. Needless to say, the mechanism is wonderfully delicate, containing an aluminium sprocket-wheel, a presser pad, a cam, a steel finger, and other comparatively uninteresting things. The camera and the projector machines are identical in principle.

` Anyone who hasn't seen Mr. Paul's amazing 'living photographs' has decidedly missed a sensational thing. Take the arrival of the Paris express at Calais station. The great train appears in the distance, and rushes forward as though to overwhelm the audience, but presently slows down in time, and discharges its living freight amid a scene of bustle and excitement. The scene at Westminster, too, with its superb equipages, high spirited horses, and passing crowds and omnibuses, fairly glows with life. Again in the Hampstead Heath set, we see the swings and roundabouts going merrily, the children skipping and 'Arry working off his traditional exuberance of spirit. *A Rough Sea at* shows the breakers rolling in majestically, and the spray is thrown up in so realistic a fashion as to make the people in the stalls actually start involuntarily, lest they should be drenched!

But the great sensation is, beyond question, the *Prince's Derby* of 1896, the most popular win the turf has ever known. Of course, Mr. Paul didn't know that the Prince of Wales was going to win the Derby; he merely went to get the finish of that great race, having less concern with the 'blue ribbon of the turf' as such, than with the black ribbon of film which should show to countless multitudes one of the most popular events of the Victorian age. At all events, our inventor was on the spot, with the result that the deposited at these offices some 80ft. of celluloid ribbon, containing about 1,280 unique instantaneous photographs of the historical race. The story of this remarkable photographic feat is well worth recording.

Mr. Paul went down a few days before the Derby to make his arrangements. Disappointed in the use of one of the stands, he at length rented a few square yards of ground from a man on the course, whose legal rights were by no means defined. The spot chosen was near Mr. D'Arcy's stand, on the opposite side to the Grand Stand, and about 20yds. past the winning post.

At five o'clock on the morning of Derby Day, Mr. Paul sets out for the Downs in a wagonette, with two assistants, and the camera shown on the first page of this article. As in the case of other expeditions, great care was taken to provide the necessary appliances. Among the impedimenta were a number of beams of wood, wherewith to shore up the vehicle, so as to take the weight off the springs. This was in order that the camera might have a perfectly steady platform. Incidentally, the beams served another purpose: preventing the total annihilation of the entire party— wagonette, apparatus and operators—by the surging thousands, who, at the finish of the race, became perfectly delirious with excitement, and were only kept from wiping out the hated intruders by being menaced with far-reaching clubs. It must have been a grand sight—the siege of the wagonette, I mean, not the race. No vehicle had ever been allowed on that spot before. Mr. Paul reached Epsom at eight o'clock, but his troubles commenced with his work. At ten his erratic landlord (who had received the rent in advance) turned up with a 'Derby-Dayish' condition, and requested him to leave. That landlord must have felt very strongly on the subject, for he spoke very strongly. Half an hour before the race, however, the man was removed, protesting.

The adventurous trio fortunately had the minor races on which to practice beforehand, so that the exact range was soon revealed by the finder. Presently the old cry was raised with its accustomed force and volume. "Off!" sounded sonorous unanimity from innumerable throats. The Derby had begun. Hearts began to beat faster. Even philosophers, ready to recognise the supreme advantage of keeping cool in all circumstances, felt a peculiar sensation thrilling through their veins. Truly the pace was astonishing. The crowd by the starting post had scarcely commenced its mad rush across the Downs in the vain hope of getting a glimpse of the finish, when the field 'began to tail', as the sporting reporters say. Tamarind and Toussaint were already out of it, and Persimmon was so full of running that his jockey could be seen taking a pull at him. Almost before one could realise the rapid progress of events, the leaders were pounding away as hard as they could down to Tattenham Corner, the purple and scarlet of the Prince gradually forging to the front. But the mighty St. Frusquin was in no humour to be left behind, and came into the straight 'going great guns' People held their breath, and wondered, with palpitating hearts, what the result would be. There was only two in it. The favourites left the others as if they were standing still, and the Derby of 1896 resolved itself into a close and desperate struggle. Cries for the Prince were already being made, when St. Frusquin made a magnificent challenge, and it looked for an instant as if the spoils were going to Mentmore after all. Only for a moment, however. The Royal Champion, full of running, answered with an invincible rush, and before he had reached the post the discerning multitude detected what was about to happen. The horses were a good twenty yards from the judge's box, but the verdict was, in the estimation of the populace, already assured. A few strides more, and there was no doubts about it. Cheering, which had already begun lustily, swelled into a surging indomitable, all conquering roar. It is easy to imagine the utter and complete abandonment of self-possession at that thrilling

Still from *The Prince's Derby* by R. W. Paul.

moment, when one united shout of semi-delirious joy broke from thousands of half-frantic spectators.

. . . Like a mariner whose vessel is in deadly peril, [Mr. Paul] stood with his hand on the wheel, looking anxiously along the vast expanse of green turf. Strange as it may seem, he commenced to turn the wheel eight seconds before the horses came into the 'field'; of course, I mean the field of the camera. At first the photos were taken at the rate of about 12 a second, but during the exciting finish the pace increased to 30 and 35 a second, or over 2,000 pictures a minute. The operator slowed down somewhat when the two favourites had passed the winning post, but the curious photos of the crowd pouring over the course were taken at about 15 a second. It took Mr. Paul exactly a minute and three-quarters to take the whole scene—the complete set of 1,280 photographs.

The inventor paid little heed to the appalling uproar that marked the finish of the race; but only turned his wheel for the dear life, and for the benefit of the public who weren't there. The moment the race was over, Mr. Paul whipped out the film, packed it up securely, and made a dash for Epsom Downs station, only regretting that he couldn't take the uproariously sequel to the race—the Prince of Wales leading in his superb horse, Persimmon. However, he had another worry on hand at the moment, for he was by no means sure that his prodigiously long negative was a photographic success.

Mr. Paul, I say, left wagonette, camera, assistants, and everything else, and hurried back to London, reaching Hatton Garden at six o'clock. The assistants, by the way, recommended operations on the next race. The great negative was developed and hung up to dry at one o'clock in the morning. Later on the Thursday prints were made and tested in the inventor's workshops at Saffron Hill, where a couple of projecting machines and a full-sized screen are always kept in readiness. Thus the same evening an enormous audience at the Alhambra Theatre witnessed the Prince's Derby all to themselves amidst wild enthusiasm, which all but drowned the strains of 'God Bless the Prince of Wales', as played by the splendid orchestra. The favourites raced in once more with a tremendous stride, checking their speed only when the winning-post was passed; next was seen the laggard horses, and lastly a seemingly illimitable multitude which swarmed over the course as far as the eye could see. In short, the great race, as depicted by Mr. Paul's Animatographe, is a veritable marvel of modern photography and mechanism.

CINEMATOGRAPH CHATS
The Warwick Trading Company

*The Talking Machine
News and Cinematograph
Chronicle,*
vol. 1, 1903–04

THERE IS A BIG FIELD AS YET UNEXPLOITED, before the Bioscope in religious and philanthropic work. How much, for example, would a series of living pictures of the actual work of the missionary enhance an appeal at Exeter Hall. With what irresistible force, on the other hand, would a living picture of the Gospel story go home to the minds of those as yet without the fold. The animated picture itself would to them appear little short of miraculous.

The Bioscope can also be used as a means of clinical education. Take the delicate and difficult operation, such as only two or three eminent surgeons would undertake—only one or two would have the courage as well as the knowledge to go through with it. You have only to Bio-scope it and you can pass on, not only their knowledge, but the actual details of the operation, step by step. No need to be in the operating theatre—no need to be within thousands of miles of the actual operation—student and medical practitioner alike can see it reproduced on the screen exactly as it happened. These particular diseases, and the operations they call for, do not occur every day for the benefit even of those who could witness them in the operating theatre for themselves. The Bioscope multiplies reproductions of them indefinitely. More, they are infinitely better than any lecture you could have, for they are a teaching power to medical students all over the world. For pictures speak a universal language: they are as well understood in one country as another.

In short, the picture's the thing, not only for recreation but for instruction as well; it beats the printed word hollow every time; the appeal to the imagination is direct and immediate. And if the picture is the thing, still more then the Living Picture, adding and strengthening it with the dramatic element, the tragedy or comedy of human action and human interests. What is the best kind of advertisement? The pictorial advertisement—an illustration of what you have to sell. What do you remember best of all 'the scenes of your childhood?'. Not the written or the spoken world, but some scene, actual or pictured, which has impressed itself indelibly on your memory, so that you never forget it while life lasts. The living picture having once 'arrived' is here for all time, for the interest of mankind in the pictorial semblance of human life belonging to all time.

*"Nature and the Cinematographer—
Mr. Percy Smith at Work.*
**Great Britain has taken the lead in bringing
the wonders of science popularly before
the public."**
From Frederick Talbot, *Moving Pictures:
How They are Made and Work,* 1912.

The World's Fair
15 January 1910

ANIMATED BABY PICTURES
Remarkable Device for Obtaining Living Portrait Albums
Home Cinematograph

ANIMATED PICTURES OF BABY at play and baby in his bath are likely to become more popular with fond mothers than posed photographs of their infants.

A London firm has started taking cinematograph portraits of children and grown-ups and producing them in a small and handy form, so that by means of an instrument resembling very much the well-known stereoscope, an actual moving picture of the subject may be seen for ever after.

This new development in portrait photography suggests extraordinary possibilities. It will be possible, for instance, for the octogenarian of 1990 to see himself laughing or crying in his cradle, or taking the first tottering steps of his life.

Or scenes in the present-day nurseries, of children romping together, can be transferred with all their living movement to photographic reproduction, and kept for the happy youngsters, to be shown to their own children in days to come.

This new 'pocket' animated photography is not, of course, confined to children. Their elders, too, are welcoming it.

Still from the Lumière film *A Game of Cards*, 1895.

Last Rubber Pictured

At the premises of the firm exploiting this animated portraiture the Daily Mirror was told that it is of frequent occurrence for two friends, or even a party of friends, to have themselves 'animatographed' before parting.

Four keen whist players, whose circle was about to be broken by the departure of one, had themselves photographed enjoying their last rubber.

Other friends parting are taken drinking each other's health. A man will be taken in characteristic attitude, smoking or reading.

The films on which these photographs are taken are 40 feet long, and show perhaps a full minute or more of actual movement.

From the film negative each picture is printed in the usual way; there are from 500 to 700 of these, and so arranged around a cylinder that they appear like the leaves of a book.

Living Portraiture

The cylinder is then placed in the kinora, as the stereoscope-like machine is called, and the cylinder made to revolve either by means of a simple spring or by clockwork.

As it revolves the pictures flash across the line of view, and the animated effect is obtained.

The cost of the first reel is 30s., and duplicate copies may be had for 7s. 6d.

The kinora varies in price, according to the type and model, from 15s. to as many guineas, the more expensive models being so designed that several people may view the pictures at the same time.

The kinora is actually equivalent to a living portrait album. A moving picture of scenes in our crinolined grandmothers' lives would fill us with amazement at the present day; to our grandchildren our moving presentments will be a matter of course.

TELL-TALE PHOTOGRAPH

Wife's Deception Discovered at a Cinematograph Show

The World's Fair
2 October 1909

A MAN NAMED JULIEN BOISTARD presented himself at the police station of Petit-Montrouge on Monday to give himself up for the murder of his wife. He had shot her with a revolver as the result of a quarrel, which arose in a curious way.

Boistard had been to see a cinematograph display in the Rue de la Gaite, and among the pictures was one representing the Rheims aviation week. On the films he recognised his wife, making merry at the buffet. His wife, who was by his side, also recognised the tell-tale picture and fainted, whilst the wronged husband cried out his woes to the audience. He had believed his wife to be spending a holiday with some relations, while he was doing his military service.

The performance was suspended, the lady taken to a chemist's and brought round. Then the couple went home, and the quarrel ensued. Fortunately for all concerned, the angry husband's aim was bad and he had not hit his wife at all. She had merely fainted again. He was set at liberty by the commissary on the understanding that the quarrel should be made up.

"THE CINEMA AS AN EDUCATIVE FORCE. Tommy (a regular attender at cinematograph shows, during the performance of a society drama): 'Is that the trusting husband or the amorous lover?'" *Punch*, 7 August 1912.

A CINEMATOGRAPHIC ROMANCE

Photographic News
24 February 1899

T ALKING ABOUT CINEMATOGRAPHY, here is the latest romance connected with this branch of photography. Some months ago an unfortunate difference in a household obliged a younger son to leave his home. As the weeks passed [there was no] trace of him despite the most searching inquiries. The father was anxious to have his son back, for he had discovered that he had unwittingly wronged him. A little later an elder brother was at a concert, which included a cinematograph entertainment. One of the pictures shown was a firemen's turn-out. Suddenly, as one of the engines was about to start, a soldier ran across the street into the foreground, and, momentarily turning his head, disclosed the features of the missing brother. He had enlisted in the army. His people were thus able to trace him and procure his discharge. The moral seems to be that if you enlist and want to assure being bought out you should get yourself included in a cinematographic picture that is to be publicly exhibited. Also you should make certain that your relatives will go and see the picture. On the whole, it is perhaps best not to enlist at all.

Above:
Chambers's Journal
25 November 1905

Below:
The Times
17 January 1914

THE CINEMATOGRAPH IN POLITICS

A NEW USE HAS BEEN FOUND for animated photography in the production of pictures to illustrate the views of politicians at election meetings. At the offices of the Primrose League a few weeks ago several animated cartoons were exhibited to the committee with a view to their liberal—or perhaps it would be better to say conservative—use in the active campaign to be waged this winter. In most cases the photographs were from acted scenes expressly produced to depict the producers' particular opinions on the subjects of current political interest; but some of the views were of actual occurrences or conditions, as in the case of those having a bearing upon the alien question. The fiscal controversy came in for a considerable share of attention; and if the views expressed by the cartoons were of a wholly one-sided character, that is only to be expected from a scheme formed expressly for party purposes. Presumably the pictures will be seen over many a platform, in preparation for the coming contest, and they should at least serve to adorn the tale and point what moral there be, even if they do not actually convince in themselves. In a circular issued by the proprietors of the venture, the cinematograph is described as a new weapon in the hands of the propagandist. 'Weapon' is distinctly good.

**Advertisement from the
Charles Urban Trading
Company catalogue, 1903.**

THE CINEMATOGRAPH AND SOCIAL REFORM

T HE PRESIDENT OF THE LOCAL Government Board and many others interested in the Poor Law reform had been invited to witness an exhibition of *Give Us This Day*, a cinematograph film which was given at the West End Cinema yesterday afternoon. The film is said to be the first of a series of eight films dealing with sociological subjects which are about to be shown in this country by Jury's Imperial Pictures (Limited); but, frankly, we hope that the later pictures will be more cheerful than that shown yesterday, for one has rarely seen a more depressing exhibition. Dickens, when he tilted against the Poor Law system, found occasional relief from the sombreness of the theme, but in this film it is all gloom which there is no Bumble to lighten.

The difficulty in accepting the film as in any way typical of Poor Law conditions in this country is that it is a Swedish production, and it is not easy to reconcile the spectacle of the heroine being taken back to the workhouse in a conveyance drawn by oxen, with a bill, made out in pounds, shillings, and pence, which is shown as the cost of apprehending her. We are inclined to wonder also what those guardians who were present yesterday thought of the guardians on the screen, whose coldness and indifference to the well-being of the unfortunate people in their charge seemed to be their main characteristic. The central object of the film is to show the misery which is involved when the children of a widow in the workhouse are taken from her and entrusted to the charge of foster-parents, and around this theme a drama which is powerful, despite its gloominess, has been built.

MR CHERRY KEARTON'S PICTURES

The Times
9 December 1913

UNDER THE TITLE OF 'NATURE'S ZOO' a highly interesting series of cinematograph films are being shown at the West End Cinema this week. The pictures, which have been secured by Mr. Cherry Kearton during his travels in many parts of the world, deal with some very varied aspects of animal life. Some of the pictures have already been seen in London at a series of special performances at the Palace Theatre, and one is impressed as much as ever with the extraordinary patience that must have been exercised by the operator. There is a delightful picture, for instance, of a couple of bears in the Rocky Mountains climbing trees and thoroughly enjoying themselves, but the result was only obtained after many wearisome hours in which the efforts were made to familiarise the animals with the clicking of the hidden camera. Again, there are pictures of a hippopotamus, a water turtle, and a crocodile in their native haunts, which speak of enormous difficulties, but there is no doubt that the result thoroughly justifies the patience that has been displayed.

"Picture Personalities: Mr. Cherry Kearton."
The Bioscope, c. 1912.

"Sport on the Cinematograph.
A new use for moving pictures."
The Graphic, 26 July 1913.

The World's Fair
3 July 1909

BIG GAME HUNTING BY CINEMATOGRAPH

How to Bag Rhinoceros in the Parlour

BIG-GAME HUNTERS will be glad to know that they can have all the sport of the chase in their own homes.

Mr. Walter Winans, the famous revolver shot and breeder of horses, has patented a contrivance whereby the cinematograph is adapted for target purposes. The big-game hunter can crouch behind an armchair, and, resting the muzzle of his gun on the chair, watch the screen and wait.

A scene flickers before him; the room fades away, and he is in Uganda 'on safari' lion-hunting. The lion appears. The armchair big-game hunter can choose his moment to shoot and the spot where his shot will prove fatal.

He fires. The picture stops, and though the lion does not drop, he remains in the position in which he stood when the shot was fired. But on the screen the bullet has made its mark, and so the hunter knows where he has shot his quarry.

All the joys of deer-stalking, the tremendous thrills of the elephant and rhinoceros shooting, and the delight of bear hunting can be indulged in without going in search of big game.

"*Picture Personalities: Mr. Herbert G. Ponting, F.R.G.S.*
Mr. Herbert Ponting, the intrepid cinematographer who accompanied Captain Scott's
Expedition to the South Pole, contemplates visiting India with his camera.
The result of Mr. Ponting's tour will be awaited with keen interest."
The Bioscope, 1912.

Herbert Ponting,
The Great White South:
or with Scott in the
Antarctic
1950, pp. 168–70

PHOTOGRAPHING IN SUCH extremely low zero temperatures necessitates a great deal of care; there are many pitfalls into all of which I plunged headlong. I had to pay dearly for some of the experiences I gained. Perhaps a few of the troubles I learned to avoid may be of interest. I found that it was advisable always to leave cameras in their cases outside the Hut. There was sometimes a difference of more than one hundred degrees between the exterior and the interior temperature. To bring cameras inside was to subject them to such condensation that they became dripping wet as they came into the warm air. If for any reason it was necessary to bring a camera indoors, all this moisture had to be carefully wiped away; and the greatest care had to be taken to see that none got inside a lens. To do so much as breathe upon a lens in the open air was to render that lens useless, for it instantly became covered with a film of ice which could not be removed. It had to be brought into warm air and thawed off; then wiped dry. Every trace of oil had to be removed from all working parts of kinematograph cameras and focal-plane shutters, as even some 'non-freezing' oil (which I had bought in Switzerland) froze. Lubricating had to be done with graphite. Several of my colour-filters became uncemented from the expansion and contraction caused by changes of temperature, and were useless; and some of my shutters became so unreliable that I had to discard them and make all exposures by makeshift expedients . . . To 'thread' a film into a kinematograph camera, in low temperatures, was an unpleasant job, for it was necessary to use bare fingers whilst doing so. Often when my fingers touched metal they became frostbitten. Such a frostbite feels exactly like a burn. Once, thoughtlessly, I held a camera screw for a moment in my mouth. It froze instantly to my lips, and took the skin off them when I moved it. On another occasion, my tongue came into contact with a metal part of one of my cameras, whilst moistening my lips as I was focusing. It froze fast instantaneously; and to release myself I had to jerk it away, leaving the skin of the end of my tongue sticking to the camera, and my mouth bled so profusely that I had to gag it with a handkerchief.

The Times
24 January 1914

PICTURES OF THE SCOTT EXPEDITION
Cinematograph Achievements

SIR EARNEST SHACKLETON presided yesterday afternoon at a private gathering at the Philharmonic Hall, Great Portland Street, when Mr. Herbert G. Ponting's pictorial record of Captain Scott's expedition to the South Pole was shown for the first time. Captain Scott was probably the first explorer to appreciate the full value of photography as an important branch of the work of a Polar expedition, and the results have fully justified the choice of Mr. Ponting as the official photographer of the party. Some of the moving pictures have been seen before, at the Palace Theatre and at the Albert Hall, when Commander Evans delivered his lecture; but this is the first occasion on which the whole series has been shown as one connected narrative, and there is the added advantage that Mr. Ponting explains the pictures in an easy conversational style.

Mr. Ponting's pictures trace, in fairly close detail, the progress of the expedition from the time that the Terra Nova first left New Zealand until the evening in November, 1911, when he bade farewell to Captain Scott, as no heavy apparatus such as a cinematograph camera could be carried beyond the point which had then been reached on the Great Ice Barrier. Many varying phases of the expedition are shown, the life on board the Terra Nova as she fought her way through the ice flows, and the arrival at the ice-foot off Cape Evans, where the explorers, the ponies, dogs, and stores were landed. The work of the sledging parties is shown, and at one point Captain Scott, Dr. Wilson, Lieutenant Bowers, and Petty Officer Evans are seen selecting a spot on which to camp for the night.

Few of the pictures show more clearly the immense patience displayed by Mr. Ponting than those depicting the penguins, the seals, and the gulls in the natural surrounding. The cinematograph pictures, as has been said, end with Mr. Ponting's parting with his leader, but the story of the expedition is rounded off with the pictures taken by Lieutenant Bowers at the Pole, showing Captain Scott and his comrades at their destination, and, with the picture of the monument erected over their bodies by the search party.

3 Cinema and Authority

THE INTRODUCTION OF CINEMA, a new means of mass communication and entertainment open to all classes and unreliant on literacy, seemed destined to draw a swift series of responses from those in authority. It was rather surprising then that the first example of direct government intervention in the industry was the Cinematograph Act of 1909 which sought to legislate for the safety of cinema patrons. Even stranger was the failure of Government to legislate in the area of censorship. The British Board of Film Censors, a voluntary organisation to which film makers could submit their works for classification, emerged in 1912 and commenced classification in 1913. On this evidence it was almost is if the cinema was dismissed as an unimportant sideshow for more than the first decade of its existence. This could not be further from the truth. The arrival of the cinema in the theatres, music halls and fairgrounds of Britain unleashed a wave of moral panics and calls for legislation. Cinema was blamed for everything from juvenile delinquency and white slavery to promiscuity and the spread of disease. The theatre and music hall had in their time been subject to the same charges. In a survey carried out by the National Council of Public Morals in 1917 school children were questioned on the potential evils of the cinema:

> *Dr. Marie Stopes*: Have you seen any picture which you thought at the time was bad to see?
> *School Child*: No, but I saw a picture once which I thought was vulgar. It was called _____.
> *M.S.*: Supposing you went into a picture house and you met a fairy at the door who told you could see any picture you liked, what kind would you like to see?
> *S.C.*: I should like to see a picture about a circus.
> *M.S.*: What sort of picture would you like best?

> *S.C.*: I should like a good drama, but not a love drama. A nice drama like Little Miss Nobody, which I thought was very nice.
> *M.S.*: Why don't you like love dramas?
> *S.C.*: There is too much fooling about in them, and there is always hatred between two men and two women.
> *M.S.*: You don't like to see two men hating each other?
> *S.C.*: Well, it is a lot of silliness. I do not think it would happen in real life.
> *M.S.*: You never got any disease at the cinema?
> *S.C.*: No, but once I got scarlet fever, but not in a cinema.
> *M.S.*: Did you ever get anything?
> *S.C.*: No, I did not catch my disease there.

Many of these rather sensational claims had their basis in real events and cases, but through the magnifying lens of the popular press they were easy fuel to those interested in imposing control upon the cinema. For example, the early sites within which the first moving pictures were exhibited were often unsanitary and potential death traps. Even after the advent of fully-regulated permanent cinemas, management handbooks offered advice on disinfecting the auditoriums with the audience in occupation.

When Members of Parliament did examine issues relating to these problems they invariably failed to find sufficient evidence to back up some of the wilder accusations levelled at the cinema. Where legislation was forthcoming, in the areas of safety, and later, protectionism of the fledgling industry, there was very real evidence that action was needed.

One of the defining events in the early history of the cinema was the Paris Charity Bazaar Fire of 4 May 1897 when 121 people died as a result of a fire started by an ether lamp at a cinematograph demonstration. The event was doubly notable because of the social status of many of those who perished and the event was widely covered in the society press. The fact that fires and explosions were a common feature of existing magic lantern entertainments which shared the same lighting technology was neither here nor there. Projectionists needed to combine a highly combustible mixture of either oxygen and hydrogen or oxygen and domestic gas to burn in their limelight lamps to illuminate their shows. These elements were combined from pressurised cylinders in a mixing bag and consequently accidents were commonplace. Lanternists were even banned from transporting their cylinders by rail for fear of accident, and often had to disguise the content of their baggage. Fatalities and mutilations were also a common feature of these exhibitions, the whole process made more dangerous by the extreme combustibility of the films used by cinematographers.

The eventual legislation imposed through the 1909 Cinematograph Act provided local councils with the responsibility of licensing all premises for exhibition of films and many prosecutions under the Act followed. However, legislation represented by the 1909 Act merely controlled the physical domain of the cinema, but the social, moral and political challenges offered by the films in terms of their subject matter were, and still are, contentious. Many early commentators, both in the popular press and from clear institutional perspectives, such as the judiciary or the church, began to articulate clear reservations about the social consequences of the cinema. A clear pattern of issues begins to emerge from the moment of the arrival of commercial cinema in 1896. Vested interests within British society regarded the cinema with deep suspicion, if not downright hostility. It was often regarded as a diversionary and potentially inflammatory entertainment, open to a myriad of abuses. These debates centred around the issues of social conformity, crime, political unrest and public morality.

It was often felt that exposure to unsuitable subjects threatened the very fabric of late Victorian and Edwardian society, and that the sense of escapism experienced by cinemagoers, the vast majority of them working class, could lead to resentment and discontent. Glimpses of other worlds, however fleeting, were not always healthy.

The symbols of authority, especially the monarchy and armed forces, were a constant feature of early cinema presentations, Queen Victoria's Diamond Jubilee of 1897, for example, proving extremely popular. Military reviews were another constant feature, as well as the yearly series of society events such as Ascot and the Henley Regatta. However, also popular were films which mocked authority figures, such as the police or clergy, and which showed alternative lifestyles, albeit from a fiercely moralising perspective. They were hardly likely to provoke mutinous uprisings, but their very presence heralded a growing tendency towards rejection of the values of class and duty.

A leading issue of the day was that of women's suffrage, and a whole genre of suffragette cinema ensued. The images of Emily Davison throwing herself under the King's horse are now familiar, but a whole series of anti-suffragette films were made as well, nearly all of them comedies. Perhaps the earliest was Bamforth's 1899 film *Women's Rights* in which two women have their skirts nailed to a fence while discussing women's issues. These films became a regular feature in the years directly preceding the first world war, revelling in titles such as *A Suffragette Inspite of Herself, How They Got The Vote, The Elusive Mrs Pinkhurst*, and *Selina's Flight For Freedom*.

One in particular, Clarendon's 1913 film *Milling the Militants* contains all the common themes, but at least this particular suffragette has the last laugh:

> The spouse of a suffragette has a sad experience after dreaming dreams of suppressing his better half —Brown is blessed with a large wife and a small family, whom he is left to look after while his better half goes forth armed with a hammer to smash, burn and plunder. Brown falls asleep and dreams that he is Primeminister and making laws to suppress the militants. Brown is gloating over a recalcitrant female when he is awakened, and his wife is upsetting a pail of water over him, at the same time scolding him for sleeping and neglecting his duties. His courage fails him, and the late 'Primeminister' begs for mercy on his knees.[1]

Other films tackled social issues, such as conditions at work, for instance Kineto's film *Day in the Life of a Coalminer*, filmed in the Wigan coalfields, drew clear parallels between the hard physical nature of the coalminers' work and the luxury of those who relied on their toil.

That the cinema had the power to inflame and incite its audience to acts of violence and raise political consciousness was without doubt. The propaganda potential of the cinema, for example, was demonstrated by the Dreyfus affair in France which began in 1894. Alfred Dreyfus, a Jewish officer in the French army was accused of spying for Germany. He was tried, convicted and exiled to Devil's Island. The affair split the French nation, unleashing waves of anti-Semitism and inciting violent demonstrations. Film-makers such as Georges Méliès were quick to provide dramatised re-enactments of the case, which toured France in 1899, causing riots at some exhibitions. These films were often banned in many regions of France well into the twentieth century. In the Jewish areas of Southern Russia in 1898, the Lumière agent Francis Doublier incited rioting by exhibiting fakes and stock-shots purporting to show the trial and exile of Dreyfus.

The manipulation of cinema for political ends after the First World War was to become an art form in itself, but already its persuasive power was more than apparent. Other events that were re-enacted for the cinema included Pathé's account of the Russian 1905 Revolution.

The relationship between the cinema and crime was another theme in this formative period. The cinema was seen both as encouraging crime and, at the same time, as a means of showing its consequences. It was even seen as a means of apprehension. Court cases involving juveniles influenced by films towards criminal behaviour were commonplace, and their punishment usually included prohibition from local cinemas. Yet the vast majority of these films showed the degradation and penalties of a life of crime. Mottershaw's 1903 film *A Daring Daylight Burglary*, for instance, showed the chase and capture of a burglar, while an article which appeared in *The World's Fair* in April 1912 outlined several occasions when the cinema had acted as an agency for the apprehension of criminals.

Whether supporting or attacking popular conceptions of authority, the cinema was, and remains, under constant scrutiny from all vested interests in British society.

---

1. *Kine Weekly,* [film released on 19 June 1913].

Cinematograph Act, 1909
(9 EDW. 7. CH. 30)

1. An exhibition of moving pictures or other optical effects by means of a cinematograph or other similar apparatus for the purposes of which inflammable films are used, shall not be given unless the regulations made by the Secretary of State for securing safety are compiled with, or, save as otherwise expressly provided by this Act, elsewhere than in premises licensed for the purpose in accordance with the provisions of this Act.

2. (1) A county council may grant licences to such persons as they think to use the premises specified in the license for the purposes aforesaid on such terms and conditions and under such restrictions as, subject to regulations of the Secretary of State, the council may by respective licences determine.

(2) A license shall be in force for one year or for such shorter period as the council on the grant of the license may determine, unless the license has been previously revoked as henceinafter provided.

(3) A county council may transfer any licence granted by them to such other persons as they think fit.

(4) An applicant for a licence or transfer of a licence shall give not less than seven days' notice in writing to the county council and to the chief office or police of the police area in which the premises are situated of his intention to apply for a licence or transfer: Provided that it shall not be necessary to give any notice where the application is for the renewal of an existing licence held by the applicant for the same premises.

(5) There shall be paid in respect of the grant, renewal of transfer of a licence such fees as the county council may fix, not exceeding in the case of a grant or renewal for one year one pound, or in the case of a grant or renewal for any less period five shillings for every month for which it is granted or renewed, so however that the aggregate of the fees payable in any year shall not exceed one pound, or, in the case of transfer, five shillings.

(6) For the purposes of this Act, the expressions 'police area' and 'chief of police' as re spects the City of London, mean the City and the Commissioner of City Police, and elsewhere have the same meanings as in the Police Act, 1890.

3. If the owner of a cinematograph or other apparatus uses the apparatus, or allows it to be used, or if the occupier of any premises allows these premises to be used, in contravention of the provisions of this Act or the regulations made thereunder, or in the conditions or restrictions under or subject to which any licence relating to the premises has been granted under this Act, he shall be liable, on summary conviction, to a fine not exceeding twenty pounds, and in the case of a continuing offence to a further penalty of five pounds for each day during with the offence continues, and the licence (if any) shall be liable to be revoked by the county council.

4. A constable or any officer appointed for the purpose by a county council may at all reasonable times enter any premises, whether licensed or not, in which he has reason to believe that such an exhibition as aforesaid is being or is about to be given, with a view to seeing whether the provisions of this Act, or any regulations made thereunder, and the conditions of any licence granted under the Act, have been compiled with, and if any person prevents or obstructs the entry of a constable or any officer appointed as aforesaid, he shall be liable, on summary conviction, to a penalty not exceeding twenty pounds.

5. Without prejudice to any other powers of delegation, whether to committees of the council or to district councils, a county council may, with or without any restrictions or conditions as they may think fit, delegate to justices sitting in petty sessions any of the powers conferred on the council by this Act.

6. The provisions of this Act shall apply in the case of a county borough as if the borough council were a county council, and the expenses of the borough council shall be defrayed out of the borough fund or borough rate.

7. (1) Where the premises are premises licensed by the Lord Chamberlain the powers of the county council under this Act shall, as respects those premises, be exerciseable by the Lord Chamberlain instead of by the county council.

(2) Where the premises in which it is proposed to give an exhibition as aforesaid are premises used occasionally and exceptionally only, and not on more than six days in any one calendar year, for the purposes of such an exhibition, it shall be necessary to obtain a licence for those premises under this Act if the occupier thereof has given to the county council and to the chief of police of the police area, not less than seven days before the exhibition, notice in writing of his intention so to use the premises, and complies with the regulations made by the Secretary of State under this Act, and, subject to such regulations, with any conditions imposed by the county council, and notified to the occupier in writing.

(3) Where it is proposed to give any such exhibition as aforesaid in any building or structure of a movable character, it shall not be necessary to obtain a licence under this Act for the council of the county in which the exhibition is to be given if the owner of the building or structure:

(a) has been granted a licence in respect of the building by the council of the county in which he ordinarily resides, or by any authority to whom that council have delegated the powers conferred on them by this Act; and

(b) has given to the council of the county and to chief officer of police of the police area in which it is proposed to give an exhibition, not less than two days before the exhibition, notice in writing of his intention to give the exhibition; and

(c) complies with the regulations made by the Secretary of State under this Act, and,subject to such regulations, with any conditions imposed by the county council, and notified in writing to the owner.

(4) This Act shall not apply to an exhibition given in a private dwelling-house to which the public are not admitted, whether on payment or otherwise.

8. This Act shall extend to Scotland subject to the following modifications:

(1) For references to the Secretary of State there shall be substituted references to the Secretary for Scotland:

(2) For the reference to the Police Act, 1890, there shall be substituted a reference to the Police (Scotland) Act, 1890:

(3) The expression 'county borough' means a royal, parliamentary, or police burgh and the expression 'borough council' means the magistrate of the burgh; and the expression 'borough fund' or 'borough' rate means any rate within the burgh leviable by the town council equally on owners and occupiers:

(4) The provision relating to the delegation of powers shall not apply.

9. This Act shall extend to Ireland subject to the following modifications:

(1) For references to the Secretary of State there shall be substituted references to the Lord Lieutenant:

(2) The provision of the Act relating to the delegation of powers shall not apply:

(3) Any of the powers conferred on the county council by this Act may be exercised by any officer of the council authorised in writing by the council in that behalf for such period and subject to such restrictions as the council think fit:

(4) In any urban district other than a county borough, the provisions of this Act shall apply as if the council of the district and the commissioners of the town, as the case may be, were a county council:

(5) The expenses incurred in the execution of this Act shall:

(a) in this case of the council other than a county borough, be defrayed out of the poor rate and raised over so much of the county as is not included in any urban district or town;

(b) in the case of the council of any county borough or other urban district, be defrayed out of any rate or fund applicable to the purposes of the Public Health (Ireland) Acts, 1878, to 1907, as if incurred for those purposes;

(c) in the case of the commissioners of any town, be defrayed out of the rate leviable under section sixty of the Town Improvement (Ireland) Act, 1854: Provided that the limits imposed upon that rate by that section may be exceeded for that purpose of raising the expenses incurred under this Act by not more than one penny in the pound:

(6) The expression 'town' means any town as defined by the Local Government (Ireland)Act, 1898, not being an urban district:

(7) The expression 'police area' and 'chief officer of police' means, as respects the police district of Dublin Metropolis, that district and the chief commissioner of the police for that district, and elsewhere a police district and the county inspector of the Royal Irish Constabulary.

10. This Act may be cited as the Cinematograph Act, 1909, and shall come into operation on the first day of January, nineteen hundred and ten.

Slide for projection on cinema screen between performances. Walturdaw Company Ltd catalogue, 1911.

L. C. C. Regulations Use of Kinematograph in Premises Licensed by the Council

1. No kinematograph or other similar apparatus involving the use of lengthy combustible film, shall be exhibited on premises licensed by the Council, until the Council has been satisfied that all reasonable precautions have been taken against accident and danger to the public.

2. Notices of any intended exhibition shall be given to the Clerk of the Council by the licensee of the premises in which such exhibition is to be given, and the licensee shall be made entirely responsible for the proper and safe use of the apparatus. Such notices shall be given at least three days before the first day of exhibition. Opportunity shall also be afforded to the Council's inspector of inspecting the apparatus before the public exhibition takes place, in order to allow time for any necessary alterations to be carried out and approved by the Council. No gangway or exit must be in any way effected.

3. The kinematographs shall stand in a suitable fire-proof room or closed sheet-iron box of sufficient dimensions to allow the operators to work freely and fitting closely to the floor, which shall be covered with fire-resisting material within such room or box. The door or doors shall open outwards and be self-closing, and one of the three windows which are necessary in the front face of the enclosure, the centre one shall not exceed eight inches square, and the windows on each side shall not exceed six inches square; a flap screen, to cover all these three holes, shall be fitted and actuated both from the inside and the outside of the enclosure; the space separating the audience and seats from the iron enclosure shall not be less than two feet in width at the sides and in the front of the enclosure, and the space at the back where the door is situated shall not be less than six feet from the enclosure. The audience shall be completely excluded from the above space around the enclosure by a suitable barrier. No unnecessary combustible material shall be within the enclosure, and as far as possible, all necessary combustible material shall be rendered fire-proof or shall be enclose in fire-proof receptacles. The part of the film immediately opposite the lens shall be provided with an apparatus which prevents the film, if kindled, from burning towards either of the spools.

4. The body of the lantern shall be constructed of wood or other non-conducting material and shall be coated inside with asbestos; it shall also have an inner lining of sheet-iron, and an air space shall be left between the iron and asbestos lining. In the bottom of the lantern shall stand an iron tray, which shall be surrounded by a vertical edge at least one inch in depth. The lantern shall be provided with a metal shutter, which shall fall freely between the source of light and the condenser. This shutter shall be immediately dropped in the event of any accident to the apparatus or stoppage of the film, and shall only be raised when the film is in motion for the purpose of projection. One of the firemen of the establishment shall be in attendance near the apparatus with a wet blanket and two buckets of water.

5. Where possible the electric arc light shall be adopted as an illuminant, the usual rules for securing safety in an electric installation being observed. Ether and other inflammable liquids shall not be employed under any circumstance for producing light. If limelight be used in the lantern, the general regulations for its safety, which are issued by the Council, shall be complied with, and any additional precautions which the Council may deem necessary for securing safety shall also be adopted. The use of acetylene gas, other than 'dissolved acetylene' is prohibited. When dissolved acetylene is used the conditions set out in Order No. 6 of the Secretary of State, made under the Explosives Act, 1875, must be complied with and the gas must not be allowed to come into contact with copper or copper alloys.

6. The space in which the kinematograph stands shall, where possible, be illuminated by electric glow lamps; but a miner's safety lamp may be substituted, if necessary. No naked gas or oil flames, or matches shall be allowed in the space. The lighting of the hydrogen flame in the lantern shall be accomplished by means of an electric lighter.

7. The films, when not actually passing through the lantern, shall be kept enclosed in metal cases. The film which is passing through the lantern shall be re-wound either automatically or by hand, upon another bobbin as fast as it emerges from the lantern front.

8. Not less than two, nor more than three operators shall be engaged with the lantern space, and no other persons shall be within the lantern enclosure during the exhibition. The whole duty of one of the operators shall consist in taking charge of the film after it has passed through the lantern.

9. The licensee shall be held responsible for the employment of competent, experienced operators, and shall be prepared at any time to supply the Council satisfactory credentials in this respect.

10. Smoking within the lantern space shall be absolutely forbidden at all times.

11. The Council reserves to itself the right of modifying any of the above regulations and requiring the adoption of any further precautions, in addition to those specified above, as circumstances may require.

G. L. GOMME, Clerk of the Council.

"The Lantern Room of a Modern Cinematograph Theatre. The operating room of the Picture House, Briggate, Leeds, showing two film projectors and slide lantern."
From Frederick Talbot, *Moving Pictures: How They are Made and Worked*, 1912.

The Times
14 November 1913

THEATRICAL LICENSES
Music in Cinematograph Halls

The Theatre and Music-halls Committee of the London County Council met yesterday at the Clerkenwell Sessions House to deal with a list of applications for music, dancing, and stage-play licenses. The list comprised 596 applications in respect of 563 London theatres, music-halls, cinematograph-halls, skating rinks, and other places of amusement. Eighty-eight of the applicants were opposed. Mr. H. J. Greenwood, chairman of the committee, presided.

Mr. Humphrey Williams, barrister, for the London Branch of the Cinematograph Association of Great Britain and Ireland, said he desired an opportunity to address the committee on the question of restricting cinematograph licenses so that the only instrumental music could be played.

The Chairman said the licenses were being granted on the same conditions as last year, and as these was no opposition in the cases there could be no need for permitting counsel to address them generally.

Dances at the Hotel Cecil

The committee decided to recommend the Council to grant a dancing license for the new Palm Court at the Hotel Cecil.

Mr. Lamb, counsel supporting the application, said that when wealthy guests wished to hold private balls the directors were anxious to place the Palm Court at their disposal. It was well adapted for that purpose, and a special floor had been laid down.

Royalty and the Coliseum

Mr. Oswald Stoll's application for a music and dancing license for the Coliseum was opposed by many bodies.

Mr. T. M. Healy, K.C., in support of the application, said that last month the King and Queen attended a performance at the Coliseum for a very important charity, and it seemed a remarkable thing that at a building which attracted Royalty ordinary refreshments could not be obtained. The performance at the Coliseum lasted several hours, and as many of the people came from a distance, it was only right they should have the means of obtaining refreshment.

Mr. C. Pinhorn, on behalf of the London Temperance Council, said Mr. Healy had referred to the visit of the King and Queen to the Coliseum, but he had not told them whether their Majesties had asked for a glass or ale or champagne. (Laughter.) It was ridiculous to use the visit as an argument to give the hall a drink license.

Mr. Pope, for the United Kingdom Alliance and other societies, also spoke in opposition, and pointed to the large capital in the business end and said it gave the big dividend of 22 (half) per cent.

Mr. Healy, said the capital had been reduced. Mr. Stoll was making that application in the interests of his patrons and not for the purpose of revenue.

The committee announced that the license would be granted subject to an undertaking that intoxicating liquor should not be sold or consumed on the premises.

The Hippodrome

In the case of the London Hippodrome, opposition was offered by various temperance bodies. Mr, Sylvain Mayer, K.C., for the applicants, said the place stood in a different position from others and an injustice had been done, because until six years ago the restriction was not imposed, and it was only by a majority of one that at the annual meeting it was so imposed.

Mr. Boothroyd said that many young people were patrons of the Hippodrome and drink temptations should not be placed in their way.

The committee granted the music and dancing license on the usual undertaking that strong drink should not be sold in the auditorium.

Songs in Cinematograph Halls

The committee reverted at the afternoon sitting to the question of music at cinematograph halls, applications for unrestricted music licenses being made by the owners of four halls at Bethnal-green—the Museum Cinema, Cambridge-road, the Victoria Picture Theatre, Grove-road, Smart's Picture Palace, Bow-road. Eventually they agreed the recommend the granting of the music licenses subject to there being only instrumental music incidental to the pictures.

The Fulham Empire

Mr. Oswald Stoll's fourth application for a music and dancing license in respect of his proposed Fulham Empire was opposed by the Granville Theatre of Varieties, Walham Green, the Variety Theatre Consolidated (Limited), owners of the Chelsea Palace, and the Grand Theatre, Fulham. Further objections came from several local clergy and the Fulham District Free Church Council, which declared that the excessive number of places of amusement severely handicapped the continuation of L.C.C. educational facilities for boys and girls, and attributed a decline of 10 or 15 per cent, in attendance during the past year to "over attraction of pure amusement".

Mr. Healy, who supported the applications, said that Fulham Empire would cost over £30,000, apart from £9,000 which Mr. Stoll had spent on the freehold of the site. He added that in 1910 the Council would have adopted the committee's recommendation and granted the license but for the objection of the Fulham Borough Council, which was dropped in the two succeeding years.

Mr. Stoll told the committee that the hall would provide high-class variety performances, including water shows. He admitted in cross-examination that he was interested in half the music-halls of London.

Mr. Tozer, chairman of the Variety Theatres Consolidated (Limited), stated that competition in the music-hall world was unhealthily acute last year, and was even worse now. The profit had gradually diminished until it had almost disappeared. The musicians' strike would make a difference of £700 or £800 a year.

Ultimately the committee resolved to recommend the Council not to grant the application.

"THE STAY-AS-YOU-PLEASE CINEMA PALACE.
Boy (to Lady just arrived).
'Please will you tell me the time, Lady?'
Lady. 'Half-past eleven.'
Boy. 'Will you please tell me it's six o'clock, Lady,
cos I've got to go out and sell papers!'"
Punch, 1 February 1911.

JUDGE ON PICTURE SHOWS

The Times
25 October 1913

AT THE LONDON SESSION yesterday Mr. Wallace, dealing with the case of a boy who pleaded guilty to burglary, said he believed that cinematograph shows were responsible for the downfall of many young people. Many of the lads who came before him owed their position to having been influenced by pictures of burglaries and thefts at such shows. The idea that there was something magnificent and bold and daring in breaking into houses, scaling ladders, and so on was doing more damage than anything he knew. These shows, as far as young boys were concerned, were a grave danger to the community. Mr. Roome, who prosecuted, said it was perhaps an example of retributive justice, that one of the houses broken into belonged to a cinematograph proprietor. He hoped the licensing authorities would take note of his Lordship's remarks. Mr. Wallace postponed sentence until next sessions in order to see if arrangements could be made to get the lad employment abroad and thus take him right away from his present surroundings.

CINEMATOGRAPH AND CRIME

The Times
5 November 1913

MR. H. J. GREENWOOD, chairman of the Theatres and Music Halls Committee, replying to Mr. E. Smallwood, who called attention to some remarks on cinematographs and crime made by Mr. Wallace, K.C., at the London Sessions, said that with all due respect to Mr. Wallace he ventured to think that the language he used was somewhat extravagant. It was obviously difficult to trace any direct connection between acts of violence and crime generally and habitual attendance of cinematograph shows. In any case the "many who came before him", to whom Mr. Wallace referred, could only be an infinitesimal fraction of those who daily visited these performances. The Council did not exercise any control or supervision over the programmes presented nor had it any power to do so. If any complaint were received of a picture shown at any premises licensed by the Council an inspector would be sent to report, and if the complaint proved to be well-founded appropriate action would be taken. In his opinion the Council's present powers were adequate.

The Storage of Celluloid

At the suggestion of the Public Control Committee it was decided to promote legislation next Session to control places where cinematograph films, celluloid and xylonite are manufactured, stored, or used. The proposals were summarised in The Times of November 3, but a new clause was added demanding that reasonable means of escape form fire should be provided in the celluloid is stored in such a way as to prejudice the existing means of escape.

The Council adjourned at 8 o'clock.

THE CINEMA AND THE YOUNG

Boys Bound Over Not To Enter Picture Theatres

The Times
13 February 1914

A NUMBER OF YOUNG LADS were before the Sutton Coldfield magistrates yesterday charged with a series of thefts, and the assertion was made that their appearance in the dock was largely due to the harmful influence of certain picture theatres. In several cases the lads were bound over not to enter a picture theatre for 12 months. The Chairman said the town had been made notorious as a den of young thieves and shopkeepers had been terrorised.

A petition, signed by clergy and ministers of religion and by the local branch of the Women's Temperance Association, was presented, suggesting the closer supervision of picture theatres. They urged that no picture should be allowed to be shown which represented violence and wrongdoing, and objected to certain posters.

The Branch expressed the hope that proprietors would be careful as to the pictures exhibited, and urged provision of afternoon performances for children.

The World's Fair
22 August 1908

THE CINEMATOGRAPH AND CRIME
Startling Police Theory

THE *SHEFFIELD DAILY TELEGRAPH* SAYS: Juvenile delinquency is on the increase, not only in Sheffield, but all over the country. How are we to account for it? Unquestionably lax parental discipline, or even, in many instances, actual incitement, to crime is responsible for much of it; but there are hundreds of cases where children of respectable families under healthy home influences, inexplicably, it would almost seem, drift into the court.

Is this a symptom of inherent depravity or merely the result of external suggestion? Two prominent Sheffield police officials, with a wide experience of criminal investigation, advance a very interesting theory bearing on the problem.

They blame the cinematograph. It is they assert, the direct successor of penny dreadfuls, only, because of the vividness with which it appeals to the senses and the emotions, through the eye, the most rapid of all sensual organs—much more potent in its influences for ill.

The child sees portrayed some exciting crime. It fires his imagination. He longs for adventures. The consequences he never considers. He essays some silly theft, and there he is—a criminal in the making, if not already made.

Do the functions of the censor of the plays extend to such cases as these?

"Boy. "Py for us t' go in, Lidy?" Lady. "Certainly not!" Boy. "Then tike us in in yer arms?" " Punch, 18 June 1913.

THE CINEMA DETECTIVE
Moving Stories of Moving Pictures

The World's Fair
13 April 1912

FEW PEOPLE WHO WITNESS THE CINEMA entertainments at the many picture-theatres scattered nowadays throughout the length and breadth of the civilised world have probably any idea of the useful purpose that these entertainments occasionally serve as a means of detecting the whereabouts of people who are 'wanted'.

"I very frequently put in an hour at the cinema shows", said a well-known Scotland Yard man to an 'Answers' representative recently, "especially when films are in the bill dealing with current public events, such as the Derby Day, Oxford and Cambridge Boat-race, Royal Progress through the City, foot-ball matches, and such things. And you would be surprised at the number of people that I recognise in the films.

"For example, the arrest of a man who had been 'wanted' for no less than four years for a forgery case was entirely brought about in consequence of inquiries which I was able to set on foot after catching a glimpse of him in a crowd at the launching of a battleship in the South of England.

Spotting a Pickpocket

"Apparently, by evading arrest so long a period he had become a little careless, and growing a beard again. I recognised the man immediately he appeared standing in a crowd outside the dockyard gates, awaiting the arrival of the distinguished patronage who were to perform the christening and launching ceremony.

"Two days spent in that particular town enabled me to trace him and effect an arrest, upon which I and the sergeant who accompanied me were complimented at the trial. No one, of course, knew how I had managed to pick up the threads of mystery which during four years had been lost.

"On another occasion I was in a West End cinema show when a Derby Day crowd was thrown on the screen, and in the picture I recognised a well-known pickpocket and swell mobsman in the neighbourhood of a lady of title who had on that day lost her purse containing not only a considerable amount of money, but several valuable rings, and a moment or two later the next picture showed me the man in the act of picking this lady's pocket.

His Female Accomplice

"When I say 'in the act' I mean that he had assumed a certain position which, to my experienced eye, told me exactly what he was about to do, but which, to the eyes of most onlookers, might have conveyed no sinister meaning. As a result we got into touch with this man, and within two days he was arrested, and a female accomplice was actually found wearing one of the rings that had been stolen.

"These are only a couple of instances of the many I could give in which the cinema show has unexpectedly proved a most valuable detective."

In conversation with one of the heads of a well-known cinematograph film company in Paris, the 'Answers' man heard one or two good 'identification' stories.

"Strong family resemblances are, of course, quite common," he said, "and we have had in our experience as film manufacturers one or two astonishingly romantic incidents.

Some Identification Stories

"Not long ago—to be exact, about nine months—we were called upon by one of the most famous members of the detective force of the Paris Police, who wished to have a film which had been recently shown at a cinema theatre on the Boulevard Rochehouart run through the lantern. Of course we were only too pleased too oblige. It happened to be a film showing a review by the President at Toulon.

"As the film was being run through, and there appeared on the screen a group of pretty Toulon midinettes, M.K., the detective suddenly cried "Halt!" and, pulling a faded photograph from his pocket, he asked us to compare the face of it with that of one of the girls in the group. I was bound to admit that the likeness was astounding. We gave every information as to the date and the neighbourhood in which that particular film had been taken, and a detective left Paris that evening to investigate the matter.

"As a result, the granddaughter of a well-known almost millionaire art dealer of Paris was discovered in the person of the girl who had posed so innocently before the camera man's camera in the streets of Toulon. The mother, whose photograph the detective possessed, had years before married one of her father's employees, and had so offended him that she was turned out of her home and lost sight of.

"The old man, in his loneliness—for his daughter was his only child—had, just prior to the time of the cinema film being taken, set on foot inquiries, with a view to discovering the whereabouts of his long lost daughter. The latter was found to have died four years previously, her husband having deceased her by many years, and this young girl—her only child—whose likeness to her mother had been the means of her being identified, had become a working-girl at one of the biggest milliner's in Toulon.

Recording a Murder

"It is not often that the cinema film records the actual commission of a crime. But I have known one or two instances of this happening. Some considerable time ago—several years—one of our operators was taking a moving picture film down the Seine at a very picturesque little village.

"The subject was a comic boating episode, and the operator's attention being naturally fixed on the approaching boat, with its occupants engaged in trying to change seats, and thus turn the craft over, he paid little or no attention to anything else happening in the neighbourhood.

"What was our surprise, however, on running the film through for test purposes after development—when, of course, the picture was enormously magnified—to see in the far distance quite distinctly two people, a man and a woman, struggling on the river's brink, and a moment later to see the man with uplifted hand knocking the woman backwards into the water.

Convicted by Film

"The figures on the screen in the distance were about six inches in height, but perfectly recognisable, and for the purpose of being quite sure as to what had taken place we threw the picture on an even larger screen, with the result of making these figures nearly a foot in height. We then clearly saw the man had some weapon in his hand, and communicated the incident to the police.

"It was found that about that date the film was taken a woman had disappeared suddenly, and two or three days later her body was found in the Seine entangled in some weeds, about five or six miles below the spot at which she had been stabbed by her assailant, and then pushed into the water.

"The man was arrested in a Montmartre cabaret, tried, and largely through the evidence of the film, was convicted.

A Valuable Witness

"The police were greatly assisted in getting up the case by the evidence of a man who passed at the same time the altercation was in progress, but, having seen our operator a little further along the bank, and having watched the comic episode in the boat which we were really engaged in photographing, had come to the conclusion—he having no knowledge of photography, and the fact that these particular figures on the bank would be almost indistinguishable to our operator—that it was all part of the show, and took no further notice of the man and woman who were quarrelling.

"So, you see, even a cinema has a usefulness over and above that of entertaining or instructing audiences, and that occasionally the eye of the camera becomes a very intelligent and successful crime detector."

"WALTURDAW" BIOSCOPE SPECIALITIES 215

Vaporisers or Sprays.

The Up-to-date Cinematograph Proprietor keeps his Theatre Sweet and Sanitary by using " Walturdaw " Hygienic Sprays and Essence.

SPRAYS FOR THE ELECTRIC PALACE, THE THEATRE AND MUSIC HALL.

Those proprietors of Theatres, Picture Palaces, Music, Concert and Dancing Halls, who have adopted the system of the " Perolin " Air Purification are unanimous in praise of it, and this is endorsed by their audiences who know how to appreciate the cool and fragrant wave of freshness and humidity in the crowded foyer or heated auditorium.

In use at—The Appollo Theatre, The Shaftesbury Theatre, The King's Theatre, Hammersmith, The Shepherd's Bush Empire, The Oxford Music Hall, &c., &c., and most of the London and Provincial Picture Palaces.

CARDIFF : 9, ST. JOHN'S SQUARE

Telephone : 1060 Cardiff   Telegrams : Walturdaw Cardiff

Advertisement from the Walturdaw Company Ltd. catalogue, 1911.

The British Journal of Photography
23 July 1897

THE PHOTOGRAPHER AND THE COUNTESS

AT THE EPSOM COUNTY Court, on the 16th inst., before his Honour, Judge Lushington, the adjourned hearing of the case in which Messrs. Claude & Co, 8, Great Portugal Street, London, sued Countess Julia Sztaray, of 2, Queen Anne Villas, Epsom, and Countess Flora Sztaray, of the same address, to recover the sum of £50, by reason of the defendants' wilful acts in overturning and destroying a photographic camera, and destroying films, negatives, and other apparatus at Epsom Downs on April 27 last.

A further action was brought against the defendants by Mr. Vernon Henry Tovey, a journalist and photographer, to recover the sum of £10. damages for assault and battery at Epsom Downs. The defendants paid £5 into court in satisfaction of all damages, but denied all liability. Mr. Tovey, on being called, stated that on April 27 he went to Epsom Downs to take photographs. He obtained permission to take his camera on to the balcony of the Epsom Downs Hotel.

After he had taken up his position there, Countess Julia went on the balcony with her daughter, and asked him if he was going to stay there all day. He replied that he supposed he could stay there as long as he liked, as he had paid for his stand. Countess Julia demurred at this, and said she had been in the habit of walking round the balcony for the past twenty years. A few minutes later he heard the Countess Julia say, "If the man gets in my way, I will throw the camera over." Soon after he was asked by her to allow her to pass, and he at once acceded to her request.

Subsequently witness was engaged in arranging to take a series of photographs of the finish of the race, and asked her to wait a minute, but she refused, and called her daughter, the Countess Flora, and told her witness would not let her pass, whereupon she took hold of witness's assistant and swung him round. She then took hold of one of the tripods, and said, "We will see all about this". She pulled the camera toward her, and a part of it struck him in the eye, injuring it seriously. The camera then fell, and was greatly damaged. The camera was worth between £80 and £100.

The defendant, Countess Flora Sztaray, stated that her mother called her, and told her that Mr. Tovey would not let her pass, whereupon she took hold of the camera, and only used sufficient force to make a clean passage to allow her mother to pass. Tovey resisted the action, and in pushing it aside a portion of the camera came into contact with Mr. Tovey's eye. She denied using more force than was necessary. She had not a hasty temper. Witness, in reply to his Honour, said her mother was an American and had married a Hungarian.

Police-constable V186 said he had great difficulty in getting the names and addresses of the defendants; it took thirty-five to forty minutes. The elder Countess, on being called, said she was in delicate health, and asked to be allowed to answer questions in a private room. Mr. Sells who appeared for the plaintiffs, strongly objected, and his Honour upheld the objection, remarking that, if she could go to race meetings, she could give evidence in open Court. Witness, in reply to questions, said she wanted to get to her daughter, but plaintiff would not let her. She was sorry he got his eye injured, but it was a very slight injury.

Mr. Powell, for the defence, said the defendants were entitled to remove the obstruction, which prevented them from exercising the right granted to them by the proprietor of the hotel.

Eventually his Honour gave judgement for the defendant, Julia Sztaray (the elder defendant), as he did not think she was responsible for the damage, and, as the younger defendant had paid £5. into Court, he should give judgement for her also, consequently the costs would fall on plaintiffs.

THE ONLY POSSIBLE EXCUSE for printing the following further enormity, perpetrated by our office boy, is the urgency of the matter to which it draws attention, and we submit this plea for a considerable judgement.

The Kinematograph and Lantern Weekly
c. 1908

Here was a young man on the Wail,
Who said, "I'll be sacked without fail
If without hesitation
A Brand New Sensation
I omit to write up in a tale".

"To avert such a horrible thing
I'll tune up my lyre and I'll sing
Of dangers from fire
To John and Maria,
When their girls to a film show they bring".

So he worked up a disinterested fury
Gainst Raymond, Ruffel and Jury,
With Gaumont and Paul
And Urban and all,
And suggested they lived in luxury

He wrote such inflammable pars,
That his readers swore by the stars,
That the dangers they ran
When the film show began
Were worse that the terrors of Mars.

He scared people from Galway to Kent-
They were frightened to enter a tent-
The Councils came round
With rules iron bound,
And receipts fell of fifty per cent.

"Commissionaire (to old lady who has been examining all the placards). 'Step inside, lady, and see the most marvellous——'
Old Lady. 'Oh, are there more inside? Well, well, I think these are quite moving enough for me, you know.'"

Punch, 23 October 1912.

The World's Fair
9 January 1909

DANGER OF FIRE

THERE REMAINS, OF COURSE, the great and all-important question of the danger that may at any moment arise from fire. As our columns have recently shown, the vital problem of how this may be adequately dealt with is at present engaging the attention of those interested in the development of the industry. But that peril has still to be overcome the awful disaster which occurred only last Saturday at Stratford abundantly proves. In such instances it is, as often as not, less the actual effects of a catastrophe of the kind than the unreasoning panic springing from alarm that one has to take into account. Until the public possesses the absolute certainty that cinematograph entertainments are free from danger there must always be the possibility of such calamities taking place as that referred to. It is a matter which calls for immediate and drastic remedial measures. If, on the other hand, as appears to be the case, recent progress has resulted in the invention of a material for film which is absolutely fire-proof, its adoption will, obviously, restore all difficulties of the sort.

Scene following the Paris Bazaar fire. *The Graphic*, 13 May 1897.

*The British Journal
of Photography*
31 March 1899

IT IS NOT OFTEN that a cinematograph accident is considered to be advantageous. A correspondent, however, sends us a cutting from a local paper of the report of Chiswick Overseers' meeting last week. From that it appears that the vestry hall keeper inquired what the Overseers would do with regard to the letting of the hall for cinematograph shows as "they were very dangerous, and there was no appliance in the hall for them. They might explode and set the place on fire". The chairman is reported to have replied: "If it was only for the destruction of the hall, I should vote for it". From this it would seem that some persons look upon a cinematograph accident more as a blessing than anything else, when it would lead to the destruction of one hall to make room for a better. In the end, however, the hall keeper was instructed to accept no applications for that class of entertainment so that there is no immediate prospect of the Chiswick Vestry Hall being destroyed by the cinematograph.

A KINEMATOGRAPH ACCIDENT

The British Journal of Photography
16 March 1899

THE HAMMERSMITH THEATRE of Varieties, in King Street West, Hammersmith, was the scene of an alarming incident about 10 o'clock at night on March 4th. A man named Andrew Wraight was giving an exhibition with a kinematograph, when there was an instant and startling flare. Wraight, who was working with one assistant, was enveloped in flames without a moment's notice, but he jumped out of the box into a wet blanket provided in accordance with the regulations of the L.C.C. At the same time the fireman turned the hydrant on. There was an immediate stream of water, which was brought to bear on the kinematograph apparatus, and almost before the audience had realised that there was something wrong the fire was out. The unfortunate operator, however, was burned on the face and hands, and was at once removed to the West London Hospital.

"THE SAFETY OF THE OPERATOR. Our Artist's idea of what will happen when the New Regulations come into force on August 1st."
The Bioscope, 1909.

A BIG HAUL OF PHOTOGRAPHIC APPARATUS

The British Journal of Photography
11 March 1898

AT THE CLERKENWELL POLICE COURT, on the 4th inst., William Henry Smith, aged twenty four, and Frank Leslie, aged twenty-two, were charged before Horace Smith, with breaking into the shop, 853, Upper Street, Islington and stealing there from seventy three cinematograph films, thirteen projecting lenses, one magic lantern, a bicycle, a typewriter, and other articles, value £200, the property of Haydon & Urry, Limited. It appears from the evidence of Mr. George Haydon, Managing Director of the prosecuting firm, that their premises were broken into on the night of February 19, and the property of the value of £200 was stolen. On the previous Thursday night, in consequence of a communication made to him, he and the manager of the cinematograph department attended at 31, Clerkenwell Green, where the two prisoners were seen to offer for sale a number of lenses and other articles included in the stolen property. Two police officers, who were within easy distances of the shop, were called, and the prisoners were given into their custody. Smith told the magistrate that he and Leslie were general dealers, and that they had purchased the articles in the Islington Cattle Market last week. The prisoners were remanded.

4 Sex, Death and Religion

CINEMA, INCORPORATING ELEMENTS of theatre, photography and magic lantern show, presented film-makers, audiences and authority with new opportunities and challenges. As films moved on from relying on the simple novelty of portraying movement to the emergence of narrative, questions arose not only about how subjects should be shown but what should be shown. Since there were, of course, no established rules or precedents, the early years of cinema were a period in which the boundaries of what and what not was acceptable on the screen were blurred. As cinema increased its influence this situation could not continue. Conflicts and tensions began to arise between film-makers and exhibitors and those, often self-appointed, guardians of morality and culture who saw film as the prime cause of a decline in moral standards. Since existing legislation proved to be inappropriate or inadequate there were growing demands for some form of censorship or even a total ban on moving films. The industry itself also began to realise that the initial free-for-all was potentially damaging and that some degree of self-regulation was essential.

Some of the earliest debates over the suitability of subject matter for the new medium revolved around the age-old question of the representation of the naked (usually female) human form. Whilst paintings or photographs of naked women were tolerated on gallery walls where they could be justified in the name of 'art', moving pictures of the same subject were a totally different matter. A number of films sold by Philipp Wolff in 1897 came in for criticism. *The Temptation of St. Anthony*, *The Artist's Model*, *A Bride Unrobing* and *A French Lady's Bath* were all deemed to be unsuitable for public exhibition since the illusion of movement made them too life-like to be classed as art. Such films, generally advertised as 'Smoking Concert Subjects', sometimes drew their inspiration from classical mythology. By placing nude women in a classical or exotic context films took on a veneer of respectability. In much the same way that painters such as Alma Tadema used settings of harems and bath houses, film makers chose fictional locations that served to justify displays of female nudity that might otherwise been thought to be gratuitous. The Pathé catalogue for 1905 devoted several pages to titles such as *Borgia Amuses Herself* (reproduced from the famous picture by Garnier), *Eastern Slave Market* and *The Judgement of Paris*. Some makers, however, abandoned any such artistic pretensions and relied on a minimal narrative involving variations on striptease or on farce—not so very different from British sex films of the 1970s. For example, *A Courageous Husband*, made in 1905, is described as follows:

> Madame is having a tête-à-tête with her lover. Everything is going on all right when suddenly they hear somebody ascending the stairs. It is the husband. What is to be done? The lover sees a bear-skin on the floor and slips under it in time. The husband enters and while he is kissing his wife the lover tries to get to the door, hidden under the bear-skin. as the husband sees his carpet moving by itself, he is overcome with fear and the lover avails himself of it to get out. leaving the skin on the landing. Still the courageous husband pulls himself together again, and running to the door, picks up the skin and carries it triumphantly to his wife who heartily laughs at the stupidity of her dear husband.[1]

France seems to have been the main source of supply for films of this type, with major figures such as Georges Méliès being involved in their production. Apart from notable exceptions such as Esme Collings's *A Lady at her Boudoir*, very few British 'Smoking Party' films seem to have been made. The introduction of mutoscope (popularly known as 'What the Butler Saw') machines at the turn of the century was to prompt a wave of moral indignation over the exhibition of 'obscene' pictures. To modern eyes these appear very innocuous in content but at the time they seemed to many to represent a real threat to the moral well-being of the country and especially to that of its young people.

Quite apart from those films intended for mainstream exhibition there was also a market for pornographic films. France, once again, seems to have been the main source for such films following on naturally from the reputation Paris gained during the Second Empire for pornographic photographs. These films contained full and graphic representations of sexual acts.

Rather than scenes showing sex or nudity, it was the depiction of violence that seems to have caused most concern. Certainly then, as now, there was a public appetite for violence and film-makers were often accused of pandering to this prurient interest by including 'sensational' scenes in their productions. In a 1908 interview for *Variety*, Thomas Edison declared "Hangings, murders and violent deaths in any form should be barred from the sheet".[2] However, his company frequently used these subjects in its films. Indeed, one of the earliest surviving films made for the kinetoscope is *The Execution of Mary, Queen of Scots*, 1895. Executions were a popular subject for early films, providing a context where violence could be justified by placing it in a an historical or documentary setting. After President McKinley was assassinated in 1901, Edison's cameramen reportedly offered $2,000 for permission to film the assassin, Leon Czolgosz, on his way to the electric chair. In the end, they were refused permission and had to make do with a studio recreation of the scene. Walter Haggar's 1904 film, *The Life of Charles Peace*, climaxes with its most controversial scene, Peace's execution at Armley Jail. A noose and a hood are seen being placed over Peace's head and he then drops through a trap door. Haggar drew the line at actually showing the body dangling on the rope but another version of the story by Frank Mottershaw, also entitled *The Life of Charles Peace*, avoided the execution scene altogether. As the catalogue desc-ription stated: "It has been decided NOT to reproduce the Execution scene, as we believe it is too ghastly and repulsive."

Not all film-makers, however, were as considerate of public sensibilities. Some films contained actual scenes of violent death, such as Charles Urban's 1904 film, *Execution of 'Li-Tang' The Chunchus Chief of Manchurian Bandits*. Advertised as "The only animated picture of a Chinese execution ever taken. Gruesome, but faithfully depicting the actual scene", this was a case of life imitating art. A sinister echo of Sigmund Lubin's film of 1900, *Beheading the Chinese Prisoner*.

Some film-makers abandoned any efforts to place violence in a justifiable historical, documentary or patriotic context, relying on sensational scenes to spice up fictional narratives. In 1907 the Kinematograph and Lantern Weekly received a letter concerning a film entitled *The Black Hand*:

> . . . a most disgusting scene in its performance is where two ruffians enter a bedroom where a little child is sleeping in its cot while its mother is doing some sewing. These two men are seen to take this young child out of its bed, tie a rope around its neck, pass the rope over a peg behind a door, and actually pull the young innocent up by its neck until its feet are two or three feet from the floor whilst he mother is kept at bay.[3]

The relationship of Church and cinema was a somewhat ambiguous one. Although members of the clergy were prominent amongst those who warned of the dangers to morality posed by moving pictures, the Church was also aware of the potential usefulness of the new medium in spreading the gospel. Since religious organisations had for many years been making use of magic lantern shows, this was hardly surprising. The Salvation Army was one of the first to embrace the new medium, setting up its own Cinematograph Department. If nothing else, film programmes were soon found to be an effective way of tempting people away from the music hall and pub.

If the Devil did not have all the best tunes, the Bible could justifiably claim to have most of the best plots. For stories brimming with sex and violence, and all in spectacular settings, film-makers need look no further than the Old Testament. As films grew longer in the years leading up to the First World War, religious subjects paved the way in defining and refining methods of narrative. From the Manger to the Cross, released in 1912, ran for an unprecedented eighty minutes.

In 1898, W. K. L. Dickson had managed to persuade Pope Leo XIII to be filmed "giving his benediction to the people of the world through the medium of his apparatus." As going to the cinema became increasingly tainted with allegations of blasphemy and immorality, this symbiotic relationship was to come under increasing strain. In 1909 Leo's successor was to prohibit members of the Roman Catholic clergy from entering cinemas. The Salvation Army, too, after its original enthusiasm, prevented its members from going to picture houses. With the rapid growth in the number of cinemas and attendance figures came a call for the introduction of some form of film censorship. When censorship did eventually arrive, the initiative came from what might be considered an unexpected source—the industry itself. Censorship sneaked into the cinema through the back door, or, more accurately, as David Robinson has pointed out, through the fire exit. The 1909 Cinematograph Act was concerned solely with fire safety. In 1910, however, a court ruling held that the act "was intended to confer on the county councils a discretion as to the conditions which they will impose, so long as those conditions are not unreasonable." This judgement effectively enabled local authorities to control film content as well as conditions of exhibition.

Rather than submit themselves to the unpredictable and often irrational decisions of local councils, the industry was prompted to put its own house in order through the introduction of self-censorship. The Kinematograph Manufacturers' Association approached the Home Office with a proposal and, on 1 January 1913, the British Board of Film Censors began its work. It is interesting to note, however, that by this date the industry was already operating a great deal of self-restraint. In its first year the B.B.F.C. examined over seven thousand films. Of these, only twenty-two were refused a certificate for exhibition.

---

1. Catalogue published by Pathé Cinematographe Co. Ltd., 1905, p. 115.
2. *Variety*, 20 June 1908, p. 12.
3. *The Kinematograph and Lantern Weekly*, 10 June 1909.

CENSORSHIP OF CINEMA FILMS

Mr. Redford's New Office

The Times
2 January 1913

THE BRITISH BOARD OF FILM CENSORS, which was established in November by the joint efforts of cinematograph film manufacturers and exhibitors, began active work yesterday at 77, Shaftesbury Avenue, where offices have been opened and a small picture theatre fitted up.

Mr. G. A. Redford is director and he will be assisted in his work by four examiners. All pictures which are sent to the Board to be approved will be first shown on a screen before the examiners, and if there is any feature for which exception is taken the film or the particular portion of it will be submitted to Mr. Redford, whose decision on any point will be final. The new body has no official status, but it is hoped that with the support of manufacturers and exhibitors it will be possible to exercise control over all pictures shown in this country, whether prepared here or elsewhere. The scheme has the approval of the Home Office. In answer to a question in the House of Commons recently Mr. McKenna stated that he thought that such an independent examination of films would be useful to the trade and do much to protect the public from any risk of the production of objectionable pictures.

From March onwards all films which have been passed by the Board of Censors will bear notices recording that fact. Mr. Redford explained yesterday that it is not his intention to take up an antagonistic attitude towards film manufacturers, and he hopes to be able to enlist their hearty co-operation. He added that whenever any portion of a picture did not meet with the approval it would not be his desire to ban the film. He would invite the producer to meet him and endeavour to get such alterations made as would remedy the objectionable or questionable portion. In his opinion the staff of examiners was well equipped for the work, and he hoped that their efforts would meet with approval.

"*Redfords of the Screen: Censors of Living Pictures.*
Judging the cinematograph films: passing and condemning new subjects . . . a writer in *The Century* says: 'The Committee of educators and exhibitors, who give their services freely, passes judgement upon more than 80 per cent of all moving pictures exhibited in the land, and determines what twelve million children and adults shall see, and what they shall not see, from week to week. Backed by no law or ordinance, the Censoring body nevertheless holds within its grasp the entire field. The Board of Censors sits four days in the week."

The Illustrated London News, 22 April 1911.

THE CINEMA HABIT

Punch
18 March 1914

THE WRITER OF THE 'IDEAL FILM PLOT', which appeared in recent issue of *Punch*, has quoted an "authority" (anonymous) for the approval of his scenario. It is quite evident that this "authority" (so-styled) must belong to the plebeian ranks of the film-world. It cannot reside in *our* suburb.

Our cinema theatre is, I venture to state, of a far superior order, both as to drama and as to morality. It is not a mere lantern-hall, close and stuffy, with twopenny and threepenny seats (half price to children, and tea provided free at matinee performances), but a white and gold Picturedrome, catering to an exclusive class of patrons at sixpence and a shilling, with neat attendants in dove-grey who atomise scent about the isles, two palms, one at each side of the proscenium (real palms), and in addition a piano, a mustel organ to accompany the pathetic passages in the films. Moreover, the commissionaire outside, whose medals prove that he has seen service in the Charge of the Light Brigade, the Black Hole of Calcutta and the Great Raid on the House of Commons in 1910, is not one of those blatant-voiced showmen who clamour for patronage, he is a quiet and dignified receptionnaire, content to rely on the fame and good repute of his theatre. Sometimes evening dress form the 'Laburnums', Meadowsweet Avenue, who are on the Stock Exchange) is to be seen in the more expensive seats.

It is unquestionably a high-class Picturedrome. True that the local dentist who is a stickler for correct English, protests against the designation, I have pointed out to him that if a 'Hippo-drome' is a place where one sees performing hippos, then surely a place where one sees per-forming pictures is correctly styled a 'Picturedrome'.

I am acquiring the cinema habit. It is very restful. Each film is preceded on the screen by a certificate showing that its morality has been guaranteed by Mr. Redford. I have complete con-fidence in Mr. Redford's sense of propriety. If, for instance, a bedroom scene is shown and a lady is about to change her gown, one's advance blushes are needless. The film will be arrested at the losing of a first hook or button. Virtue will always be plainly triumphant and vice plain-ly vanquished. When on the screen we see Daisy, the flighty college girl, borrowing without per-mission her friend's gown, shoes, necklace and curls in order to make a fascinating display before her young college man, it is certain she will be publicly shamed by her friends and dis-credited in the eyes of her lover whose affections she seeks to win in this unmoral fashion.

On the screen we shall be sure to meet many old friends. The young American Society nuts, in square-rigged coats, spacious trousers, and knobbly shoes, will buzz around the pretty girl like flies to a honey-pot, clamouring for the privilege of presenting her with a twenty-dollar bouquet of American Beauty roses. The bouquet she accepts will be the hero's; and the other nuts will then group themselves in the background while she registers a glad but demure smile full in the eye of the camera.

The hero, however, loses his paternal expectations in the maelstrom of Wall Street. Throwing of his coat—literally because at the cinema we are left in no doubt as to his intentions,—he resolves to go 'out West' and retrieve the family fortunes.

Our old friends the cow-boys meet him at the wooden shack which represents the railway sta-tion at Waybackville, registering great glee at the prospect of hazing a tenderfoot. We know full well that he will eventually win their respect and high regard—probably by foiling a dastardly plot on the part of a Mexican half-breed—and we are therefore in no anxiety of mind when they raise the dust around this feet with their six-shooters, toss him in a blanket and entice him on to meek looking, but in reality record busting bronco.

In the middle of the drama we look forward to the 'chases', and we are never disappointed. Our pursued hero, attired in the picturesque bandarilleros of shaggy mohair and the open-throated shirterino of the West, will race through the tangled thickets, of the picadoro-trees, thunder down the crumbling banks of amontillados so steep that the camera probably gets a crick in the neck looking up at him; ride the foaming torrent with one hand clasping the mane of this now tamed broncho, and the other hand triggering his shooting-iron; and eventually fall exhausted from the horse at the very doorstep of the ranch, one arm, dangling hopelessly by his side. (It is, by the way, always the arm or shoulder; the camera never allows him to get it distressingly in the leg or in the neck.)

In the ultimate, with the wounded arm in a sling, he will tenderly embrace the heroine, through a hundred feet of film, she meanwhile registering great joy and trustfulness, until the scene slowly darkens into darkness, and the screen announces that the next item on the programme will be No. 7, Exclusive to the Picturedrome.

We are greatly favoured with 'exclusives'. It may be possible that other suburbs have these films, but it must be second-hand, after we have finished with them. The names of the artistes who create the roles are announced on the screen: *Captain Jack Reckless—Mr. Courcy van Highball*, or it may be *Juliet, Miss Mamie Ruffles*, Or is it a film taken at the local regatta or athletic sports, and the actors in it include all the notabilities of the district. We flock to see how we (or our neighbours) look on the screen and enjoy a hearty laugh when the scullers of *The Laburnums* register a crab full in the eye of the camera, or *The Oleanders* canoe receives a plenteous backwash from a river-steamer.

But the staple fare is drama—red blooded drama, where one is never in doubt as to who is in love with whom, and how much. Sometimes, to be frank, there is a passing flirtation, due to pique, between a wife and a third party, leading to misunderstandings, complications and blank despair on the part of the husband: but as there is always a 'little one' somewhere in the background we are never anxious as to the final outcome. It will end with the husband embracing the repentant (but stainless) wife, and at the same time extending a manly hand of reconciliation to the third party.

We also like the dying fiddler (with visions) and the motor-car splurges—especially the latter. In our daily life we are plagued with motor-cars, cycle-cars and motor-cycle side-cars, being on a highroad from London town to the country, but on the screen we adore them.

The cinema is very restful. There are no problems to vex the moral judgement; no psychological doubts; no anxieties. It will be 'the mixture as before' ending in the loving, lingering kiss.

Say what you will of Mr. Redford, he never deprives us of the kiss.

From *Photograms of the Year*, 1897.

The Times
3 August 1899

DEMORALIZING MOVING PICTURES

Sir,

Will you allow me to call the attention of the public, through your columns, to a new source of evil which has recently sprung up at our popular watering places? I refer to vicious, demoralizing pictures shown in penny-in-the-slot machines . . . I understand it is difficult to obtain a conviction unless the outrage is of the grossest kind, but surely the local authorities can, at least, prohibit such exhibitions on the foreshores of seaside places which are under their control. It is hardly possible to exaggerate the corruption of the young that comes from exhibiting, under a strong light, nude female figures represented as living and moving, going in and out of baths, sitting as artists' models &c. Similar exhibitions took place at Rhyl in the men's lavatory, but, owing to public denunciation, they have been stopped. Is it not possible to do this in other localities? . . . If nothing is done to stop this, we shall see a rapid decay of English morals to the level of Paris, with the same deadly results on the life of the nation.

I remain yours faithfully,

Samuel Smith.

Viewing Mutoscope machines at the seaside, 1912.
National Museum of Photography, Film & Television.

MUTOSCOPE PICTURES

The Times
2 October 1901

JOSEPH COWLEY, AGENT OF THE MUTOSCOPE COMPANY, was summoned at the Newcastle Police-court yesterday morning to show cause why certain pictures should not, on account of their obscene nature, be destroyed by the police. The pictures in question, according to the evidence given, by Superintendent Fyfe and Sergeant Besgick, were shown in one of the mutoscopes in the hall of the old art gallery, Grainger-street. When the sergeant visited the pictures, the charge for viewing which was 1d, there was a small boy in attendance, who said the pictures labelled 'The Artist's Model' and 'Special Extra' had been on show for about a month, whereas the defendant said he had shown the pictures for over a year without any objection having been made. Cowley said he did not think that the pictures could be objected to. Sir Riley Lord said the Bench had examined the pictures. They did not object simply to the nudity of the figure, but they considered that the suggestion conveyed was decidedly obscene and most immoral in its tendency, and an order would be made for their destruction. Upon this decision Cowley pleaded guilty to having unlawfully and wilfully exposed the pictures, and in extenuation he said the description 'Special Extra' had been placed on the pictures by the boy who was assisting him without his knowledge or consent. A fine of £5 and costs, with an alternative of one month's imprisonment, was imposed.

MORAL DANGERS OF CINEMATOGRAPH EXHIBITIONS

The Times
7 March 1913

THE LIVERPOOL SPECIAL COMMITTEE which was appointed last October, to consider the proposed new rules for premises licensed for cinematograph exhibitions state in their report that "from time to time complaints have been made of indecency having taken place in cinematograph halls, and it is obvious that such offences may be facilitated by the darkness in which some of the halls are kept while the pictures are being shown". The committee also deal in their report with the question of objectionable film, and mention is made of a censorship board which will examine the films submitted. Those passed for children's performance will certified for "universal exhibition", and those for adults will receive a certificate for "public exhibition". The committee are, however, of opinion that this form of censorship does not go far enough. The proposed rules provide that if there should be three or four more well-founded complaints against any particular hall during the period for which the license is granted there should be power to cancel the license. The committee recommended that children under 14 should not be allowed to attend an evening performance unaccompanied by parent or guardians. The educational value of the films shown, they consider, have been greatly exaggerated, and a rule has been included to exclude from the halls children of a certain age when infectious disease is so prevalent in the immediate district that children of that particular age are excluded from attending public elementary schools. The report will be considered at a meeting of justices next Tuesday.

The Manchester City Council have decided that children apparently under 14 years of age shall not be allowed inside places licensed the Cinematograph Act between 9 and 11 in the evening unless accompanied by their parents or guardians. Sir Thomas Shann (chairman of the Education Committee) stated that teachers in the elementary schools complained of the late hours which were kept by the pupils.

Despite vigorous protests by several ministers, the Middlesborough county bench yesterday granted a seven-day license to a new picture hall. The police-superintendent supported the Sunday opening of the halls, saying they took young people off the streets and kept others out of publichouses. Since the other halls had opened on Sunday evenings the streets were much quieter than they used to be. One minister objecting, said there was a rush from churches to the halls after evening services, which was unseemly.

Still from *Lady in her Boudoir*, by Esme Collings, **1896.** *BFI Stills, Photos and Drawings.*

"*First Suburban Nut.* 'I say, you chaps, did you see in the papers that the rotten old censor is going to stop crime being shown at the cinemas?'
Second Suburban Nut. 'And dog-fights!'
Third Suburban Nut. 'And prize-fights! Why, dash it, it's enough to drive one into the Territorials.'"
Punch, 13 November 1912.

INCENTIVES TO VICE

To the Editor of *The Times*

The Times
1 June 1901

Sir,

I address you upon a subject of the utmost gravity, a subject which has entirely outgrown public control, and now constitutes an evil which Parliament, law, or the public are powerless at present to stop, or even to check—namely, the debauching pictures and stories in the low cheap papers sold freely by newsagents throughout the kingdom.

To these horrors are now added the lewd pictures in mutoscopes or kalloscopes, which have grown up in our midst, and which are especially to be seen by the score on seaside esplanades, piers, or any place of holiday centre.

An occasional prosecution, a rare seizure, a still rarer fine (soon recouped by holiday pennies from Sunday school treats), and the whole thing goes on more briskly than before.

The whole country is now fairly gripped by all these indecent incentives to vice, and that quite openly. It seems no one's business.

The religious Press is heartily taking the matter up, and is now warning school treat managers to inquire carefully beforehand, either of the local authorities or the caterers, as to whether the place to which they are taking their children is or is not infected with these scandalous shows, for far better for children is a day in God's green fields than at some seaside place or holiday centre that is planted thick with penny illustrated guides to vice.

Against all such outrages, pictorial, literary, mutoscopic, we turn primarily to Parliament; Parliament refers us to the law; and the law, when appealed to, is found to rest, oddly enough, upon the amount of it which popular opinion insists upon having.

Then, again, there is a line by which these moral pirates have to steer, by law; but the steering is so accurate that all this deadly harm is being done to the nation within this line laid down by law; thus is the law at present helpless.

This position, quite apart from any religious aspect, is tearing education to shreds, for here we have the Forster Acts in full swing, established at immense cost of money and anxious thought, with schools fitted elaborately with pictures and diagrams illustrating the subjects best designed to improve the mind and elevate the character of the young children of the nation, and, directly school is over, they flock out into the streets, and there, facing them in the shop windows, are those shocking papers, or pictures, or else mutoscopes.

Therefore, Sir, the instinct of self-preservation compels us to turn once more to our civic mother, Parliament, and implore that a Royal Commission may be granted to inquire into the whole of this immense subject, and to devise means to put an end to this new régime of vicious incentives, which though within the line, is baffling every law of God or man.

Yours obediently
    Robert P. C. Corfe

CINEMATOGRAPHS AND THE CHILD

To the Editor of *The Times*

The Times
12 April 1913

Sir,

The writer of the interesting article on the cinematograph on April 9 says: "Whether in this extraordinary greed of the eye we are to see reason for alarm or not we do not know"; and after suggesting that the cinematograph may after all be helping us in our "fumbling towards some new form of art which is to have movement and shape", he adds "In the meantime we have a fury for seeing and remain happy, greedy, and terribly indiscriminate". As to our happiness I cannot agree. Those of us who know what a large proportion of the spectators are children between four and 14, and that before these children's greedy eyes with heartless indiscrimination

"Lady Godiva rides through Coventry. (*Tableau arranged by the Bio-cinematographic Co.*)
IF THEY HAD LIVED IN THE DAYS OF GOOD KING GEORGE."
Punch, 7 June 1911.

horrors unimaginable are in many of the halls presented night after night, are the reverse of happy. Terrific massacres, horrible catastrophes, motor-car smashes, public hangings, lynchings, hell fire and the tortures of the damned, &c., are passed before them, and become such realities that they cannot sleep at night and have been known to implore the policemen to guard them on their way home from "the horrid man with the beard".

Those of us who know that these same children, after sitting in the cinematograph hall till 11 o'clock at night, come weary and listless to school the following morning, who also from police and magisterial reports are informed that, many children become petty pilferers to get pence for admission to the show, others actually begin their downward course of crime by reason of the burglary and pick-pocket scenes they have witnessed, cannot help feeling very real alarm. It remains to be seen in Mr. Redford, the film censor, can work the change for the better that many film-makers desire. Meantime I dare to suggest that all who care for the moral well-being and education of the child will set their faces like flint against this new form of excitement, shall insist that no children under school age be allowed to go to these shows in the evening unless accompanied by their parents or guardians, and that our civic authorities should be called upon not to license any cinematograph hall that will not undertake to give afternoon shows for children on Saturday afternoons, at which all films shall be fit for a child to see.

Yours truly,

H. D. Rawnsley

KISSING BY CINEMATOGRAPH: AN AMUSING CASE

The British Journal of Photography
31 March 1899

AT NEWCASTLE COUNTY COURT last week, an action was bought by F. W. Dodsworth, Collingwood Street, Newcastle, against the Rev. B. Stone Spencer, Curate of St Paul's, Gateshead, to recover £1 16s. in respect of a cinematograph entertainment given at the parish hall of the church. Mr. D. E. Stanford was for the plaintiffs, and Mr. Hick for the defendant.

Mr. Stanford said the usual charge for the entertainment was £2 2s. but in this instance the agreed to take £1 16s. On arrival at the hall the plaintiffs' man was asked by Mr. Stack, the vicar, if the pictures to be exhibited were in order and fit to be shown. The answer was "Yes". The man referred to one picture. This showed a man at one side of fence tarring it, and a man at the other whitewashing it. They concluded by tarring and whitewashing each other. This, the man said was " a dirty scene". (Laughter.)

The Judge: One half of it. (Laughter.)

Mr. Stamford: Both.

The Judge: The whitewashing would not be dirty. (Laughter.)

Mr. Stamford added that, towards the close of the exhibition some pictures were shown which appeared to have created a terrible sensation in Gateshead. (Laughter.) One represented a fisherman sitting under a rock, and three or four properly attired boys who were anxious to bathe. (Laughter.) The boys succeeded in throwing the fisherman in the water. Then there was depicted a scene in a garden in which there was three seats. Upon the middle sat a lady. A gentleman came up slyly behind and kissed her. That was the picture objected to as unfit to be shown to an audience.

His Honour: It is an indecent assault. (Laughter.)

Mr. Stamford went on to read a letter from the defendant to the plaintiff, dated February 16. The epistle said the writer was sorry to have to say that he had to report more than unfavourably of the entertainment. It had been the cause of very serious complaint. The writer believed that it was the bathing scene, but this he did not recognise at the time (laughter) as it was so indistinct. Some mentioned it afterwards and expressed some surprise that the picture was not stopped. The second part of the programme was not finished. It was stopped because of the picture which was called Courtship. The vicar interfered, and told the operator to withdraw it, but the man refused to show any more, and commenced to pack up. The vicar at the outset said "We are very particular, and not only do we not want anything indecent, but nothing low or vulgar". The man would not give a list of subjects, but said the worst picture was that showing a man tarring on one side of a fence, and another whitewashing on the other side. The picture called Courtship had done a lot of injury to the parish. He (Mr. Stamford) supposed that the parishioners had been so injured that it would be impossible to get them redeemed (laughter). The entertainment had been given in many places. At Longhurst the pictures were shown, and the Rev. R. Proctor expressed great delight, and said his people were pleased.

Mr. Hick said the case rested entirely upon a question of breach of contract. They objected to one of the pictures, and said it could have been taken out and the entertainment proceeded with.

John Bolton, who was in charge of the apparatus, stated that he did not refuse to exhibit. When the kissing picture stopped, he did not turn to the audience and say that he could see no harm in it. What he did say that he was extremely sorry that the vicar should have interposed. He was excited when the picture stopped, but not until then. It was not necessary to swear at the machine, because it was one of the latest. (Laughter.)

Mr. Hick argued that the vicar was perfectly justified in insisting upon having the kissing picture taken out. The vicar objected to kissing.

The Judge: Do you mean that kissing is less known in Gateshead than elsewhere, or that it is so well known that they want to stop it? (Laughter.)

Mr. Hick: I say a picture of that sort at a parish hall is one thing and the same picture at a music-hall another.

The Judge: If you call the picture Courtship, it does not seem to me to be indecent. If the girl was a stranger to the man then it would be indecent. (Laughter.)

Mr. Hick: But it cannot be ascertained from that picture. (Laughter.)

The Judge: If it is intended for courtship, where is the indecency?

Mr. Hick: It is not exactly a question of whether it is indecent or not, but whether the vicar liked to have such a picture shown.

The Judge: I should be astonished to find that the vicar is such an unreasonable man as you are making him out to be. Here is a machine that cannot be stopped, when started, without difficulty, and you ask me to say that he ought to have it stopped as he chose. He ought to have asked for details beforehand.

Mr. Hick: My instructions are that he did ask for them, but did not get them.

Mr. Stamford: That is not the fact.

Mr. Hick submitted that there was no reason why the entertainment should not have been completed. His contention was that the plaintiff's man, when told to go with his performance, ought to have done so. Not having done so he had broken the contract.

The Rev. J. Stack (Vicar of St Paul's, Askew Road, Gateshead) said he asked the plaintiff's man to let him have a look at the pictures and he said he had not got them. Witness told him that he was very particular and the operator said he would give him the names of the pictures adding "Do you think I would bring anything here that you would not approve of?" He said the worst picture was that which had been mentioned of two men tarring and whitewashing. Witness said that, if that was the worst, he was quite satisfied, but added, "Remember, if there is anything improper I will stop it". He not only objected to things wrong in themselves, but to anything at all vulgar, "such as kissing matches". He mentioned it particularly because it was a common thing in such entertainments. The kissing picture was "a most violent windmill performance" with their arms in a most elaborate and grotesque style, and was utterly low. When he saw this picture being thrown on the screen he went to the plaintiffs' man and said, "I told you I would not have anything of that kind and you must stop it". The operator said, "What for?" Witness replied, "Because I wish it", and put his hand in front of the machine, but did not touch it, knowing that it would have been dangerous to do so. The plaintiffs' man then stopped the machine, and witness told him to take out the objectionable picture and to go on with the next. He declined and made a speech to the audience, saying: "Our worthy vicar objects to this picture. I suppose he does not approve of kissing. I can see no objection to it". (Laughter.) Witness said, "That is no business of yours; I object to the picture. Go on with your performance". Witness added that "if he did not go on with the performance, he would not pay for it". He could bring evidence that the men were swearing at the machine. Besides the kissing picture there was another that people said they were surprised he had not stopped. He prohibited the scene because he did not know what it was coming to. "You never do with these pictures." (Laughter.) "The courtship picture is a wild kissing match and nothing else." (Laughter.) "They don't court that way in Gateshead; they may in Newcastle." (Laughter.)

The Judge: There are things all right in one place and entirely wrong in another. (Laughter.)

Mr. Stamford said the plaintiffs' were not guilty of breach of contract, because it was the vicar and not they, who stopped the entertainment. His Honour had seen the picture which had been submitted to him, and he did not think he had found anything wrong in it.

The Judge said he thought it was entirely vulgar. He had no doubt that part of the audience would have enjoyed the picture extremely, but that was no reason why those who were trying to raise them should not have the right to object. He thought the vicar was within his rights in putting his hand in front and stopping the pictures. He could not come to any other conclusion than that the contract was not completed. It seemed monstrous to suppose that gentlemen in the position of the vicar should have no power in their hands in such circumstances, but were to leave it up to the discretion of others as to what they were going to exhibit. Judgement must be for the defendant.

Slide for projection on cinema screen before performances. Walturdaw Company Ltd. catalogue 1911.

PRIESTS AND THEATRES

Pope Prohibits Attendance at Kinematograph Shows

The World's Fair
24 July 1909

WHILE IT IS WELL KNOWN that Roman Catholic clergy are not allowed to go to theatres, their attendance hitherto at kinematograph entertainments has not been questioned, says the *Morning Leader*.

On Tuesday, however, the Cardinal-Vicar published the following decree: "It is among our duties to see that good habits prevail among the clergy and to protect their morality. Having ascertained that members of the regular and secular clergy attend kinematograph spectacles, many of which offend religion and morality, we informed the Holy Father, who authorised us to remind the clergy that they may not frequent theatres, and that they are particularly ordered not to attend kinematograph exhibitions of any kind. Any clergyman contravening this order will be liable to canonical punishment, including suspension from the celebration of mass and the divine offices."

THE POPE AND "KINEMACOLOR"

The Times
11 July 1913

MR. CHARLES URBAN HAS JUST GIVEN the first "Kinemacolor" entertainment at the Vatican, and the Pope, who is stated to have expressed his cordial approval, has ordered it to be repeated at an early date. The entertainment was given in one of the Throne Rooms of the Papal Suite, and amongst the spectators were the Pope's two sisters, his niece, the Secretary of State, and about 20 prelates of the Papal household. "Kinemacolor" pictures are to be made of daily life at the Vatican and kindred subjects, and the operators who are to make the films have already arrived in Rome.

The Times
21 March 1913

A CLERGYMAN ON THE CINEMA

THE NEW BRIXTON PALLADIUM PICTURE PLAY HOUSE, which is situated near the Town Hall, was opened by Mr. Davison Dalziel, M.P. yesterday afternoon. It has accommodation for some 2,000 people, the architects being Mr. Gilbert Booth and Mr Albert . . . and the proprietors Messrs. Sedger and Laurillard. Mr. Laurillard presided at the opening ceremony, and there was also present Mrs Davison Dalziel, the Mayor of Lambeth, Mr Hayes . . . M.P., the Rev. A. J. Waldron, vicar of Brixton, and members of the Borough Council.

A performance was subsequently given, the proceeds being devoted to the Brixton Nursing Home, Brixton Dispensary, and the Brixton Orphanage. In thanking the management for their kindness. Mr. Waldron said he was the chaplain of the local theatre and of the Empress Theatre of Varieties. In future he would become chaplain of the Brixton Palladium. He commented: "We must have enjoyment, and we want the best we can get. I am never ashamed to take my own boy to the picture palace. I am never ashamed to him to the theatre or music-hall if the play is clean. I am chairman of the religious section of the Cinematograph Show which opens at Olympia on Saturday, and shall speak at two conferences on the use of the cinema for educational, social and religious work. But don't think that because I am a parson I am out to say that you must have instruction and instruction only. That is perfectly absurd. I shall come into this picture palace, and I hope sometimes I shall be able to forget the worries of the parish and everything else".

The World's Fair
28 January 1911

WHAT IS A SACRED PICTURE?

Sequel to a Policeman's Visit to Cinematograph Show

WHAT IS A SACRED PICTURE? was the question debated at the Royton Police Court on Wednesday, when Thomas William Hall, the manager of a cinematograph show which is held at the Oddfellows' Hall, Shaw, was summoned for a breach of the Cinematograph Act.

Police-sergeant Taylor stated that he visited the hall on Sunday evening, January 8th, and afterwards asked the manager to point out any part of the programme which was of a sacred nature. He replied, "Morally I cannot". Witness told him that the would have to report him, and Hall said he made a practice of showing sacred pictures each Sunday night. Two of the films were entitled *Even the Police are Interested* and *Two Wrongs Never Make a Right*. The pictures were not of a sacred nature, but more of a sporting or dramatic character.

Mr. Waddington (for the defence): Have theses pictures a good moral?—I do not think so.

The police did not shine in these picture? (laughter)—I do not think so.

Continuing, the officer said that one of the pictures depicted a policeman kissing another man's wife whilst her husband was being run in (laughter).

Mr. Waddington: Didn't it suit?—It suited the audience.

Was everything orderly?—It was not; it was disorderly. The audience was shouting and laughing.

The Clerk: The question is, are these pictures of a sacred character or not?

Mr. Waddington held that the defendant either showed sacred pictures, or semi-sacred ones with a moral. There were only three absolutely sacred films to be got hold of today. It was for the magistrates to use their discretion as to what was a sacred picture. It might be a sacred or semi-sacred picture if it had a moral although it might not be a Biblical picture.

The Clerk: I suggest that the defendant undertakes not to show any picture other than a sacred one.

Mr. Waddington: What do you mean by sacred?

The Clerk: Well, I don't know, but a policemen is not a a sacred picture, you know.

Mr. Waddington: Well, policemen may be brought in on the scene in Palestine (laughter).

Defendant promised not to show any but sacred pictures in the future, and was told if he was brought there again he would have to pay £20.

A PATRON OF THE MUTOSCOPE

The British Journal of Photography
15 August 1901

WE ARE AS INTERESTED as the most puritanically minded M.P. could wish in the suppression of all photographs of an indecent or suggestive character. It is a misfortune that so beautiful an art should allow of such degradation, and it behoves all photographers to do what they can to see that such a stigma shall not attach to their calling or hobby. At the same time, it is doubtful whether public interest and private morality is served by undue exaggeration which only too often accompanies the attempts of misguided but well meaning enthusiasts to suppress everything which to a too prurient mind can savour in any way of suggestiveness. 'To the pure all things are pure' is a truth these individuals often forget. An instance of this was to be seen in the House of Commons last week, when Mr. Caine dwelt upon the disgusting nature of certain mutoscope pictures publicly exhibited in London. We cannot help wondering how these people acquire their altogether abnormal scent for the improper and the offensive. Mr. Ritchie remarked that on a previous occasion Mr. Caine urged him to see an exhibition in the Strand. One day he paraded up and down the Strand one whole afternoon but failed to detect anything. He said that he spent August Bank Holiday on Hampstead Heath, where he had been told that disgraceful exhibitions were on view. He saw many of the instruments in the Vale of Health, surrounded by urchins, and spent several pennies in order to have a peep, but the pictures he saw did not shock him in the least. We can add our testimony to that of the Home Secretary. We have never seen a picture in the a mutoscope that could be fairly described in the words employed by Mr. Caine, nor one that would shock anyone less sensitive that the proverbial maiden aunt. It only remains for the tradesmen who have received Mr. Ritchie's pennies to announce themselves as "under the patronage of His Majesty's Secretary of State for Home Affairs."

Postcard, c. 1910. *Collection of the Author.*

The Times
15 January 1913

KINEMATOGRAPH AND THEATRE

Sir George Alexander on Sunday Opening

SIR GEORGE ALEXANDER, who was accompanied by Lady Alexander, opened the New Gallery Kinema, Regent-street, yesterday, in the presence of a large audience.

Sir George Alexander said that the occasion was a significant one. Ghosts haunted that building and they were clad in the robes of Art. The genius of Burne-Jones, of Sargent, and many others had been associated with the New Gallery, which was now quite certain to be one of the most important centres of the Kinematograph: and the kinematograph, already the amusement and instruction of scores of millions all over the civilised world, was in its development destined to have an immense and tremendous effect on the minds and characters of those millions elsewhere. Its influence on the opening and widening of intelligence, in the formation of character, could not be over-estimated. They knew what the stage had done, and he believed that the stage, which had had the services of his life, was destined to do much more. Neither as a pure art, nor in intensity of effect would any ingenious development of mechanical photography ever compete with the theatre of living and speaking players. But the kinematograph theatre would do on the educational and moral side, with less intensity, but over a wider surface, what the other theatres had done and were doing. The swiftness of the action, the chance of seeing a vast number of scenes, all that added to the possibilities. The moral effect, especially on the young, would be very great, and he hoped that producers would never be afraid of being "goody goody", but always remember that their shows were essentially places in which a man should be able to take his wife and children. Some of them might be wondering if he, as a manager of a theatre and actor, might not be doing princely homage to his eventual conqueror. He believed, however, that so long as the manager was able to produce good plays, and had them well acted, he need fear no competition at all. On the contrary he believed that the kinematograph, by exciting and fostering a taste for the drama, would send more people than ever to plays worth seeing. Even if he thought otherwise, he would be the last person to attempt to discourage or depreciate that new art, for fair competition was the soul of human endeavour.

The question of Sunday opening was a most difficult problem. People might be rightly afraid of what was called the Continental Sunday, but when he had watched the quiet and simple way in which the great majority of people enjoyed themselves on a Sunday in the cities on the Continent known to him, the Continental Sunday seemed no such terrible matter. Others were afraid of workers having no day of rest, but that question, at least in the kinematograph theatre, would be easily settled by the licensing authority. One thing made emphatically for the wisdom of opening the kinematograph theatre on Sunday. They were assured on unmistakable authority that since its advent the attendance in the public houses had been greatly diminished, and not even the most extreme advocate of beer would deny that seeing a good kinematograph show was a better way of spending an afternoon than having a succession of pots of beer. If there was something to be said against Sunday opening, there was much to be said in favour of it, and after all, the man or woman whose conscience was offended could stay away. He believed that the theatres would never be opened on Sundays, though the thought that there was no doubt that a large section of the most intelligent people desired it. Certainly the work done by the Stage Society and others on Sunday had been of inestimable utility in furthering the cause of intellectual drama.

Sir George Alexander mentioned that from proceeds of the opening play at least 50 guineas would be contributed to the League of Mercy, one of the few charities of London, which during the past year had been able to keep up the amounts subscribed to it.

THE EDITOR'S CHAIR

Photographic News
14 January 1898

WHEN THE HUMOURS OF PHOTOGRAPHY come to be written, if ever they are written, space will no doubt be found for the following episode, which occurred recently in a chapel not far outside the metropolitan area. If not wholly true, the story is certainly a good specimen of the tales that are credited to Mr. Benjamin Trovato.

The narrative runs thus: In the chapel referred to, and for the benefit of its funds, it had been determined to hold a bazaar, and as a prime attraction, a gentleman skilled in the cinematograph had been engaged to give a demonstration of living photographs. When the eventful evening arrived it was arranged that the showman was to call out the title of each picture, after which a lady volunteer would strike up on the piano appropriate music whilst its subject ran its frisky course upon the scene.

In an evil moment the pastor of the chapel asked to examine the list of subjects to be shown, most of which met with his ungrudging approval; but his pious horror, when he came to the *Skirt Dance by Mdlle. X*, was piteous to behold. He would have none of it, and even were he to so far forget his duty as to countenance such an exhibition, he was convinced that half of his congregation would forsake him in disgust.

Now, it so happened on this particular picture the cinematograph professor much prided himself. It was the only one of his collection which was coloured, and it was invariably received by an appreciative public with thunders of applause. To omit it would be suicidal, but yet it would not do to offend the chapel authorities. Moreover, this picture, or rather ribbons of pictures, were attached to the other films to be shown on one spool, and it [would be] extremely inconvenient, on this ground alone, to leave it out. And so, for more reasons than one, it grieved the professor sore to omit from exhibition this attractive item.

At length the hour came for commencing the show, and the exhibition proceeded with the greatest success, the pictures being not more jumpy and headachey than is usual on such occasions. And when the time came for showing the tabooed *Skirt Dance*, the resourceful professor announced it as *Salome Dancing before Herod*. To say that this particular item of the programme was enthusiastically received, is to give but a faint idea of the *furore* it created. None of the audience thought of taking the least exception to it, and the pastor himself failed altogether to identify it with the picture which he had prohibited. The only comment upon which reached the professor's ear was that of an old lady, who thought it quite the best thing shown that evening, adding: "Well, we live and learn; I never knew until tonight that they took photographs in the time of Herod".

Letter to the *Nottingham Daily Express*, quoted in *The Kinematograph and Lantern Weekly*
4 July 1907

Sir,

Where will animated photography stop? A few nights ago I was at a kinematograph entertainment when a film was shown depicting the body of a fisherman being cast up by the tide. Surely this is too revolting to be popular with the crowd, and too morbid to be termed 'entertaining'. If it served any good purpose none would object, but the tragedy of the sea is too well known to need any reminder in this way. A few months ago I saw a kinematograph picture, which, if anything, was even more morbid than the one I have just mentioned—a scene in a lunatic asylum. Yet another—that of a suicide by hanging. A considerable sensation was created a short time ago by a series on 'The Birth of Christ'. To say the least it was indelicate, and from a religious standpoint blasphemous. At the time I expected some protest, but none came. Personally I feel there is a need for a strong expression of public opinion on the subject.

I am, etc.,

G.S.B.

Still from *The Passion Play of Oberammergau*, **1898.**

The Field Officer
October 1906

ARMY CINEMATOGRAPHS

IN MANY CORPS CINEMATOGRAPH exhibitions have proved of great use, especially on a Saturday night. Pictures appeal to everybody, and rightly, and they can win souls for God and The Army as effectually as words, written or spoken.

"The foolishness of preaching" is not foolishness when it bring sinners to the Cross; and the simpleness of "a picture show" assumes an air of wisdom when it keeps lads and lasses from the music-hall, interests their fathers or mothers in the Salvation Army, and finally attracts some of all ages out of their homes on the Sunday to the same place where they had been on the Saturday, there to hear of salvation and find the Saviour.

God directs such efforts, if taken up in the right spirit, and they are full of surprises. Not long ago, for instance, in a North-Eastern city, the whole performance came to a standstill while a man, who had been a terrible character, and not long before had attempted to take his life, came forward for salvation. The Officer can conduct the whole programme with an idea to save souls, and the audience can be easily induced to remember that they are in a building where Salvationists are accustomed to seeing souls born into newness of life.

As to laughter and merriment, God meant His people to be happy, and, just as the devil has no right to all the best music—let alone the 'catchy' tunes—no more has he any right to a monopoly of pictures grave and gay, or modern improvements on the magic lantern of our youth, which used to show us highly coloured views of an impossible . . . and on a white sheet at the missionary meeting! . . .

The Officer
March 1897

ANIMATED PICTURES

A Nineteenth Century Wonder. To Go Round the Provinces.

DURING THE SALE AT CLERKENWELL, visitors were generally surprised at seeing bills round the building, announcing a show of "Animated Pictures" on the building, and when they afterwards saw the thing itself, their surprise was lost in wonder. There the pictures were, moving on the screen as if they were living—the children played so happily on the sea-shore, there the waves came rolling, and further out shops were sailing to and fro. That was marvellous indeed, and gradually the nineteenth century spirit of enquiry was evident—everybody wanted to know

How it was done.

Adjutant Howse, who is the "showman" of the affair, gave us all the information we wanted, and we reproduce it below for the benefit of our readers.

The 'Animated Pictures' are the greatest marvel in limelight-work up to date. It must be seen to be believed. To see a fine limelight-picture is a treat in itself, but when you see the figures in it suddenly commence to move about as naturally in real life, then you see something which defies the understanding of the average man. And yet it is all very simple—when you know it.

The apparatus is founded on the principle which we perhaps may call persistence of vision. Anything that moves quicker that one-eight of a second cannot be seen distinctly with the human eye. Take for instance a stick, which is lighted at one end, and swing it round rapidly in a circle. You will then see, not the point of the stick shifting position, but an illuminated unbroken circle, which is, of course, an illusion. Upon that illusion is the machine founded.

What, you see on the screen is not one picture, but an immense number of pictures—in some cases up to a thousand—revolving so rapidly that to the human vision it looks like one. These pictures are taken on a long photographic film. The photographic apparatus is focussed to the scene you want reproduced, and the film is reeled through it very quickly so that about fifteen different photographs are taken every second. It is obvious that every movement of the focussed objects in that way is arrested on the film in a progressive scale, and when the negative afterwards is developed and printed on another film, and that is drawn through a limelight apparatus sufficiently quick, the thousand pictures will show all the movements of the figures as one living picture.

Several men claim the honour of this invention which seems to have a great future before it. Adjutant Howse thinks the Frenchmen Lumiere can claim to be the first on the market, and it is his patent we use.

Salvation Army Pictures

"Have you any Salvation Army pictures Adjutant?" we asked, knowing that unless linked up with the Army it will not get its proper place in Army circles.

"We have none for the present, but as soon as the fine weather comes, it is our intention to get a series of S.A pictures. The machine we are making will be able to take photographs as well as show them."

(What splendid things the future has in store for us! By-and-by, we shall be able to enjoy the sight of the grand march-past at the Crystal Palace from a comfortable corner of our barracks.)

"It is the intention to go round the Provinces with the machine, I understand?"

"Yes. We will give everybody a chance. Our terms are very favourable. Any Officer can book us in conjunction with an ordinary Limelight Service—which we ourselves provide. We do all the advertisement ourselves. The admission will be threepence—we take two-thirds and leave one-third for the Corps, if we only get, say, 500 people, it will mean quite £2 for the Corps."

"And can the Corps chose the subject for the Limelight Service?"

"Certainly. We shall be glad to make arrangements with D.O's or F.O's as soon as possible. Those that come first will get first served. I am confident it will prove a great success."

The Field Officer
January 1906

THE CINEMATOGRAPH
Its Spiritual and Financial Value

ADJUTANT ERNEST SUTTON, South Tottenham: I was led to commence Cinematograph services, first, in order to draw the right class of people into my Hall on Saturday nights. I saw that the Cinematograph attracted crowds elsewhere, and as, of course, there is nothing wrong in the employment of a picture, provided the picture is consistent with our principles, I resolved upon adopting the 'Kine' to my work. In this I have not been disappointed. Fully an hour before the service commence the crowds begin to flock in a constant stream until the Citadel is crowded.

Then, I felt the need of fresh means to aid me in financing the Corps.

I would like to say that fully £8 is needed per week to cover the Senior Corps expenses, and when taking over the command I found there was fully £2 each week short of this amount, in addition to which the Corps had a liability of nearly £120.

That the venture has proved a success from a financial point of view is beyond doubt, for between £3 and £4, and sometimes nearly £5, net profit, is handed over to the Corps funds out of the Saturday night's service. The financial burden in now a thing of the past, the Corps is clear of debt, and I can enter upon my Sunday meetings without a single care with regard to

"A Cinematograph Drama in Paris: The Condemned Man being dragged to the stake in the centre of the arena, immediately facing Nero, to await the coming of the lions." *The Tatler*, 3 May 1905.

the collection, devoting myself entirely to the needs of the people and the spiritual welfare of the Corps. This alone, from an Officer's standpoint is an inestimable blessing.

I began 'all in a hurry.' My Local Officers were rather against the idea, but I begged them to work with me for one month and they agreed. That was just six days before I announced my first night. I then got out posters, small handbills, illuminated posters for carrying up and down the main streets, and visited as many Soldiers as I possibly could, leaving bills for them to distribute. I then went into the Walturdaw Company and booked up four Saturday nights, paying £2 10s. for each night.

The first Saturday I took just enough to pay the bill; from that time it has grown until now we are always sure of a full Hall. I keep the subjects as varied as possible. To take one subject only right through the evening gets very monotonous. There are a great many subjects one can use to great profit, e.g., cities of various countries, panoramic views of the great cities of the world, railways, canals, etc. The industries of the world, e.g., logging in Canada, coal mines, fishing, brickmaking, hop gardens, harvesting of all kinds, ship-building, a day in the cotton mills, silk mills, cloth mills, a few humorous stories, especially where children figure in the pictures, such as The Children's War, Children's Pets, Stolen Cake. These never fail to interest, and are quite harmless, and help to brighten up the evening. Then there are the Bible subjects: Life of Christ, Moses, Joseph, Samson, Gideon, Prodigal Son, and a host of other subjects that are ever increasing as the days go by.

I have never experienced any difficulty in getting suitable films. The Walturdaw Co., 3 Dean Street, High Holborn, London, have practically an endless stock of all kinds, as well as a very good idea as to what is, or is not, suitable for Salvation Army purposes.

My expenses, on an average, run to £2 per week. This includes hire of Cinematograph and accessories, two gas cylinders, and one large spool of films, about 1,600 feet, short stories with slides, illustrated songs, and printing.

The following is a programme of my Saturday night's service:

1. Opening song—*War Cry*; band leading.
2. Prayers.
3. Selection by Band.
4. Officer reads out programme for evening.
(here lights are lowered and sheet drops).
5. Illustrated song—'Rock of Ages'.
6. Cinematographs: *Mountaineering in Switzerland* and *Logging in Canada*.
7. Recitation: 'The Road to Heaven', Illustrated by Limelight Views.
8. Cinematograph: *Rescued by Rover*.
9. Illustrated song: 'Oh, God our help'.
10. Cinematograph: *Nell and the Burglar*.
11. Reading: 'Life of General Gordon'. Limelight Views.
12. Cinematograph: *Life of Moses*.
13. Doxology (thrown on sheet).

Our attendance on Saturday nights before the Cinematograph was between fifty and sixty; now it is from 500 to 700—the latter figure is the extent of our seating.

Our Sunday night meetings were never as well attended as now. Most Sundays we have to turn people away, and without a doubt this is partly due to the Cinematograph.

A gentleman in thanking me for the Saturday nights, said, "We find them very helpful. I have a large family of ten. The Saturdays, previous to your starting the Cinematograph, were a great cause of anxiety to my wife and I, but now we can bring the whole of our children with us where they are under our eye, and now we have a little joy in coming out." This man and family are constant attendants at our meetings, and only yesterday asked for an interview with regard to spiritual matters.

Last Saturday a whole Roman Catholic family I discovered, are now attending our Saturday nights, whereas they formerly spent it in the pub. Moreover, there is a likelihood of this family becoming Salvationists.

Finally I would say that organisation is very necessary to complete the success of the Saturday night's service. This is how we manage at Tottenham:

1. A Sergeant is appointed to take over the entire charge of tickets, keeping order, putting people into seats, etc. He has a dozen men at his disposal.
2. Two Brothers are my right-hand men. One attends to the machine, gas etc; the other looks after the readings and slides and illustrated songs, he is also responsible for getting and returning the same. I attend to the films myself.
3. Two Sisters are always responsible for the refreshments.
4. Eight Brothers, during interval (four for the gallery and four for downstairs) serve out the refreshments on trays.
5. A Brother is appointed to attend to the lights, lower and raise, as needed, also the same for the sheet.
6. The Bandmaster does the musical side of the meeting. We always have a good Band up. They do the open-air, opening song, selection after prayers and play during the twenty minutes interval.
7. One thing I find very helpful, and that is a rehearsal of the spool of films on Friday night, generally after the night's meeting. The advantage is: first, you get to know the character of the films shown, and should any portion of it be not suitable, it can be left out. Second, it is almost necessary if you desire to explain the pictures, and if you wish to give a moral with each picture.

Then, and specially, the effect on my Sunday congregations is excellent. We have Soldier in the Corps who were first attracted to the Army by this means.

W. T. Stead
'The Church's Picture Galleries: A Plea for Special Sunday Cinemas'
The Review of Reviews
November 1912

AT A TIME WHEN there is so much discussion with reference to Sunday entertainments, whether in Theatre, Music-hall or Cinematograph Hall, we think it of a very great interest to print the following article by the late Mr. W. T. Stead, in which he advocates Sunday Cinema shows under the auspices of the Churches. In this he saw a possibility of enormously enlarging the sphere of religious activity, and an educational and moral development of the highest importance.

There are said to be 4,000 Picture Palaces doing business in the United Kingdom. Of these at least 3,500 are closed on Sunday. The local authorities quite properly refuse seven-day licenses to exhibitions which are as much speculations run for purposes of private gain as theatres or music-halls. The operators and employers of the Picture Palaces, which now number about forty thousand men and women, have as much right to a six-day week as any other class of the community. The Picture Palace, is however, allowed to open on Sundays in certain places under certain restrictions; as, for instance, in London, where proprietors are free to open their shows after six o'clock on condition that they hand over their net profit, after deducting their working expenses, to some local hospital, charity or some other public fund. It is complained that the proprietors sometimes over-estimate their working expenses, relying upon the impossibility of any strict audit, and that in consequence the do succeed in making some commercial profit for themselves by trading on the Lord's Day. Even when the profits, or some proportion of them, are handed over to charity, there is still considerable opposition to the Sunday picture show on the part of the spiritual pastor and the vendor of the spirits, as at present, parson and publican have a monopoly of the right to cater to the public need on Sunday. Whatever may be the reason, the fact remains that of 4,000 Cinema halls 3,500 remain empty and useless on the one day in the week when the masses have leisure to attend them.

Average Daily Attendance 4,000,000

If we take the average attendance at each picture hall at 1,000 a day for a performance that begins at two and goes on till ten—no excessive estimate, seeing that the average capacity of a hall is about 600—we may estimate the average attendance at Cinema shows at 4,000,000 every week-day, and only 500,000 on every Sunday. If all the halls were open on Sundays as on week-days the attendance would probably be over rather than under the week-day average. That is to say, there are about 4,000,000 persons who, if the Cinema were open on Sunday, would go to see the pictures; but, as the Cinemas are shut, they walk about the streets, go the public-house, stay at home, or in a few cases, go to the church or chapel.

These 4,000,000 are at present not reached by any ethical, educational, or evangelical agency. This seems to indicate that there is screw loose somewhere in our machinery for making the most of man.

The Cinema show as it at present exists is one of the most popular institutions in the modern world. Although it is but of yesterday, it has sprung up all over the two hemispheres. While churches and chapels are bewailing their empty pews, the Cinema show is crowded to the doors. Attendants at places of worship would mutiny if the minister protracted the service ten minutes beyond the usual time. A Cinema crowd would consider that it was exceptionally favoured if it were treated to an extra quarter of an hour of the show. The utmost efforts of a host of zealous workers fail to induce the average citizen to attend church, where the ministration is without money and without price. But these average citizens who flock in crowds to the Cinemas gladly pay threepence or sixpence for the privilege of admission. There is surely a lesson in this notable contrast which it may be well worth while to endeavour to discover.

The Attraction of the Cinema

The answer to that is easy. The attraction of the Cinema is Life. It is the living picture that appeals to the eye of living people. The magic-lantern slide often produces far more artistic effects than can be obtained from the Cinema film. But it is not Art that draws the multitude. It is Life. The Cinema show represents Life as it is lived to-day—Life caught in the act of living, and made to reproduce itself before the Cinema crowd. All kinds of life—life real and life faked, life savaged and life civilised, the life of the desert and the poles, the life of animals and birds and insects, the wonder and glory of Niagara, the sublimity and terror of the Atlantic in storm, the pomp and panoply of glorious war and wars by no means glorious, the stately splendour of Royal pageants—every phase of the life of man from the cradle to the grave the Cinema presents to the crowd. This endlessly varied and constantly changing living panorama of the world, and of all the things that live therein, attracts the multitude by its novelty and holds them by its interest.

That is the good side of Cinema. It has another side. It is no more an unadulterated boon and a blessing to men than is the newspaper, which it much resembles. Much of the spectacle provided at Cinemas is mere sensational spectacle, and some of the pictures are as bad as the piffling drivel that fills so many of our cheaper comic papers. But even here, where coarseness is often substituted for humour and vulgarity for wit, the Cinema show is no worse than many comic prints, and it makes the same kind of appeal to the same kind of people. Thanks to the rules of the Film Manufacturers' Association the plague of filthy living pictures has been stayed. Some of the films are suggestive, but none are obscene. The Cinema show may be vapid, it may be silly, it is seldom unclean. For which we may well be grateful.

Eye-pleasing, Mind Tickling, Time Wasting

Taken at its worst, the Cinema provides millions of men, women, and children with a means of spending their leisure hours more pleasantly than they used to do ten years ago, with less

The Adoration.

Healing the Blind.

The Flight into Egypt.

The Last Supper.

Turning Water into Wine.

The Betrayal.

A CINEMATOGRAPH LIFE OF CHRIST.
(Such a film should be singularly suitable for showing in the Cinema halls on Sundays.)

Illustration accompanying 'The Church's Picture Galleries: A Plea for Special Sunday Cinemas'
by W. T. Stead, in *The Review of Reviews*, November 1912.

incitement to extravagance and to vice than either the public-house or the music-hall. The Cinema may be, and often is, a temptation to spend time pleasantly which ought to be devoted to study or to social service; but, as all police authorities attest, it has diminished drunkenness and immensely facilitated maintenance of law and order in the streets. The chief fault that can be found with the Cinema is that it is too stimulating. The rapid and constant succession of moving pictures leaves no time for reflection. You see life as from the window of an express train. You have not even opportunity to recollect the impression of the scene. The Cinema public is like a child whose only literature is picture books; it is apt to be satisfied with looking at the pictures and never learns to read. The approach to the mind is solely through Eye-gate; the approach by Ear-gate is entirely neglected. The Cinema challenges, but does not fix attention. It excites wonder; it does not allow time for reflection. "It is an eye-pleasing, mind-tickling, time-wasting thing", say its critics. To which I reply: maybe so, maybe not; but it draws. Is it not possible to utilise what there is good in it, and to leave out what there is bad in it, so as to make the Cinema useful for instructing, inspiring, and saving the people . . .

In brief, what I propose is that there should be instituted at once a National Cinema Sunday Mission for the utilisation of the closed Cinema palaces for ethical, educational and evangelical purposes. What scheme of Church Extension can for a moment be compared with this opportunity of suddenly exploiting in the service of religion 4,000 buildings, situated in the very heart of our densest population, which are the favourite assembling places of four million of our people. It is not a case where we have hunt for sites. Cleverer and smarter men than we have selected them already. The buildings are already erected. Their week-day congregations amount to millions. We have only to open the Cinemas on Sunday with the right kind of pictures presented as parts of an ethical, educational, and evangelical service to reach millions who at present never "darken the doors of the house of the Lord"

The Picture Gallery of the Universal Church

It would, I am convinced, be quite possible to run a Cinema Sunday show in many places on lines as distinctly religious as the service, let us say in the Lyceum Theatre. Those who prefer sticking to the old ways and limiting the utilisation of the Cinemas on Sunday to the salvation of the souls of their people could do so, and everyone would rejoice over their success. But in putting forward this suggestion of a Cinema Sunday Mission I am at least as anxious to utilise the Sunday for ethical, educational, and evangelical purposes as I am to exploit the Cinema Halls which are at present unused. The worst of services run on strictly devotional lines is that no one attends them but strictly devotional people. Now the great note of the Cinema Sunday Mission should be the excessive width and breadth of its appeal. It should be the picture gallery of that universal Church which Longfellow described as being:

As Lofty as the Love of God
And wide as are the wants of man.

It should adopt the motto of the Son of Man: "I come that ye might have life and have it more abundantly". As the heavens declare the glory of God and the firmament showeth forth His handiwork, as the world and all things that are therein were the work of His hands, the Cinema would endeavour to set forth before the eyes of the man in the street on Sunday some pictures of the glories and the splendours and the marvels and the miracles of the world which God has made. And as History is but the continued manifestation of the evolutions of the embodied thought of God, and the events of the day are history in the making, so there would be an attempt to make the Cinema represent the realities of that drama "whose scene-shifter is Time and whose curtain is rung down by Death". The word that was spoken to Peter, "Call thou nothing clean or unclean", may be addressed to cavillers who may object to using the Sunday Cinema to rouse men to a realisation of the truths of science, the inspiration of history, and the infinite marvel of the universe.

5 Art and Artifice

CINEMA IS CONCERNED WITH THE creation of illusion, of convincing its audience to suspend belief. Yet it is equally reliant on replicating and reflecting versions of reality. If something appears 'real' we are inclined to take it more seriously, even if what we see on the screen is preposterous, fantastic or impossible. Many forms of artifice were practised before the camera, and trick films and shots perfected by George Méliès, Ferdinand Zecca and Robert William Paul proved extremely popular in this early period. These illusions, created for the cinema, had a long theatrical tradition and relied heavily on well-tried stage routines. These were coupled with the technological capacities of the cine camera which enabled a far greater control to be exercised over the visual spectacle presented to audiences. Time could be frozen, people and objects substituted, magnified or diminished, time reversed or speeded up; yet with clever editing the audience experienced everything in continuous, real time. The following description provides some idea as to the content of many of these films:

> The baby is chewed up by gee-gee with his hay right in front of your eyes. You see it go down a mouthful at a time. Baby missed. A rumpus. Baby's cries heard coming from the horse's stomach. The veterinary surgeon at work. A life or death operation upon the horse. The horse completely empty inside. The baby drawn out whole in triumph, and the horse none the worse for his experience. Length 275 feet. Price £5 10s nett.[1]

Perhaps George Méliès, originally the proprietor of the Robert Houdin Magic Theatre in Paris, deserves recognition for creating some of the most arresting and fantastic films of this period. His pioneering adaptation of the tradition of theatrical illusion for use before the cine camera inspired many emulators, but none matched his early skill, or the grand scale on which he practised his techniques. His sets were hand built, and every trick tirelessly rehearsed and choreographed.

Unlike theatre or the magic lantern show, cinema's main strength, and an obvious difference, is the degree of pictorial realism it creates. Audiences were drawn by this particular quality which no other medium offered, but were equally aware of its limitations in its capacity to replicate images from real life. Maxim Gorky was not the only commentator to draw attention to the grey, soundless and flat world the subjects of cinema inhabited. As a form of visual representation the cinema was naturally compared to existing entertainment and art forms. Its status within this debate was under constant review and one early commentator explored the relationship between cinema and art, drawing parallels between the individual work of the artist and the prolific but limited appeal of cinema:

> One critic has said that if photographers would turn their attention to the recording of historic events like the Jubilee, or of vanishing buildings, they could do an immense service to art. In one way this is true; in another it is not. Surely this critic would be the last to suggest that the cinematographic 'pictures'—the whole twenty-two thousand of them, shown at the Empire, I think—are equal to one picture of a procession by Carpaccio, painted centuries before we had any photographs. No doubt twenty-two thousand artists would be required to secure as many views of the Jubilee procession as were obtained by the cinematograph, and their employment might have been too much of a good thing. But if, say, half a dozen accomplished artists had been commissioned, and allowed to do what they wanted, might we not have a record of some artistic importance? As to the photographing of old buildings, which would the architect rather have, an etching by Piranesi or a photograph by one of the most revolutionary of the 'Salon' photographers?[2]

Like photography before it, the cinema was regarded as a useful tool for artists, but generally rejected as too low-brow to constitute an art form in its own right. In many respects it was also pitched between opposing camps within the art world, between the debate about realism and the growing trend towards forms of abstraction. In its infancy the cinema's capacity to articulate and reflect reality was crude, often seen as functioning as an undiscriminating recording device. The operator in fact acted as mediator between reality and the unreality created on the cinema screen. It was the space between these two worlds upon which the audience's imagination worked.

As the medium evolved its practitioners began to develop the means of more subtly controlling the sets of images the camera was recording. Film makers consciously began to explore the relationships between sets of images, some staged, some documentary and form simple narratives by the ordering of these images or scenes. These progressions allowed for more and more complex narratives to be formed within the body of films.

The first commercially exhibited films were less than a minute in length and shot in single takes, in real time. Yet even within these constrictive circumstances we can see the basis of basic narratives, stories in miniature. The 1895 film *The Sprinkler Sprinkled* by the Lumières, with the familiar image of the boy standing on the gardener's hosepipe and ultimately drenching him when he looks down the end of the nozzle, is a perfect example. Contained in these fifty or so seconds is a single self-contained story. Within ten years films were over ten times as long, with as many joined scenes, utilising spatial and temporal manipulation to aid the story telling. As films grew longer and more complex it also became necessary to guide audiences through often complex narratives, either by providing a running commentary or by the use of inter-titles which described the action. These were dependent on whether patrons could read or not, and were tested further by a report in which lip-readers had determined whether the silent utterances of actors matched the story or not. Many early narratives were adaptations of existing stage or literary works and provided ready material for film makers, as one early commentator pointed out:

> 'Narrative Animatography'
> We passed a pleasant half an hour at Messrs. Maskelyne & Cooke's entertainment the other evening, and were interested to observe that not the least appreciated part of the programme was the exhibition of animated photographs. One of the series, which lasted some minutes, was of a humorous character—being, in fact, a kind of little farce of a grotesque description. The reflection occurred to us, that, so far, little has been done to tell a connected story or narrative by means of animatography, and that probably the idea is capable of considerable development. Plays without words could, in fact, be reproduced by means of the Kinematograph, pending the arrival of the time when Mr. Edison's alleged idea of associating the phonograph with animated photography is realised.[3]

These texts were drawn not only from the theatre, and literature, but from magic lantern narratives as well. Robert Paul's *Buy Your Own Cherries*, a temperance film, was adapted from a much older series of magic lantern slides and follows it scene by scene. It was not long, however, before famous literary figures such as George Bernard Shaw and H. G. Wells were courted by film makers to provide material for films, and artists like Sir Hubert Von Herkomer were to lend respectability to cinema, transforming its popular perception from that of mere artifice to an art.

1. *The World's Fair*, 1 December 1906.
2. *The Contemporary Review*, December 1897.
3. *The Photographic News*, 8 April 1898.

"Mr. Punch's Own Cinematograph."
Punch's Almanack for 1901.

THE FOLLOWING CONVERSATION overheard in the train has prompted me to give a short survey of the progress of the Cinematograph.

'A Great Traveller'
*Historical Review of the
Cinematograph*
anonymous pamphlet, 1910

First Passenger: "I gather, sir, from what you have told us, that you have seen a great deal in your travels?"

Second Passenger: "Why, of course I have".

"I was present at the King's funeral and had a splendid view both in London and at Windsor. I was also present at that memorable Derby when his late Majesty led his winning horse through the crowd. I have also seen him, too, at the Great Review in Spithead, Yachting at Cowes, Trooping the Colours at the Horse Guards, visiting the sick in the Netley Hospital and I can't tell you how many more places. Then I was present in the stadium when Dorando staggered in the real winner of the first Marathon. I've seen the Derby annually, also the Boatrace, I have been at the reviews at Aldershot, War Dances in Tahiti, and a Durbar in Calcutta. I have sailed up the Yan-Tse-Kiang, travelled the Great Pacific and the Trans-Siberian Railways, seen log rolling in Canada, mustang taming in Mexico, pig sticking in Chicago, apple packing in New Zealand, diamond getting in Kimberley as well as twinkle footed geishas serving tea to British men-of-war in Yokohama. Of course I saw Beirut crossing the Channel, and the late Mr. H. C. Rolls and Mr Graham White rising on their aeroplanes in many places. I have seen suffragettes at the House of Commons, the Presidential Election mob on Broadway, a bull fight in Madrid. Nor have I missed the Passion Play at Oberammergau, the procession of Palms in St. Petersburg, that of Corpus Christi in Rome or our dear Lord Mayor's Show in London. I have even penetrated wild Tibet to see the Tiger God or Golden Fire, have reached the Pyramids of Ghizeh, the Madhi's tomb at Khartoum, the Mosque of Omar, the Villages of Jehosophat, the Mountains beyond Jordan, the Sea of Galilee, the Mount of Olives, the Pool of Siloam, the Golden Gates, Solomon's Temple, the Via Dolorosa, Golgotha itself and the Calvary's Tomb!"

First Passenger: "What great expense you must have been put to?"

Second Passenger: "Not at all", he replied, "if you know the right way to go about it. For my part I have seen all those things and a great deal many more sitting in a comfortably upholstered seat in a CINEMA PALACE and the cost to me has been THREEPENCE A TIME. *Cayley Calvert.*

A Revolution in Entertainments

In the history of public entertainments no revolution has been so rapid and startling as the very veering of public taste in the direction of the Cinematograph. Ever since the days when the ancients varied the monotony of daily toil by dancing orgies held in honour of pagan deities, the first form of indulgence in public entertainment, no change has been so sudden and sweeping as this.

The Cinematograph Come to Stay

The Cinematograph has come. It has moreover come to stay. The public has welcomed it broadcast. It decidedly promises to become a standard and institution of our latter-day civilisation.

Yet in its Infancy

Many say it is as yet in its infancy. They look to the 'Cinema Habit' growing until it becomes an integral part of our daily avocations. They dream that we shall enter the Cinema Theatre to watch the unfolding of the events of the hour in their habit as they take place, just as we now have to be satisfied with a cold and uninspiring account of them in the evening paper.

Its Influence

The question then arises, what is the influence of the Cinema? Is it for the general good of the community who patronise it in such vast numbers, or is it calculated to debase and degrade them. To this question those who have been in the habit of attending Cinematograph Theatres can unhesitatingly and conscientiously answer an emphatic "for the good!"

Entertainments of the Past

And no one would be foolish to assert that all the entertainments of past have been scrupulously for the good of the people. Those where riot was allowed to run and may have been swept away. The cruel sports which delighted our forefathers, such as cock-fighting, bull baiting, and the rest have been shamed out of countenance. But the public entertainments of the stage have sometimes left much to be desired and it has often been a question with the managers whether vice in an attractive form did not pay better than virtue in the fustian.

An Entertainment For All Classes

The object is to please all classes and all ages. To delight all patrons and offend none. Thus all repellent, degrading or even gruesome subjects are strictly barred by those providing the films. Subjects are most carefully selected so as to run no risk of offending the susceptibilities of the most fastidious, and their treatment kept on a high plane of elevation. And the public generally have shown their full appreciation of such treatment. They are usually satisfied when they get the best.

Its Power for Good

Hence it follows that the Cinematograph Entertainment is not only the greatest source of innocent recreation yet offered the public, but it is one of the most powerful engines for good. It is undoubtedly the most potent adversary the public house for instance, has yet to contend with. The comfort and luxury and sense of case it offers apart from its most excellent show, and all at such a modest figure, must contend successfully with the attractions of the bar-parlour.

Distinctly a Family Entertainment

One has only to note the screams of delight with which the variety of pictures are greeted to know how they are appreciated by the young folks. And this brings one to another point. The Cinema is essentially a FAMILY ENTERTAINMENT. Not only do parents feel safe in the assurance that nothing will be seen or done to contaminate the morals of the young, but the humour requires no technical or topical knowledge to understand it. It is simple and good, and being acted can't fail to appeal to all. Then the pictures are in themselves so faithful and so interesting they can appeal to the youngest as well as to the oldest minds. Its power is therefore universal. It shows life and scene as they are and anybody who can see can appreciate.

Its Teaching

And with all this the deepest sentiments of human nature are actually played upon. Stories are portrayed inculcating the noblest heroism. Incidents which teach warmest compassion for one's neighbours. Scenes depicted which stir deep notes of pathos and breathe the spirit of human charity. The grandeur of fortitude under dire distress, the triumph of virtue and right, the overthrow of sin and wrong, such are amongst the many lessons taught. No one can sit through such an exhibition and come away without feelings one's better instincts have been stirred and one has benefited by the experience. And the enthusiasm for which such stirring of the higher susceptibilities are received proves how they lay hold of the audiences and go home to their hearts, and what good precepts they must carry away with them for future guidance. By reason of their life-like truth they become indelibly fixed on the mind and training to especially, youthful intelligencies is obvious. All honour to the authors of such moral teaching pictures and to the managers who encourage them.

To Support the Cinema a Duty

It is indeed fortunate that the Cinema has fallen into such good hands. That its progenitors have chosen this, the proper course. What if it had been otherwise! But no, they determined on giving their entertainment void of a sign of offence. To maintain this attitude all films are offered to the censorship and judgement of the projectors before being played on the market and any film of questionable taste would not have the slightest chance of being exploited. In their determination not to pander to any lower instincts they are solid and impregnable. Decidedly it behoves every person with the good of the community at heart to support and encourage them in their work of retaining the high standard of taste and morals and to assist them by all the means of patronage to their exhibitions they can give to the continuance of so ennobling a policy.

Harmless and Enjoyable

Time was, when moral upholders of our race looked with some misgiving on public entertainments, and, if the truth be admitted, not without cause. Rather than endeavour to discriminate, or run the risk of encountering shocks to their moral sense, they abstained, many of them, from attending the customary theatrical entertainments altogether. To such, the Cinema would prove a boundless boon. A relaxation they can take without fear of qualms of conscience, and with a certainty of being educated and amused. And it therefore becomes the bounden duty of all such to help all they can this antidote to moral laxity or shameless frivolity.

Boon to the Working Man

But another to whom the Cinema should prove an inestimable blessing is the Working Man. The small charges for admission permit him of taking mamma, the baby, and the "kids". And a pleasant sight it is in any suburban Cinema theatre to see whole families of the industrial classes sharing the enjoyment of the evening. If anything should sweeten the delights of home life it should be this.

Origins of Entertainments and Religious Rivalry

Public amusements began with the observance of religious rights at festivals, and religion and amusement were for a long time intimately associated. Shepherds and peasants first danced and buffooned at these celebrations until Thespis added by Susarion drew some picked ones on to the platform he had devised a travelling cart, so that the use of the stage and touring commenced simultaneously. Then when the theatre proper started into being, it was customary to burn incense on the stage and for the performers to offer up prayers. This was the custom of the early Greeks. The Nautch Girls of India, the public dancers, belong to the temples still. In England entertainments commenced by copying the festivals of the Greeks and Romans, followed by Mystery and Miracle plays performed by the clergy in the churches. Even St Paul's Cathedral had its Sunday afternoon plays. The drama commenced and generated a rivalry between the Priests and the actors which caused a rupture that no 'Church and Stage Guild' or any kindred society, has been able to fully breach over to this day.

Cinema Outside this Rivalry

But the Cinema is outside this rivalry (which has proved good neither for Church or Stage, but far the reverse). It is unimpeachable, flawless and with no back history to load with prejudice. But there is one point on which it comes into contact with the clergy, beyond the fact of bidding strongly for its support, and that is the Sunday Question. Cinematograph proprietors whilst they require no member of their staffs to be on duty seven days per week consider that they should deprive the worker of seeing the pictures on what is often his only opportunity, on Sunday. And looking at the vast crowds that otherwise lounge around the streets, pack into public houses, or are ready for any mischief on Sunday evening, to take them into a well conducted Cinema Theatre where they can see improving pictures, to the music that charms the savage beast, must appear to any, but those saturated in Sabbatarian prejudice, a Christian thing to do. The Lord of the Sabbath did not hesitate to violate the strict law of the Jews in this matter, and severely rebuked his disciples when they called His attention to the fact. There is no rivalry in this instance, so it is devoutly to be wished that Church and Cinema may work hand in hand in permitting the toilers of the week a little helpful and harmless recreation on the Sabbath.

Victor W. Cook
'The Humours of 'Living
Picture' Making'
Chambers' Journal,
vol. III, 30 June 1900

"PLEASE SEND SAUSAGES AT ONCE". There was something so frankly vulgar about that telegram, lying naked and unashamed on a table littered with scientific memoranda, that it held attention and stimulated curiosity to make wild guesses at its possible import. The rest of the study contained not the least suggestion of pork-butchering, while the view from the windows comprised grassy, tree-grown slopes, vivid with the verdure of the spring. In one part of the grounds was a chalybeate well, to whose bitter waters St. Ann has lent her name and patronage.

St. Ann's Well and wild gardens have a reputation in the sister towns of Brighton and Hove as a pleasant summer resort; but very few people, even locally, are aware what strange cargoes go to and from the well and London every day, and how world-wide are the dealings of Mr. Albert Smith, its proprietor. For in this quiet retreat is carried on what is, outside the United States, probably the largest manufacture and development in the world of the crowning marvel of the closing century—the 'living picture'.

It was as the inquirer subsequently discovered, a big London firm who were so impatient for Mr. Smith to "send sausages at once". That apparently vulgar telegram referred of course, to a very popular picture, in which vigorously protesting pigs, cats, and dogs are unceremoniously bundled into a sausage-machine, while a gentleman with a beaming face turns them out as sausages as fast as they go in.

Our inquirer was on the point of asking how this feat was accomplished, when Mr. Smith asked, "would you like to see a 'Kissing' film?" Where is the man with soul so dead that he would not like to see a 'Kissing' film? One could merely endeavour not to betray too much haste in answering, "Oh-well-if it really wouldn't be troubling you".

"No trouble at all. Here you are—seventy-five yards of kissing". Mr. Smith stepped up to a shady corner of the room where there stood what at first glance looked like a hat-stand hung with a couple of wet waterproofs. Closer inspection showed it to be one mass of delicate narrow celluloid films, yard upon yard, running up and down the long folds. It looked as if there might be a mile or so of it altogether. Beside it, on a table, lay a lot of small round tin boxes. Indeed, the room seemed everywhere full of these little tins. From one of them Mr. Smith took what to the casual eye looked like a roll of black tape closely perforated each side with small holes. For yard after yard Mr. Smith unwound it, and then held a foot or so up to the light. Each inch was a tiny picture, every detail perfect in sharpness and clearness. The scene was a lady and gentleman in a railway carriage. As the roll was passed through Mr. Smith's fingers, you could see how the gentleman took off his hat by hair-breadths, and the lady turned up her face with a charming good-nature.

Hairbreadth by hairbreadth the faces drew closer, and then there were 'times' in that railway carriage! . . . Not so many months ago people were roused to astonishment by *The Astronomer's Dream*, or *The Haunted Castle*, where folks vanished into thin air, demons appeared in flame and smoke, witches danced and skeletons gibbered, and

104

"G.A.S." FILM SUBJECTS.

Arranged and Photographed by G. ALBERT SMITH, F.R.A.S.

Works, Laboratory and Studio:—SOUTHWICK, BRIGHTON.

HUMOROUS FACIAL EXPRESSIONS.

Of the best Photographic quality. One of the most successful series of humorous productions on the market.

Price 21s. per 50 feet lengths.

3500 ... LET ME DREAM AGAIN
A humorous facial expression picture with surprising climax. An elderly beau flirting with maiden at masquerade ball, wakes, and finds himself in bed bestowing unexpected caresses upon his "old missus." **Length 75 feet.**

3501 ... GRANDMA THREADING HER NEEDLE
Succeeds after many attempts, whilst the cat contentedly washes by her side. Excellent photographic quality. **Length 50 feet.**

3502 ... SCANDAL OVER THE TEA CUPS
A famous subject. Two maiden ladies at afternoon tea relate shocking secrets of society with mingled horror and pleasure depicted by their expressions. **Length 75 feet.**

3503 ... THE POLITICAL DISCUSSION
Two ardent politicians of rival views discuss with much earnestness and heat the situation as set forth in their favourite newspapers. **Length 50 feet.**

3504 ... A GAME OF NAP
The excitement and surprises of the game vividly depicted by a couple of old sports. **Length 50 feet.**

3505 ... GAME OF CARDS
Similar to preceding film, but with more incident. **Length 125 feet.**

3506 ... GOOD STORIES
Told by two jolly good fellows. Most amusing expressions. **Length 100 feet**

3507 ... THE LAST BOTTLE AT THE CLUB
Two old club cronies at a late hour are remarkably mellow and affectionate. **Length 50 feet.**

No. 3523 "Mary Jane" . . .

**Description of George Albert Smith's films,
Charles Urban Trading Company catalogue, 1903.**

generally 'black art' was rampant. There were even ghosts, of a transparent and unsubstantial texture, that performed various weird and alarming pranks. How did they come? The method is ingenious and yet simple enough. Suppose you want to make a man vanish, at the right moment you stop the handle of the camera, wait till the man has walked off, and then go on. When the pictures are thrown on the screen at the rate of sixteen a second, with no stoppage, the effect is as if the man simply ceased to exist. In the same way, if the man is to appear, you stop the machine until he is at the required spot, and then resume. If he is to fly through the roof, he jumps up, and you stop at the moment when he reaches the highest point. This simple process is the key to all sorts of fantastic jugglings. The picture alluded to in the 'sausage' telegram is one of their simplest 'fakes'. All that is required is a wire-covered trough placed behind the machine, so that the machine hides it entirely. The pigs, dogs, &c. run off along the trough, and are ready to make more sausages when required . . . Ghosts, in the raising of which Mr. Smith is a specialist, are more difficult to produce than Astronomers' Dreams or Haunted Castles. The secret of their manufacture is that two exposures are made of the same film; but Mr. Smith has introduced several cunning little devices in spirit-raising that he preserved a discreet silence about. It may be mentioned that some of his spirits were exhibited before the Queen and the Royal Family when such productions (the spirits, not the Royal Family) were quite a novelty, and the august spectators were immensely interested.

"Now, this is what I call a really beautiful ghost; though I say it who shouldn't," said Mr. Smith. "It cost me a good deal of pains to get her; but she is the prettiest spirit I have seen anywhere. Notice her perfect transparency".

He unrolled a few yards of film setting forth the story of *A Guardian Angel*, as Mr. Smith calls it in his trade lists. A gambler, after losing at cards and dismissing his friends, takes a pistol, and is on the verge of suicide, when his wife's spirit comes down the staircase. The spirit sadly takes up the cards and pleads with the gambler. The result, when the picture is thrown on the screen, is a beautiful photographic effect, for the 'spirit', though perfectly transparent, is full of detail. Upon her disappearance one of the gambler's guests returns and suggests that play shall be resumed. But the gambler's resolution is made. He seizes the cards, hurls them at the tempter, and bids him be gone.

'Fakes' that are not always so beautifully 'transparent' are those dealing with public events. People want to see the Oxford and Cambridge boat-race, the launch of a new battleship, or the latest royal visit. It is obvious, however, that an event of this kind, once recorded by Animatograph, may be made to do duty over again as many times as are desired. One Royal procession is much like another; battleships, at a distance, and naked as they slide from the contractors wharf, have little to distinguish them from one another; while, as for boat-races, Mr. Smith remarked that when the 1899 race came on, the principal English firm declined to send to Animatograph it. They had previous boat-races, and saw no use in risking the money necessary to record this one, more especially as the day was very foggy. So last year's films were requisitioned again.

A little while ago a good many people were stirred to wonder by realistic descriptions of how trains were fitted up with Animatograph developing apparatus, which enterprising persons and arranged in order to prepare pictures of the events in the far provinces of England for show at the London music-halls the same night as they occurred. Mr. Smith's visitor innocently asked if this were not smart work. Mr. Smith, with the look of one who 'winks at 'Omer down the road', answered, "Yes, it was very smart work indeed. The trains," he added smiling, "were all fitted up as announced; but the films—pictures of similar things that had occurred before— were all in London before the event took place!"

While speaking of 'fakes', it may be observed that some of the most curious and diverting effects of the Animatograph are to be obtained by putting long films through backwards. Thus a man eating an apple becomes a man biting at a piece of an apple until it grows into a whole one; the fag end of a cigarette flies up from the pavement to the mouth of the smoker, and he draws back the wreathing smoke until the cigarette has grown to its original size. The capabilities of the invention in this respect have inspired some humorous pictures. Many persons will have seen the guileless countryman at a restaurant who eats a huge pile of sandwiches; the bill is presented; it staggers him. You can imagine him protesting at the charge, and finally up goes his and to his mouth; a sandwich gradually emerges and is placed on the counter, another and another follows, until all are back again.

So with the Kinematograph one can compass that impossibility—to eat one's cake and have it. An action that perhaps looks the queerest of all when presented backwards is a high drive. There is the crowd, expectantly gazing into the water. Presently the feet of the diver merge, accompanied by a prodigious splashing. His body follows gradually, and up he goes into the air, feet foremost. At the highest point his body arches round in a graceful semi-somersault; and lo! he descends elegantly on his feet on the end of the diving-board.

"Surely things must be rather lively at times at St. Ann's well?" we inquired.

"Well, they are," Mr. Smith responded reflectively. "I'm afraid my poor gardeners have a rough time of it. Now and then they have to vary their agricultural pursuits and sacrifice themselves to make an English holiday. Sometimes every man, woman, and child in the place has to be pressed into the service to make up a 'crowd'".

So much has been said of the occasions when the Animatograph does not tell the truth, the whole truth, and nothing but the truth, that the result may have been to convey an exaggerated notion of its capacity for setting forth the thing that is not. Like many of the great inventions that have broken upon the end of this century, it is as yet comparatively undeveloped. So far we have used it as a scientific toy for the entertainment of the public; but the days are not far distant when it will play an important part of the life of the community. Already it is possible to make a genuine pictorial record of any event occurring within reasonable distance of the metropolis, and show the 'living picture' the same evening. But something more than this is in store. For one thing, the newspaper aspect of 'living pictures' making is going to develop immensely.

"I look upon the Animatograph as the illustrated newspaper of the future," said Mr. Smith. "There can be no doubt that the time will very quickly arrive when the public will expect that not only at the music-halls, but at other places, all events of public interest shall be shown to them as they occur. It will become as customary to reserve places at public functions for the Animatograph-man and his camera as it now is to set a place for the newspaper reporters".

Other developments there are in store, concerning some of which it would be as yet premature to speak. For one thing, Mr. Smith's firm has interpreted a drawing-room adaptation of the 'mutoscope', which may be loaded with any films that are desired, and passed round the table for inspection. Mr. Smith mentioned another development which of itself alone gives one some idea of what the Animatograph may do for humanity.

"One of the most distinguished surgeons in Paris," said he, "whom numbers of English doctors go to consult, has fitted up a special instrument in his operating-room, and performs the most intricate surgical operations in front of the Kinematograph. Not much has been said about it; but he has had pictures taken in this way for some couple of years. The result has been a perfectly unique collection of Kinematograph pictures of the most difficult, and what I may call the most prodigious, operations. The pictures are not, of course, such as could possibly be shown; but their success has been remarkable. Such pictures will be to surgical science, as it is easy to see, of the greatest possible value. Where one distinguished surgeon was previously able to effect a cure, or to demonstrate before a small number of students, it will in future be possible to obtain faithful record of the whole delicate operation, which record can be duplicated and shown in every clinique in Europe. The arrangements are not yet sufficiently complete to speak of; but the pictures are in the hands of my firm, and when I have printed off the positive films down here they will be supplied to qualified clinical lecturers in all parts, so that surgical science everywhere, and humanity in general, may benefit from the work of this Parisian surgeon".

T HE ACHIEVEMENTS OF MÉLIÈS AND PAUL set a very high standard of excellence
in trick pictures. Their popularity precipitated a 'trick film' fever. The market became
inundated with so-called magic pictures, of which the majority were inane or conventional. The
inevitable happened; the public appetite became satiated. Consequently, to-day, the popular
taste demands extreme novelty.

Unless the subject is original in theme, and the atmosphere of mystification is sustained, the
effort is regarded with indifference, if not with absolute contempt. On the other hand, a first-
class trick film commands the highest admiration, is regarded with as much satisfaction as were
the products of the past masters in cinematographic magic of fifteen years ago, and when once
seen is not forgotten very readily. There are certain producers who specialise in trick films with
considerable success; but their number is small . . . Of course, a film of
this character demands considerable preparation, and photographing it
occupies a long time. The picture is built up incident by incident, in the
same way that a picture play is produced, there being an interval of time
between each series of exposures to permit the arrangements for the next
episode to be made; and each phase is rehearsed over and over again
before being filmed. When the pieces of film are connected to form a
complete band, the continuity in action is so perfect that the public is
unable to detect the points where the sequence was interrupted.

A film which created a sensation when it appeared was The Automobile Accident. A workman, who has imbibed not wisely but too well, is
homeward bound, and describes grotesque geometrical patterns as he
advances along the thoroughfare. Presently he is smitten with an irresistible desire to sleep. Although the couch is hard and dangerous he lies
down in the middle of the road, and in a few seconds is in the arms of
Morpheus. While he is sleeping peacefully a taxi-cab comes along at a
smart pace, and, not observing the slumbering form of the roisterer, the
chauffeur drives over him, cutting off both his legs. The shock awakes
the man rudely, and he is surprised to find his lower limbs scattered
across the road-way. The chauffeur is horrified by the unfortunate accident; but his fare, on the contrary, a doctor, is not much perturbed. He
descends from his carriage, picks up the dismembered limbs, replaces
them in position, assists the afflicted man to his feet, and after shaking
hands each proceeds on his separate way, the workman resuming his
journey as if nothing had happened.

The requirements for this terrible calamity were very few. They consisted of three actors, to take the parts of the intoxicated workman, the
driver, and the doctor respectively; a cripple who had lost both legs
through an accident, and for the properties a taxi-cab and a couple of
artificial limbs. The legless cripple is, of course, the key to the whole sit-

"The producer giving instructions to the principal actor
and his double, the legless cripple. The dummy legs in
the foreground."

uation. The great difficulty was to find such a luckless individual, and, when he had been discovered, to bribe him to participate in a picture play. Probably the unfortunate had never before
found his misfortune so profitable to him.

In a trick-film like this, success depends essentially upon what may be described as the 'Stop
and Substitution' action.

When the legless cripple was found, the leading actor was made up in such a manner as to
be his exact counter-part. The company then proceeded to the scene of the accident, which was
in the Bois de Vincennes. The camera was set up and the producer outlined the story to the
participants.

In taking the film the operations were as follows: The leading actor, dressed like a French

Frederick Talbot
'Trick Pictures and How
They are Produced'
from *Moving Pictures:
How They are Made
and Worked.*
1912, pp. 211–15.

"The taxi-cab running over the sleeper and apparently cutting off his legs, but in reality displacing the legless cripple's property limbs."

workman, ambled down the road simulating inebriation, and presently prepared his couch in the dust. While he was lying prone and asleep, the taxi-cab drove up quickly in such a way as to run over the sleeper's legs just above the knees. Of course, this did not actually take place, the chauffeur drawing up a short distance from the prostrate form. At precisely this point the camera stopped working, and the cab slowly continued its way until its front wheels touched the prostrate man's legs at the required point. The tracks of the vehicles wheels were plainly visible on the road.

At this juncture the producer stepped forward with the legless cripple mounted on his self-propelled wheel truck, from which he was lifted. The principal actor now got up and left the scene. The cripple took his place in the road, and the artificial legs were laid against his stumps in a natural position. Care had to be taken that the cripple occupied exactly the same position as that of the actor he has displaced, so that no sign of the substitution could be observed on the film.

The cab was now backed to its former starting point and then re-started, the chauffeur making it follow the tracks made by its wheels on the former journey. As the automobile reached the point where it had stopped in the previous picture, the camera started working again, and the cab ran over the prostrate cripple, cutting off both his legs—in reality displacing the dummy limbs and tumbling them across the road.

Suddenly awakened in this rough manner, the sleeper beholds his severed limbs with dismay, and then hops after the vehicle which had been the cause of his disaster.

Left: **"The roysterer after being run over by the taxi-cab sitting up and brandishing his severed limbs."**

Right: **"The legless cripple being prepared for the act. The second artist is made up as the cripple's double."**

The cab stops, the doctor alights, picks up the severed limbs, and, while the cripple is seated on the ground, restores the displaced artificial limbs to their natural positions.

The camera now stopped working once more. The cripple was restored to his wheeled carriage and transported out of the picture, while the dummy legs were thrown on one side. In the place of the cripple the principal actor reappeared, and when the camera started again it photographed him sitting upon the ground. He is helped to his feet and resumes his journey.

In this picture we have seen two 'stop and substitution' movements, once when the principal actor was withdrawn from the scene to make way for the legless cripple, and again when the reverse was made. Owing to the neat and skilful manner in which the change from actor to the cripple, and back from the cripple to the actor, is effected, the public fails to observe either the stop or the substitution, and thinks that one man has acted the role throughout. The fact that the accident occurs on the high-road, and the possibility of a man being run over in this manner, helps the deception.

The 'stop and substitution' movement is probably practised more extensively than any other artifice in cinematography. In the picture dramas where a situation is presented such as the throwing of the villain over a cliff, or before an approaching train, or some other scene impossible to picture without sacrifice of life, the camera is stopped immediately before the incident. The actors engaged in the scene become rooted to the spot when the 'stop' call is given, signifying the fact that the camera has ceased its purring. At this juncture the villain disappears from the picture, a lay or dummy figure being substituted for him. When the camera resumes operation the episode is completed with the dummy.

Top: **"Observing the effects of the disaster, the doctor proceeds to replace the severed legs."**

Bottom: **"The limbs replaced, the patient and doctor shake hands."**

INQUEST

The Times
23 April 1907

AT CROYDON, YESTERDAY, AN INQUEST was held on the body of Wilhelm Zeitz, who was killed last week on the railway at Stoat's Nest whilst acting a part in a train-wrecking scene intended for reproduction on the bioscope.

Mr Austin, on behalf of the London, Brighton, and South Coast Railway, said he wished to state before any evidence was taken that the occurrence took place without any knowledge or sanction on the part of the railway company's chief officials. Directly it came to their knowledge all the railway men concerned in the affair were suspended.

Mr Price, on behalf of the Clarendon Film Company, said he wished to express the firm's deep regret for the accident.

Henry Lawley, a partner in the firm, said their object was to get a film picture in which a dog should play a prominent part. The idea was that the ganger on the line discovered three men placing sleepers on the railway line with the intention of wrecking a train when he was struck down and rendered unconscious across the line. His dog, seeing his master's danger, was to return to his home for assistance. Being unable to get assistance, the dog was to pull a cord of the signal and set it at danger, thereby stopping the train. To work out this scheme he went down to Mr. Bromley, the station master at Stoat's Nest, and showed him a written copy of the plot. He explained it to the station master and asked his permission to act it on a siding at Stoat's Nest. Mr. Bromley consented. On Wednesday last Mr. and Mrs. Zeitz and four other men met the witness and his partner at Stoat's Nest. The station master escorted them to the siding, and the first scenes of the pictures were taken. Mr. Bromley then left them. As the train started out of the station into the siding for one of the later scenes Zeitz lay down on the line just beyond the sleepers. The witness had arranged with Mr. Bromley that the train should draw up 20 yards before it got to the sleepers. Instead of stopping as arranged the train passed the mark and the guard iron caught the first sleeper, which struck the second sleeper, this in turn striking Zeitz. Zeitz threw himself on his back in the four-foot way. A sleeper caught his chest and dragged him along about 20ft., his head bumping the other sleeper. The usual driver was driving the train. The witness said that they thought it was possible to stop an engine within 6in. of any spot they wished. They never anticipated the least possibility of danger. There was no mention of remuneration, either directly or indirectly, of the officials.

Perceval Stow, partner of the last witness, agreed with the evidence, and said he rode on the engine, and he told the driver he could enter the picture fairly quickly. The train pulled up very suddenly, and one of the men came up and shouted, "You have run over the man", and the engine was then reversed. In reply to Mr. Tytte (for the driver), the witness denied that the driver said afterwards, "You have blinded and deceived me". The driver made two different statements; on one occasion he said he did not know there was a man on the line, and on another occasion he said he thought that the witness had gone with him to tell him where to stop. That was not a fact. In answer to Mr. Austin, the witness said it was true that he told the driver that the faster he came into the picture the better.

John Samuel Bromley, station master at Stoat's Nest, said he gave permission for the picture to be taken. He was not promised any payment. It was not explained to him that the man was to be left on the line. No sane man would have taken an engine down, and no station master would have allowed him to do so if he had known the man was lying on the line.

William Podmore, the driver of the engine, said he was told by the station master that he was to run his train down the siding because Stow was to take a snapshot. He turned to Stow and asked him what he wanted, and the station master then pointed down the siding and told him he was to run down it and stop dead. He did not see the sleepers on the line. Stow told him he wanted him to go up as far as he could so that he could make a good picture. Both the witness and his mate were to keep out of sight as they did not want them to appear in the picture. They were to stop at the camera.

The Coroner: After running over a man?—I did not know the man was there, or any obstacle whatever.

The fireman of the train gave evidence, agreeing with the driver that he was told to pull up at the camera. He did not know there was to be a man on the line.

The jury returned a verdict of accidental death.

'Blair', the star of the Hepworth film
Rescued by Rover, 1905

SUICIDE CINEMATOGRAPHED

Parachutist who Resolved to Die Sensationally

FURTHER DETAILS OF THE BERLIN parachutist's fall form the column of victory are given by the *Daily News and Leader* correspondent.

Erich Bittner, aged 19, it appears tested his invention with a life-size doll, and secured the permission of the police to try the descent, but not from the Siegesaale, over which the police have no authority. Armed with the police permit Erich thought out the best means of advertising his invention. He composed a cinematograph drama, which began with a love affair. The hero was to attempt a descent in a parachute, which was to fail at the critical moment, hurling the hero to death at the base of the column of Victory. Thereupon the hero's fiancee was to commit suicide.

He explained the plot to a friend owning a cinema camera and also to a well known film firm, inviting the latter to send an operator to take a picture. He imagined that he would receive world-wide advertisement for his parachute.

Precisely what happened on the Siegesaale is uncertain. An eye-witness says that Erich had the clumsy apparatus tied on his back across his shoulders. It was fastened together with string in order to lie flat under his cape, so as to escape the notice of the custodian of the column. At the moment of leaping from the parapet Erich did not even unfasten the string.

This account is contradicted by another, which says that he laid the apparatus on the coping of the parapet and grasped it with both hands, raising it over his head. Erich explained to the cinematographist the apparatus would only open after dropping some 40 feet. The fall would then be checked suddenly for an instant and then the parachute would glide gently to the ground. The cinematograph picture was only to reproduce the first part of the drop, but the operators actually recorded the whole terrible disaster.

On Monday night it was asserted that Erich knew he was going to hurl himself to his death. It was his third attempt at suicide, and like other suicides before him, he had determined that it should be as impressive as possible, and, moreover, should be perpetuated on a cinematograph film at the centre of the drama which would bear his name as the author, principal actor, hero, and victim. If this strange but not impossible psychological desire is true Erich has achieved his desire.

PLOTS FOR PICTURE PLAYS

Concocting Thrilling Dramas and Farcical Fakes for the Cinematograph

WHO HAS NOT ASKED THE QUESTION after a visit to a 'picture palace': "I wonder where and how they get their ideas?" says a writer in 'Answers'. On the screen you have seen the intensely dramatic, lugubriously pathetic, and the uproariously farcical stories told clearly and lucidly.

In the columns of a weekly paper devoted solely to the interests of the theatrical profession, I saw, some months ago, and insignificant three-line advertisement, asking for plots for cinematographs. I knew absolutely nothing about the technicalities of picture-making, but his ignorance did not prevent my submitting a scenario of what I believed would make a picture play. It came back, and with it a letter containing valuable suggestions and hints of things to do, and things not to do, in picture-plot writing, and concluded with a kindly word of encouragement to try again.

I visited many picture shows—not for amusement, but to 'study' the films and, with no more literary ability than the ordinary man, I have succeeded in 'placing' several of my plots, and hope to continue doing so.

The story of a picture, humorous or dramatic must be very clear and easily followed. A simple line of progressive action, through a series of scenes must be maintained until the climax is reached, each scene having a delicate connection with the story.

Do not introduce too many important characters, and—this most important—try to arrange your scenes 'real exteriors'—as gardens, streets. lanes, sea-beach, &c. When it is necessary to introduce an 'interior' have it as simple as possible. Film manufacturers keep a stock company of experienced actors and actresses, but it must be remembered these people, clever as they may be, are limited entirely to 'dumb show' and pure pantomime to tell their story.

Work your plot out in numbered scenes, each one having a definite incident. The probability of acceptance is greater with light comedy stories, with just a touch of pathos, in a picturesque setting.

There seems little chance with plots of the extravagantly farcical 'chase' type. The idea of one man, for some ridiculous reason, running after another, and picking up at every turn all sorts and conditions of humanity—with a few stray dogs thrown in—until there is an assorted army of a hundred or two strong 'on the warpath' is not a brilliant idea, nor is it in demand.

Although nothing seems impossible in the picture business, the beginners at plot-writing, will be wise to avoid 'trick' stories. The notion of an aviator beginning his adventures by falling out of his airship down the chimney of an Anarchists' lodging-house has innumerable possibilities for exciting elaboration: but to handle successfully the style of story requires a thorough technical knowledge of film making, and is too wildly extravagant for the beginner.

If the amateur plot writer will study those films—and this kind of study has its attractive side—which by their simple story makes a direct and successful appeal to an audience, and bear in mind the humble suggestions give here, there seems no reason, if possessed of the average share of imagination, why he should not succeed at writing plots for cinematographs. And it will be as well to remind him that 'picture shows' are very popular with the children.

The pay is good, the work pleasant, and, so far as my experience goes, the firms with which one has to deal are singularly courteous and encouraging to the would-be schemer of moving picture plots.

"*Our Village Cinema.* Showman: ''Ere, I say, it be 'orses' 'ooves, not 'orns or 'ail-storms.'"
Punch, 19 February 1913.

MR. WELLS AND THE CINEMATOGRAPH

The Times
10 January 1914

THE CONTRACT WHICH MR. H. G. WELLS has entered into with the Gaumont Company for the right of presenting his works on the cinematograph is of a very comprehensive nature. It applies to all Mr. Wells's library work of the past and to any matter he may write in the future, and it is also hoped that Mr. Wells will construct stories especially for cinematograph productions. It has not yet been decided which books will be first employed, though it is obvious that many of them are admirably suited for the purpose, and the Gaumont Company's experts are now endeavouring to make a selection. It is not likely that any of the films thus obtained will be shown in public until next summer or autumn at the earliest, as the company have a great amount of work on hand at present.

Although such a contract as has been made with Mr. Wells is not new—a well known writer of melodramatic stories recently bought himself out of a similar contract entered into some years ago—it is interesting as showing that a successful author can hope nowadays for an additional source of revenue beyond literary and dramatic rights. It is generally admitted among film manufacturers that, while a good plot is essential, its value is generally enhanced if there is associated with the production the name of a famous author. The fact is recognised in most of the contracts which are now made. An Actor, whose name is a house-hold name when he agrees to appear in one of Shakespeare's plays for the cinematograph, further undertakes that he will take part in no other Shakespearean film for a rival company for a given period of time, as it is felt that his appearance in a second film, even though the story is totally different, would militate considerably against the success of the first. It is apparently the actor, therefore, more than the story that the picture palace audience goes to see.

THE CINEMA AND THE DRAMA

The Times
29 April 1913

AS PART OF THE JOINT CELEBRATION of the Shakespeare Commemoration for the Shakespeare Reading Society and the London Shakespeare League, Dr. William Martin lectured last night in King's College on 'The Camera in its relation to the Drama'. Sir Sidney Lee presided.

Dr. Martin said that the cinema, while possessing plasticity, was less suitable than the stage for the expression of lyrical emotion. Whatever fears might exist regarding cinematography's becoming a serious competitor of the playhouse, there was little doubt that, in the main, it was complementary, having a sphere of its own. He suggested that the interpolation of dialogue between the scenes on the screen deserved serious attention, and held that the cinemas were peculiarly fitted for dealing with things which were not yet capable of expression on the ordinary stage. It would take them right into the realm of imagination, and satisfactorily exhibit the eerie fancies to which the human mind was so prone. The cinema could never be approached by the theatre in the exposition of the natural surroundings of forest, desert, or country life, where the rural background was objectionable. He mentioned that in London alone there was nearly 400 picture palaces, while in the United Kingdom the number approached 6,000, the invested capital being two and half million.

Sir Sidney Lee said all that had watched this enormous growth, this eruption of course, of picture palaces, that now covered the earth—he would not say encumbered it (laughter)—and so far as his observation went they had certainly added to the gaiety of nations. Whether they had done more was a matter of opinion, but certainly their omnipresence justified consideration of the theme dealt with by Dr. Martin.

Above and below:
Georges Méliès's studio at Montreuil-sous-Bois, France, c. 1902.
National Museum of Photography, Film & Television.

THOSE WHO FEAR THAT THE KINEMATOGRAPH is, or ever can be, a serious rival to the interests of the drama, or those engaged in the animated picture industry who imagine that the future of drama will possibly be in their eventual keeping, are rather wide of the mark. The drama can never be affected by the popularity or otherwise of the kinematograph for the simple reason that it has not more to do, as a counter attraction, with the living and spoken drama than has a glove fight at the National Sporting Club, or a Cup Tie football match at the draughty, overgrown greenhouse known as the Crystal Palace. It seems rather late in the day to have to repeat the evident truth that the drama can have no enemy but the one that comes from within, and that so long as it is true to itself, and produces the right kind of play, all the picture palaces of the world can have no effect upon box-office receipts. The 'superior' lover of the drama who dislikes the kinematograph is deluded in this matter, as indeed he is in most other matters, and probably takes his cue from the present popularity of what is known as the picture play. He deplores the fact that thousands of persons go to see What Happened to Mary at the local picture palaces who do not care a brass button about What Happened to Jones at the local Theatre Royal, and quite ignores the obvious explanation that one section of the populace is going to see a kinematograph display and the other a spoken drama acted by actually-present persons. The two publics are at present wide apart, and the average picture lover can be no more tempted to sit out at a play than can the inveterate theatre-goer be persuaded to descend to what is to him the ghastly frivolity of 'seeing the pictures'. The 'superior' lover of the drama also grounds his fears upon something even more simple and obvious—something, moreover, which those interested in the picture industry will do well to lay to heart—and that is, that the imitation article, however apparently real, will never out-rival the appeal of the real article. A living person, inspired by human thoughts and passions, is always infinitely more attractive than your mere automaton, or moving photograph; and nothing on earth can ever dethrone the value and beauty of the spoken and acted word. This also seems rather a superfluous thing to say, but is necessary for more than one reason. As has already been explained in this article, the kinematograph is as yet in the early days of its development, and is feeling for ground, as it were, upon which to erect the lasting foundation of its future existence. This is proved, if proof were needed, by the extraordinary diversity of the subjects it exercises its ingenuity upon, and the peculiar, if somewhat rough-shod, facility with which it exploits and assimilates them. Its present appetite would seem to be just as rapacious as that of a growing child, and just as liable to be injudicious. What more natural, therefore, than that, like a greedy boy, it should sometimes turn its eye away from that sustenance best suited to its constitution, and cast a sheep's eye at the biggest and oldest fellow's plate? It would be idle for even the most devoted worshipper of my Lady Kinema to enter upon a whole-hearted defence of the picture play in its present phase. Some are good, some merely indifferent, but a vast number, it must be confessed, are hopelessly crude and sensational. Moreover, many of them have a most deplorable lack of continuity, which is emphasised rather than dissipated by a form of interruption that can only be described as an aggressive resurrection of the old-fashioned theatrical aside or Greek chorus—that of the explanatory word thrown on the screen to serve as a sort of connecting link between scene and scene. If for that little circumstance alone, pregnant as it is with something of the pathos of a dumb man trying to make himself understood, it should be obvious that the kinematograph can never replace the spoken drama. That several leading actors have recently succumbed to the golden persuasions of picture-producing firms can discomfort only those theatrical whole-hoggers who possess not the seeing eye, or what the Americans call horse sense. Nor will the device of exploiting a theatrical 'star' benefit the film producer in the long run, because it is quite certain that the entertainment-seeker is not going to look for a famous player upon the screen if he can see him in the flesh round the corner. In the same connection, also, the entertainment-seeker may be disinclined to go back to the picture palace when once he has tasted the play it induced him to see, for once a playgoer always a playgoer is one of those axioms which admit no argument. The film exploiter, therefore, is going against

Arthur Coles Armstrong: 'My Lady Kinema: The Eleventh Muse' *The Stage Year Book,* ed. L. Carson (London: Carson & Comerford) 1914

his own ultimate interests by encroaching, or endeavouring to encroach, upon the Tom Tiddler's ground of the drama, and by creating a public, which, it is reasonable to suppose, will eventually leave him for the theatre. Owing to the comparatively modest capital he requires for his enterprise, he can penetrate into districts where the average theatrical manager would fear to tread, even with a fit-up. He is, therefore, moulding the tastes and desire of an entirely new public; is it to his ultimate interest that he turn their thoughts towards the drama by giving them snippets of popular plays, or featuring famous players? Is he not, by so doing, acting simply as a sort of an advance agent for the theatrical manager? When the picture man has extricated himself from the uncertain desires of adolescence, none will recognise this truth more readily than he; for the kinematograph, like the drama, like variety, can only hope to succeed by assiduously ploughing its own particular furrow. It legitimate sphere in anything approaching drama must lie solely in the pictorial representation of those stories, novels, themes and broadly comic effects which are too large for the restricted and concentrated canvas of the dramatic stage. In other words, the kinematograph must stick to its task of realising the pictorial worth of a herd of cattle, for instance, and leave the concentrated beef essence suggested by such herbivorous quadrupeds to the skill of the theatrical dramatist. At its best the kinematograph cannot give the soul of a play; and to see, as one has recently seen, prominent actors mouthing the words of Shakespeare, is anything but a pleasing experience. Surely the real value to humanity of such productions, excellently produced as most of them have been, is in a theatre for the chronically deaf, or in a storehouse of future records in the British Museum! And, speaking of the British Museum, what would the present generation of drama-lovers give to be able to spend an afternoon in Great Russell Street in the filmic presence of the great historians of the past? To see Garrick, Siddons, the two Keans, Kemble, Macready, Phelps, Irving—all the giants of the sock and buskin in their full habit as they fretted their brief hour upon the stage, and then were seen no more! Could anything make that old thief Time look more stupid than that! Such an experience is reserved only for our more fortunate descendants. For the present, my Lady Kinema will surely not take it amiss if some of us make the most of the contemporary player while he is yet with us in the flesh, and refrain from paying him the questionable compliment of anticipating his demise by looking for him only on the screen.

The World's Fair
9 January 1909

ADVANCE OF THE CINEMATOGRAPH

Its Place in the Entertainment World

IN THE WORLD OF ENTERTAINMENT the cinematograph has already conquered for itself a prominent position. Although in a rude and elementary form it may be traced back some fifty years, its practical development is limited to the past decade. It would appear also that it had reached little more than the starting-point of its career. Only the other day, for instance, we referred to the demonstration made by Mr. G. Albert Smith before the Royal Society of Arts, when the gentleman set forth the results of his researches and experiments in the production of animated photographs in natural colours.

For the moment, however, we are more concerned with the question that an industry is fast growing up amongst us which is destined to appeal markedly to pleasure-seekers. And it is largely to their histrionic sense that that appeal will be made. Miniature theatres are being constructed where plays are to be given in action, while with the view of considering these are realistically effective as possible, the co-operation of some of the leading actors and actresses has been secured. In this country, at any rate, the enterprise is still in its infancy, but its boundaries are daily being extended. Further, as complete success has so far attended the efforts of the promoters—as the results from a financial standpoint are eminently satisfactory—it may be taken for granted that the ball thus set rolling will quickly assume larger and still larger proportions.

Electric Theatres

How far is the movement destined to affect the regular theatres? That, of course, is a problem which only time can solve. It may be contended on the one side that it will merely serve to increase the taste for the theatres, that it will only prove a stepping stone to a better appreciation of the drama itself. On the other hand it may be argued that these cinematograph performances are all sufficient, that they are much more likely to wean the public away from, than to send it to, the theatre proper. Whatever the final outcome of the situation may be it is indubitable of the newcomers—electric theatres or palaces as they are called—in the field of amusement are doing very well. Without taking into account those minor places of entertainment where only one penny is charged with admission. London at present boasts some half a dozen, of which, however, the greater number are situated in the suburbs. There is one, for example, at Shepherd's Bush, another in Camden Town, a third at Walworth, a fourth at Peckham, and a fifth at Hammersmith. There are also the Egyptian Hall, in Piccadilly, controlled by Pathe Freres, a second theatre just started on the Strand, and another among the latest opened and the largest in Oxford Street, close to the Marble Arch. Consider the conditions under which these places of entertainments are run. To begin with they owe allegiance to nobody, provided, of course, that their owners have satisfied the requirements of the London County Council surveyor. The initial and chief drawback is the difficulty of finding a site at a reasonable rent. The difficulty obviously increases the nearer one draws to the heart of London. The Electric Palace in Oxford Street to come to a concrete example, possesses a length of 150ft., a height of 14ft., and a width of 30ft., while the provisions in regard to exits and other means for ensuring the safety of the public are of the most thorough-going description. Manifestly such a building is not easily to be met with on easy terms within Central London.

The Entertainment

What does the public get for its money? In the place just referred to the charge for seats is 1s., 6d., and 3d. The building is open from two in the afternoon until 10 p.m. and if anyone desires a surfeit of animated pictures he can remain in his seat all the time. As one entire series takes just upon fifty minutes for exhibition, he would have, however, to witness the same performance some half a dozen items in succession. Thus the audience, like the riders in a omnibus, is constantly changing, a fact upon which, the proprietors, of course, rely upon. The entertainment comprises humorous sketches—pictorial presentments of journeys by land and water, athletic competitions, and so on; in short, as everyone knows, it forms an illustrated record of current events. Above all, and this brings us to the kernel of the matter so far as it touches the interests of the theatre, it includes brief compressed dramas, played by actors of the first rank, in which a story is set forth clearly, impressively, and succinctly by means of action, not dialogue. It may be added that the latter, however is not to be entirely neglected, for by the employment of a synchronised gramophone, pantomime is at places reinforced by speech. In point of fact the performance promises at no very remote date to possess most of the features of a theatrical entertainment, or at least a series of vivid dramatic sketches.

Growth of the Cinematograph

It may not be uninteresting briefly to trace here the growth of the industry. Chatting the other day with Mr. Ivatt, London Manager of Pathé Frères, certain instructive particulars were furnished by him. Nine years has sufficed to bring the business to its present position. The number of people employed in their manufactories at Vincennes and Joieville-le-Pont is close upon 3,000. The actual output of films, which they claim to be the largest in the world, reaches the astonishing aggregate of eighty miles per day! In practically every large town in Europe and America they have their own agent or representative. In the United States they have established a factory where films are turned out at the rate of 100,000 feet per day.

"Can you give me any idea", I asked of how many films, dealing with the same subject, you will sell?!"

The Sphere,
2 August 1913.

THE RISE of the FILM.

Professor Sir Hubert von Herkomer's Cinematographic Endeavours at Bushey

As an Old Woodcarver

Professor Sir Hubert von Herkomer acts the part of the old woodcarver himself in a mediæval drama

It is certainly a sign of wonderful progress in the past and of promise for the future when an artist of Professor Sir Hubert von Herkomer's standing takes such an interest in cinematography as his theatre at Bushey shows. Sir Hubert has been thinking of the wonderful possibilities of the cinematograph for the last year or so, and about six months ago decided to start the actual making of films himself. He has fitted up a glass theatre large enough to take two scenes at once, and has also built elaborate houses and scenes of the fourteenth century for two of his most important scenarios. The professor's own work now is as a kind of super-manager; he edits and criticises the films generally, and in the evenings discusses with his son, Mr. Siegfried Herkomer, who is his manager, the dramatic possibilities of the scenarios and the general arrangement of the scenes. The professor sometimes has a

As a Witch

Professor Sir Hubert von Herkomer acts the name-part in a film entitled "The White Witch"

rehearsal before breakfast, then works on the portraits of a couple of sitters, again rehearses in the evening, and after dinner there may be a projection of the morning's work on the screen.

The staff are at present engaged on some very varied scenarios. Sir Hubert is very enthusiastic about the splendid settings and backgrounds he is able to find at Bushey; already his famous house has been used with great effect. The professor himself acts the principal parts in *The Old Woodcarver* and *The White Witch*, his "make-up" being most effective in the two plays. The stories are really charming ones and allow Sir Hubert full play for his dramatic abilities. Mr. Siegfried Herkomer and his assistant, Mr. Cielery, look after the practical side of the stage-managing and the general film business. Some of the Bushey films, it is hoped, may be seen in the early autumn.

Professor Sir Hubert von Herkomer and his son (on right holding film) examining results of the morning's work

Taking a Film of "The Old Woodcarver" in Professor Sir Hubert von Herkomer's New Cinema Theatre at Bushey

These illustrations have been specially drawn for "The Sphere" by Clement Flower

"That, of course", Mr. Ivatt answered, "depends entirely upon the importance and popularity of the subject. Take, for instance, the recent Marathon Race. We disposed of 1,800 copies, each 600 feet in length. But obviously, this was quite an exceptional case.

Miniature Dramas

"What we are aiming at now is to increase and to satisfy the demand for miniature dramas, such as those now being exhibited at the Alhambra, under the title of *La Moulin Rouge*, *L'Arlesienne*, and *La Mort du Due de Guise*. With this view, we have already built four theatres, and are now constructing two more at, respectively, Versailles and Montrouille. There the plays which we have chosen for treatment are duly rehearsed by a company of artists selected from various Paris companies. This is not all, however. The advance in the taste of the public, as in the means of pleasing it, has been enormous since the early days of the biograph, when audiences were content with a number of comic scenes imperfectly mounted. What they want now is something more absolute in its realism, and of a more refined character. To meet this desire we carry the members of our companies to the actual scene described by the author, and there, on the very spot of its occurrence, the story is rehearsed in every detail. In fact, we go one better than the author himself, for even by the most graphic descriptions he can never arrive, either in his book or on the stage, at the perfection or verisimilitude which, naturally, the cinematograph is able to attain to. Difficulties there are, of course. Occasionally we find the authorities opposed to us. But we don't in the least mind setting the law at defiance in order to obtain results. Again and again we have had to pay fines for our hardihood: but by the moment the police appear upon the scene we have secured the desired film, and we are quite willing to go on paying fines to the end of time on the conditions."

"Written in Water"

"It has been often said that the art of the actor is written in water. By the combined help of the cinematograph and the gramophone that reproach no longer holds good. A hundred years hence it will possible for the public to study the methods and to listen to the tones of the leading artists of the day. We ourselves have secured the monopoly of the services of practically every important actor and actress in Paris. Let me mention, to cite only a few among many, the names of Le Bargy, Sarah Bernhardt, Coquelin, Albert Lambert, Rejane and Jeanno Granier. What we are doing in France we are also doing in Germany, and hope before long to accomplish in England. You can obtain at the Alhambra every evening a fair impressions of our aims. At this moment we have Sardou's *La Tosca* in hand, and in two or three weeks time we shall be able to provide a indelible record of Sarah Bernhardt in her famous part of the heroine of that play. Works by Victor Hugo and Zola are also shortly to be dealt with, and here again we shall show the actual scenes. The most celebrated French artistes and authors have, without exception, signalled their readiness to fall in with our wishes, and we ourselves have created a Societe d'Auteurs et de Gens de Lettres whose members are pledged to supply the material we require. There is not a French writer of any importance who stands outside the circle. Their business is to supply us with a piece, as it is the business of the artists to act it. The arrangement is that all rights in the negatives are vested in ourselves, while we pay the society a royalty for every metre sold. Striking broadly, we calculate that a film of 200 metres will bring the author from 2,000 to 3,000 francs in fees, and naturally, should the subject be more of ordinary interest, the amount is materially increased.

English Artists Co-operate

"As I have hinted," continued Mr. Ivatt, "we have every hope and intention to bring English artists within the charmed circle. That, however, is not so easy a matter as in France, where the spirit of combination is much stronger than here. Still, I confidently trust that before very long we shall be able to secure records of say, Sir Charles Wyndham as David Garrick, of Sir John Hare in *A Pair of Spectacles* or in *A Quiet Robber* of Beerbohm Tree in one of his most striking characters. Shakespeare and Dickens we can always have for the asking; what we cannot get in the same terms is the artist in his portrayal of Caliban or of a Fagin. What, indeed, would we of today give to be able to look upon Edward Kean, Mrs. Siddons, or Garrick in one of those which have served to make their name illustrious for all time? Remember, too, that a film is cosmopolitan, that it recognises no barrier, that it can overleap all obstacles. And if, as Hamlet declared, the Players are the abstracts and brief chronicles of the time, could anything be more interesting or more edifying than that the methods, the manners, and the fashions peculiar to each successive generation should be enduringly placed on record for the benefit and the instruction of those who follow in their footsteps."

❋

The World's Fair
14 December 1912

CHILDREN WHO CAN "READ" MOVING PICTURES

Film Secrets Revealed by Lip-Readers

The most critical patrons of a cinematograph show in all London on Thursday were a lady in a long grey fur cloak and two school children, a boy and a girl, both aged fourteen. For this party of three, the films were not only moving pictures, but talking pictures, and every one of the trio—unlike the rest of the audience—understood exactly what the actors were saying.

The lady in the grey cloak was Mrs. G. Sibley Haycock of Fitzroy Square Training College for teachers in the oral instruction of the deaf and dumb, and the two children were pupils at the school attached to the college.

All three, although deaf, are expert lip-readers. They visited various picture-palaces in the neighbourhood of Oxford Street at the invitation of the Express for the twofold object of proving or disproving the statement that three deaf persons who can lip-read are able to understand anything that film-actors might be saying; and discovering whether film-actors suit their words to their actions.

The statement as to lip-reading was proved in the affirmative up to the hilt despite the difficulties of flickering film, bad enunciations, or averted faces, under which the lip-readers laboured.

The first secret of the film surprised by Mrs. Haycock and the two children, Raymond and Florrie, was in connection with a film entitled A French Spy. French soldiers, Arabs, and Turks, costumed with marvellous realism, appear to figure exclusively in this film, the scene of which is laid in Egypt.

The French soldier, who is the hero of this film, had scarcely been confined in his cell at the fortress before Mrs. Haycock said, "Why, he's talking English! He exclaimed just now, "It is a woman's voice!" as plainly as speech could say it".

It was Florrie who called attention to the next discrepancy, pointing out on her writing-pad that the picturesque swarthy turbaned sheikh had just answered to the French spy, "You will be killed and this woman will be mine". This was confirmed by Raymond who, writing also in the dark, put down the same words.

The experiment showed that in many, if not most cases, the actor's speech actually is relevant to the film, the dialogue fitting the gesture and action perfectly.

PICTURE THEATRES

1,000 Cinematograph Shows

The World's Fair
30 October 1909

Effect on the Drama

SEVERAL EXPLANATIONS have been given of the bad theatrical business in the provinces, reports of which daily reach the managers most concerned in sending out companies. The experience of London managers this autumn is the opposite of that of those interested in the provinces. In London, the playhouses are flourishing; in the provincial cities and towns and in the London suburbs complaints are general, says the London *Daily Mail*.

Mr. George Dance, who has as much experience of the business side of the theatre as anyone in England, is inclined to think that the comparative effect of cinematograph shows and skating rinks has been exaggerated. In his opinion the theatre has been injured by the policy of managers, who are rarely prepared to allow fair terms for the sending out on the road of well-cast and well-equipped companies. So-called attractions are constantly "billed" at provincial theatres which will not draw the people who pay for the higher-priced seats, and have no chance of competing against the music-hall for the classes that patronise cheaper seats. "The theatre is being starved" he says, and there seems some ground for his opinion, for reports from the provinces are to the effect that nearly all the companies that went out this autumn with London actor-managers at their head have played to much smaller receipts than a few years ago.

Music-hall opposition is a recognised fact in the country, but many managers now see a serious competitor in the cinematograph show. It is calculated that about 1,000 of these places are open in the United Kingdom, at prices of admission varying from a penny to a shilling. They give living-pictures displays of events more or less topical, a representation of a play, and always some comic incident that has been "staged" by one of the film-supply companies. The character of these "picture theatres" ranges from the display in a black-lined tent to the "theatre" in Piccadilly where there is music and tea.

Profit of £100 a Week

One or two in London are reputed to be making a profit of £100 a week, and although many of the provinces are playing to receipts that leave as good a margin for their proprietors as a prosperous music-hall. The business is attracting the capitalist. One company expects to open forty provincial cinematograph houses before Christmas and to extend the number up to 150 before the end of next year. Each of these houses will cost from two to three thousand pounds, and will have tea rooms.

One inventor of cinematograph machines and appliances, Mr. Charles Urban, has produced a new screen which is rid of the present necessity to have the display in a dark house. With his screen, a large mirror with a chemically-etched surface, the pictures appear as well as in a lighted room, and the danger of panic in the dark is obviated. Mr. Urban has enormous faith in the future of the cinematograph. He thinks every school should have an outfit for educational purposes, and cites the Naval School at Whale Island, where a cinematograph is used as an aid to gunnery instruction.

The machine that photographs objects for the cinematograph takes 1,920 pictures a minute, and sixty feet of pictures are generally passed on the screen in the same space of time. The picture films vary in length according to the subject, but one prize fight took 2,700 feet of film to record, and a film designed to illustrate the romance of the railway measured 3,500 feet.

A cinematograph machine costs from £35 to £50, and films are sold at 4d. a foot. A man may set up business in a white-washed hall, hiring some chairs, two operators, a man to sell tickets and lecture during the show, a "shouter" to stand at the doors, and a girl to sell programmes. It is estimated that 20,000 people are employed in the cinematograph business in these islands.

Mrs. Henry Mansergh
'An Idyll of the
Cinematographe'
Windsor Magazine
February 1898

THERE ARE SOME PEOPLE who require a course of education before an idea penetrates to their brain; there are others who clutch greedily at a discovery while it is yet in the air, and are instant to realise the service which it may render to themselves.

Mark Robson belonged to the latter class. He was a private detective, moderately successful in business, yet cherishing a grudge against fate, insomuch as he found himself at a constant disadvantage as compared with his brothers of the magazines. Lords and Ladies consulted him in his office, but showed no disposition to take him to their social bosoms; there was no intelligent young gentleman ready to share his midnight journeys and play the part of his assistant, free of charge; while, so far from being pressed to relate his experiences, his friends yawned and showed unmistakable signs of boredom when he threatened a recital. But, as has been said, Mark Robson was a sharp fellow, and his day was coming. He studied the newspapers assiduously, digesting the news of the nations with an undercurrent of questioning as to how he could make any particular event serve his own ends, which, as every sensible person knows, is the only spirit by which a business man can hope to make his way in the world. And suddenly he had a brilliant inspiration. The cinematographe was the novelty of the hour; all the world flocking to see it; Mark Robson flocked with the rest; and it was while watching the entrance of the Czar and Czarina into Paris that he suddenly clapped his hands together, to the amazement of the beholders, took up his hat and rushed hurriedly from the building.

Two days later a large-typed announcement was added to Mark Robson's advertisements in the London dailies: Cinematographe slides of private individuals taken without their knowledge, and forwarded secretly to any quarter of the globe.

❦

After fifteen years of hard labour beneath an Indian sun, John Webb found himself in the position to fulfil his engagement to Daisy May. Fifteen years before he had said "goodbye" to Daisy in the drawing-room of the old house in Liverpool and again in the cab—because she ran down to the gate at the last moment and refused to be left behind—and again on the landing-stage and again -oh, the knell like sound of that bell!—when the very last moment had come, and the tender was about to return to the shore. He had leant over the side of vessel gazing at Daisy as the tender bobbed up and down, and Daisy had held out her arms to him with a gesture of longing so child-like and winsome that he had groaned aloud and hidden his head in his hands. Fifteen years ago! And he had written to Daisy once a week ever since: "My own precious darling!" "Darling Daisy!" "Dearest Daisy!" "My dear girl!" . . . Ah me! if we could only eat our cake while the appetite is keen. Fifteen years is a long time, and a continued course of curry has a hardening effect on the masculine animal.

John had written home asking Daisy to come out to be married in the following autumn, and though this was the object for which he had been working for so many years, it is certain that his difficulty in composing the letter was caused less by excess of rapture than by the problem of making the request sufficiently warm to please Daisy, and at the same time honest enough satisfy his own conscience. After the letter was finished he took up the latest photograph which he had received from his fiancee and studied it with critical eyes. Daisy had been a pretty girl and the face which looked at him now seemed almost as young as the one he had kissed in farewell.

"But its all nonsense" grumbled John to himself. "I know these present-day photographs. She will be forty in a couple of years, and it stands to reason that she can't look like this. Why does she always send vignettes? Can it be that she is growing—fat? She was always a trifle inclined that way; and it there is one thing more than another that I do bar—Fat, fair and forty! O Lord!" He threw the photograph on the table, and picked up the newspaper with an expression of anything but appropriate for a bride-groom elect, and the first thing on which his eye lighted was the advertisement of Mark Robson with that insidious large-typed edition!

When the boy came in an hour later to collect the sahib's mail he carried away two letters addressed to London, one of which bore the name of Miss Daisy May and the other that of Mr. Mark Robson, the detective. To such depths of iniquity will men descend when temptation is pressing and the chance of discovery remote!

Some months later a carefully-packed box was delivered to Mr. Webb's residence in Calcutta, and a local photographer was summoned who busied himself in preparing a magic-lantern exhibition of such enthralling interest to the master of the house that he denied himself to all visitors, and was fairly apoplectic with excitement before the critical moment arrived.

Whir-r! A curious rattling noise came to his ear, and there upon the sheet was the picture of the old-fashioned English room where he had wooed his love. The chintz-covered chairs and the maidenhair ferns under the glass domes were all there complete, not a detail was changed, from the beadwork bannerette pendant from the mantelpiece to the case of stuffed birds on the chiffonnier. How was it possible for furniture to stand still while the world moved so fast? Webb felt he has lived through a dozen incarnations since he had looked his last upon this old-world scene. And Daisy—poor little loyal Daisy, with her petals already beginning to wither and lose their dainty flush! In what a narrow garden she had passed her youth! It was a touching thought, and John's heart swelled with a throb of the old devotion to the love of his youth. What if she had lost some of the early bloom? Could such a trifle as that weigh against the faithful devotion of a lifetime? The lines of a sweet old ballad came into his head, and he hummed them in tender tones:

> Though would'st still be mine own, as this moment thou art,
> Let thy loveliness fade as it will;
> And around the dear ruins each wish of my heart . . .

The whirring sound continued, and curious spots and blemishes appeared upon the sheet. It was by no means a perfect exhibition, but accurate enough for the purpose for which it was required. And presently the door opened and a stout lady came into the room. She wore a dark dress, which fitted closely to her exuberant figure, and her hair was coiled tightly round her head. There was no nonsense about this good lady, no dallying in dressing-gowns, no waste of time with ironing-tongs or crimping irons; from which the bunch of keys which hung at her side to the pile of account-books under her arm everything breathed of method, order and decorum. The stout lady drew a chair to the table, and dipped her pen in the ink. It was evident that she was about to over-look her weekly accounts; but it was not until she bent forward to take a book from a shelf on the wall, and in doing so turned her face more fully towards him, that John Webb realised that this was Daisy—this stout bustling, middle-aged woman, the little Daisy with the withered petals and the drooping head, about whom he had been sentimentalising a moment before!

From out of the magic sheet she stared at him, sentient, breathing, the keen eyes fixed, the lips pressed together in frugal calculation. At the sight of the figures at the bottom of the page a frown contracted her forehead and her fingers rapped the table; anon she smiled, and a network of wrinkles showed around her eyes.

The photograph had lied—basely lied!

She looked older than her age, and old with a cut-and-dried, old-maid-like severity which

"Mr. Harry Furniss superintending a marriage ceremony for the cinematograph."
The Sphere, 7 September 1912.

struck ice into Webb's soul. Fifteen years of bachelor life in India, no woman in the house to consider, what in the world would—er—Daisy! (Why could people not christen their children by sensible names?) have to say to his free and easy ways? John Webb lay back in his chair and stared at his fiancee, and his fiancee went on with her work in methodical unconsciousness. The little books were checked off one by one; she drew the ledger towards her and began fumbling in her pockets, and clapping her hands over various parts of her dress as if in search for some article which persistently refused to be found. Something in her gestures brought a vivid recollection of his old mother to Webb's mind, and his heart beat with a sickening fear. Could it be that Daisy . . . ? Already? Alas it was but too true. The good lady produced a leather case from some hidden receptacle and fitted a pair of spectacles over her ears. Daisy—in spectacles!

If she had looked her age before she looked fifty now—sixty, a hundred—any age you like to mention, and formidable enough into the bargain to frighten the life out of a poor defenceless bachelor.

The writing was finished. Miss May put away the ledger and rose to cross the room. Her figure advanced towards him, nearer and nearer, larger and larger, with such startling, convincing reality, that he seemed to hear the tread of her feet, the rustling of her garments. The spectacles were still on her nose; the short skirts stood out well around the stout figure. She tried to take a short cut between the chiffonnier and the table, and failed because—O Daisy, Daisy!

Webb burst into a roar of hysterical laughter. "The dear ruins!" he cried aloud. "My dear ruins!" and clapped his hands together like a maniac.

"That's all, sir", said the photographer, coming forward into the room. "The impressions don't go any further."

⁕

Now Mark Robson, as has been said, was a shrewd man of business, and when he received a commission from India to secure a cinematographic photograph of Miss Daisy May, he reasoned with himself that if Mr. Webb were interested in Miss May, Miss May would be naturally interested in Mr. Webb, and that it was absurd to be satisfied with one client, when it was possible to secure two. He therefore selected one of his specious circulars, in which special reference to made to agencies in India and the Colonies, posted it to the lady's address in an envelope marked "private" and awaited the course of events. Miss May read the circular, re-read the circular, and carried it away to show her bosom friend.

"It doesn't seem altogether fair", she said.

"I don't like the idea of spying upon on him unawares; but still—"

"But still, my dear, when the happiness of a whole life is concerned", said the bosom friend solemnly. "I am told men degenerate terribly in India."

"He asks me to come out in October", faltered the fiancee. "He has always been most kind and thoughtful, and I have no reason to believe—"

"You see this Mr. Robson says that his agents arrange with the servants, by means of a smaller gratuity, to introduce the camera into the room, so that Mr. Webb would be none the wiser. Marriage is a serious step."

"It is, Maria, it is. And I am such a wretched sailor—I am afraid the fee would be very high!"

"It would be cheaper than a trousseau, and the fare out- and back again, if he ill-used you. It seems to me like the leading of Providence."

"Poor dear Jack!" sighed Miss May pensively, for ladies may still cherish sentimental memories though they be stout and middle-aged. Daisy had a tender place in her heart for the love of her youth, but fifteen years—that dreadful voyage—and at the other end the heat, the discomfort, the serpents, worst of all the strange man, who might turn out to be so painfully different to the Jack of her dreams . . .

"I'll do it!" she cried desperately, and Mr. Robson heaped a handsome profit by her decision, the black 'boy' in Calcutta also, though his sahib was far from suspecting his business one evening, five or six weeks later on, when he roared at him to cease fidgeting about the room and to take himself off to his own quarters.

The days of John Webb's bachelorhood were drawing to a close, and he set ever increasing store upon those long lazy evenings, when he could loll at ease, undisturbed by feminine prejudice. It was not precisely the moment he would have chosen, however in which to make his appearance before two maiden ladies at home, who had spent their lives in a narrow and rigid environment.

Miss May started violently as she beheld the counterfeit presentment of her lover, and the surprise did not appear to be pleasurable.

"He is—a great deal changed! He used to be such a—pretty boy!" she faltered . . .

"I never thought he would grow so plain."

"He is getting bald. He used to have such lovely hair, Maria—all little, tight curling rings, like a woolly lamb." Then her eyes wandered around the room. "I don't see the chair-back I sent him, or the sofa blanket . . . Is that my portrait on the table? Your eyes are better than mine."

"She has on a white dress, I don't think you were ever taken in white, dear", said the bosom friend sweetly. "Had he always that very-er-eadaverous appearance?"

"Its the liver, I suppose. They suffer from it in India", said the fiancee sadly . . .

"I wish he wouldn't crumple up those cushions. It's a shame to treat them like that such handsome embroidery . . . Dear me his is terribly thin. Do you think he can be quite strong? A delicate man is a great responsibility . . . I tell you solemnly, Maria, that if he had walked on board the boat to meet me I should not have known him from Adam . . . Here's the native servant coming to see what is wanted . . . Poor benighted heathen! I hope Jack is kind to him, and remembers that if he is black, we are all brothers . . . Oh Maria! O heavens! How could he do it? . . . To throw the book at that poor creature's head in that savage manner . . . Its sinful. If I had not seen it with my own eyes I would never have believed it . . . A brandy bottle! Why, he had just finished what was in the glass! I thought it was lemonade. No wonder his liver is out of order. And then that cigar . . .

"They will never the smell of smoke out of those curtains," said the bosom friend. "I know what it is. You will find it a little difficult to get him out of your ways, dear, but you must be firm. Those violent tempered men always give in in the end, if you worry long enough . . . Now he is falling asleep . . . Very dangerous lying there, with his head hanging over the chair . . . I shouldn't wonder if he had apoplexy some night and died off suddenly . . . There I knew he would waken himself if he nodded like that . . . Here's the black man again . . . He keeps calling for him all the time. You will never be able to keep your servants . . . What is he wants? Another brandy and soda! . . . My poor dear Daisy!"

"It's the second he has had in the last half hour!" cried Miss May wildly, and burying her head in her hands, she bursts into a passion of tears.

Miss May wrote to Calcutta to state that upon mature reflection, she had come to the conclusion that it would be wiser to bring the engagement to an end—lapse of time, change of disposition, etc,—and John Webb sent back a straightforward, manly letter, commending her candour, and agreeing in the wisdom of her decision.

⚜

For the time being both are inclined to bless Mr. Robson and the cinematographe for being the means of their deliverance, but as the years pass by one is inclined to doubt whether they will remain of the same opinion. The loss of the weekly letters will make a blank in Webb's life, and there may come an hour when the joys of a solitary life pall upon him, and he thinks longingly of Daisy—poor Daisy, who was faithful to him for fifteen long years! And Daisy too may weary of her account-books, and her dusting and mending and polishing up, for, ah, dear me, however well garnished the house, it is bare indeed if love be not in it, and companionship and sympathetic smiles. She is bound to think of Jack, and to torment herself by useless questionings, for she is a woman, and he was the lover of her youth. Was she right in playing the coward at the last moment? "For better, for worse." He was all alone, poor fellow, and she might have helped him . . .

But Mark Robson, the detective, grows fat and flourishes.

"*Picture Personalities: Mr. T. A. Welsh.*
**Mr. Welsh is the popular head of the Gaumont
Company, Limited, in England, and is an enthusiast
on the future of colour films.**"
The Bioscope, c. 1912.

The Times
9 April 1913

CINEMATOGRAPHS

Truth and Fiction

AT THE PRESENT MOMENT the popularity of picture palaces and the reason for it are directing a good deal of attention to the state of the public mind. But these sudden crazes are not new: 30 years ago it was croquet, 15 years ago it cycling, ten years ago it was roller skating. It seems that from time to time, like a person lying long in bed, we turn over and try a new position. Nevertheless, whenever it happens, the more thoughtful part of the race becomes alarmed, collect statistics, and wonder what this development, which it chooses to call back-sliding is caused by. We have lately been told that picture palaces are preventing us from going to church, from going to the theatre, from going to public houses, and from reading novels. On the other hand, we may find encouragement in the fact that the number of people who use works of reference is increasing.

One need not be thoughtful, or specially anxious about the future of the race, or a great believer in the value of statistics, and yet one may wonder as one walks down the Strand or Oxford Street or Tottenham Court Road why these excessively brilliant doorways which may star the pavement such short distances apart prove so irresistibly attractive. It is true that the management often provide tea for nothing, the carpets are very thick, and the attendants are finely grown as Royal footmen, and all these things are good; but without any such attractions, when the door is unlit, and down a back street, and the seats are hard and the attendants meagre, we sit there until the first picture begins to come over again, and directly the programme is changed, which is not as often as it should be, we pay our sixpence and go once more.

But what is the reason for this? Why do we invariably find the hall full of men and women, old, elderly, and young, paying their sixpence, listening intently, going away and coming again! No doubt we are all feeling much the same thing, and are driven to drop in by some such experience as this.

After trudging for an hour and a half in and out of tubes, shops, omnibuses, hard pavements for the feet, grey sky between the houses, windblown, with uncharitable people to confront, there comes a moment when it is no longer to be home. Wherever you are, whatever your tastes, you stop at some street corner and declare that you must immediately escape. The only question is whether is shall be to a church or to a picture gallery or to a public house or to a library. Each of these offers some kind of relief from the stony superficiality, the inhospitality, the impersonality of the street. Each offers some kind or resting room where you may recollect your human soul. At the same time each demands a certain effect, a certain chaffing and stamping if one may so call it, before one is comfortably aglow. It is now that the lighted doorway presents itself. The picture palace offers immediate escape with the least expenditure of energy. You have only to lean back in a well-wadded chair, and you are floated upon some ambling dance tune down southern streets, or to the dusty jungle where the lion crouches, or to the centre of some public pageant where merely to trace the expressions of the faces is to be in the making of history. The street is only a few yards away, and five minutes ago you were cold and wind blown like the rest; but now that is nothing, or a dream. You are now in the position most comfortable to man—sitting at ease, observing, speculating, ruminating, imagining, with hardly any trouble to yourself. All the work seems to be done for you. The marvellous way in which an illusion, strong enough to defeat circumstances, is created at once, without any effort of imagination, must be attributed chiefly to the fact that the pictures move. You never have time to be bored by one picture before it changes, becomes another picture, becomes not only a picture but a story, something which has a separate life of its own. Meanwhile you are being worked upon, as indifferent music that goes straight for the obvious emotion does work upon one, and made to feel without willing it rather more than is reasonable.

But this is only part of the secret, for the stream of traffic outside has no such power to please. A great part of the enchantment must lie in the fact that the most trivial scene—let us say a meet of coaches in Hyde Park—when cut off from its surroundings becomes for some queer reason significant, even emotional, as it seldom does in reality. Looking up from an arm-chair in a darkened room you see as you have never seen before. The horses and the woman and the trees appear on the sheet as if they had nothing to do with future or with the past, as if the whips would never descend, or the grooms swing up behind, or the horses trot off down the road to Richmond. Let alone the strange way in which isolating something from its context heightens the meaning, there is also the sheer excitement and curiosity of the sites themselves. For the first time we see wild beasts creeping down to the pools to drink, or ice-fields grinding each other in the Polar sea. We might almost say that for the first time we see flowers unfolding and waves breaking on the beach.

Indeed the only grudge we have against the management of picture palaces is that they will go to any amount of trouble and expense in dramatizing romantic stories which take place, we believe, in cardboard castles in the outskirts of Paris, when the streets are full of pictures at once more comic, more tragic, and possessed of the incomparable recommendation that they are true. (Suppose that, instead of inventing an improbable love story complicated by a couple of fierce brown bears in the Rocky Mountains, which has to be conveyed by trained actors carefully made up and craggy steeps that fail to convince, we had simply 12 o'clock yesterday in London, Paris, Moscow, Madrid, New York, Rome. The effect would be far more striking, and we must suppose a tenth part as expensive. Those half-dozen pictures of real people going about their businesses in real streets on different sides of the world, with all the little oddities and incidents that one would delight in detecting, would set up an image of the earth and mankind that would surpass all the lovers and the bears in America.

The versions of famous novels and imaginary adventures which fill three-fourths of the programme appeal, of course, to our love of story-telling, and if they tend to be a little monotonous they have the advantage that moving pictures are simpler, quicker, more direct than the best printed prose can ever hope to be. Whether in this extraordinary greed of the eye we are to see reason for alarm or not, we do not know. We are inclined to suspect that the eye in England has been rather cruelly starved. At the present moment, at any rate, it will take anything you choose to give it, as long as it moves quickly and is exactly like life. We are ready to look at places, people, animals, plants, waves, things that never happened, things that were written about, things that could not possibly happen anywhere. What the brain does with all this material is to difficult to say. Judging from personal experience, we should be inclined to believe that it remains quiescent during the greater part of the time, amused but not stimulated, that there are scattered moments of pure revelation; and that, for the rest, a marvellous confusion reigns, a welter of music, of facts, of fiction, of forms. It is not life, it is not art, it is not music, it is not literature. Whether, all the same, we are fumbling towards some new form of art, which is to have movement and shape, to be like life and yet, to be selected and arranged as a work of art, who can say? In the meantime, we have a fury for seeing, and remain happy, greedy, and terribly indiscriminate.

❄

6   The Biograph in Battle

MILITARY SUBJECTS DEPICTING troops on parade or manoeuvres were among the very first presented as moving pictures. As early as August 1896, Robert Paul had filmed *The Gordon Highlanders Marching out of Maryhill Barracks, Glasgow.* Sadly, the world did not have to wait very long for the first films showing armed conflict. The late Victorian and Edwardian era offered many opportunities for the cinema and warfare to become better acquainted. The Spanish-American, Boer, Russo-Japanese and Balkan Wars, amongst other conflicts, were all to be captured by the infant cinema. Scenes from the Greco-Turkish War of 1897 were recreated in the Montreuil studio of Georges Méliès whose épisodes *les plus sanglants* included titles such as *Les Massacres de la population Cretoise* and *Combat naval en Grece.* Now, for the very first time, however, it was claimed that films were made at the seat of war itself. Frederic Villiers, war artist and special correspondent, was despatched to the Balkans to cover the war for *The Standard* and *Black and White.* He took with him two novel items of equipment—a bicycle and a cinematograph camera. Villiers claims to have used his camera to record the siege of Volo. Unfortunately, however, no films have survived to verify his claims. Villiers was a legend in his own lifetime, a larger than life character who had no qualms about sometimes embellishing the truth a little. His anecdotes about filming the war, recounted on his autobiography more than twenty years later, must be read with caution. The very next year found Villiers covering another, very different, war, accompanying Kitchener's march to Omdurman in the Sudan. Once again he had his cinematograph camera with him. This time he claims that his camera tripod overturned in the middle of filming, exposing and ruining the film so that he had no option but to fall back on his trusty pencil and sketchbook. A suspicious mind might conclude that Villiers' misfortune was somewhat convenient. Villiers, however, was not the only correspondent to have a cinematograph camera in the Sudan. Alarming Queen's Company of Grenadier Guards at Omdurman, filmed by John Benett-Stanford in September 1898, was exhibited in Britain from November, with much attendant publicity. Unfortunately, no print of the film is known to have survived. On the other side of the world the Spanish-American war in Cuba was also covered by a number of cameramen.

It was the Boer War, however, that was to have a profound effect on the development of the cinema in Britain. It was during this conflict that fundamental issues of authenticity, realism, censorship and propaganda were raised. These are issues which remain with us to this day. There was an immediate and practically insatiable demand for films depicting every aspect of the war. A demand which meant that producers such as the Warwick Trading Company and the British Mutoscope & Biograph Co. Ltd. lost no time in sending their most experienced cameramen to South Africa. At home, too, the fledgling film industry received a massive boost as domestic production was geared up to record the training, embarkation and return of troops and provide dramatised recreations of incidents from the war.

Capturing front line scenes showing actual fighting presented the cameramen, no matter how intrepid, with insurmountable problems. Early cameras were comparatively bulky and clumsy to operate and could only film for about a minute before they needed reloading. Mostly hand-cranked they were also static, requiring a tripod for support. The Mutograph camera used by Dickson during the Boer War was powered by batteries but was also extremely cumbersome. When Dickson sailed to South Africa he needed to take three-quarters of a ton of equipment with him. Camera operators were extremely vulnerable and made very conspicuous and tempting targets. Despite their undoubted bravery, and the addition of bullet-proof shields mounted on their cameras, they could hardly be expected to be effective in the thick of the action.

Neither was the task of the earliest war cinematographers helped by the transformation in the art of warfare. Recent developments in military technology meant that fighting was rarely conducted at close range or hand-to-hand. As Charles Urban, commenting on the total absence of 'real' battle films, lamented: "You cannot get them; nobody can. Modern battles are at long distance; the bullets go 'zip, zip', but you can't see the men who fired them; they are too far off. In the olden days it would have been different, when everything was at close quarters. But there were no Bioscopes then". The use of telephoto lenses such as those developed in the 1890s by Dallmeyer was one possible solution but such lenses could not be fitted to most cine cameras of the time. The war films sent home by the likes of Dickson and Rosenthal were inevitably less impressive and stirring than the images of battle drawn by the illustrators employed by the popular press. No matter how representative of the actuality of war these films were, they simply could not compete in the public's mind with such idealised and heroic images. War pictures, usually secured behind the front lines, were simply not exciting enough for people who were used to reading the reports of the special war correspondents.

However, since action was what the public wanted, action was precisely what the public got. If the camera could not get to where the fighting was, then the fighting would have to be brought before the camera. Battle scenes were staged behind the lines (with British troops dressed up as Boers) but more commonly at home which had the combined advantage of being both more convenient and, of course, cheaper. It was costly to obtain equipment and travel around a war zone, if, indeed, one could get there at all. Films then had to be processed and shipped back home which took several weeks. Far better then, to simply make them at home. By producing such fakes producers were also able to respond far quicker to the demand for topical films

relating to events fresh in the public's memory. Usually referred to by their makers as 'dramatic representations' or 'reproductions of incidents', sham war films were made with Sheffield doubling as Manchuria and Lancashire as South Africa. One of the most famous of these films, James Williamson's *Attack On A China Mission, Bluejackets To The Rescue*, an incident from the Boxer rebellion was actually filmed in his own garden in Hove. They were undeniably effective and very popular, giving the public a far more graphic representation of war than any 'actual' footage could provide. Made with varying efforts to give some aura of authenticity, such films can seem to us to be incredibly crude and primitive.

It is all too easy to say that audiences of the time were naive or stupid and to assume that most people did not realise that they were being fooled. As Ian Christie has pointed out, however, this is to ignore the wider context of the popular press of the day and the way in which news was reported. What, after all, is the difference between an engraving in a magazine 'based' on a sketch from a special artist and a war film 'arranged under the supervision of an experienced military officer from the front'? Film as yet played only a very small part in the way that the public interpreted events as Christie says: 'moving pictures started by functioning as illustrations to what were still predominantly verbal narratives.' The commercial value and intrinsic superiority of 'genuine' films was, however, recognised by many. The Warwick Trading Company boasted that all its films were the genuine article and warned exhibitors: "Do not discredit your Exhibits and the General Animated Picture Business by trying to fool the Public with Faked Films. You will be the loser in the long run if you do."

The Boer War saw an increasing awareness of the potency of film as propaganda. A popular magazine of the day, *Today*, noted with foresight that the biograph "will reveal bravery as no despatch may do, and will tell the truth in all things, owing neither loyalty to chief nor submission to esprit de corps. How far this truthfulness will please the authorities remains to be seen". Staged films, of course, often carried a very crude propaganda message with brave Tommy performing his heroic duty for Queen and Country against the evil, blood-thirsty Boer.

Actuality films too, however, through a process of selection, omission and emphasis could be used to promote a cause. It is interesting to note that whilst all Boer War films were shot exclusively from a British point of view (the Boers had photographers but no cinematographers) they were used to press both causes in different countries depending on their political sympathies. As the century progressed, war cinematographers found themselves battling increasingly against another problem. A problem that they themselves considered far more serious than any technical difficulties, hardship or physical danger, was censorship. During the Russo-Japanese War of 1904–5, censorship was rigidly imposed by both sides. All films that made it back to London had to be shown at the Japanese Embassy before they could be exhibited for the public. The Russians were, if anything, even stricter, confiscating camera equipment and deporting correspondents. Rosenthal, filming the siege of Port Arthur was reduced to sending out films wrapped in cabbage heads to evade the eyes of the authorities.

The result of all this censorship was quite predictable. More and more fake films of the war were produced in order to satisfy public demand. The growing public appetite for news saw the creation of newsreel companies such as the Pathé Journal and the Topical Budget and more and more cameramen being sent to battle zones. Over twenty operators were assigned to cover the Balkan War of 1912 where they came into daily conflict with the censors and the military authorities. In many ways the Balkans, however, proved to be merely the tragic curtain raiser for the war into which the world was to be plunged in 1914. This time, the authorities were to act quickly and decisively. Not only did the War Office place a virtual ban on all film cameramen within thirty miles of the front line but it also prevented exhibitors from showing any films whatsoever connected with the war. A committee of prominent Belgians appealed that films would provide valuable evidence of German atrocities in their country ("the camera would render a service to humanity by giving a true and honest account of things"). A true account was however, the last thing that governments wanted.

*The Optical Magic
Lantern and
Photographic Enlarger*
1898

A NEW MILITARY CINEMATOGRAPHIC PICTURE

WHEN AT THE OFFICES OF MR. PHILIPP WOLFF, of 9 Southampton St., [London] WC, a few days ago, Mr. Hessberg, the manager, informed us that they were about to publish a remarkable cinematographic picture taken in the Soudan by a well-known war correspondent. We give, with permission, an extract from an explanatory letter written to Mr. Woolf [*sic*]: "The cinematographic film which you have was taken by me on the battlefield of Omdurman the day before the battle. It is the only genuine Soudan film as nobody else had a cinematograph with them. There was a rumour that the dervishes were advancing to attack us, and all the men were told to lie down and be in readiness to fall in for anything. I therefore fixed my camera on the Grenadier Guards (Queen's Company) and when the brigade-trumpeter, whom you see in the photograph, sounded the call, I took the men standing up, fixing bayonets, and marching off . . ." Mr. Wolff is to be congratulated on having the publishing of this valuable film.

"A Cinematograph Operator giving instructions to a Commander-in-Chief before a battle."
Punch's Almanack for 1912.

Albert E. Smith
Two Reels and a Crank
1952, pp. 64–68.

THAT EVENING A SOLDIER TOOK ME TO ONE SIDE. "Better be up bright and early tomorrow morning", he whispered. "Something's doin'."

Long before daylight Blackton and I were afoot with camera, tripod, and film cartridge boxes, ready for the business of the day.

At the first hint of dawn the Rough Riders, paced by Roosevelt and Davis, started towards the hills. Our equipment slowed us down considerably, I with camera and tripod slung over a shoulder, and Blackton with a load of film. Ever inching forwards as they were, it was all we could do to keep behind Roosevelt and Davis.

The colonel carried a Krag-Jorgensen rifle taken from a dead Spaniard. Davis was searching trees with binoculars for snipers who, we were warned, had fallen into the evil practice of letting the men pass, then shooting them in the back.

As daylight came we saw indications of our plan of attack.

Other regiments were moving through the brush in a sort of crouch, a long irregular arc converging on a point in the farthermost hills, where the tops of enemy blockhouses were visible.

The thin line of Rough Riders halted, fired, advanced slowly, more picking their way through the heavy thicket than charging. This was the assault. Nothing glamorous or hip-hip-hooray or George M Cohan; the mean vicious deadly business of tracking an enemy who at any moment might be leisurely drawing a bead on the small of your back.

It was not until Blackton and I returned to New York that we learned we had taken part in the celebrated 'charge' up San Juan Hill. Many historians have given it a Hollywood flavour, but there was vastly more bravery in the tortuous advance against this enemy who could see and not be seen. Historians have embroidered a most dramatic scene—Roosevelt springing to the front of his Rough Riders, flashing his sword and crying, "Forward, charge the hill!" From the start the intrepid Teddy was never anywhere except in front of his soldiers. Nor did he ride a horse in the charge, as is popularly believed. He walked! One account I have before me reads: "His (Roosevelt's) horse was shot, but the rider fell upon his feet and, seizing a rifle, climbed up, firing as he went. That hill, also, was captured."

Near the San Juan ford we encountered a line of regulars relaxing on the ground.

When Roosevelt came up, an officer rose, saluted. "General Shafter's compliments, sir. The general wishes that the Rough Riders will go no further," he said.

Historians quote Roosevelt as returning Shafter's compliments, then saying: "The Rough Riders are going up the hill."

I was right behind Roosevelt, and this is what he said: "To hell with General Shafter—come on, boys, we're going up."

And we did.

While we were on the move our equipment forced us into a kind of awkward stoop, made much more difficult for because I could carry my camera only one way, over a shoulder. At frequent intervals we heard a thin whistle sound.

"Tropical bugs", I said, and Blackton nodded.

Whenever we set up camera for pictures, its black head poking above the heavy growth, the bugs became particularly bothersome.

We came upon a Rough Rider, very young, lying near a bush. He was wounded and seemed unable to speak. His eyes followed us as we put down beside him. One corner of his mouth turned up a little in an effort at a smile. He was of a prominent New York family; he died there a few hours later.

Suddenly that whine again, then several more.

Blackton flogged the air angrily, "Damn those bugs."

The young soldier was grinning. "Bugs, hell! Spaniards!"

The "bugs" were bullets from Spanish Mausers.

I had rested the tripod and camera upright on the ground, and as the soldier spoke I reached to lower them to safety. A moment too late! Two Mausers pierced the wooden door of the camera but, fortunately, coursed past the mechanism.

Up to this time we had a nervous curiosity as to what might happen. The shattered camera door brought with it the realization that bullets, not bugs, were whining past our heads. I appeared to be foolish to go on in the same manner, namely, shooting picture out in the open, calling to Rough Riders to stand up so we might get a better shot. You couldn't operate an old fashioned tripod camera from a belly position, and now our open-air technique seemed curiously lacking in logic.

I talked it over with Blackton. More accurately, I had barely suggested it when a verdict was reached: Vitagraph would retreat.

We had gotten what we came to Cuba for. Besides, we told each other, piling reason on reason, our film supply was running low. Even though it was now American-held ground I remember with what marvellous caution we picked our way back to the camp, moving in a half crouch until we were well toward the rear.

We were eager to return to New York and develop our film as quickly as possible, for we saw our adventure looming up in the film world as quite a tour de force. We boarded a transport leaving for Tampa that afternoon. An hour or so from Siboney the low distant thunder of heavy guns reached our ship. We speculated on whether the troops had captured the ridge and were now shelling Santiago. This, we learned upon reaching Tampa, was not the case. Admiral Cervera, bottled up in Santiago by American Warships, had tried to make a run for it. The rumble was American cannon fire lambasting the Spanish Armada.

News of the naval victory had reached New York, and the port was buzzing when we arrived. Blackton and I agreed to keep mum about what we had photographed in Cuba, not an easy restraint for a twenty-two-year old sorely tempted to assume the air of a conquering hero. A number of reporters, hungry for information, gathered around us. To our shame we patronizingly doled out a mere tidbit or two, making it a point to mention Colonel Roosevelt's name frequently and in a most familiar way: "Yes, we camped in with Teddy and the boys", or, "It was when we got to the San Juan ford that the colonel knew we were in for some rough times . . ."

I was thinking of the land fighting.

"Did you get other shots?" a reporter asked.

"What do you mean?"

"The sea-battle the American fleet pasting Admiral Cervera."

At this precise moment, flushed with triumph, I think we would have taken credit for any phase of the Cuban campaign.

"Certainly, certainly", I said, and then Blackton nodded solemnly as if I had spoken a simple irrefutable truth. After extracting a little more admiration from the reporters with veiled comments, we rushed past the wide-eyed group with the magnificent hauteur of two youths in their finest hour, or so it appeared at the time.

Once in our office, we knew we were in trouble. Word has spread through New York that Vitagraph had taken pictures of the Battle of Santiago Bay! To caller after caller we said we had not yet developed any of the film, that we were not sure what we had, that it would be some time yet inasmuch as the film had to be processed in order. We sat down and looked at each other. How to get out of this one? Vitagraph, not too well off as things were, could ill afford to reverse itself.

Blackton said we could fake a sea battle and I said he was insane, but as the minutes passed the idea got better and better. Why not?

At this time the street vendors in New York were selling large sturdy photographs of ships of the American and Spanish fleets. We bought a set of each and cut out the battleships. On a table, topside down, we placed one of artist Blackton's large canvas-covered frames and filled it with water an inch deep. In order to stand the cutouts of the ships in the water, we nailed them to lengths of wood about an inch square. In this way a little "shelf" was provided for each ship, and on this shelf we placed pinches of gunpowder—three pinches for each ship—not too many, we felt, for a major sea engagement of this sort.

For a background, Blackton daubed a few white clouds on a blue tinted cardboard. To each of the ships, now sitting placidly in our shallow 'bay', we attached a fine thread to enable us to pull the ships past the camera at the proper moment and in the correct order.

We needed someone to blow smoke into the scene, but we couldn't go too far outside our circle if the secret was to be kept. Mrs. Blackton was called in and she volunteered, in this day of nonsmoking womanhood to smoke a cigarette. A friendly office boy said he would try a cigar. This was fine, as we needed the volume.

A piece of cotton was dipped in alcohol and attached to a wire slender enough to escape the eye of the camera. Blackton, concealed behind the side of the table farthermost from the camera, touched of the mounds of gunpowder with his wire taper—and the battle was on. Mrs. Blackton, smoking and coughing, delivered a fine haze. Jim had worked out a timing arrangement with her so that she blew smoke into the scene at approximately the moment of explosion. Brave soul though she was, Mrs. Blackton turned and fled with each blast of gunpowder. Jim waited until she returned, whereupon he would ignite another mound and Mrs. Blackton would blow in the smoke, then flee. Consequently, the lapse between Mrs. Blackton's flight and return made it impossible for Blackton to 'shoot' in rapid-fire order. We knew this was a serious compromise of the real battle, but it was hardly a time to weigh deceptions.

The boy at the other side of the table was not faring as well, the cigar quickly proving too much for him, though he held to his post in fine military fashion. Blackton was the busiest setting of the powder, drawing one ship then another into the scene, and stirring up little waves.

It would be less than the truth to say we were not wildly excited as to what we saw on the screen. The smoky overcast and the flashes of fire from the 'guns' gave the scene an atmosphere of remarkable realism. The film and the lenses of the day were imperfect enough to conceal the crudities of our miniature, and as the picture ran only two minutes there was not enough time for anyone to study it critically. Deception though it was then, it as the first miniature and the forerunner of the elaborate 'special effects' technique of modern picture making.

Pastor's and both Proctor houses played to capacity audiences for several weeks. Jim and I felt less remorse of conscience when we saw how much excitement and enthusiasm were aroused by the *Battle of Santiago Bay* and the thirty-nine-minute-long *Fighting With Our Boys in Cuba*. Almost every newspaper in New York carried an account of the showings, commenting on Vitagraph's remarkable feat in obtaining on-spot pictures of these two historic events.

Dairy entry—March 30, 1989: Filmed miniature of Windsor Hotel fire with rubber figures jumping out of windows of cardboard model. Ignited gunpowder for fire and smoke. Used toy squirt guns for steaming of water. Film very successful among Vitagraph customers.

The notoriety we received from the Cuban films yielded another dividend; it brought to our door, for the first time, the great Edison Company. Nibbling, as we were, at the fringes of a field in which Edison was the dominant figure, even casual recognition of us by 'the Wizard of Men Park' was something we hadn't dared dream about.

Still from *The Battle of Manila Bay*. Vitagraph 1898.

*The Optical Magic
Lantern Journal and
Photographic Enlarger*
March 1900

SHAM WAR CINEMATOGRAPH FILMS

ACORRESPONDENT HAS ASKED US how he is to know real from sham war films, see-ing that several subjects are made up at home from life models? The subject lends itself so well to life model work that one has to a great extent to rely on common sense; for instance, in one film we have heard about, there is a hand-to-hand encounter between Boers and British, all realistic in its way, but the effect is somewhat spoilt by reason of a fringe of an audience appear-ing on the picture occasionally. Thus, when one sees gentlemen with tall hats, accompanied by ladies, apparently looking on, common sense would at once pronounce the film of the sham order. The same thing may be said of films showing soldiers lying and firing behind 'earthworks' composed of nicely arranged straw.

**Joseph Rosenthal in South
Africa, 1900.**

*The Photographic
Chronicle*
1 August 1901

CINEMATOGRAPH IN WAR

AWRITER IN THE *MANCHESTER WEEKLY TIMES*, says: "Of course, the cinemato-graph has been 'at the front', but the results are far from satisfactory. A battle is not the picturesque affair it used to be in the old days. It would be difficult to tell from a photograph where the battle was being fought, for what with subtly constructed trenches, where the soldiers hide, and smokeless powder, there is practically nothing of a spectacular nature. The cinemato-graph operator who was sent to South Africa had every facility to do his work. Lord Roberts gave assistance in crossing the rivers, and some capital views were obtained on the march, but of actual warfare it was difficult to obtain anything of any value. The operator had a bullet-proof chamber made, by which he was enabled to get within two miles of the scene of opera-tions, but was generally the target for the Boers, and was struck time after time. Although telephoto lenses were used nothing but splashes of sand where the bullets struck the ground were to be distinguishable. The cost of these pictures was enormous, and may be gauged to some extent when I say in conclusion, on the authority of Mr. Thomas, who is representing Messrs Edison in Manchester, that the pictures of the Sunday School processions in Manches-ter, on Whit Monday alone, cost about £500.

"Picture Personalities: Mr. 'Joe' Rosenthal."
The Bioscope, c. 1912.

MR. W. K. LAURIE DICKSON, who followed the war in South Africa as the representative of the Biograph Company, was fortunate in securing several pictures of engagements, &c.: in fact, most of his pictures were taken under fire. It would be impossible for me to give anything like a brief account, or, indeed, a list, of his experiences out there—they would fill many numbers of the *Black and White Budget.* As a matter of fact he has written a most interesting book, *The Biograph in Battle,* in which he deals at length with his experiences in South Africa. It is a diary kept from the time he left England, and in it he relates many experiences and incidents which it has not been the privilege of many civilians to participate in.

**Pat Brooklyn
'Biograph Operators—
Some of the Risks
They Run'
*Black and White Budget***
1 June 1901

'The Camera on the
Battlefield'
*The Photographic
Chronicle*
15 August 1901

IT HAS BEEN SAID on several occasions of late that the present war in South Africa is in many respects the most scientific campaign ever fought, and having regard to the new and wonderful appliances which are now being for the first time tried in a great war, this is in a measure correct.

In no direction, however, is the development more striking than in photography. If anyone had suggested twenty years ago that the camera would shortly be used to photograph the British Army on the battlefield, he would probably have been laughed at, and yet this is what has come to pass, and in the present war the camera has been extensively used both by war correspondents and artists and the Intelligence Department of the Army.

It has long been obvious that for some purposes, such as snapshots of positions and portions of the country, photography in war time would be of great advantage to the commanding officers, while it would prove a useful auxiliary to those whose business it is to provide accounts either pictorial or otherwise for the newspapers, but this usefulness of the camera was limited by the fact that only things which were comparatively close at hand could be photographed, but, thanks to a recent invention, this has been to a great extent overcome.

This invention consists, broadly speaking, of the adaption of the principle of the telescope to the camera, and was invented by Mr. Dallmeyer. It is obvious to all that, for instance, photographs of actual fighting could never be taken by means of an ordinary camera in these days of long-distance weapons, for by the time the operator got within focus of the contending forces he would be too much occupied in providing for his own safety to think of 'pressing the button' or anything of that kind.

By means of Mr. Dallmeyer's invention, it is possible to take excellent photos at a distance of two or three miles, so that all the enterprising photographer has to do is to select a nice lofty position within about a couple of miles of where a battle is raging, and he can take his photos as comfortably as though he were in a London studio. This, of course, refers more especially to South Africa, where the air is remarkably clear and free from vapour, for mist would be fatal to telephotography, as this process is called.

The invention consists in its essential part, of a kind of telescope about six or eight inches long and two inches in diameter, fixed to where the lens would be in an ordinary camera.

The first Government to examine and adopt this instrument for use with its Army and Navy was the progressive Administration of Japan, and in 1894, during the war between that country and China, it proved of considerable assistance. Sine that time other Governments have adopted telephotography for use in war time, including Spain and Italy, while Russia and Germany ware experimenting with it at the present time. True to its traditions, the British War Office has so far lagged behind, and has so far contented itself with a casual examination of the instrument, and such tele-cameras as are being used in the field at the present moment have been provided by the officers themselves.

Another important development with regard to photography, which has been brought about during the present war, has been in connection with the 'moving pictures' which have been so popular of late years. As many people are aware, at the outbreak of the war the Biograph Company sent representatives to the front to procure scenes from the campaign, many of which have since been exhibited in London. The takers of these pictures, however, have laboured under some disadvantage owing to the fact that the censors of the press messages and pictures have insisted on opening the cases containing the photographic films to see that nothing else was in them. This exposure of the undeveloped photographs to the light of day has, of course, ruined them. It may be mentioned with regard to telephotography that this invention cannot be fitted to the biograph cameras, owing to the fact that with these machines an extreme quickness of lens is required, and so it comes out that we cannot yet sit at home in England and watch the actual fighting taking place before our eyes, but his will probably come to pass within the next few years.

Many telephotographs of the troops in action have, however, already arrived in this country and have been published in some of the illustrated papers.—*Military Mail.*

Cameramen under fire. *Le Petit Journal,* 1911.

[Crete 1897]

Frederic Villiers
Villiers: His Five Decades of Adventure
1921, pp. 181–83, 302–03.

LUCKILY I WAS WELL HOUSED during the fighting in front of Volo, for the British consul insisted on my residing at the consulate. To me it was campaigning in luxury. From the balcony of the residence I could always see of a morning when the Turks opened fire up on the Velestino Plateau; then I would drive with my cinema outfit to the battlefield, taking my bicycle with me in the carriage. After I had secured a few reels of movies, if the Turks pressed too hard on our lines I would throw my camera into the vehicle and send it out of action, and at nightfall, after the fight, I would trundle back down the hill to dinner.

When this little war broke out I had ingeniously thought that cinema pictures of the fighting would delight and astonish the public. The cinema camera was then in its infancy, so at considerable expense I took one to the front, as I have already mentioned. It was a laborious business in those early days to arrange the spools and change the films; and I sweated a good deal at the work, but managed to get touches of real warfare.

It was a great disappointment, therefore, to discover that these films were of no value in the movie market, for when I returned to England a friend, generally of ordinary intelligence, said to me:

"My dear Villiers, I saw some wonderful pictures of the Greek war last night."

By his description I knew they were certainly not mine. I wondered at this, because my camera was the only one to pass the Greek customs during the campaign. Then he described one of the pictures:

"Three Albanians came along a very white, dusty road toward a cottage on the right of the screen. As they neared it they opened fire; you could see the bullets strike the stucco of the building. Then one of the Turks with the butt end of his rifle smashed the door of the cottage, entered, and brought out a lovely Athenian maid in his arms. You could see her struggling and fighting for liberty. Presently an old man, evidently the girl's father, rushed out of the house to her rescue, when the second Albanian whipped out his yataghan from his belt and cut the gentleman's head off."

Here my friend grew enthusiastic. "There was the head", said he, "rolling in the foreground of the picture." Nothing could be more positive than that.

I did not raise my voice or smile derisively; I calmly asked him, "Have you ever seen a movie camera?"

"No", he replied.

"Well, you have to fix it on a tripod", said I, "and get everything in focus before you can take a picture. Then you have to turn the handle in a deliberate, coffee-mill sort of way, with no hurry or excitement. It's not a bit like a snapshot, press-the-button pocket Kodak."

"Now just think of that scene you have so vividly described to me. Imagine the man who was coffee-milling saying, in a persuasive way, 'Now, Mr Albanian, before you take the old gent's head off come a little nearer; yes, but a little more to the left, please. Thank you. Now, then, look as savage as you can and cutaway'. Or 'You, No.2 Albanian, make that hussy lower her chin a bit and keep her kicking as ladylike as possible'. Wru-ru-ru-ru-ru!"

A famous firm outside Paris made those films, and since then many others of a similar nature have delighted the movie 'fan'. Barnum and Baily, those wonderful American showmen, correctly averred that the public liked to be fooled.

[The Balkans, 1911]

The Bulgarians sent word to the correspondents assembled at Mustapha Pasha that the execution of two Turkish spies was to take place the following morning. Execution of spies is always brutal and not particularly a happy subject for illustration, and I thought I would not go. But my servant told me that all the other correspondents intended to be there, and then I felt bound to show up, as I was for the moment directing a moving-picture operation called 'Kinemacolor'.

The ghastly little tragedy took place in a orchard by the side of a shed which had been the dumping ground of a bivouac and stunk horribly. When I arrived to take up position, I found two spies being harangued by a Bulgarian officer who was reciting their appalling deed to them while they stood bound by the wrists under the shade of some fruit trees, over the stout branches of which were slung two ominous-looking ropes.

One of the condemned was a short, sandy-haired Turk, the other was a tall black-haired man with Jewish features and the most wonderful poise and indifference as to what was going on. Indeed I felt that he would like to say, "Oh! please stop the cackle and get on with the show; don't you see the audience is waiting?"

Before the final kick-off, a tin can was offered the culprits to dip in an adjacent bucket of water for the ablutions all good Mussulmans perform before prayer. The sandy man waived his privilege, but the other religiously went through the whole ceremony, even to the washing of the feet. Now the crowd was becoming impatient and I think the tall Turk was playing with his audience, for he had a sly, cunning look in his dark eyes.

At last he washed his toes and threw away the cup. Then followed a scene that was indescribably disgraceful. The camera men—and there were legions—crawled up the trees, mounted the roof of the barn, and occupied every coign of vantage. Bulgarian children, dressed in gala attire and accompanied by their fathers and mothers, crowded up to the gallows trees to gloat over the misery of these wretched men. I became so nauseated with the disgusting sight that I closed down my machine and fled.

Ward Muir
from **'Photogramerriment
and Songs of the Camera'**
The Photogram
July 1900

'THE KHAKI-COVERED CAMERA'

We've songs about Pretoria (which rhymes with Queen Victoria):
We've patriotic photo-frames and soap and statuettes;
For war we are all glutton, e'en to wearing portrait buttons,
And decking out with tri-colours our harmless household pets;
But the khaki-covered camera is the latest thing,
To use the Emerald language, "its the natest thing!"
Your Kodak's in disgrace
If not in a khaki case,
For it's positively quite the up-to-datest thing!

The Special Correspondent need never be despondent
If a khaki-covered camera forms a portion of his kit,
For the mere fact that it's there will save him from the snare
Over over-gory writing in the wish to make a "hit".
Yes, the khaki-covered camera is the latest thing,
For saving printers' ink it is the greatest thing;
Each exposure states a fact,
Plain, unvarnished and compact;
As historian it's quite the up-to-datest thing!

But every blessed journal,—monthly, weekly or diurnal,—
Is filled with "our exclusive snap-shots of the Transvaal War";
And it all is very clever, for our "artist" often never
Heard a louder cannon's thunder from Fleet Street's traffic roar!
But he's got a khaki camera—it's the latest thing;
For absolute straightforwardness the straightest thing.
You can make a "Scene at Paard-
eburg" in your own back yard
If you understand this truly up-to-datest thing.

Then the dizzling kinetograph and its brave undaunted staff
Who've rented a secluded park not far from gay Paree;
Their methods, though dramatic, are a little bit erratic,
For they can't resist the joys of making British soldiers flee!
Their khaki-covered camera is the latest thing,
As a fabrication-mill it is the greatest thing:
Two hundred lies a minute!
Why, Kruger isn't in it
With this quite unanswerable film-beats-platest thing!

The Times
4 September 1914
IN CONFORMITY WITH THE WISHES of the Secretary of State, and of the Press Bureau, the British Board of Film Censors has decided in order to prevent the exhibition of films dealing with the present crisis in an inopportune or improper manner, that during the war all such pictures, whether topical or otherwise, shall be submitted for censorship.

THE CENSOR AT WORK—A MISMANAGED PART OF THE WAR

The Times
21 November 1912

NO ONE FOR ONE MOMENT can question the right of a nation engaged in fighting for its very existence to impose whatever restrictions it may deem needful on the presence of mere spectators, however deeply interested. War is not waged for the purpose of providing a cinematograph show, nor is the bedside of a dying Power the place for a writer of short stories; and I may turn aside for a moment to say here that while I believe I have as keen an appreciation as any one of the natural desire of human kind to see and to hear all about the doings of the human race, especially in its most supreme trials and triumphs, I could not but sympathise with the indignation expressed to me by men, taking active part in what was to them the greatest tragedy in their own life and in that of their country, that whirring cinematograph machines should make a side-shoe out of their sufferings. In a London music-hall the other night, a few days after my return from the tragedies of the battlefields and the hospitals, I saw cinematograph pictures of regiments of poor devils of prisoners being trotted at a grotesque pace before a blasé audience to the tune of a ragtime march. I choked with indignation, and remembered with joy how I cheered when I saw a captured Turk hurl his fez at a photographer who was taking a 'fine film' of the misery and humiliation of himself and his dejected companions. The extent and the methods of the restrictions imposed on duly accredited and accepted onlookers must be carefully considered by the censors simply as a matter of international policy. I believe I am right in stating that this has never been completely done in any war. The Censorship is not a branch of military science and study. It is high time it was made so. Invariably it is an afterthought regarded by the General Staff as a mere incident and considered a nuisance by the average military officer, concerned only with his immediate business of winning the war.

The war correspondents' camp
at Port Arthur.
The Illustrated London News,
17 December 1904.

Bradford Telegraph and Argus
September 1914

BRADFORD MAN'S ADVENTURES

An Eventful Three Weeks

MR. ROWLAND G. HIBBERT OF BRADFORD, endeavouring to get cinematograph pictures of the military operations in France, has had a series of experiences which he will not soon forget.

He is only twenty years of age, but was particularly daring until his enterprise was cut short and he was 'captured' by the authorities who sent him back to England, his camera being confiscated.

After arriving at Dieppe he intended going to Crepy-en-Valois, but as he was travelling in the train he saw two French aeroplanes chasing a German Taube. The latter was brought down. He alighted at the next station and went to the spot the same evening. He returned the following morning at daybreak, hoping to get a picture but found that the French Transport Corps had dismantled the machine, whilst the villagers had taken what remained as souvenirs.

On reaching Crepy-en-Valois he met the famous war correspondent, Mr. W. B. Maxwell, formerly of Bradford, but the following day Mr. Hibbert was arrested by the military for coming to the town with a camera. He was kept under guard for three days, and was only liberated after some Englishmen in the town had guaranteed his bona fides. He got back to Paris, and next went to Creil and Senlis.

Tragedy at the Front

His next journey was made in an ambulance van to Braisne, where he got right amongst the English artillery, who were advancing to the battle of the Aisne. Between Braisne and Soissons he saw considerable firing. Bridges were being blown up, whilst he declares that he crossed one field which was almost covered with dead bodies. It was here that he picked up part of a German shrapnel shell which he has brought home.

Again going back to Paris he managed to get back to Hazebrouch (via Calais), travelling in an empty troop train, and he witnessed the passing of the Indian troops, of whom he secured several pictures. He was again caught by the military authorities and taken to the English headquarters and placed in the guard room.

When taken out the next morning he was in charge of eight armed soldiers, a sergeant, and two officers. Going through the streets the people imagined that he was a spy, and they hooted him.

Hooted as a Spy

Similarly on his journey to Paris, accompanied by soldiers, demonstrations were made against him, and things were getting to look serious till a French soldier told the people who he was.

Later, he had to give a written undertaking that he would return straight to England. He got back to Bradford on Friday.

Opposite: **Second Lieutenant Bertram Brooks-Carrington, British official cameraman, with a Moy and Bastie camera and a German anti-tank rifle, c. September 1917.**
Photo: Imperial War Museum, neg. no. IWM Q111226

7   The Cinema and Royalty

THE CLOSING YEARS OF THE NINE-teenth century and the reign of Edward VII were to witness the climax of empire and dynastic monarchy in Britain. The embryonic cinema was quick to realise the potential appeal of members of royalty and state occasions as film subjects. Throughout this period, such subjects remained favourite topics for actuality films. There was to be no shortage of events to be covered. Major topics were Queen Victoria's Jubilee (1897) and her funeral (1901), the Coronation of Edward VII (1902) and his funeral (1910), the Coronation of George V, the Investiture of the Prince of Wales and the Delhi Durbar in 1911.

The first occasion that a member of the British royal family was filmed occurred on 27 June 1896 when Birt Acres filmed the Prince of Wales (the future Edward VII) on a visit to Cardiff. Taken without the Prince's knowledge but shown following his consent, this very first film provoked much comment over the possible damage such pictures would do to the image of royalty. That the Prince was shown seemingly scratching his head was felt to attack the dignity of the monarchy and Acres was described by the popular press as a "photographic fiend". In his defence Acres pointed out that:

> . . . there are millions of British subjects all over the world who will probably never get the chance of seeing the Heir to the Throne of this Empire, and have to content themselves with ordinary portraits; but my invention makes it possible for millions in all parts of the world to see His Royal Highness and others exactly as they are, and move and have their being'.[1]

On 21 July 1896, Acres was invited to give an exhibition of his animated photographs to the Prince and Princess of Wales and their guests after a dinner given in honour of the marriage of Princess Maud to Prince Charles of Denmark. A marquee was erected in the grounds of Marlborough House and the royal party and their guests were entertained with a programme of twenty-one films, including *The Derby, 1896*, *The Boxing Kangaroo* and *Niagara Falls*. The highlight and conclusion of the performance was a showing of the film of the Prince and Princess of Wales in Cardiff. This was not the first time that Royalty had seen moving pictures. In May 1896, the Duke of York had seen the Lumière Cinématographe in Paris and, on 13 July, only a few days before the Marlborough House show, the Prince of Wales and the Duke of York had seen a film of the 1896 Derby at the Alhambra Theatre. This was, however, the first time that members of the royal family had the chance to see themselves on the screen: "The reception was most enthusiastic. as each of the royal family . . . recognized himself on the screen, moving just as in life, he burst into applause and merriment".[2]

The public's first opportunity to see Royalty on film came on 25 August when the film of the Cardiff visit was shown at the Metropolitan Music Hall in London's Edgware Road. A contemporary account noted that: "During the exhibition of the picture the orchestra played 'God Bless the Prince of Wales' and at the close the audience loudly cheered the operator and his work."[3]

Queen Victoria had always taken a keen interest in photography. In October 1896, the royal photographer, Downey, visited Balmoral in order to photograph the visit of the Tsar and Tsarina. Downey had recently acquired a cinematograph camera and requested the Queen's permission to take some animated photographs. The Queen's journal for 3 October records: "At twelve went down to below the terrace, near the ballroom, and we were all photographed by Downey by the new cinematograph process, which makes moving pictures by winding off a reel of films. We were walking up and down, and the children jumping about."

The Queen did not see the results of Downey's work until 23 November when she wrote in her journal: "After tea went to the Red Drawing-room, where so-called 'animated pictures' were shown off, including the groups taken in September [*sic*] at Balmoral. It is a very wonderful process, representing people, their movements and actions, as if they were alive." Nicholas and Alexandra's visit was very much a private affair and the film was never intended for public consumption. The following year, however, there occurred an event upon which the entire British film industry was to direct its undivided attention.

The procession through the streets of London on 22 June 1897 to celebrate Queen Victoria's Diamond Jubilee was covered by almost every film producer in Britain. Never before had an event been filmed so extensively. Films of the Jubilee procession were included in every dealer's list and were to appear on practically every programme. By the end of the year there could have been very few people who had not witnessed the event on screen. The importance of the Jubilee as a boost to the fledgling British film industry was profound. A comparison can be drawn with another royal occasion, over fifty years later, when the Coronation of Elizabeth II marked a watershed in the history of British television.

There was, of course, intense competition amongst producers to be the first to show their films. Robert Paul first included his Jubilee films in the programme at the Alhambra, Leicester Square, on 25 June but his efforts seem positively sluggish when compared with that of the Bradford firm of Appleton's who succeeded in getting a film of the event to Bradford in time for a public performance on the evening of the day itself. Reviews of Jubilee films were generally favourable and their importance did not go unrecognised:

> We owe much to the recent development of scientific photography; and by the invention of the cinematographe a means has been discovered for the preservation of what is to all intents and purposes living representations of memorable events.

Our descendants will be able to learn how the completion of the sixtieth year of Queen Victoria's reign was celebrated in the capital of the country. [4]

The Duke and Duchess of York visited the Alhambra on 14 August to see the Jubilee films. Queen Victoria herself, however, waited until 23 November, when a special command performance was given at Windsor Castle. She was not particularly impressed. Over the next few years film performances were to be given at most royal residences, including Balmoral, Sandringham and Buckingham Palace. After about 1907, when film was searching for social acceptance and beginning to find a home of its own, royal patronage of cinemas was very important in promoting the ethos of middle class respectability. Royalty began to go to the film rather than film come to Royalty. On 11 May 1912, for example, King George V and Queen Mary visited the Scala Theatre to see Charles Urban's Kinemacolor films of the Delhi Durbar.

The public's appetite for films of newsworthy events was such that if film of actual events could not be obtained then they would often be recreated for the camera. Such fake or sham actuality films were common in the early years of cinema. State occasions were not to be exempt. For the coronation of Edward VII in 1902, cameras were not allowed in Westminster Abbey. Undaunted, the Warwick Trading Company commissioned Georges Méliès to restage the ceremony for the camera. Méliès built a set of the interior of the Abbey in his garden at Montreuil and filmed the mock coronation with a waiter playing the role of the King. Such attempts at reproducing actual events were to find their greatest expression in films such as W. G. Barker's 1913 production, *Sixty Years A Queen*. This epic film of Victoria's reign covered events that were so recent as to hardly qualify as history and was conceived more as reconstruction than drama. Enormous care was taken to ensure historical accuracy and the cast were chosen for their resemblance to the characters they were playing. As *The Graphic* reported:

> The most ambitious attempt yet at 'filming' history is now being carried out by an English manufacturer of motion pictures, the idea being to illustrate the life of

Queen Victoria from her Coronation until the end of her reign. Historical accuracy is being adhered to in every detail, and when the film is finished, a matter of many months, it will be submitted to experts in the history of the period, any part pronounced inaccurate being re-cast and re-photographed.' [5]

The First World War was to bring about irrevocable changes in the fortunes of Royalty in Europe. In Britain, too, the status of the monarchy and their imperial role was never again to approach that of the last years of Victoria's reign. Increasingly aware of the enormous power of the cinema, monarchs now had to work with the media and cultivate the image of them that it put forward. As Stephen Bottomore has keenly observed: "modern society had seen a fundamental shift of emphasis from the royal palace to the picture palace".

1. Letter to *The Globe*, 31 August 1896.
2. *Daily Mail*, 31 July 1896.
3. *Cardiff Western Mail*, 26 August 1896.
4. *The Era*, 24 July 1897.
5. *The Graphic*, 30 August 1913, p. 413.

ed. G. R. Buckle
The Letters of Queen Victoria
1932, pp. 87–88, 105

BALMORAL, 3RD OCT. 1896. At twelve went down to below the terrace, near the ball-room, and we were all photographed by Downey by the new cinematograph process, which makes moving pictures by winding off a reel of films. We were walking up and down and the children jumping about. Then took a turn in the pony chair, and not far from the garden cottage Nicky and Alicky planted a tree. In the afternoon drove out with them, alas! for the last time, and went to Invercauld and back by the Balloch Bhui. It was rather showery and dark. Took tea with them on coming home. We dined *en famille*, including Daisy and Patsy, at a quarter to nine.

At ten dear Nicky and Alicky left, to my great regrets, as I as so fond of them both. Arthur and Louischen went with them and are going abroad. The girls remain here. Went to the door to see our dear visitors leave. There was again the Highlanders bearing torches but no pipes.

23rd Nov.—After tea went to the Red Drawing-room, where so called 'animated pictures' were shown off, including the groups taken in September at Balmoral. It is a very wonderful process, representing people, their movements and actions, as if they were alive.

THE ROYAL PROCESSION

Reproduced in Bradford
Animated Photographs

at

The *Argus* Office

A Unique Exhibition and a
Triumph in Science

The Bradford Daily Argus
23 June 1897

LOYAL BRADFORD, BRAVE YESTERDAY in its Jubilee decorations and enthusiastically celebrating the long and happy reign of the Queen, as well as the city honour which Her Majesty has graciously been pleased to confer on this year of jubilee of the incorporation, was the only city in the United Kingdom whose people had the privilege of seeing with their own eyes a vivid reproduction of the magnificent ceremony which had that day taken place in the Metropolis. From the cinematograph at the *Argus* office was flashed forth before midnight a living picture of the pageant which stirred the heart of the whole Empire to the depths, and aroused in every patriotic heart a feeling of deepened and affectionate fealty to the Queen, and all the ideals that she embodies as a good woman. No such additional incentive was needed to arouse the loyalty of the masses who filled Bradford streets until the early hours of the morning, but the cheering with which the crowds greeted the moving panorama of London's pageant, and the heartiness of the strains of the National Anthem which it evoked, were eloquent proofs that on the great question of fealty to the throne, to the Empire, and to the flag, the heart of the people of this district beat high.

The exhibition of the cinematograph as the *Argus* office, which will be represented in a greater state to-night, possesses several unique features, apart from the small lapses of time between the London procession and its photographic representation here. It is the first exhibition which has been afforded gratuitously to the public of Bradford, and it is an instance of enterprise in journalism which the progressive citizens of Bradford may be relied upon to thoroughly appreciate. The chief idea of the *Argus* management was to obtain a continuous photograph of the Queen's Jubilee Pageant in London, and to reproduce the great event for the edification of Bradfordians the same evening, a feat of evening journalism which will bear comparison with any of the up-to-date attributes of 1897. Not content with publishing a long description of the historic parade,

Poster advertising animated photographs of Queen Victoria's Diamond Jubilee, 1897.
National Museum of Photography, Film & Television.

The Bradford Daily Argus, actually gave a series of pictures which portrayed the changing scenes in all their vividness and picturesque effects. To bring about this achievement plans had been very carefully prepared. A couple of the best seats along route of the procession were secured in the name of the *Argus*, on the magnificent stand which Sir Westman Pearson had erected for the benefit of St. George's Church, and there, amid the great excitement which characterised the festive occasion Mr. R. J Appleton and his son, of the well known Bradford firm of photographers, added further to their efforts in the advancement of that particular phase of scientific research . . . The operators secured a good negative, and with that treasure in their close keeping they left the busy scene, and hastened across London to St. Pancras. At the station all was in readiness to carry out the scheme which had been devised at much labour and expense during the week. Special arrangements had been entered into with the Midland Railway Company to facilitate transit, and the work of completing the undertaking. A carriage had been expressly reserved for the purpose. This carriage had been arranged and provided with apparatus, and although the area was very limited, and the motion more eccentric than agreeable, the accommodation was utilised to the best advantage as a laboratory. Some hundreds of people crowded round to see the operators transfer their strange impediments to the dungeon-like compartment, and to gaze upon the mystic legend, *The Bradford Daily Argus* 'Photographic Laboratory', and when the huge milkcan full of water was hoisted into the carriage to provide the liquid for the 'bathe', there was much speculation as to the capacity of the two men who could 'drink all that'. The label was read with curiosity wherever the train stopped. As soon as they had settled themselves in their new quarters Messrs. Appleton proceeded to develop the film which bore the

Thousands of Photographs

intended to be reproduced in Bradford the same night, and as the train sped on from the Metropolis to the City of Bradford, they were kept busily and constantly engaged. This process of development was an extremely irksome part of the process, for the carriage had been made light-tight and practically air-tight as well. When the reader bears in mind how hot the weather was yesterday afternoon he may have some little conception of the heat in that dark and ill-ventilated space wherein the work was being conducted. Despite the difficulties, however, the process successfully accomplished, and by exercises of great care and skill the artists were enabled to slowly but surely draw nearer and nearer to the object of their efforts . . . So it was that the realistic and animated view of the procession of Her Majesty through London was shown to Bradfordians

With a Few Hours

of the actual happening of the function as seen by millions of people in London . . . As the hour at which the London train was due drew nigh there was a feeling of great expectation manifested. When ultimately the life-like pictures of the Queen was seen driving through the streets of London with her brilliant escort and pageantry, and the *Argus* orchestra struck up 'God Save the Queen', the thousands of onlookers joined in the National Anthem with great heartiness. The difficulty of producing the cinematograph pictures and the general blaze of illuminations in Forster Square may be readily conceived, but the precautions and the provisions for an efficient display were on a complete scale, and the whole scheme was worked out with a success which was in the highest degree gratifying.

The whole of the street which leads to the *Argus* publishing department had been covered in, and stretching across this improvised roofing was the picture-screen, an immense sheet of whiteness upon which the pictures were so excellently represented that the exhibition could be seen to advantage last evening, both from the front and from behind it.

There was a changing crowd of

Many Thousands of People

to witness the proceedings and the exhibition was by general consent voted a huge success.

John Munro
**'Living Photographs of
the Queen'**
Cassell's Family Magazine
July 1897

I CONFESS THAT I AM STRONGLY tempted to write a glowing description of the now historic pageant which so many of us had the good fortune to watch last month and enjoy; but the eloquent journalist who never employs one word if six will do, has already flooded the land with streams of print, and I shall only try to give an account of a certain humble onlooker. He was the possessor of a glass eye and a mechanical brain and he passed almost unnoticed in the crowd. Nevertheless, he observed more sharply than the vigilant pressman, and furnished a truer report of the ceremony than any shorthand notes—I mean the animatographe.

No doubt, many of our readers know something about the character of the automatic spectator, who is destined to play an important part in life and literature by treasuring up the 'fleeting shows' of the world for the delight of thousands in distant countries and in future ages; but I shall probably be forgiven if I devote a few words to it by way of introduction.

When a boy whirls a firebrand in the darkness he sees a continuous ring of light—bright golden hoop, as it were. Why so? Because an image lingers for the tenth of a second on the retina of the eye and the spark at the end of the brand glides so rapidly through the air that all images which it leaves on the eye appear blended into one. For the same reason, when we are travelling by a fast train, we can see the country pretty well across the rails of a fence. The glimpses which we get through the gaps in the fence are superposed and combined into a single view. Obviously, then, if we can bring a number of separate pictures or photographs of the same scene before the eye, with sufficient quickness they will coalesce on the retina and seem one picture. Moreover, if the object is living or moving, and the pictures represent it in successive instants, the resulting picture will seem to be animated or in movement. This, of course, is done in the old and well-known toy called a zoetrope, or 'wheel of life'. The zoetrope is the germ of the animatographe, but it is only the germ. It has about as much resemblance to the animatographe as a costermonger's donkey bears to a winner of the Derby, such as Persimmon. In the zoetrope you have crude pictures wheeling past the eye. In the animatographe you have instantaneous photographs taken on a transparent film, magnified thousands of times and projected by a beam of light upon a distant screen after the manner of a magic lantern, so that a large number of persons can see the object full size, living and moving, so to speak, before them.

Mr. R. W. Paul, of Hatton Garden, has brought his animatographe to great perfection and his living photographs of the royal pageant are the finest I, for one, have ever seen. They were taken from three positions, and give a much more interesting and artistic effect than if they had been obtained at a single point of the route . . .

The first of the films . . . were taken at the corner of York Road, Westminster and shows the head of the procession with the gigantic Captain Ames leading his troopers, the colonial procession and the Canadian and other troopers, and the royal cavalcade. The next two were taken by Mr. Paul himself from a window on the south side of St. Paul's Churchyard, and represents the Cape Mounted Rifles passing St. Paul's, the dragoons, the arrival of the royal cavalcade and princes, the Indian escort, and the Queen's carriage entering the Churchyard. The fourth also depicts Her Majesty's arrival at St. Paul's, but from the opposite point of view, and was taken by Mr. Hunt, one of Mr. Paul's assistants, from the front of the Maskelyne pavilion, on the north side of the Churchyard. Not until the service was begun and everybody kept their places was the ordinary camera sufficient to portray the ceremony.

Let us now glance for a moment at the interior of the animatographe which Mr. Paul has kindly opened for our inspection and which was photographed for our illustration. It is, of course, a camera, but of a special construction and the film on which the instantaneous photographs are taken is not a fixed plate, but a moving ribbon or band or transparent celluloid, made particularly sensitive in order that good pictures may be obtained even under a cloudy sky. Luckily, the Clerk of the Weather is an official who understands what her Majesty requires, and, as we all know, the sun shone bravely as she approached St. Paul's, so that with the help of 'stops' to the lenses, the pictures were of a marvellous distinctness.

The film is drawn past the object glass by means of an electric motor of one-eight horse-power, and passes from an upper reel, or spool, to a lower. In doing so it is carried past the object glass by a train of wheel-work, the holes along its edges engaging in the teeth of several wheels. A tachometer, or speed indicator, tells the number of pictures being taken in second or any moment, and a revolution counter shows the number taken during the whole time the instrument is at work. There is also a view 'finder' which gives a horizontal picture on a screen of ground glass corresponding to that impressed on the film, and shows the photographer what he is to expect. The working speed of the camera, that is to say the number of pictures taken in a second, is controlled by altering the strength of the electric current, and consequently the power of the motor, by a switch and 'rheostat' which is a sort of sluice-gate for the current.

The camera could be slewed horizontally so as to follow a moving object and keep it in the centre of the field of vision by means of a horizontal worm wheel. It could also be tilted in any direction with the aid of a spherical seat on a short tripod which supported it. In brief it was under complete management. Now as to the method of eclipsing the light and thus taking a row of separate pictures on the same film. This was done by a revolving shutter between the film and the object glass. It was revolved by the wheelwork that moved the film and once in every revolution it cut off the light for an instant. About thirty pictures were taken in a second or, in other words, from 1,500 to 2,500 a minute which is so much faster than the twinkling of an eye.

This remarkable instrument could take a series of such pictures for half an hour at an stretch. It contained 2,500 feet of the film, and, as sixteen pictures go into a foot, it was capable of taking 40,000 pictures. The adjoining illustration shows the inventor Mr. Paul putting it in operation.

The development of the negative photographs taken in this way was begun on the morning after the ceremony (Pardon the word, O generous reader! for although it has been done to death of late, I cannot think of a better), and a complete set of positives taken from them was ready on Thursday evening. These positives were taken on a similar celluloid film and are exact copies of the original negatives. Each of them is one inch long and three-fourths of an inch wide, or about the size of a postage stamp, as it will be seen from our reproductions. Next evening, on Friday, June 25th, they were shown, amidst the greatest enthusiasm, to an immense audience at a well-known theatre, before Prince Rudolph of Austria, a detachment of the Bornco Native Police, and others who had taken part in the actual procession three days before.

For this purpose they were it is needless to say, magnified enormously and thrown upon a great white screen, so that everybody in the amphitheatre could see, by an apparatus like that shown in the accompanying illustration. Essentially it is merely a camera like that which we have already described, but it works backwards, if we may so express it. The transparent film, with its row of positive pictures, is drawn past the object glass by a train of wheels, and a powerful beam from electric arc lantern is sent through it in such a manner as to project the picture on the screen. The picture is magnified 56,000 times in the process, and from a miniature the size of a postage stamp becomes a life-like view, nearly twenty feet wide.

By this time these living pictures of the Queen have evoked the loyalty and admiration of many thousands of Her Majesty's faithful subjects of all races and in every clime, thousands out of the hundreds of millions whose thoughts were turned towards her on that memorable day. But it is not only the present generation which will have the opportunity of seeing them. Mr. Paul has taken steps to lodge a series of pictures in the British Museum. The films will be packed in asbestos, and sealed in glass tubes, in order to preserve them for the gratification of posterity.

Still from *Sixty Years a Queen*, 1913.

The Times
9 December 1913

SIXTY YEARS A QUEEN

A Pictorial Record of the Victorian Era

A PUBLIC PRODUCTION OF AN IMPORTANT cinematograph film is rapidly becoming as interesting a social function as a theatrical 'first-night'. Last night *Sixty Years a Queen*, the pictorial record of the Victorian era which has been arranged by the Barker Motion Company (Limited), was given at the New Gallery Kinema, and an audience thoroughly representative of many phases of London life gave the new film a notably enthusiastic welcome. We have not the slightest doubt that this series will long stand out as one of the most remarkable accomplishments in English cinematography, for the amount of Labour that has been put into the film is beyond comprehension until one has actually seen it. It is impossible to conceive any other way in which in two hours, the leading events of a reign of 60 years could be marshalled and passed before the onlooker in a series of vivid and abiding pictures. The mere work of singling out the incidents considered worthy to represent an era crammed with events of historic magnitude must have been enormous, but the task of recreating those scenes with their wealth of detail sounds an impossible one. After the enthusiastic applause which greeted the pictures last night, however, it will be generally conceded that the Barker Motion Company have carried through to success their great undertaking.

The scenes open with the announcement to the Queen of the death of William IV, and cover every conceivable kind of happening until her Jubilee in 1887—her Coronation, her engagement and marriage, the attempt on her life by John Francis, the christening of the Prince of Wales, the departure of troops for the Crimea, the opening of the International Exhibition of 1851, the inauguration of the first National Rifle Association meeting at Wimbledon, and the thanksgiving service in St. Paul's Cathedral for the recovery of the Prince of Wales. But it is not merely the incidents of her reign at home which are depicted, for there are stirring scenes of the Indian Mutiny, and the death of General Gordon, while the horror of life in the trenches during the Crimean War is shown with almost painful realism. After the Jubilee there is a big jump in the sequence of events from 1887 to 1900, due possibly to considerations of time, but in the closing moments of the film there are incidents of the defence and relief of Ladysmith and a beautiful scene showing the aged Queen reading peacefully in her garden at Osborne, which is portrayed with great charm by the unnamed actress to whom the part of Queen Victoria was entrusted. *Sixty Years a Queen* is an all-British production, and it affords welcome proof that the British film manufacturer nowadays has not the slightest reason to fear the competition of his foreign rivals.

"Early 'news-reel': *Queen Victoria's Funeral*, 1901. King Edward VII, hearing the camera, stops the cortège." From *Came the Dawn* by Cecil Hepworth.

Daily Mail
31 July 1896

THE KINEMATOGRAPH'S INVENTOR
His Royal Highness Albert Edward of Wales and Mr. Birt Acres

SCIENTISTS AND THE PUBLIC AT LARGE are just as considerably agog over that very entertaining instrument, the kinematograph and its developments. It is curious to learn, writes a Daily Mail representative, that the kinematograph is not an invention of either an American or a Frenchman, as every one supposes, but of an Englishman.

The name of this English inventor is Mr Birt Acres, and the credit of calling public attention to this fact belongs to none other than his royal highness the Prince of Wales.

The story of this invention is most curious, but the story of the life of the inventor is even more so.

I found Mr. Birt Acres in his workshop just after his return from Marlborough House, where he had exhibited his invention before many members of the royal family at the express personal desire of the Prince. He is a tall, broad-shouldered man, with clear blue eyes and a simple, engaging manner. He seemed a little embarrassed at my visit and said that newspaper notoriety was the last thing he had striven for, and, as for one of his inventions, the kinematograph, he had long been content to let others claim the honour, believing that in the end things would right themselves. He has never tried to exploit himself commercially, he added; he has been too busy.

"I commenced to devote myself to inventions when I was only ten years of age", said Mr. Acres, in response to a question, "and I am still at it at 40. One of my first devices was a centre-board for a yacht, which I employed and subsequently abandoned. One day, many years after, an American yacht-builder showed me the scheme of his new patent centre board, and, strange as it may seem, I recognised my own invention, after so long a period."

"How did you come to think of the kinematograph?"

"It was in this way. Years ago—I shouldn't care to say how many—I constructed an elaborate sort of zoetrope—which is the guiding principle, you know, of the kinetoscope. I have devoted myself to photography in all its branches, until I have now thoroughly mastered its very detail, and the application of photography to the zoetrope was, as I may say, a process of evolution. When I had completed my screen-kinetoscope I determined to show it before the Royal Photographic Society, of which I am a member. This was last August, many months before M. Lumiere's invention was exhibited. The society, like most bodies of its kind, is very conservative, but when I had projected my first picture, a boxing match on the screen, they burst into such laughter and cheering that made me doubt whether I was in Hanover Square or a music hall."

"What then became of your invention?"

Mr. Acres seemed to desire to change the subject, when pressed, he said: "I do not like to indulge in recriminations. All I can do is to claim that I was first in the field, as the minutes of the Photographic Society will amply show. I went to Cardiff and made a series of kinematographic photos of the Prince of Wales and the royal family there. Later on his royal highness, expressing great interest in my invention, had a marquee erected for my express use in the grounds of Marlborough House, and it was there, on the eve of the royal wedding, that I exhibited the many animated pictures I have taken."

"Were they well received?"

"The reception was most enthusiastic. As each of the royal family, including Prince and Princess Charles of Denmark, recognised himself on the screen, moving just as in life, he burst into applause and merriment. Afterwards I was graciously permitted to make photographs of royalty performing various actions; and these the public will see perhaps in due course. I need hardly say they are most lifelike."

Nothing can exceed the interest and pains which Mr. Acres takes in his work. In his eyes the kinematograph is not a toy, but a method of instruction and historical record hardly as yet appreciated. *London Mail.*

CINEMATOSCOPED ROYALTY

Sir,

As I am the "photographic fiend" alluded in your article headed 'Cinematoscoped Royalty' I should be glad if you would allow space for some explanation. The series of photographs of HRH the Prince and Princess of Wales and Princesses Victoria and Maud, taken at Cardiff, were certainly taken without the knowledge of the Royal party; but before these photographs were exhibited to anyone I submitted a complete copy (about two thousand photographs) to his Royal Highness, with the result that I was invited to show these pictures and others at Marlborough House on the night before the wedding of the Princess Maud to the guests assembled at the dinner party given by his Royal Highness in honour of the wedding. I showed 21 separate series of pictures taken from life, including Niagara Falls, the opening of the Kiel Canal, Henley Regatta, the Derby of 1895, and also the Derby of 1896, finishing up with the series that has called forth your article. The result was that it was well received, and although the Royal Party had sat through three-quarters of an hour of animated photographs, an encore was required for this series. At the conclusion of the demonstration His Royal Highness gave me special and exclusive permission to take a series of animated photographs in grounds of Marlborough House on the following (wedding) day, and I succeeded in obtaining several excellent pictures. The allusion to his Royal Highness scratching his head is wrong in fact. the movement referred to is simply a momentary placing of the hand to the ear, probably to brush away an intrusive fly. There is, however, another side of the question which you quite overlook, and that is that there are millions of British subjects all over the world, who will probably never get the chance of seeing the Heir to the Throne of this Empire, and have to content themselves with ordinary portraits; but my invention makes is possible for millions in all parts of the world to see His Royal Highness and others exactly as they are, and move and have their being. I have always aimed at taking interesting historical events, and not going in for comic knock-about scenes.

I am, yours faithfully

Birt Acres

Fellow of the Royal Meteorological Society.
Fellow of the Royal Photographic Society.
Hedley, Herts, August 29.

Birt Acres and his wife, no date.
National Museum of Photography, Film & Television

Photography
30 July 1896

ANIMATED PHOTOGRAPHS AT MARLBOROUGH HOUSE

O N TUESDAY EVENING, THE 21ST INST., Mr. Birt Acres had, by command of HRH the Prince of Wales, through Sir Dighton Probyn, the honour of giving an exhibition of some of animated photographs. The demonstration was given in a specially arranged marquee in the grounds of Marlborough House, and took place after the dinner given by their Royal Highnesses the Prince and Princess of Wales in honour of the marriage of HRH the Princess Maud of Wales to HRH Prince Charles of Denmark, the following being present:

Their Royal Highnesses Prince and Princess of Wales, Crown Prince and Princess of Denmark, Duke and Duchess of Sparta, Prince and Princess Christian of Schleswig-Holstein, Princess Victoria of Schleswig-Holstein, Princess Louise (Marchioness of Lorne) and the Marquis of Lorne, the Duchess of Albany, Princess Elizabeth of Waldeck Pyrmont, Prince Christian of Denmark, Prince Charles of Denmark, Prince Harold of Denmark, Princess Ingeborg of Denmark, Princess Thyra of Denmark, the Duke and Duchess of York, Princess Louise (Duchess of Fife) and the Duke of Fife, Princess Victoria and Princess Maud of Wales, Prince and Princess Philip of Saxe-Coburg, Prince and Princess Frederick of Schaumberg-Lippe, the Duke of Cambridge, Prince Christian Victor of Schelswig-Holstein, Prince and Princess Edward of Saxe-Weimar, Duke of Teck, Princess Victoria of Hohenlohe-Langenburg, Countess Feodora and Helena Gleichen, Prince and Princess Adolphus of Teck, Count Gleichen, etc., etc., making in all a total of about seventy-five.

The programme consisted of twenty-one pictures, as follows:

1. *Capstone Parade, Ilfracombe.*
2. *Children playing.*
3. *Great Northern Railway; Departure of an East Coast Express.*
4. *The Derby, 1895.*
5. *Niagara Falls* (in three tableaux). No. 1. 'The Upper River just below the Falls'. No. 2. 'The Falls in Winter'. No. 3. 'The Whirlpool Rapids'.
6. *The German Emperor reviewing his Guard previous to the opening of the Kiel Canal, June 1895.*
7. *Carpenter's shop.* Scene, 'Refreshments'.
8. *The Boxing Kangaroo.*
9. *The Hunt of a Pickpocket.*
10. *A visit to the 'Zoo'.*
11. *Yarmouth fishing boats leaving Harbour.*
12. *Golf extraordinary.*
13. *Tom Merry (Lightning Artist) drawing Mr. Gladstone.*
14. *Lord Salisbury.*
15. *Boxing match in two rounds by Sergt. Instructor Barrett and Sergt. Pope.*
16. *Highgate Tunnel.*
17. *Henley Regatta.*
18. *The Derby, 1896*: 'Clearing the Course'; 'The Preliminary Parade'; 'The Race'; '"Persimmon" Wins'; 'Wild enthusiasm, hats waving, etc.'
19. *Broadway, New York.*
20. *A "South-wester"*
21. *HRH The Prince of Wales, accompanied by T. R. H. The Princess of Wales, Princess Victoria, and Princess Maud, arriving at the Cardiff Exhibition, June 27th 1896.*

All the pictures were received with applause, but in the last picture Royalty recognised themselves as they had never been portrayed before, the result being that this picture was enthusiastically received, and as their Royal Highnesses were shown life size on the screen, and the portraits were clear and distinct, this last picture had to be repeated, although the programme was such a long one.

At the conclusion, HRH the Prince of Wales personally thanked Mr. Birt Acres for the exhibition.

The disc thrown on the screen was perhaps the largest ever attempted in this class of work, measuring nearly 11ft. by 8ft. 6in.

Mr. Acres obtained permission from HRH the Prince of Wales to take kinetic photographs at Marlborough House on the following day (the wedding of Princess Maud with Prince Charles), and succeeded in obtaining excellent pictures of the departure of the wedding party from Marlborough House, the return of the Royal wedding party after the ceremony at Buckingham Palace, and finally taking up his position on the lawn at Marlborough House, obtained an excellent picture of the departure of the Royal couple for Sandringham.

Mr. Birt Acres says that he cannot speak too highly of the uniform kindness exhibited towards him by their Royal Highnesses, every facility having been granted by him to ensure satisfactory results, both at the exhibition of pictures on Tuesday night and in taking the photographs on the wedding day.

Still from *The Royal Family at Afternoon Tea in the Garden of Clarence House*, 1897.
National Museum of Photography, Film & Television.

*The British Journal
of Photography*
(Supplement)
4 February 1898

M R. BIRT ACRES SHOWED his ingenious little instrument, the Birtac, to a large audience at the Croydon Camera Club on 25th inst. Subsequently, in acknowledging the vociferated thanks of his audience, Mr. Birt Acres told how, when he was asked to photograph the arrival of HRH the Prince of Wales to open the Cardiff Photographic Exhibition, and was shown where the ceremony was to be held, he said it was impossible to kinematograph the function, "for it would necessitate knocking a hole in the wall". To his surprise, the Exhibition Committee immediately ordered the wall to be partly demolished! Subsequently the moving picture was, by special command, shown before eighty guests—half of whom were princes and princesses—at Marlborough House, where all at once the whole assemblage burst into hearty laughter. He (Mr. Birt Acres) could not imagine what could be the reason. However, the Duke of York, with sailor-like impetuosity, exclaimed "We must show that again!" And they did. On the second time of showing it, Mr. Birt Acres kept his eye on the scene, and when he saw HRH step from the carriage, and consequent possibly on the kinematográph being at work, pause for a moment in doubt, push aside his hat, and seek with the same hand for inspiration amongst the locks of his head, the Royal amusement was explained. Any one who has ever noticed his little trick, which seems to be characteristic of His Royal Highness, will better appreciate the joke, and realise how little personal habits passed unnoticed become so drolly noticeable when projected on the screen.

The Chester Observer
20 March 1897

THE CINEMATOGRAPHE AT CHESTER PANTOMIME
Alleged Miserable Exhibition

H IS HONOUR SIR HORATIO LLOYD was occupied several hours at Chester County Court on Thursday in the hearing of an action brought on James William Carter, proprietor of the Royalty Theatre, Chester, against Maurice Edward Bandmann and Robert Malcolm Wallace, of London, to recover £15 damages for nonfulfillment of contract in connection with the recent engagement of the cinematographe at the Royalty Theatre. Mr. E. Brassey was for the plaintiff, and Mr. S. Moss (barrister) represented the defendants.

Mr. Brassey said that after the Chester pantomime had run a few weeks, Mr. Carter was looking about for fresh attractions, and his eye lighted upon an advertisement of the cinematographe as the 'same machine as shown at Marlborough House by special command, and highly commended by His Royal Highness the Prince of Wales. This is the only machine showing a distinct picture of the Prince, which was taken by his permission.' As the result of the correspondence, Mr. Carter engaged with the defendants to give an exhibition of the cinematographe of eight performances of the pantomime for 25 guineas. It was agreed that no less than 12 high-class pictures, including that of the 'distinct picture of the Prince' should be sent with the machine. At four o'clock in the afternoon of the 1st February a man turned up at Chester Theatre from Liverpool with the machine, and the screen itself a dirty rag. The performance was a wretched affair, and could easily have been beaten by an ordinary magic lantern. Only seven films instead of twelve were shown, and the films appeared to be worn out, as the pictures were all blurred. One scene depicted a race, and it was a good job the stewards of the Jockey Club were not present, else a number of persons would have been ordered off the course. (Laughter.) The horses started at the winning post and ran in the wrong direction, to the amusement of the audience. (Renewed laughter.) 'The only distinct picture of the Prince of Wales' was absolutely unrecognisable, and the machine made a disagreeable vibrating noise. The whole thing was a disgrace, and Mr. Carter was so grumbled at about the exhibition that he wired to the defendants stating that the exhibition was a failure, and the films agreed upon had not been shown. The defendants wired that they would send another machine and a man to work it, and the exhibition would be perfect afterwards. The new machine did come and although it was an improvement it did not comply with the terms of the contract. After the expiry of the engagement the defendants wrote saying that they had ascertained that the cause of Mr. Carter's so-called disappointment was that the exhibition was fixed at such a time as not to leave sufficient time for the operator to get his apparatus ready. They now found that there was no reason for Mr. Carter's complaint, and no necessity for their sending another machine.

James Wm. Carter, the plaintiff, stated that on account of the exorbitant price he paid for the cinematograph, he expected to do very good business that week, and he largely advertised it, incurring about £19 special expenses in this respect. When the man arrived at four o'clock with the machine, witness asked him why he was so late, and he said he had been on a spree all the week with the manager of a Liverpool Theatre, and he looked like it. (Laughter.) The effect of the pictures on the sheet was disgraceful in every respect. The pictures might have done very well for a bazaar or a Sunday school treat. (Laughter.)

Cross-examined: He considered that his reputation as a theatrical manager had been damaged by this cinematograph.

Robert Jones Williams went to see the cinematographe either on the Thursday or Friday. He sat in the stalls. He only saw five film. He had seen the cinematographe in London. The pictures shown at the Royalty Theatre were all very poor, wretched thing, and most confused except the train picture and that was rather good. The Prince of Wales was not shown.

Wm. Mulliner, City Road, John Henry Price, John Sadler, scenic artist, and Wm. Fox, stage carpenter, also gave evidence.

Ernest. J. Pritchard, assistant manager, said there was an exceptional delay in the throwing of the pictures on the sheet, and the exhibition was most unsatisfactory.

One of the defendants, Maurice Edward Bandmann, theatrical manager, London, then gave evidence.

Harold Aylmer said he came to Chester with the machine on the occasion in question, arriving between one and two o'clock. It was not true he was under the influence of drink, or that he told Mr. Carter he had been on the spree. The stage arrangements were not such as to enable him to give a perfect show. He was not allowed sufficient time to make his arrangements, and another thing that militated against the success of the exhibition was that he could only get soft lime instead of hard lime as was necessary.

Cross-examined: He considered the display at Chester was a first-class one with the exception of the first night.

J. W. Campbell, manager to the defendants, deposed to coming to Chester and seeing the show, at which he was very satisfied.

Mr. Moss, for the defence, said there could be no doubt that on the Monday night there was some defect in the performance, but that was caused entirely by the defective arrangements of the plaintiff, which did not permit the fixing of the machine. The reason twelve pictures were not shown at the first two nights was that the advisability of not occupying too much time was impressed upon the electrician in charge of the machine (Mr. Aylmer) by Mr. Kemble, who they alleged, though the plaintiff denied it, was Mr. Carter's stage manager. Possibly the show had not come up to the advertisement, but he maintained that defendants had fully carried out their contract.

His Honour reserved judgement.

Slide for projection. Walturdaw Co. Ltd. catalogue, 1911.

Daily Telegraph
20 June 1902

THE CORONATION BY CINEMATOGRAPH

ON THE NIGHT OF THE CORONATION at many theatres and places of entertainment throughout the country there will be on exhibition a 'living' photographic representation of the ceremonial at Westminster Abbey. It may at once be frankly explained that, in respect of all out-of-door pageantry, the records will be the faithful reproduction of the moving incidents of the day. But up to the present science has failed to solve the problem of registering upon the sensitive surface of even the most rapid film the light and shade of a picture which will, at the best, be viewed in a dull light. Even the wonderful fluid lens of Dr. Grün cannot master the difficulties, and, notwithstanding that Dallmeyer has produced an optical objective 'working' at F. 1, this large aperture would be comparatively useless in the 'dim, religious light' of the Abbey. In actual fact, a photograph could not be taken in the interior, with the most rapid lens obtainable, in less than three minutes, and, having regard to the exclusion of daylight by the surrounding structures, artificial light equivalent to 50,000-candle power would be required for cinematograph purposes. Though recourse may be had to electricity as an illuminant to a limited degree in the transepts, there never has been any hope of utilising it to the extend demanded by the instantaneous camerist.

Another difficulty presented itself—that of the impossibility of employing an absolutely silent machine. Obviously, the whirr of wheels would be altogether out of keeping with the solemnity of the occasion. Yet it was recognised by the authorities that a pictorial record would have a value of its own, and would be appreciated by hundreds of thousands of people who would have necessarily to depend upon written descriptions of the historic scene, supplemented by the

Georges Méliès's *The Coronation of Edward,* 1902. *BFI Stills, Posters and Designs*

Charles Urban (centre) with cameramen at the Delhi Durbar, 1911. *BFI Stills, Posters and Designs.*

impressions of this artist or that. There was only one way to accomplish this result—to photograph a rehearsal. But again the difficulties applied, rendered, indeed, all the greater by the unfavourable climatic influences prevailing, and the only course left open was to 'reconstitute' the scene, or, rather, intelligently to anticipate events, with every official assistance. Then came a question of the locale of this representation, and the superior actinic light—the governing feature of the problem—at command in France led to the transfer of the whole operation across the Channel.

It was at Montreuil, fourteen miles from Paris, that a huge 'property' Westminster Abbey was built up, at great expense, the whole front being left open to the daylight. The point of sight was chosen so as to give a view of the High Altar, the theatre, the entire north transept, with its great window, and a part of the choir stalls, with two of the four great pillars in the centre of the church. The camera occupied a position corresponding to that of a peer in the south transept—one of the very few spectators who will actually view the details of the ceremonial. In constructing the scene regard was had to the necessities of photography, while the actual lighting of the subject was preserved. Real and very substantial galleries were constructed for the peeresses, and above them, the members of the House of Commons, with their wives. Other spectators were seated in the triforium. But, by the illusion of scenic art, the first rows only of the chairs were actually filled with representatives of the nobility of England robed in crimson and ermine. One of the most startling effects of the display is at the moment when the duchesses and countesses assume their coronets. the ceremony itself, however, is taken as the main subject. Mr. Urban, the managing director of the Warwick Trading Company, was his own operator, and he was guided throughout by the desire to give a faithful transcript of the ceremonial in all its essential details, but confining himself to that portion only which was capable of being recorded by the lens. Actually it was found that in seven minutes the chief incidents could be enacted, and therefore photographed. Amateur photographers may be interested to know that a lens of no greater aperture than F. 5.6—such as many hand cameras have—was necessary, the focus being 2¾ inches, and that 350 feet of film was used up, pictures being taken at the rate of sixteen per second. Of course, these are very small—the size of a postage stamp— but the definition is so very good that great magnification is possible upon the bioscope screen.

In matters of detail the camera does not lie. Therefore the outlay upon the incidentals of the picture has been great—about £1,200. Thus the representative of the King has been dressed in Field Marshal's uniform, complete to the last order, and the portrait of the Earl Marshal is astounding in its fidelity. Uniforms, robes, ribands, crowns, coronets, and jewels had all to be supplied, from data verified to the day of the mimic Coronation—Saturday last. And, although the picture is necessarily in black and white, regard was paid to the difference of colour, the King being arrayed first in crimson robes, and then clothed with the Imperial mantle. Cloth of gold was specially obtained, and nothing was left to the imagination which came within 'principal focus'. All the theatres of Paris were drawn upon for the actors and actresses, and rehearsals were carried out with the exactitude of the Théâtre Français or the mise-en-scène of the Opera, in anticipation of a gala night. One hundred and fifty artists travelled by special train to Montreuil daily, and so perfect were they in their parts that Mr. Urban suddenly determined to 'take' the last rehearsal on his film. A trial bit of it was developed in the darkroom on the spot, and it was found so satisfactory that the rest was brought to London and was put in hand the same night, with the result that every picture was found perfect, each negative beautifully graded, promising most pleasing results upon the screen.

It was considered advisable to begin the photographic record with the Presentation of the King at the four corners of the Theatre, when the Archbishop of Canterbury (together with the lord Chancellor, the Lord Great Chamberlain, the Lord High Constable, and the Earl Marshal) speaks to the people, the King meanwhile standing up by his chair, the Archbishop saying, "Sirs, I here present to you King Edward, the undoubted King of this realm; wherefore, all of you

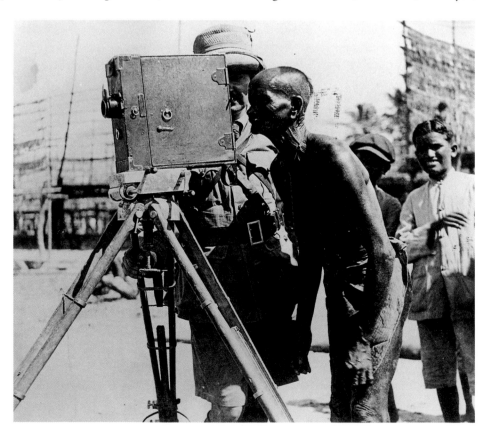

Filming the Delhi Durbar, 1911.
National Museum of Photography,
Film & Television.

who are come this day to do your homage, are you willing to do the same?" To which the people cry, "God Save King Edward", whilst the trumpeters sound a fanfare. His Majesty is then seen going to the 'chair of repose', placed for him, with a second for the Queen, south of the altar. In the bioscope representation the Regalia is now borne to the altar and deposited thereon. The Coronation oath is administered, his Majesty is relieved of his crimson robe, and is conducted to St. Edward's Chair, while four Knights of the Garter hold over him a pall of cloth of gold. The Dean of Westminster proceeds to take the ampulla and spoon from the altar, and the Archbishop anoints the King on the head and breast and hands. His Majesty is then clothed with the Colobium Sindonis and the Supertunica, and is girt with the sword by the Lord Great Chamberlain, which is afterwards placed upon the altar and redeemed by the Swordbearer. The King comes forward under the golden canopy, and he is clothed with the Imperial mantle, and, sitting down, receives the orb, the ring, and the Royal sceptre, which are brought in upon cushions. Lastly, the crown is taken from the altar, and placed by the Archbishop upon the King's head, the peers and peeresses at the same moment putting on the coronets. Then his Majesty is shown passing from the sacrarium to the Chair of State, south of the altar.

At this point a variation is introduced designedly. The Queen's coronation is taken as having been performed, and the bioscope version concludes with the homage of the archbishops, and bishops to their Majesties. This is for the sake of an effective finale, as it is obviously impossible to transfer the scene to St. Edward's Chapel, behind the high altar, in which the actual ceremonial closes.

"How London sees the Durbar day by day. Durbar pictures have been the great attraction at the Hippodrome during the week."
Black and White, 31 January 1903.

William James Coffin
'The Cannibal and the
Kinetoscope'
Bradford Daily Argus
28 April 1897

"WHRRING!" "Hello, there's the telephone," said the King of the Cannibal Islands, who was enjoying a quiet game of cribbage with his Royal Consort, Queen Ever-hungrie.

"Oh let the old thing go," said the wife.

"It's probably no one but that everlasting Prime Minister. I must insist upon you finishing this game, Masticator."

"Very well," said the King, meekly; "I've only four to go, and it's my deal."

So saying, he dealt the cards, and turned up the jack of hearts.

"Two for his heels," he said, moving up his peg two holes on his elegantly-carved cribbage board, which formerly occupied the position of right shin bone of the Rev. Plumpleigh Wellfed. The King had relished this gentlemen so very much that he had had one of his shin bones made into a cribbage board in order that he might be constantly reminded of his old friend.

"Seven," said the King, putting down the seven of spades.

"Fifteen two," said his wife, promptly covering it with the eight of clubs and counting her two points.

"Twenty-three and a pair," said the King, chuckling with glee.

"Twenty-eight," said the Queen.

"Thirty," said the King.

"Go," said the Queen.

"Out!" shouted his Royal Highness Masticator the Fifth, rushing to the telephone and stepping on his wife's pet porcupine on the way.

"Hello," he shouted, after taking down the 'phone and applying it to his ear.

"What's that?" he said, and then roared, "Begin again, and talk plain or I'll have your stuttering tongue out."

"Now Masticator!" warned the Queen, "be careful. It might be some ambassador."

"Oh shut up!" said the King aside. "What's that?" he continued into the 'phone. "That's good; we'll have him for dinner to-morrow. A what? Say that again. Say, look here! Come up and talk to me about it. I can't hear anything through this telephone—those electric ears make such a noise."

"Hungrie, my dear," said the King, returning to his wife. "Servility Broadnose telephones to say that there's a new white man in town. He says that he arrived yesterday and put up at the Masticator Arms last night. Strange I wasn't informed of it before. He also says that he had some sort of machine to exhibit. What have we for dinner to-morrow?"

"Well, we were going to have that missionary baby, but let's have this person and ask a few friends in," said the Queen.

"Good idea," said the King, who was knocking the balls around on his billiard table.

The King's chief delights were to eat, play billiards and cribbage, and to sign death warrants.

He had a record of three hundred and sixty an hour signing the latter, which was excellent considering that he had to sign his full name, Masticator P. Dahominy.

At this point the footman entered, bearing to cards upon his salver. The King looked at them and then put down his cue.

"Hungrie," he called, "Broadnose is in the drawing-room with the white man. I'm going down to see him. Please wait supper for me."

The King then straightened his necktie and hastily descended the stairs to the drawing-room.

There he found Mr. Broadnose, the Prime Minister, waiting for him, and with him was a young white man whom Broadnose introduced as Mr. Jones, from Orange, New Jersey, United States of America. The necessary interpreter was also present, and conversation speedily commenced.

"Young man," said the King. "I may as well tell you right here I have read Trilby; I am not buying any hideous chromos; my wife has all the hair pins she can possibly use; I don't want any lightning rods; I have no need of a comfortable rocking chair; we are supplied with plenty of lamp chimney cleaners; in short, I will buy nothing of you. The Royal Exchequer is too low to warrant any unnecessary expenditure. I owe three ivory tusks to the grocer now." And then he added very suggestively, "I am my own butcher."

Mr. Jones was considerably flustered by this harangue when interpreted, but Mr. Broadnose put in a good word for him.

"Sire," he said, "this young man is exhibiting a wonderful machine. He wishes to be allowed to astound you with the wonders of science as applied by a Mr. Edison, of his town in the United States."

"All right," said the King, "go on with the astounding."

Mr. Broadnose then signified to Mr. Jones through the interpreter, that the King was graciously willing to look at his wonderful machine.

Jones went to the door and summoned a negro attendant, who brought in Mr. Edison's wonderful invention called the Kinetoscope, with all its paraphernalia. He then proceeded to set it up, the King watching him curiously. When he finished, he motioned the King to look into the aperture, but his Royal Highness smelt a mouse.

"Oh come on!" said he, "you can't fool me on anything like that. I've been there before. The son of the last missionary we had showed me something like that, and when I looked into it he blew a lot of dust into my eyes. He was a plump lad that boy!" he said, licking his chops, thoughtfully.

An idea seemed to strike the King suddenly, and he touched the electric button on the wall. A footman appeared, and the King beckoned him to approach. Then he commanded the luckless menial to apply his eye to the orifice. The man sank on his knees in an agony of terror.

"Oh, sire," he wailed, despairingly, "spare me, spare me for the sake of my wife and thirteen children!"

The King dragged him to his feet and forced him to look into the machine. Jones put it in motion. The savage gave one astounded glance and then bounded into the air, throwing off the King. When he came down, he started for the door on a dead run, every tooth in the string around his neck standing up with horror.

"Hem!" said the King. "That's very queer."

By this time his Royal curiosity was excited, and he determined to brave the dangers of the Kinetoscope.

"Shut the door," said he to Broadnose; fearing that the Kinetoscope would have the same effect on him as it had had on his footman.

Then he took off his coat, rolled up his sleeves, gritted his teeth and approached the machine with a look of determination upon his face. He was about to look into it when he stopped, and turning to Broadnose said:

"Good-bye, old friend. This machine may make an end of me. If it does, tell my wife I died with my boots on, in the interests of science. I appoint you Regent for little Reginald. I want Openmouth Swallower to have my cribbage board; and now, old friend, once more adieu!"

They fell into each other's arms weeping copiously.

Then the King straightened up, and assuming his former manly look, advanced on the instrument.

"Turn her on!" he commanded, and then applied his eye to the hole.

Jones had put in an Indian war dance. The King took a long look. Then he began to work his hands convulsively and show evidences of great excitement. Presently he called out without taking his eyes from the machine,

"Broadnose, hustle up to my room, and bring down my sandbag. It's under the pillow. Get an everlasting hump on you too!"

Broadnose made a hurried exit and speedily returned with the weapon.

"Now!" said the King as he grasped his trusty sandbag, "just bring on your blooming Injuns and I'll give you a South Sea lesson in manners! Teach 'em to come cutting up their shines right

The King and Queen watching a film of themselves outside Government House, Calcutta. *The Illustrated London News,* 3 February 1912.

before my eyes. Where are they?" he demanded, shaking his sandbag in Jones's face.

Jones hastened to explain, through the interpreter, that there weren't any real Indians. Then opening the Kinetoscope, he took out the roll of film and passed it over the eyes of the dumbfounded savage.

After a time it began to dawn on the brain of the King that there really weren't any Indians, and that the whole business was a clever invention of an American. Then his delight knew no bounds. When Jones put in another film of a prize fight, the King became too full for utterance. After watching this for a time, he sent up for the Queen and Master Reginald Dahominy, the heir to the throne of Cannibalia.

The Queen came down attired in her best earrings, and very latest style of shoestring belt. The King explained the instrument to her as well as he was able. She was delighted with the prize fight as was also Master Reginald. The latter suggested that he would like to get his teeth into the smaller pugilist.

As soon as the prize fight began to pall, Jones put in a film of a skirt dance. The King, taking advantage of his kingly position, took first peep. His wife, seeing his evident delight and excitement, pushed him aside enough to get one eye at the hole. She gave one horrified look, and then securing her hubby by the ear, marched him away from the instrument.

After that, the King was not allowed to see anything unless it had first obtained her approval.

At last Jones exhausted his repertoire, much to the King's sorrow. He asked the young man what he could do for him, and was told that he would like to be protected from injury while exhibiting the Kinetoscope through Cannibalia.

The King called for his fountain pen and some paper, and wrote out the following certificate:

"The bearer, T. T. Jones, is hereby protected from all injury during his sojourn in my Kingdom. He is protected from all barbarous practices, harsh sports, and other entertainments of that description. Is entitled to free transportation on the Cannibalia trunkline and all its branches. He is also exempt from hotel bills and restaurant charges. Anyone in anyway molesting him from fulfilling his mission will be executed without trial by the Masticator Execution Co.

"Given under my hand and seal this the tenth day of December, in the year of our sacred stone idol eighteen hundred and ninety four, King Masticator."

This paper he handed to Jones with a beaming smile, and slapping him on the back, said in a very friendly tone:

"It's my opinion, my boy you've got a good thing there. Push it along!"

Then in the fullness of his heart he sat down and wrote out a cheque for five hundred ivory tusks, which he gave to Jones as a slight testimonial of his everlasting affection and regard.

And these are the reasons that the Kinetoscope has had such a boom in the kingdom of Cannibalia.

Cinematograph camera no. 2, used by Robert W. Paul to film Queen Victoria's Diamond Jubilee procession in June 1897. *National Museum of Photography, Film & Television.*

Catalogue for Lumière films, 1897. *James Offer.*

Right: **A souvenir programme, printed on satin, for the Royal Command Film Performance given at Windsor Castle in November 1897.**
National Museum of Photography, Film & Television.

Below left: **Programme for the Palace Theatre of Varieties, London, October 1899.**
National Museum of Photography, Film & Television.

Below right: **Poster for a Bioscope show at the Public Hall, Epsom, 23 September 1905.**
National Museum of Photography, Film & Television.

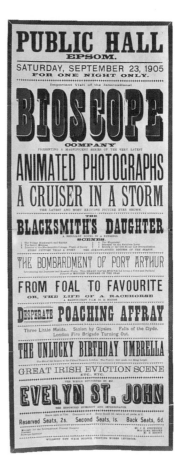

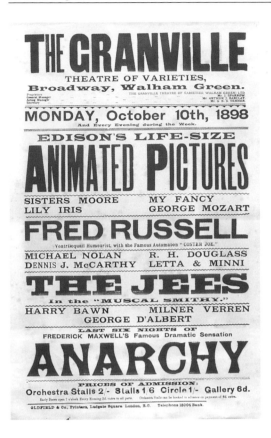

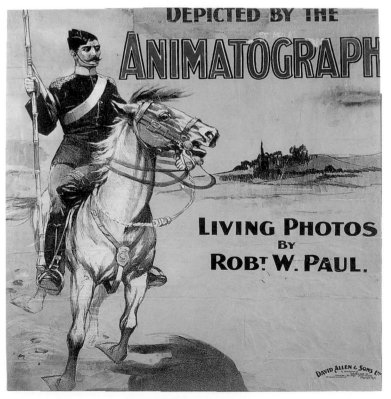

Above left: **Poster for Animated Pictures at the Granville Theatre of Varieties, London, 10 October 1898.**
National Museum of Photography, Film & Television.

Above right: **Poster for the Max Linder film *Max Fait de la Photo*, 1910.**
National Museum of Photography, Film & Television.

Left: **Poster advertising Robert W. Paul's Animatograph, 1896.**
National Museum of Photography, Film & Television.

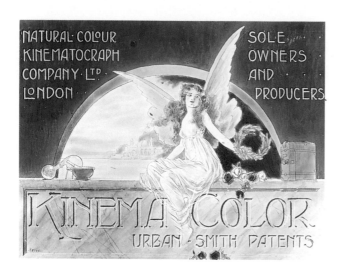

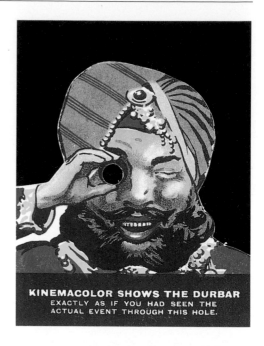

Kinemacolor ephemera, 1912–1914. *National Museum of Photography, Film & Television.*

Caricature of Charles Urban. *Vanity Fair*, c. 1912. *National Museum of Photography, Film & Television.*

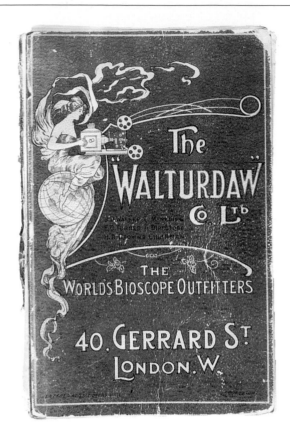

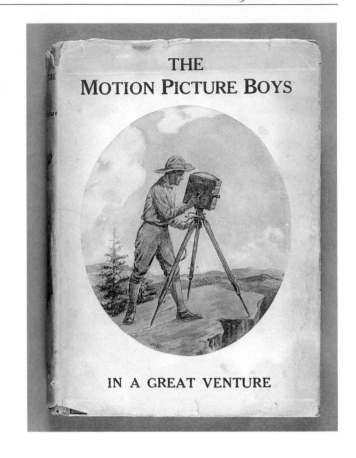

Top left: **Walturdaw Co. Ltd. catalogue, 1911.**
National Museum of Photography, Film & Television.

Top right: **The Motion Picture Boys in a Great Adventure
by Elmer Tracey Barnes
(Ohio: The Saalweld Publishing Co.) 1917.**

Right: **'The Director.'** *Judge* **magazine (New York) 1915.**
National Museum of Photography, Film & Television.

Postcards, c. 1910–1916. *Collection of the Author.*

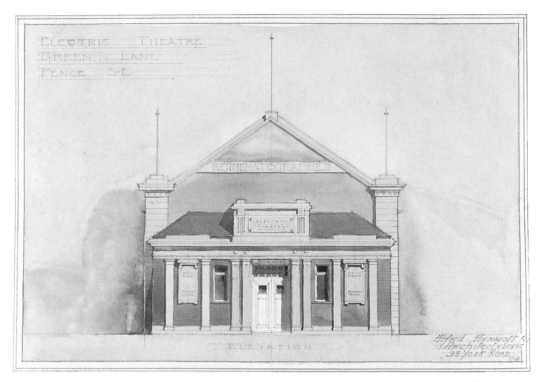

Plans for a Proposed Electric Theatre, Penge, 1909. *National Museum of Photography, Film & Television.*

Au Cinema **by Eug Forel, 1914. Oil on canvas.** *Christie's South Kensington, London.*

8 Both Sides of the Camera

After many months of waiting I have seen the biograph men at work, but I did not succeed in getting into the picture. I was on an omnibus in Piccadilly and we were stopped near the Automobile Club in order that the start of a reliability trial car might be registered for all time on the films. two men worked the apparatus, each turning a little handle very slowly. It was like a blessed noiseless organ. Meanwhile the driver of the car sat in uneasy self consciousness.

I suggested just now that I wanted to figure in a biograph picture. This was, of course, not a genuine ambition; I want nothing less. I was once horrified at the Palace to recognise a friend in a prominent position in one of the pictures. He is a man of some authority, but his nervousness turned him to a waiter in this scene.[1]

AT FIRST THERE WAS NO SUCH thing as a film actor. film recorded actuality and people were just there. Not performing, but appearing as themselves, going about their business in front of the camera. The very first film to be presented publicly on screen, Louis and Auguste Lumière's, *La Sortie des Ouvriers de l'Usine Lumière*, probably taken in September 1894, showed workers at the Lumière photographic factory in Lyons leaving for their lunch break. Similarly, *Arrivée d'un Train*, showed just that - people waiting on a station platform and entering or leaving a train. If some form of rudimentary narrative was required, then friends, relatives or employees of the film-maker would be persuaded, bribed or ordered to perform for the camera. Another early Lumière film, *L'Arroseur Arrosé* (*The Gardener Sprinkling and Being Sprinkled*) is a good illustration of this practice. M. Clerc, a gardener employed by Mme. Lumière, is somewhat type-cast as the gardener. The mischievous young boy who stands on the gardener's hosepipe was played by a fourteen-year-old apprentice at the Lumière factory named Duval.

Professional performers did appear on screen but it was very unusual for these to have a background in legitimate theatre. More usually, these were from the world of music hall or circus. Georges Méliès, who began his career as a magician and illusionist before discovering film-making, brought to the cinema all of the experience that he had gained at the Théâtre Robert-Houdin. At first, in common with most other early film-makers he relied on his friends, family and employees, often appearing himself. Aware that these 'non-professionals' often appeared uncomfortable in front of the camera, he began increasingly to turn to other performers. In 1902 Méliès produced what was perhaps his most famous film *Voyage dans la lune*. He was later to recall:

> The people employed in *Voyage dans la lune* were all acrobats, girls and singers from the music hall, theatre actors not yet having accepted to play roles in films because they considered films as much below the theatre. They only came later, when they learned that the music hall people earned more money playing in films than they did working in the theatre . . . In the cinema they could earn double. Two years after this, my office was every evening full of theatre people wanting jobs . . . I remember that in *Voyage dans la lune* the moon was Bleinette Bernon, a music hall singer, the stars were ballet girls from the Châtelet, and the men, Victor André, from the Théâtre de Cluny, Delpierre, Farjaux, Kelm, Brunnet, music hall singers and myself. The Selenites were acrobats from the Folies-Bergère. [2]

As films became longer, the need for narrative plot increased. The stage was the obvious source for ready-made characters and plots. As early as 1896, Esme Collings had filmed a scene from the play *The Broken Melody*. Primarily as documentary records of classic stage performances the work of some noted thespians found its way on to film, most notably Sir Herbert Beerbohm-Tree's version of *King John* in 1899 and Sarah Bernhardt's famous interpretation of Hamlet the following year. Having turned to the repertoire of classical and popular drama for material it was a simple and logical step to use the same actors who appeared in them on stage. Fred Storey, a professional actor, had played the title role in R. W. Paul's 1896 film *The Soldier's Courtship,* but before about 1908 it was comparatively rare for actors with an established reputation to appear on film. This was partly due to the legitimate theatre's low regard for cinema but also because of film-makers understandable motivation to keep production costs as low as possible—actors, after all, cost money. When professional actors were used it was often because the film-maker came from a theatrical background. For example, when William Haggar made *The Maid of*

Cefn Ydfa he used members of his own theatre company (eight of whom, it must be said, were Haggar's own children). On other occasions, professionals were used to supplement other members of cast made up of family and friends. Cecil Hepworth used paid actors for the first time in 1905 when he made *Rescued by Rover*. A cast which included Hepworth, his wife, his baby and, of course, his dog—the eponymous hero of the film—was augmented by two professionals from London. These were paid half a guinea each, including expenses. In contrast, in 1911, Will Barker had to pay Sir Herbert Beerbohm-Tree an unprecedented £1,000 to play Cardinal Wolsey in his production of *Henry VIII*. Established and recognised theatrical figures such as Beerbohm-Tree brought with them a degree of public appeal. More importantly, however, they also conferred on the new medium with a degree of status and artistic respectability, raising cinema to the same level as the theatre. Although the first texts on screen acting, such as Frances Agnew's *Motion Picture Acting* were to appear before the first World War, it was not until 1927 that a separate professional acting association, the film Artistes' Guild was formed.

---

1. *The Tatler*, 23 November 1904.
2. Quoted in David Robinson, *Georges Méliès. Father of Film Fantasy*, London: British film Institute, 1993, p. 40.

Photographs of studios from George Pearson's *Flashback: The Autobiography of a British Film Maker*, 1957.

Above:
Portland Street Underground Studio, London, 1913.

Left:
Alexandra Palace Studios, London, 1913.

George S. Guy
'In a Biograph Theatre:
Humour, Pathos and
Sensation on the Film'
The Strand Magazine,
February 1911

AS YOU SIT IN AN ELECTRIC THEATRE watching the pictures on screen, sometimes moved to tears by a sympathetic scene, sometimes to laughter by a humorous one, you have no time to wonder how these effects are brought about. But when you leave the building you may feel that you have would like to know how it is all done.

In the first place, the actors and actresses who perform the piece before the camera in order to obtain the film are, many of them well-known people on the music-hall or regular stage. So great is the demand for films that special buildings have been built in order that pictures may be taken indoors as well as in the open air. One of the finest of these, belongs to the Hepworth Manufacturing Company, is situated at Walton. It has twenty arc lamps, each producing a light of six thousand candle-power, so that when they are all alight no less than one hundred and twenty thousand candle-power of light is produced, permitting and indoor scene to be photographed. The company employs a complete staff of scenic-painters, carpenters, and scene-shifters. No expense is spared to make the pictures as realistic as possible, and the setting in some of them costs several hundred pounds. The expenditure on a single film sometimes amounts to nearly a thousand pounds. But the cost of an ordinary comic picture is much lower that this—say, on average a hundred pounds. Very large salaries are paid to certain artistes who have become public favourites. It has been stated that a certain actress in America has received over two thousand pounds a year for acting for film-pictures of this kind.

The first thing, of course, is to obtain a really good plot. After this has been secure, it is divided into different scenes, and it is no uncommon thing for an ordinary comic film to be divided into fifteen or twenty scenes. The stage-manager then calls the company together, explains the plot to them fully, and allots the different parts. After each has been 'made up' to represent his or her character, the company starts, rehearsing. The mind of every artist must be concentrated on his work. He must know the time he has come to into the picture to the very instant, for as the operator is taking photographs at the rate of sixteen per second, it is easy to understand that the slightest mistake will ruin the whole picture.

Imagine that the operator is waiting for the word to start. "Are you ready?" he calls. "Go!" The machine buzzes merrily round, the artistes act as if before a crowded house, while the stage-manager is shouting warnings and directions. When the taking of the first scene is complete the scene-shifters are busy preparing for the next scene. So the work goes on until all the scenes are finished. It may be several days before the whole film is completed.

"Acting a dramatic scene
before the camera."

The length of the film varies, but one of a thousand feet, which is considered a full length contains no fewer than sixteen thousand separate pictures and takes about an hour and three quarters to develop. The time taken to display this picture on the screen is nearly twenty minutes.

So much for indoor work. But many scenes are taken in the open air. The artistes who devote their time to this kind of work are more liable to serious accidents than those who work in the more tranquil atmosphere of the theatre. An accident that happened in Surrey is probably still fresh in the public mind. A man was tied to the railway lines, and it was arranged that train should approach as near to him as possible, when he was to have been rescued just in the nick of time. Owing, however, to the greasy state of the metal, the train was unable to stop dead, the train was unable to stop dead and the engine passed over the unfortunate performer. Fortunately, this kind of accident very seldom happens. Another case that might have had an unhappy ending was that of a young lady who was depicted as being thrown into the water by the villain of the piece and then rescued by the hero from a watery grave. The impression was that she could swim, but when she was immersed the operators soon found out their mistake, for to their consternation it was some time before she reappeared, half-drowned and scarcely conscious, on the surface. Happily she was soon rescued, and quickly recovered.

Only a short time ago a scene from the *French Revolution* was being acted. A guillotine had been erected by the roadside, and a howling mob had assembled about it. The mimic execution was going on in the most lifelike manner. The dramatic moment had arrived; the condemned man, with the priest beside him, stood under the glittering knife, the savage-faced mob waved its arms in fierce exultation—when a touring car swept round a curve in the road. Some ladies in the car, finding themselves face to face with this extremely realistic picture, broke into piercing screams, while the startled chauffeur brought his machine to a stop. The disturbance was too much for the actors, and the condemned man, the priest, and the mob turned round to see what was the matter. The motorists soon found out the situation and sped away, but the film was ruined.

On another occasion a picture was just about to be started a little way out of London, when along came a very pompous old gentleman who wanted to pass.

"Excuse me, sir," said one of the company, "but you can't go through now."

"Can't go through? Why not, indeed?" thundered the old gentleman.

"Because we are just going to start," replied the actor.

"Oh, really!" snapped the old man. "Oh really! I'm a ratepayer and I'll see what this constable has to say on the subject." He walked up to a near-by constable and demanded the meaning of it all.

"Can't 'elp it, sir," said the constable, stolidly, barring the road as he spoke. "These people have bought the road for a time, and you can't pass."

And he didn't notice till they had finished, nor did he discover that the constable was an actor ready for the part.

We stated at the head of this article that we proposed to say something about the humour, the pathos, and the sensation of what has now become one of the most popular of all entertainments. Let us, in the first place, consider the subject of humour. It will be readily understood that where the whole play consists of action without words anything like subtlety of wit is out of the question. The effects must be of all the broadest possible kind, bordering on horseplay. It has been said that in the theatre the most sparkling epigram is less effective than the spectacle of a man sitting down on his hat—and this is entirely the kind of humour on what the biograph theatre has to depend on for its effects.

Perhaps the most popular series of films of this nature are those which, are known as *The Adventures of Foolshead*, in which a person whose character is well conveyed by his name through a series of most astonishing adventures and comes to grief in a score of different ways.

Foolshead is an assistant in a large store and is so enamoured of the pretty daughter of the proprietor that he neglects his duties. He is so preoccupied that he knocks over a lady customer with a roll of cloth, and when she buys it wraps it so badly that she complains to the proprietor. The latter finds Foolshead talking to his daughter, and angrily throws him out of the shop with such force that he is carried across the road through the chute for the parcels in the basement, where he lands on a pile of hat-boxes . . . Recovering his senses, Foolshead laboriously climbs up the chute to the shop, when seeing the proprietor coming into view with a party of customers, he hides behind a pile a furniture and carpets, which by an unlucky movement, he precipitates upon the party. He next gets behind a big stall of plaster statuettes, and the crash here, as the others appear, is greater than ever. finally Foolshead opens the door of a large cupboard, into which the pursuers rush, whereupon the door is slammed to, and he and his sweetheart sit on the overturned cupboard and parley with the father until his consent is given to an early marriage.

**"Humour—
'The Adventures of Foolshead.'
Foolshead is thrown down a
parcel-chute."**

His adventures, however, are by no means at an end, and another picture shows the great little comedian as a chauffeur, whose car breaks down in a busy thoroughfare. Water being required for cooling purposes, he obtains a supply, but in a leaky watering-can. Petrol is next required, which he obtains in his usual hurry, knocking two policemen into a tank in the process. The petrol is no sooner [in] the tank than a tyre bursts. He now goes off in an even greater hurry for a tyre, upsetting . . . the contents of the shop before being suited. On his way back he meets a friend. They celebrate the occasion, and when Foolshead returns—of course, without the tyre—the car is blazing furiously.

As might be expected the modern sport of roller-skating offers Foolshead an exceptional opportunity for the exercise of his unique gifts. It is his weakness for the fair sex which leads him into trouble. Meeting a lady in the street, nothing will satisfy him more but that they should go rinking together. Foolshead signalizes his entry by bowling over a couple or rinkers, and then, seeing his lady friend skating towards the refreshment room with another cavalier, he gives chase. In a outer room he keeps his feet with difficulty by clinging to the curtains at the doorway . . . and then, venturing away from their support, saves himself by grasping the long white beard of an elderly skater, whom he wheels round several times before bringing him to the floor with a crash.

The lady and gentleman skate gracefully between the chairs an tables in the refreshment room, but Foolshead, following, brings furniture and diners down together, and leaves inextricable confusion before he again reaches the floor . . . This exhausts the patience of the manager, and Foolshead is thrown into the street. He lands outside a house door, where stands one of the large wicker arrangements used by children learning to walk quickly. Creeping inside this, he progresses down the street in triumph, save for one tumble caused by unexpectedly meeting his late fair companion and her new attendant.

We now pass on to another favourite of the biograph theatre, Max Linder who impersonates a youth supposed to be smitten with the charms of two damsels. Timidly, yet with a certain amount of determination, he follows them through the streets and all hints that his presence is not desirable are lost upon him. Annoyed at his presumption, the two girls resolve to make him pay for his audacity. With very little effort he is lured into a confectioner's shop and compelled to consume a quantity of unwholesome cakes as a penalty. A visit to the dentist follows, and before he is well aware of it he has lost a couple of good teeth.

He is full of pluck, however, and continues the chase, with a handkerchief pressed to his face, and is soon inveigled into smoking some cigarettes which they press upon him. These, however, as another photograph shows, put the finishing stroke to his discomfort, and the young lady-killer is finally vanquished.

The humorous side of the question has detained us so long that we have scarcely space to touch upon the pathetic and the sensational. However, of the former, let us take as a typical example the film entitled *The Call of the Heart*. It tells the story of a widowed mother, who, finding herself near death, instructs her little daughter to trust God and seek a shelter where He may direct her. She pins a note to the little one's dress, telling of her mother's death, and soon after the child has left the mother dies. By some strange disposition of Fate the child is led to the comfortable home of a hard-fisted miser who thinks of no one but himself. The little girl is cared for by the housekeeper and taken to the old man, who has just awakened from a dream, in which his conscience has been aroused. He realizes his hard-hearted meanness, having been brought by his dream to an appreciation of the blessings of charity. When he sees the little

orphan and the note she has brought with her, the old
fellow cannot resist her winning ways. He takes her too
his heart and home and becomes a child himself.

Now, finally, in a sensational scene, of which as good
an example as any is that entitled *The Power of the Press*.
Bill Mason, mayor of a small American town, is on bad
terms with a local editor, whom he has succeeded in driving out of the town. John Marsden, the new editor,
arrives, and Mawson attempts to make him his tool. On
Marsden refusing, the mayor starts a conspiracy to get rid
of him, but his niece, Nettie, overhears the plot and
warns Marsden. He refuses to fly, and is soon afterwards
'held up' by some masked men, among whom he recognises Bill Mawson, the mayor. They drag him to a tree
and put a rope round his neck, as shown in our last picture, but he still refuses to obey the mayor. Everything is
ready, when Nettie dashes up with the police and rescues
her lover from death. Marsden takes Nettie in this arms
and graciously intervenes for the release of Mawson, who
extends his hand and promises to mend his ways.

Such, then, is the quality of the fare provided by the
biograph theatre, and if it true that it does not appeal
essentially to the 'superior person' but to an infinitely
wider public, there is no reason why it should be
regarded as any of the worse for that.

"**SENSATION**—'The Power of the Press.'
Nettie rescues her lover from death."

I N THE ENDEAVOURS TO OBTAIN startling and sensational cinematograph films, the
cinematographer often has to run no little personal risks, and an illustration of this could
have been found during the recent storm in Sunderland. Messrs. Mitchell & Kenyon, who are
celebrated for their films, received the news that a terrific storm was raging on the North East
coast, and Mr. Kenyon at once caught a train to Sunderland, prepared to take 1,000 feet of pictures of the storm. To a photographer the scene was awfully grand, and no time was lost by the
enterprising picture man in making arrangements for taking scenes of the boiling waters. From
the foot of the lighthouse on Roker Pier, about 300 feet of pictures were taken, and then Mr.
Kenyon removed to the very end of a little jetty running into the sea and commenced operating on the wild seascape from this coign of vantage. He had nearly finished and was intent upon
his work when a tremendous wave came along and swept past the cinematographer, and in the
backward rush, hurled the camera out of his grasp, and very nearly dragged him with it. Knowing that a fortune was encased in the camera in the shape of unique and valuable films, Mr.
Kenyon yelled out the offer of a big reward to anyone who recovered it. The old caretaker of
the lighthouse lent the cinematographer and his assistant some grappling irons and hooks, but
all they succeeded in securing was the leather case of the camera, the more valuable contents
being washed up in the tide, all battered and useless, on the Saturday morning. The chagrin of
the operator can be well imagined when he saw, the same day, several children flying cinematograph ribbons round the streets of Sunderland. What a pity it seems that there was not
another camera at work, taking pictures of the exciting scenes.

The Showman
29 November 1901

"On the Rhine. First Tourist. 'Care to use these glasses?' Second Tourist. 'No thanks. Seen it all on the cinema 't 'ome!'"
Punch, 17 July 1912.

John Palmer
'Mr Bunny'
The Saturday Review
11 April 1914

MR. BUNNY IS MORE FAMOUS than Sir George Alexander. He is even more famous than Harry Lauder. Not to know Mr. Bunny argues oneself unknown—at any rate among that vast public which pays sixpence a stall. Mr. Bunny's fame is international. It transcends the barriers of language and race. When Mr. Bunny laughs, people from San Francisco to Stepney Green laugh with him. When Mr. Bunny frowns, every kingdom of the earth is contracted in one brow of woe. When Mr. Bunny shuts one eye, the old world and the new winks familiarly back. When Mr. Bunny is perplexed, a grimace of tortured bafflement puckers town and country. Yet, though Mr. Bunny is a universal friend, and the most famous man in all the world, his lovers never see him, or hear his voice; his admirers are content, indeed they are compelled, to worship and to watch his shadow.

Mr. Bunny has an extensive and extremely flexible face. When he smells a piece of Gorgonzola cheese there is no doubt whatever that his nose has been very seriously offended. When he sees for the first time a pretty and eligible young woman, there is no doubt whatsoever that he is immensely excited and moved with intentions so extravagantly honourable that they seem almost too grievous to be borne. Mr. Bunny's emotions are all there on a grand scale. His despair is incredible. His grief is unendurable. His smile is an ignis fatuus. His pleasure can be palpably be seen to spread from the ends of his hair to the soles of his feet. His wrath is apoplectic. His terror is the panic of the whole army. His congratulations wring one's hands till circulation is for the moment suspended. We know at once why Mr. Bunny never speaks. He could not possibly find words to convey the extremity of his feelings. It is enough that he should open his mouth. He opens his mouth so expressively that mere language must destroy rather than add to his appeal. When Mr. Bunny's jaws are in travail, imagination boggles at suitably fitting them with any sort of verbal parturition. Mr. Bunny's unuttered words would exhaust the means of ordinary language. The futurists might fit him with a speech in his hours of comparative ease and mildness; but Mr. Bunny's conversation is beyond the resources of tongues which still retain qualifying adjectives and modifying adverbs. It is surprising, indeed, that Mr. Bunny does not vigorously protest against the feeble efforts of his producers to describe his conduct in mere English. His appearance is often preceded by a verbal synopsis of his emotions flung upon a screen—"Mr. Bunny is surprised to find..." Really this seems hardly fair to Mr. Bunny. We do not need to be told that Mr. Bunny is surprised. When Mr. Bunny is surprised his face is no longer a face. It is a note of exclamation.

Mr. Bunny, of course is not always a funny fellow. The man on the film is sometimes a handsome soldier, and sometimes he is a sweet ingenue of seventeen, or a beautiful, unhappy wife whose husband has been falsely imprisoned for forging cheques or breaking into a safe. Then, if you are an impressionable young man or woman, you must buy a picture postcard at the door and feed yourself into sentimental affection for a shadow. These picture postcards of the film player are a last pathetic evidence of the need of men and women to adore a complementary image of themselves. When I think of thousands of small mantelpieces where, above the tobacco and a match-box, lovely and appealing ghosts stick forth from the edges of the mirror, and when I see thousands of small dressing tables where, amid hairpins and a pincushion, in a self supporting frame, a regimental shadow fronts a sanctuary of feminine mysteries, I am filled with a sense of tears in mortal things. What shadows we are and what shadows we pursue! Is it not better to love an image we have never beheld than never to have loved at all? What though that dimpled chin and most excellent teeth have never in the solid flesh been seen? What though that sternly beautiful brow and light moustache have never tangibly been bodied forth? These visions, delectable, and fair, have flickered mysteriously into our lives as we sat among the shadows where Mr. Bunny reigns. Let us capture the fair illusion and cherish it, tinted or plain.

These shadows of the picture houses must be very real when their portraits are sold for pennies at the door. One is tempted to imagine things unutterably sad. Pygmalion loved a statue; but his tragedy was comparatively simple and bearable beside the tragedy of the clerk who loves a girl on the film. The conception is Dantesque in its enormous horror. The torment of Tantalus is mere innocent foolery compared with this more modern doom. That the victim should yearn into the eyes of a ghost is only the beginning of his woe. Conceive him treading wearily upon his daily visit to the palace where she mysteriously comes and goes. He must

**"*Picture Personalities: Mr. John Bunny.*
That popular Vitagraph artist, Mr. John Bunny, who is paying England a visit, will, it is said, appear as 'Pickwick' is a series of picture plays based on the famous 'Pickwick Papers'."
The Bioscope, c. 1912.**

submit to behold her—his adorable shadow—moving amongst shadows like herself. She speaks with them, but he cannot hear her voice. She embraces them in a ghostly embrace which he can never hope to enjoy. He beholds her wasting her sweetness upon beings like herself, and he is powerless to intervene, to affect her exits or her entrances, to claim her from the spectres who, happy and blessed in their privilege, are able to live with her upon the same screen and retire into the darkness whence she has issued to bewitch him.

Personally, I only seldom desire to enter upon speaking terms with people who live on the film. They exist at too high a pressure for me. I am sure their conversation would not be restful. I can't help feeling that the girl on the film, if she really took a fancy to you, would be extremely exhausting. I have seen her fall in love with a ghost. The ecstasy of her countenance would blast an ordinary mortal. I have seen her embrace her husband. No mortal man could stand it. Then, of course, there are her friends. Their faces are too expressive. Any sort of social life would be quite impossible with people who cannot help looking exactly what they think of you. Silent disapproval is always a little galling; but the silent disapproval of an ordinary polite citizen is not actionable. The silent disapproval of Mr. Bunny would be quite another matter. I have seen him expressing it. I have also seen him express silent incredibility. If you were an ordinary polite citizen, and if you told Mr. Bunny a story, and if Mr. Bunny expressed silent incredibility in the way he usually expresses it, you would in self-respect be compelled immediately to serve a writ. This would make Mr. Bunny angry, and Mr. Bunny's silent anger is not to be lightly encountered. Or Mr. Bunny might forgive you and shake hands. I have seen Mr. Bunny shake hands. I would rather put my hand under a steam-roller than give it into the grasp of Mr. Bunny. Besides, it might not end with shaking hands. Mr. Bunny might claim you for a good fellow and an acquaintance with a hearty thump between the shoulders.

No: The risks are too great. Mr. Bunny is an excellent fellow upon the screen, but, in the flesh, I do not desire his better acquaintance. I am not quite sufficiently robust.

"He (carried away). 'See that?' (No answer) 'Now they've bound 'im, they'll gag 'im' (No answer) 'So as he can't shout. See?' She (with great difficulty). 'They ought to 'ave some of this toffee of yours to give 'im.'" Punch's Almanack for 1913.

THE CINEMATOGRAPH, SIR HUBERT VON HERKOMER'S VIEWS
To the Editor of the *Daily Telegraph*

Daily Telegraph
21 December 1912

Sir,

It is now some twenty years since Mr. Muybridge came down to me to lecture to my students on animal locomotion, bringing his camera with him, and a most interesting demonstration it was. Those photographs were a great revelation, and were probably the beginning of the picture film of today, hidden though it was from the mind of man at that moment.

But who can tell from where an idea starts? And now the growth of film shows has almost become an epidemic. It is time, in view of this state of things, that we should look around and ask ourselves some questions as to the future. We take it that the cinematograph has come to stay; then what is its present status? Technically it has certainly been vastly improved, and morally it is improving. For a long time there had been too hasty catering to a rather low class of people, and that is difficult to eradicate, as the idea is afloat that there is money in it, and for money the caterers have gone; hence the moral side has had to take care of itself. But, strange to say, it has done so, as show after show has gradually given more and more attention to natural history and drama, and less and less to silly jokes and murderous subjects.

Presence of Children

I cannot quite find out why such young children have become frequenters of these places. I am told that in Germany they are not allowed to attend under nine years of age, and I am quite in favour of that. The little mind is very impressionable, and it is impossible to say what the effect on it would be of one of those blood curdling stories. These enacted scenes are far more dangerous to the young mind than a copy of the old-fashioned Police News would have been. I say, therefore, emphatically that children should not be admitted to every kind of subject, and the managers of shows should be responsible for the selection of subjects for young and old, rich or poor. If it be not possible to combine these elements in one audience, let there be different days at different prices.

Need for Censorship

A censor is needed on this, more than any licensing of a play. But I want to know on what grounds the censor is to judge a film. He cannot judge a scenario; he must see the film on the screen, and film makers have by then gone to all the expense and trouble of getting the scenes together, a matter that sometimes runs into many thousands of pounds.

I was present the other day at a private view of that new film Les Miserables. The audience, I was told, was mostly composed of managers of shows; there was a sprinkling of actors and actresses. But from remarks made around me I could see they took neither the acting, the stage management of the scenes, nor the selection of backgrounds seriously; it was to them something purely artificial. Yet these living pictures were much more real and convincing to me than reading the book. To a literary man I know this is heresy.

The Future

The cinematograph has already shown itself such a potent factor in our daily life that anything may be expected of it in the future, and I should be sorry to prophesy what it will not yet do educationally, artistically, dramatically, and even commercially. But before it can attain to its full development the strong prejudice still existing against the cinematograph amongst better-class people must be overcome. So strong is this prejudice that some people would almost as soon confess to entering a gin-palace as a picture-palace.

If one might indulge in a little chimerical phantasy, I should say the day will come when the one film will take up form, colour and sound, and reproduce all these simultaneously; that a cinematograph will be laid on in every home, as your gas or electricity is now laid on; that the world's stories will be brought to you in a pictorial and dramatic form, such as one has not yet dreamed of. Every child will be taught geography, natural history, and botany by screen pictures, rather than by books; actors and scripts will be recorded for all times; the progress of any great engineering feat will be recorded accurately. In short the future will be made of recorded facts. I will not venture to say it is all for the good of mankind, but man is getting more and more 'subjective' and his inventive faculties lean altogether that way.

That the cinematograph is not encouraged in Germany lies probably in the fear that theatre may be damaged, as they are mostly state subsidised. There was a great outcry in this country by the theatres against the growing influence of the music hall. But although the music hall is a vastly different thing to what it used to be, it is the music hall that is now beginning to groan under the yoke of the ever encroaching cinematograph.

Artistic Sobriety

What is to be the next move in the commercial aspect of the entertaining world? I can only hope that it will be towards artistic sobriety in all film-subjects; a reduction in the sensationalism generally, and an avoidance of criminality. Great books revivified is a movement in the right direction and English literature should not be neglected by the English. Tennyson's *Idylls of the King*, Browning's 'Pied Piper of Hamlin' are great and eminently suitable subjects. It is the public that must help in making the cinematograph one of the greatest powers for good so far placed in the hands of man.

I thank-you for your courtesy in printing my letter, and I am, Sir, your obedient servant,

Hubert von Herkomer

Lululand, Bushey, Herts. Dec. 20.

"We are growing so accustomed to cinema tragedies in our midst that we run the risk of some day failing to recognise the real article when we find it."
***The Graphic*, 15 November 1913.**

IN A LARGE STUDIO, with glass roof and walls, singing pictures—known to the general public as vivaphone films—are made. The studio belongs to the Hepworth Manufacturing Company; Mr. Hepworth's individual invention having produced the first really successful combination of living pictures and vocal sounds—otherwise the 'Vivaphone'.

The erratic behaviour of the Hepworth Company, whose studio is in Walton-on-Thames, causes intense amazement and amusement to that 'village'. If the inhabitants were permitted a glimpse of the interior of those glass-walled studios, where singing, dramatic, and farcical films are born, their amazement would be doubled, and their amusement know no bounds.

A cinema studio is a truly wonderful place. Just a large, very bare room, in which light and space are the most desirable attributes. The stage is merely the deal-boarded floor: footlights are nil—unless the arc lamps suspended right and left above the edge of the camera's eye can be so called. Behind the camera the room narrows; the after-part, utilised for 'props', overflowing with chairs, tables, and other paraphernalia. At the Hepworth studio the camera is an amazing affair—a combination of wheels and cords, gearing together a gramophone and an ordinary bioscope camera. A length of cable connects this machine with electric current, both machines, together or separately, being worked by electric power. In the Hepworth studio all the 'turning' is done by mechanism, not manual labour.

With a singing-picture in rehearsal the studio shelters a unique scene. The stage represents a garden, the realistic effect being gained by dried hay scattered lavishly, small trees suspended from the roof, other trees stuck into tubs, skilfully hidden, a large gate flanked by pseudo-iron railings all painted black and white, and made of light wood, while at the back a 'cloth' representing a ghost-like street of grey-white houses fills in the picture and blots out the 'scene-dock' beyond. Prehistoric life is led by Londoners in this garden, and a dozen men and girls in crude pink tights, woolly garments and flowing locks are prancing gaily round a tin hip-bath containing two scared ducks—the lake in the ancestral park! Some of them are wearing very up-to-date overcoats, or shawls, and look weird figures from some phantasy as they skip and gesticulate, opening their mouths as if singing, but making no sound. The stage-manager gives a few directions, or pulls them up when anything goes seriously wrong. The principal singer stands facing the camera in a flimsy muslin garment, with a thick tweed coat over it and high-heeled shoes, repeating, with much mouthing, the words of the song as revealed by the gramophone. Movement is rather restricted; but having rehearsed the two verses of the song, with business, successfully, the record is ready to be 'filmed'. . .

The arc lamps are switched on, and Mr. Hepworth sees that the gramophone and camera are properly geared together. 'Ready?' he inquires. Suddenly, as a switch goes down, a purring sound begins, and at the same moment the introduction of the song is heard from the waxen record. The camera and gramophone are working together! On come the players, dancing and smiling; and then all that took place at rehearsal is repeated, with the sole addition of that purring sound, and the figure of Mr. Hepworth behind the camera. The voice that made the record rings out clearly, and it is strange to watch all the actors' mouths moving, with no sound. In the middle a contretemps occurs, for the ducks, scared by the antics of fierce 'prehistorics', leave their 'lake' and make a dash for the wings and safety. They are 'shoo-o-ed' back by prancing stage hands and the stage-manager, and flutter into the bath again, disappointed tragedians!

The gramophone record ends; up goes that switch, while the purring ceases—and a record of another singing picture reposes in the narrow box above the camera! While the players change for another song the stage-manager begins ruthlessly rooting up that lovely garden, to rebuild a typical 'Lovers' Lane', stile and all, in the same space. . .

In a series of marvellous 'dark-rooms' the films are prepared for public use. Every day something like 25,000 feet of film is turned out by the Hepworth Company. And a small room contains round tin boxes, stacked high and numbered, holding film No. 1, taken thirteen years ago, and film No. 8000, taken last week, with every intervening number! Such is the magnitude of this amazing enterprise.

Margaret Chute 'How Singing Pictures are Made' *The Graphic* · 30 March 1912

Margaret Chute
'Cinemitis: The Fury of
the Film Exposed!'
The Graphic,
15 November 1913

IT IS A NEW DISEASE, AND DEADLY INTO THE BARGAIN. It may be caught in palaces of dazzling white and glittering gold, guarded by Gulliver wearing a mongrel uniform. It abounds among folk who earn a livelihood by indulging in exotic emotions before a one-eyed machine in a wooden cover. Germs may be found, fertilising merrily, in millions of miles of perforated celluloid, generally labelled 'film.' When hatched, these germs produce a dire disease, which leads sane people to perform insane acts, and turns casual, everyday citizens into raging fanatics.

'Cinemitis!' For want of a better word, let us call it by that name. Entre nous, it's all I can think of at the moment. Anyhow, it's original, and the patent has been applied for. 'Cinemitis!' It's new to you, today. So far, you are untouched by its awful fingers. As yet, the syllables come hesitatingly to your tongue. Cin-e-mi—Yes, it's a tricky word! But you'll get used to it. If I haven't succeeded in familiarising it by the end of this article—provided, of course, that your premature removal to the hospital has not occurred ere then—do not be alarmed. You will learn all about it in time. When appendicitis burst upon us in all its glory, you may remember that we were quite a long while recognising it as an ancient enemy under a modern appellation. Well, 'Cinemitis' is not precisely an ancient enemy. It has not existed, in an active state, for many months. But what I am striving to convey to your brain-centre is the fact that, strange though it sounds, you know all about 'Cinemitis' already, without any further elucidation on my part. Which is exactly why I propose to go on elucidating.

It is intimately connected with that amazing thing, the Cinematograph: called, during moments of relaxation in the family circle, the Cinema. It attacks, with dastardly virulence, those who work for the 'Movies'—a term of endearment not without significance. Not content with victimising actors and actresses it seizes members of the audiences, producing raging cases of 'Cinemitis' in the cracking of a nut. This simile depends, obviously, on the use of a hammer, somebody's best back tooth rendering it inappropriate. The heel of a boot is also useful, failing other appliances.

You are sneering at 'Cinemitis'—don't deny it! Anyhow, I must write another 500 words; so it suits my purpose to imagine you are sneering. The process does not suit you; and besides, don't be too confident. Though free from taint today, you may be one of the world's worst cases tomorrow. Every time you enter a white-and-gold palace, you risk catching the disease. So be careful. And, if you have the Cinema habit badly, take my advice—use blinkers!

'Cinemitis' to come to the third act of the drama in one terrific bound, is a craze for performing dangerous actions before the Bioscope. Now we can really get on. When Kinematography first crept into our hearts, and made holes in our weekly sweet-money, it was gentle, tame, and domesticated. It pictured humble folk, like ourselves, at work and play, falling in love and out again, surrounded by the dog and family Bible.

Then the worst happened. The desperate Drama began its insane career. Runaway bicycles began it, roller skates came in a good second, and wheelbarrows followed in hot pursuit. Then came an avalanche of Horse-Horrors. Hero and heroine, on one galloping steed, pursued by Villain and Co; rivers to swim, trees to climb, walls to jump—and so to safety and the final curtain. Motors next; thousands of valuable 90 h.p. cars hurled to destruction over precipices, into rivers, and under the wheels of monstrous engines. The fate of their drivers is not recorded. Then we got reckless. 'Cinemitis' seized the entire population of Bioscopeville; every producer, actor, actress, and operator in the business set to work to provide ultra-dangerous ideas, and carry them out.

The man who thought of 'bricking up' the heroine alive in a cellar, and then puncturing the main water-pipe, received a medal and a pension for life. The actress who allowed herself to be cast adrift in a burning boat, chancing a rescue by the hero from a handy parachute, got badly singed, but received due monetary reward. And the boy who leapt from the crow's next of an Atlantic liner, to wrest the missing 'clue' (plot, please) from the raging waters, was arrested as a criminal lunatic. He didn't care—the film was a record! Then came aeroplanes. Hanging by her teeth, a sweet creature swung between two aerial machines, 3000.957 feet, and the rest of the decimals, above ground. That was nothing—a mere pin-prick. Clinging to the stationary portion of the propeller—4000.84 (and the rest) feet in mid-air, a man travelled with his rival to that gentleman's destination, secured the incriminating documents, and married the girl (serial and other rights preserved). Was she worth it? How do I know?

Every day it grows worse. Houses are blown up, shops are blown down, trains are wrecked, loss of life and limb is risked, blindly. And all for an infernal one-eyed machine—a noisy demon, too. Only last week the leading lady of a certain film firm, reading the plot, discovered that she had to dive off Westminster Bridge, drive a racing car over the Shakespeare Cliff, be run over at Piccadilly Circus, and dance to a barrel organ in Whitechapel. She took a holiday.

Daily, hourly, beholders of cinema plays are stricken. The horrible fascination of it—the awful inspiration of it—grips them, in their 6d stall. And as there are millions of cinema theatres in the world, the disease is increasing at the rate of . . . Never mind: my statistics won't stand the strain!

Stage setting for Kinemacolor films of the Delhi Durbar at the Scala Cinema, London, 1911. *National Museum of Photography, Film & Television.*

KINEMACOLOR
The Scala

The Tatler
2 August 1911

THE BEAUTIFUL SCALA THEATRE is an architectural example of casting pearls if not before Christmas porkers at any rate among them. Anything more unlovely than Charlotte Street and its immediate neighbourhood I don't want to be lost in, ever: and the smells—oh the effluvia! Chemists must do a roaring trade in scents now that the whole of London is flocking to the Scala to see the wonderful new series of royal events in "natural colours." The "creature," who always thinks herself so attractive that Death must be simply perspiring to get hold of her and cannot perceive even the faint and delicious odour of onions without at once thinking that she will shortly be called upon to die, marched along with her face buried—'happily' you might add if you saw it—in her pocket handkerchief.

Charlotte Street

It is a good thing we are not able to see Charlotte Street painted in its "natural colours" or there might be a congestion of pedestrian traffic in the district. It is a very weird affair. If you woke up suddenly you might think that Fate had plopped you down in the slums of Strasbourg after a polony beanfeast. Most of the inhabitants spend their time hanging on to the area railings; they talk a strange jargon and carry in their hands newspapers the printing of which looks as if it had been done in the Ark. They are a very sociable lot these inhabitants of Charlotte Street. Those dressing in the second-floor fronts are delighted to hold converse with those squatting on the front doorstep or in the house opposite. The result is very gay and animated, and one sees quite a lot, thank you. The street is full of clubs—quite "clubland" in fact—and the members hang out of the windows and round the front door in a manner that denotes a somewhat unexciting interior. Sometimes we are told the police visit these clubs, and quite a lot of real ladies and gentlemen pay a visit to Bow Street. But that time is not yet; this is only the afternoon.

The Wonderful Invention

In this unlovely district full of frizzled sausages and "*zimmers zu valeeren*" stands the Scala Theatre. Of course, it can be reached by way of the Tottenham Court Road—the way everybody gets there—but then, of course, you miss that pleasant sensation of foreign travel to be obtained if you come by way of Greek Street and Soho. It is certainly the loveliest theatre in London and until Messrs. Smith-Urban brought their wonderful invention, Kinemacolor, from The Palace it was one of the most lonely. Now, however, everything is buzzing and humming, and what opened with poetical drama is more than content to harbour moving pictures—and who shall say that everybody is not the merrier?

Kinemacolor

Kinemacolor is an extraordinary invention. It is colour photography and must not be confused with coloured photography. The latter, I understand, is photography coloured by hand. Kinemacolor is photography coloured by the sun's rays. "In the following diagram you will observe..." Oh bother! I thought I was giving a lecture. How it's all done I haven't the least idea, and am quite content not to know seeing that I can watch all the results amid beautiful surroundings for sixpence or a shilling. These results—well, they really are astounding. Of course, all the colours do not come out with the same brilliance. Blues, greens, and reds are very vivid; yellows, greys, and the fainter shades are less pronounced. Still-life gives some of the most lovely pictures imaginable; but the coronation processions and the investiture at Carnarvon of the Prince of Wales are perfect pageants of glowing colour. Certainly the next coronation I shall let the 'views of the procession' go hang and simply buy a stall at the Scala. I shall see it just as well and better, and I shall have a comfortable seat, faint music floating through the air, and a cup of tea. Could anything be more peaceful and undisturbing? There will come a time perhaps when the great events of the day will all be thus posed before the cinematograph and there will be no fearful fuss about anything.

The Pictures

Of course it is the coronation procession and the investiture at Carnarvon which are the great attractions. They are printed in large type and I suppose have the place of honour on the programme; but what was far more amusing and interesting were the studies of animal life. A procession is always a procession, and I am not sure that even seeing the King and Queen popping into the picture every few seconds is half so thrilling as to see a real fight between two insects that look, one like an elongated wasp and the other like a frisky spider. It was the most uncanny spectacle. The 'creature' was very restive for a long time afterwards with that peculiar restiveness usually associated with a visit to a booth at a fair. For myself all Balham has been wakened by my roars of terror, and how the master dreams of 'hawful hanimals' is quite the topic of the kitchen.

Dramas

People talk a lot about cinematographs ruining the theatres, but if there is anything more unutterably dull than a wordless drama I should not like to see it. Kinemacolor gives us as few of these as possible in view of the public demand, but what it presents are really very exciting and well arranged. There were none of those clattering horses over miles and miles of country in the wake of a stolen heroine or dying children being rescued by the angels from a starving mother who in the next play may be anything from an Indian squaw to the Empress Josephine. The Kinemacolor dramas are terse, beautifully reproduced, and commendably short. Still, as far as I am concerned, the whole lot of them are not worth one of the pictures of animal life, scenes of foreign parts, and incidents in flower life which make up the bulk of the programme. These make the entertainment unique and are well worth dozens and dozens of visits to the lovely Scala Theatre.

'THE MAKING AND EXHIBITING OF LIVING PICTURES'
by Mr. Birt Acres
(Thursday, February 11, Mr. Stroh in the Chair.)

Journal of the Camera Club
May 1897

MR. BIRT ACRES COMMENCED HIS LECTURE by briefly sketching the evolution of animated photographs, and the apparatus for exhibiting them, from the old 'wheel of life' or zoetrope, mentioning the instruments and processes of Prof. Muybridge, who first successfully projected living pictures on the screen about nine years ago; Prof. Anschuz; Friese Greene who was the first to use a film, Demeny; Marey, Edison's kinetoscope; and Lumiere. He claimed, and said that he could prove, that he was himself the first to attempt to take, and to succeed in taking, photographs of events as they were happening, rather than 'got-up' scenes in a studio or elsewhere, of which he gave a short exhibition at a meeting of the Royal Photographic Society in January, 1896, his apparatus having been privately demonstrated as early as August, 1895. Messrs. Lumière, he admitted, had beaten him, and their instrument was a very fine one, but he thought they had followed a bad policy in placing it upon the music-hall stage.

In his experimental work he had met with considerable difficulty in connection with the preparation of the film upon which the photographs were to be taken, great exactness being necessary in cutting it to size and in punching the perforations required to ensure registration. It was absolutely essential that the celluloid should thoroughly seasoned in order to prevent shrinkage, and the only satisfactory variety that he had been able to find was manufactured by an American company, having agents in London. Apparatus had been recently mentioned which was said not to require perforated films, but in his opinion the perforations were essential to the accurate registration of the pictures, for the length of the film was subject to alteration by variations of temperature, and the register was thus impaired.

Mr. Birt Acres then proceeded to explain the action of the camera with which the pictures were taken. In the construction of this instrument the chief problem was to devise a method of moving the film forward at a very rapid rate, bringing it up to a dead stop for an extremely short time, and then moving it on again. To meet this requirement the system of jerking the sprocket-wheel was advocated in certain quarters, but he preferred his own system, for which he took out a patent two years ago, and the action of which he now exhibited and explained. The system was constructed to carry a spool containing 250 feet of film, upon which photographs were

Birt Acres, date unknown.
National Museum of Film,
Photography & Television

taken at the rate of twelve per foot, the exposed portion being wound on to a second spool; in projecting, also, the film which had passed through the lantern was received upon an empty spool, instead of being run out loose into a box or basket, as was the case with some apparatus. The camera was fitted with a simple form of revolving shutter, and a finder was placed on the top, the whole being enclosed in a box which could be readily carried, and all that was necessary for taking the pictures was to turn the handle on the outside. The entire process had been reduced to the upmost simplicity, for in taking the negatives, printing the positives, and showing them in the lantern, nothing had to be done but to turn the handle.

Choice of subject must be left entirely to the experience of the operator. The speed at which the photographs were taken must depend, of course, upon the nature of the subject. A regiment of soldiers, marching twenty feet from the camera, and at right-angles to it, would require perhaps twenty views per second, but he had for some time been endeavouring to show the movements of clouds, and for this purpose he took about one negative per second, thus exaggerating the movement but retaining the form. He preferred to work with the sun directly behind the camera. If one were photographing, say, a street scene, and after a short time the street became practically clear, one need not waste film when there was nothing of interest to photograph, but the exposure could be temporarily stopped and continued as desired.

For the development of the film Mr. Acres used a wooden frame in which were fixed a number of pegs, about one and a half inches apart, round which the film was wound, a hundred feet of film requiring a frame about 30 in. x 24 in. This frame fitted into an upright dish containing the developer, and he was able in that manner to develop a film up to 200 feet in length absolutely evenly from beginning to end. To print the positive the two films were placed together and exposed by turning the handle in the same manner as when taking the negative, the speed depending upon the rapidity of the sensitive coating, the quality of the light, and the density of the negative. The films could be dried upon similar frames to those used for developing, but a better plan was to wind them upon drums, and the drying could be accelerated by rapidly revolving the drums.

The lecturer thought that the system of animated photographs, and their exhibition by projection, would be something more than a "nine days wonder," and that it afforded excellent opportunities for the production of results of great artistic value. He was now pursuing a series of experiments with the object of adapting the three-colour process to his apparatus and had nearly completed an instrument by means of which it would be possible to take the photographs and to project them in natural colours.

At the conclusion of the lecture several series of photographs taken by Mr. Birt Acres were exhibited by means of his projection apparatus.

A cordial vote of thanks was passed to Mr. Birt Acres for this lecture and demonstration, and the proceedings terminated.

HOW TO BECOME A BIOSCOPE MODEL

**George Edgar, ed.,
*Careers For Men, Women,
and Children.* Vol. i.
1911, p. 104–10

TO BE A BIOSCOPE MODEL is a very modern form of employment, about which there are prospects, though, at the moment, it is only to be counted as means of income on a supplementary basis. The business of animated pictures calls for the model, whose duty it is to assist in working out the ideas which are placed before the public in animated picture shows. Models are not required, as a rule, for nature studies, or photographs of events; their employment is largely confined to the production of the picture plays which are so much a part of the cinematograph business to-day.

The nature of the work is best seen by examining photographs as they are presented to the public. It is an examination which may strike the model strange to the work with misgiving. Some of the modern pictures shown on the screen are quiet little plays, in which the work of the actors would be comparatively easy to experienced people; but the most of these plays are comic, and the comicality of the cinematograph world is full of robust action. While it lasts, the playing of a comic conception for the camera must put a heavy task on the physical strength of the model. Judging from the average of such shows, the model has to run helter-skelter up and down stairs and across country; he is expected to fall as often as possible down steps, off bicycles, and into water; he is frequently covered with soot and flour by the way, and usually be-laboured and pulled about at the end of the journey. To take part in the comic situations realised for animated photography is, to say the least of it, a strenuous business.

A Supplemental Employment

The employment must be considered as a supplemental one, undertaken by workers connected with the stage. As such, it is useful as a means of adding to income, but there will be few people who make a living entirely out of this work. It is a summer employment, much of the work being done when things are dull on the stage for the rank and file workers in that profession. During the winter months there is little demand for models in England, the absence of sunlight making it impossible to take successful photographs. Even in summer it is a precarious occupation. It is true there are many large cinematograph firms and numerous smaller ones scattered all over the country, but the people who look out for the work very much outnumber the people wanted. The fact that there are so many people with qualifications for the work makes competition very keen.

The people who are employed are mostly comedians, actors and actresses out of work, and other unemployed workers of various grades in the theatrical profession. They know their business well enough to be able to enact a play in pantomime, which has to be broad and convincing, after one or two rehearsals, which do not as a rule take place under favourable conditions. Very often short plays and sketches are photographed on the day when the parts are handed out, after a brief rehearsal, and under the best circumstances little time is wasted. The average rate of payment for the work is 10s. per day, and half the sum for rehearsals, which never exceed one or two. Ten shillings a day, as supplemental income to an actor either in or out of employment would be a satisfactory addition if the work were of a permanent character, but it can never be looked upon as regular source of income. Considerable skill is demanded of the model. In merely dramatic passages of the domestic order, any experienced actor would find the work simple; but to carry out a part in a series of incidents performed at breakneck speed, and often of an unpleasant character, demands a great deal of resource, to say nothing of endurance. Models who are not experienced in the rough-and-tumble work of the stage would hardly think of securing work of this character, and if they did would not get it. Only experience people are engaged.

An Income for Theatrical People

As time goes by, a different class of film is being produced, aiming at greater realism and a finer type of art. For this purpose understudies of famous theatrical folk are sometimes secured to play the leading parts and higher remuneration is offered to them. Some days before the actual photographic production the book of the play is handed to these principals, and they simply attend the actual representation of the play before the recording machine. For such performances fees of from £2 to £3 are paid. It is along these lines that a lucrative development of the film-making business may be anticipated by the artist. Already leading French players pose to the camera in plays more ambitious than the run of animated picture plays of the past, and the probability is that sooner or later personality will count, even in this field of theatrical presentation.

Models are engaged in many ways. Advertisements appear in theatrical papers such as the Era and the Stage, and engagements are also made by the different theatrical agents. The common way of securing work of this type is the best—that is, to make a list of a number of firms engaged in the animated film business and to call on them personally. Note is taken of the applicant's name and address, his experience and qualifications, and when engagements are available he is asked to call. Expenses out of town, for plays which have to be produced under exceptional natural circumstances, are usually borne by the organisers of these enterprises.

"Cinematograph Operator (filling the only gateway):
'Now a pleasant smile, please.'"
Punch, 26 February 1908.

HOW TO BECOME A BIOSCOPE PHOTOGRAPHER

The man who takes the pictures for bioscope purposes is a development of the photographer, of comparatively recent growth. The performance of such work is interesting, apart from the fact that men find it a means of livelihood. Like the press photographer, the taker of animated or moving pictures leads a very strenuous life, and only a photographer with a taste for adventure and a strong constitution would care to follow it. Every day, in every part of the world, subjects are being photographed for animated picture shows, and behind the camera there must be an operator.

Unusual qualities go to the making of a successful operator for cinematograph purposes. For instance, he must not be a man who studies his own comfort overmuch, or he would not be in the business at all. The operator must be prepared to see little of his home. In the summer months, when his work calls him here, there and everywhere, photographing the great panorama of events, he lives very strenuous days. Not only is he constantly travelling, a wearing process, but the actual work involves in many cases both difficulties and dangers. The operator visits the jungle to photograph natural history pictures; he has joined hands with the correspondent, in appearing where there is war; and from these exciting pursuits in out-of-the-way places to the simpler tasks performed at home he encounters many dangers and overcomes many difficulties. It is quite an ordinary item in the day's work for a photographer to cover two or three hundred miles by rail, obtain the desired pictures perched on some perilous vantage-ground, and return to headquarters within forty-eight hours. In addition to carrying about his heavy equipment from place to place, he has all the anxiety of getting favourable positions for his work. It will thus be seen that the operator must be a strong man, prepared for the spice of dangerous adventure, and almost tirelessly resourceful and ready to act in constantly recurring emergencies.

The Tricks of the Trade

Although the actual taking of an animated picture looks simple enough, it is by no means commences and ends with the mere rapid turning of a handle. All the knowledge required by the expert photographer is necessary, for focus, time exposure, and other technical details, and this would be acquired before entering the service of a firm of film makers. The tricks of his trade must be picked up through the actual experience gained by doing the work. There is no school where the knowledge can be acquired and firms who produce films do not want to try some expensive experiments. A wrong focus or some trifling neglect of detail may lead to heavy loss. Photographs are taken at a rate of sixteen a second, and five pounds worth of film can be rendered, useless in as many minutes. In addition, the picture is lost and the opportunity of getting the subject, in many cases, may not occur again. The work entails much nervous strain, especially on the big occasions, such as a horse race for reproduction the same night, or a royal function, which has to be handled in the same rapid manner. The important incidents are over quickly, and if anything goes amiss with the camera at the critical moment, the operator is face to face with failure.

For this work the operator does not get heavy rate of pay; indeed, his income does not reach the rate of pay given to a press photographer. While the latter may be paid from £4 to £12 a week, the cinematograph operator only receives a salary of from £2 to £5 per week, though he may get a percentage of his negatives, which in some instances, amounts to a considerable sum. For particularly risky employment, such as a trip to the jungle or service during war, the operator, would, of course, make special terms and get higher pay. The position is not easy to obtain. Only skilled operators are taken, so that the candidate for employment in this field must learn his work by hook or crook, before any company will engage him. At present the supply of such men exceeds the demand. In the United Kingdom there are seven or eight large firms of film makers, but they only employ the services of four or five camera men each, while dozens of smaller firms are represented by one or two. All alike insist on the skilled man, and will not try experiments with unskilled operators which might prove expensive. Beyond the interest and excitement of travelling and recording passing events of considerable importance, the work of an operator has many drawbacks and cannot be reckoned as one of the most profitable careers. With the rapid development of the business and the need for greater individuality in the pictures shown, this is one of the occupations which might improve for exceptionally capable men.

HOW TO BECOME A BIOSCOPE SUBJECT INVENTOR

A new source of income has been developed by the growing popularity of the bioscope and the needs of entertainers who depend on the attractions of moving pictures. The picture theatre is a very modern development, but it has come to stay, and those who know the most about its business side assert that only the fringe of its possibilities has been reached. In other articles this work deals with employments arising out of the new business, but there is one form which can hardly be called an employment, and yet opens up possibilities of supplemental incomes to men and women possessing the right type of mind.

The bioscope theatre, if it has to succeed, must in future depend upon the interests of its pictures. Of these there are at present three classes: topical events, which usually force themselves on to the attention of the film maker—the Derby or the University boat-race are typical instances; out-of-the-way phases of life—big game shooting in Africa or whale fishing might be used to illustrate this class of subject; and as a last class, the subject picture, which is a little play in pantomime form and has to be originated and reproduced in action for the purposes of the camera. Of these three classes the topical event is usually appreciated at its proper value by the film maker without any reference to outside workers. The out-of-the-way phase of life is suggested both by people interested in the business of film-making and people outside the trade interest; but a suggestion of this kind has little or no value from the point of view of income. The third class opens up a new field of work for the man with the creative mind and calls into play faculties which are associated, more or less, with the making of drama. In the origination and planning of these subjects there is opportunity of making income, perhaps limited at present, but undoubtedly displaying possibilities for the future.

Studying the Subjects Necessary

The quickest way of gathering the needs of this new interest is to visit the many bioscope theatres which are now to be found all over London and its provincial cities and towns, and so learn exactly the kind of thing required. A common item in the programme is the play in pantomime. It usually tells a story—broadly comic or obviously dramatic. There is a definite plot behind the construction of such a sketch, demanding the power of originating stories and developing them by action, which is seen in its highest form in the works of the dramatist. The demand for plays is an increasing one, and competition in the trade makes it necessary to continually produce novel forms of this kind of photographic entertainment. Naturally the more subjects of the type are used the more difficult it becomes to invent them. Further, the limits of the camera are so strictly defined that only a proportion of the ideas available can be used, excellent ideas having to be rejected because it is found impossible to work them out before the camera. Good, practical, working ideas are in demand, and the man or woman who has the knack of inventing a story full of situations, life, and action, likely to please the public, ought to find a constant market for such ideas. film makers usually employ men thoroughly acquainted with

Costume department of the Méliès, c. 1900.
National Museum of Photography, Film & Television.

the work of the trade who may be depended upon to invent subjects, but it is so obviously just as likely that still better plots for plays may be suggested by people who have no acquaintance with the business side of this new industry. The man who can keep on inventing comic situations is, at the moment, invaluable to the bioscope business if his subjects come within the limits of photographic reproduction.

The Limitations of the Camera

At first sight the work of inventing subjects for treatment in the bioscope theatre seems so easy that every one is likely to be tempted to it as a home amusement. Almost every form of creative work appeals to the inexperienced, who turn light-heartedly to the production of short stories, plays and poetry, under the impression that one has only to begin to produce successful work. Experience teaches that such a light-hearted approach only leads to failure. The same may be said of the possibilities of inventing bioscope plots and plays. Only men and women who really study the matter and have the inventive temperament are likely to succeed in this work. The majority of people who try it fail because they have no critical faculty which will enable them to compare their happy ideas with successful work actually produced—i.e. they cannot tell whether their ideas are commonplace and impracticable or whether they are original and practical. They seem to think that if the chief characters in their plays or sketches get into impossible situations, or undertake ridiculous things, that the camera will do the rest. As a matter of fact, ideas must be good, tell a clear story, possess originality, and make a certain appeal, and they can only be created by inventive-minded persons who have some idea of the obstacles in the way of success. Then again, it is not sufficient to invent ideas and leave the camera to do the rest. The camera can only do certain things; and if more is asked of it than it can do, by the play submitted, the idea fails to find a market, no matter how brilliant it may be.

There is a demand for this type of work which is going to increase rapidly. Comic subjects are preferred, and are rarely offered in the right quarters. Next in popularity is the little drama with a strong domestic incident and plenty of homely pathos. The plot of any play should be simple and capable of being graphically represented in pantomime. The highly sensational plot makes a third bid for popularity. Such ideas should be worked out carefully, and should appear in MS. almost like a skeleton of ordinary dramatic literature, with every detail indicated—story, characters, scenery, grouping of figures, and incidents. The whole should be neatly typed and sent to any one of the firms employed in making films, most of whom advertise in the theatrical papers. It is not suggested that there is a living to be made in this class of work, but it is worth considering as a supplemental form of income. Most firms engaged in the work invent their own plots—so little do the outside public grasp what is needed. Suggestions are carefully considered, and usually a cash offer is made. A guinea for a mere suggestion is the usual price, but complete plots with all the detail worked out bring just what they are worth—anything from three guineas upwards. The practice of producing pictures on a royalty basis is hardly in vogue at present, but this is a development which must take place sooner or later.

"People we admire. **The cinematograph actor, to whom this sort of thing is an ordinary day's work."** *London Opinion*, **21 February 1914.** *Stephen Bottomore.*

Bernard. E. Jones, ed.,
*The Cinematograph
Book: A Complete
Practical Guide to the
Taking and Projecting of
Cinematograph Pictures*
1915, pp. 32–35

ACTUAL OPERATION. Assuming everything is ready for exposure, the operator starts turning the handle, in the same direction as the hands move around a clock. This must be done steadily and evenly, at the rate of two turns per second. It will be as well to practice turning beforehand with an empty camera, using a watch having a seconds hand as a guide to the rate of turning, unless, of course, the camera has a speed indicator.

The operator should form, if possible, a rough idea of how much film he wishes to expose on a particular subject. If the whole spool, there is nothing to do but continue turning until the handle suddenly runs easier, thus showing that all the film is through; whereas, if only a portion of the spool is wanted, the outside measurer must be watched and the turning stopped directly the desired figure is recorded. It is usual to indicate the end of the exposure in such a case, either by operating a punching device or by opening the camera and nicking a small piece out of the edge of the film with a scissors. During operating an eye must be kept on the subject, to see that everything continues right and that no person or obstruction gets in the way.

'Topicals'. Something may here be said about topicals, or 'newsy' films, including such things as processions, pageants, reviews, athletic displays, opening ceremonies, cricket or football matches, and so on. Quite the most important consideration with such subjects is the selection of a good standpoint. Sometimes, this may be arranged beforehand by application in the right quarter, or by making friends with officials, but more often the operator has to put up with the best he can get and to take his chance with the public. The only advice that can be given it to come reasonably early, to keep on good terms with the crowds or rival operators, and to accommodate oneself readily to any requests made by the police or others in authority. Pliability and a conciliatory attitude in the last respect often leads to special facilities being offered, whereas the contrary spirit may raise up unexpected obstacles. A standpoint slightly elevated, so as to above the heads of the people, is desirable, though occasionally it is better still if one can get right in front. When need arises, additional height may be got by fully extending the tripod legs, standing on a box or other convenient support to operate. Possibly the camera case will have been made strong enough to serve.

As far as possible, the distance should be judged at which the pageant, procession, or whatever it may be, will pass or take place. The camera should then be focused upon that distance, or the lens set to it by means of the scale which is, or ought to be, provided. For most topical subjects not actually close to the camera and in a fairly good light, so that an unusually large stop is not needed, it will be about right to set the lens scale to a distance of 100 ft. When the subject comes in sight, the camera is promptly pointed in the right direction by means of the tripod adjustments, the handle being instantly started and the object of interest kept in the picture by watching the outside finder and working the turntable if necessary. When a long procession of pageant is filmed, it is seldom that the whole of it is taken, unless of exceptional public attraction and warranting the expenditure of so much film. It is more usual to expose only on the principal features or most striking portions, stopping the handle when one of these has passed and starting it again when the next appears. The sections of the film should not, however, be made too short and too abrupt.

If the film is to be disposed of, what follows must be done quickly. Preparations should previously have been made for its prompt reception, development and printing, and the speediest way back should have been ascertained. Nowadays, if a topical film is to have much value, it has to be shown publicly on the screen within the briefest possible time after the actual event.

Staged Subjects and Story Pictures. These are scarcely within the scope of the amateur or the worker on a small scale. Except in such incidents as can be acted suitably in outdoor surroundings, a well-lighted studio with ample room is indispensable. This should preferably be on the top of a house, or, at least, in open surroundings. There should be liberal glazing for the admission of daylight, while, unless the work is to be hindered by time and weather, an adequate installation of mercury-vapour or arc lamps is also required. The scenery and accessories are much the same as for the ordinary theatre, save that backgrounds, etc, may be in monochrome instead of colour. Usually professional artistes are engaged for the different parts. The larger film-producers keep stock companies, including a certain number of "stars," but smaller firms, or those who only go in for an occasional staged subject, are content to secure the spare-time services of a few averagely good performers from a local theatre. The conditions for good film-acting are somewhat different from those obtaining on the ordinary stage. Since words are practically lost, gesture and expression become of primary importance, but these should not be exaggerated, except in farcical or comic films. The part should be spoken as well as acted, however, even though the wording may be more or less impromptu, in order to get a natural effect; and special distinctness of enunciation is desirable at all dramatic moments, as it much improves the realism of the film if the public can gather a few key explanations or sentences by watching the movements of the mouth. Care must be taken that the actors keep within the field of view of the lens and make their exits properly outside it. As an aid to this, it is advisable to draw two diverging chalk lines on the floor from the position of the camera to indicate the space within which all action must take place. Careful planning and repeated rehearsal are always necessary, to secure that everything shall be done in the minimum time, in order to avoid waste of film.

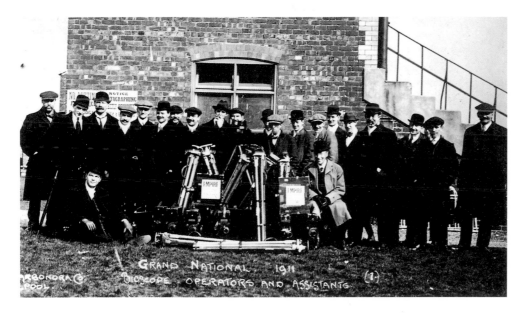

Bioscope operators and assistants at the Grand National, 1911.
National Museum of Photography, Film & Television.

STAGE CELEBRITIES IN CINEMA
RELATE THEIR EXPERIENCES BEFORE THE CAMERA

Mme Sarah Bernhardt

The Strand Magazine
December 1915

MME BERNHARDT regards the cinema enthusiastically. "It is the wonder of the age," the French tragedienne remarked recently. "I must confess that it was the novelty of the idea which first led me to act before the camera. But since then I have become greatly impressed with the utility of moving-pictures, and although I have acted before the camera so little that I feel somewhat diffident about venturing an opinion, I really do think that the cinema is a great aid to an actor's art.

"When I first acted before the camera in *Adrienne Lecouvreur* I was afraid the film would be far from successful. the confined area in which I had to act in order to keep within the focus of the camera, the absence of audience and words, seemed so unreal that I could arouse no enthusiasm. However, I proved to be a bad judge of effects, and was agreeably surprised at the result."

Sir Herbert Tree

Particularly interesting are the views of Sir Herbert Tree, who first appeared in a picture-play four and a half years ago, when he played for the films in *Henry V* and *King John*. It is, however, as Svengali in *Trilby*, produced in the picture world by the London film Company, that Sir Herbert perhaps shows to greatest advantage on the screen.

"I think," he said, "that the cinema is creating a new appreciation, a new love of the romantic in the people. So far it has not helped the theatre, so that we must hope that in time the people may be led from their attendances at picture-palaces to tolerate the drama. I can see, however, that the cinema might be of great service to the actor in recording the works of producers for future generations. It might thus become an invaluable instructor, for at a moment's notice the past-masters of the art could be projected on the screen for the benefit of the student's attention, and he could in this way learn from his models and their experience."

Referring to his own experience and sensations when acting before the camera, Sir Herbert mentions the curious fact that when he played Wolsey in *Henry VIII*, and came to his downfall, he felt he must speak the words, and did actually recite them to the mute camera. "I simply couldn't help it," he said, when relating the incident. "To act without speaking was a strange experience for me, I admit. But I fell into the business quickly enough. In playing for the films, however, I found that an entirely different method is required, as different as sculpture is from painting. Looking at the pictures of myself afterwards, I thought I was quite passable—thanks to the operator."

Miss Sydney Fairbrother

Mr. Tearle's confrere in *Quinneys* at the Haymarket, Miss Sydney Fairbrother so long associated with Fred Emmey in that funniest of sketches, *A Sister to Assist Her*, has also acted for the pictures, and confessed to us that when she first saw her picture on the screen in that highly-successful Davison's film Sales Agency's picture drama, entitled *Iron Justice*, she could scarcely believe it was herself. "Surely," I said to myself, "that is not me making these deliberate and pronounced actions, forgetting that in cinema acting everything is done so broadly. There are no subtle touches in cinema acting. Whereas on the stage, for instance, you would say, with a quick indication of the hand, 'Take a chair,' in cinema acting you would move in a slow deliberate manner, saying, 'Ta-a-a-ak-a-a-cha-cha-cha-ir', prolonging the agony so to speak, in order to give the operator time to record the proper effect. The operator's instruction's are at first very bewildering to the stage actor, and I remember I was very amused when the man behind the camera talked to me something like this when I was acting in a certain scene:

"'Move across to the hero; embrace him; sit down; get up; shake hands; look into his eyes; show agony; clutch your throat; faint'; and so on. It was like drilling a child, but the operator was merely indicating the time he wanted me to take according to the camera.

"I find the rehearsing is very tiring and tedious at times, while jumping backwards and forwards from one scene to another is apt to confuse you. Sometimes it is necessary to rehearse a part many times to get the proper effect. For instance, in *Iron Justice*, I tried a certain fall twenty-three times before I got it correct from the operator's point of view. I had to fall so that the picture was in perspective and the hands, feet, or head did not unduly predominate."

In answer to another question, Miss Fairbrother said that her experience was that cinema acting was in no way detrimental to stage acting. "In fact," she said, "I am inclined to think that it is beneficial, inasmuch as it revives little matters of technique which one may have forgotten."

"Sir Johnston Forbes-Robertson, whose great impersonation of Hamlet has recently been recorded by the cinematograph." *The Bioscope*, c. 1912.

**Theodore Waters
'The Escape of the
Convicts: On the
Biograph'**
The Strand Magazine
June 1906

FIRST A WORD OF EXPLANATION as to how the writer came to be arrayed in the clothes of a convict, and to be depicted on the film of a biograph in the act of escaping from prison.

Time was when people were satisfied with views of strange places at home or abroad, but lately the taste has run to melodramas and light comedy scenes, so that the makers of biograph pictures, instead of sending abroad for views, are compelled to invent them at home, which means a staff of pantomime actors, companies of actors to play the parts, scene-painters to give them the proper settings, and numerous other appurtenances, human and otherwise, of a regularly-equipped theatre. "But," said the camera-man in explaining these things to the writer, "there is just one way to learn the moving picture game, and that is to take part in it. We are about to take a series showing an escape from prison. There will be plenty of excitement and much shooting about the country. How would you like to be one of the convicts?"

I thought I would like it very much, and so one bright day I found myself in an office building clad in stripes and hard at rehearsing the scene which is now about to be described. Although classed as an interior, our cells were not even enclosed. The stage-carpenter had painted an ordinary flat with two barred doors in it and a partition 'wall' between the doors extending from the flat across the middle of the stage toward the camera. Thus the cells had neither fronts nor sides, but that fact did not appear on the moving-picture films. Besides, the arrangement could be adapted to make a jail courtyard scene, as will become evident later on.

Panzer, the restless prisoner in the cell next to mine, was pacing back and forth like a caged animal. The moment which for days we had waited was approaching, the moment when if all was propitious, we would make a break for liberty. But it was a question of the restless prisoner's preparedness. If he could tune himself up to the proper pitch this day, he would signal me to be on the look-out for the warder, and when the latter approached I would signal back through the cell wall so that he, my neighbour, could have time to feign the sleep that would throw the warder off his guard and give him a chance to spring upon the official from behind. Oh, we had planned if all went well we would be safe in Panzer's cottage by night, for he was as desperate as he looked, was my neighbour; his wife and children were waiting for him even then, and if we could but reach them . . . !

Hark! It was the signal. Panzer was ready. I rushed to the door of my cell and gazed steadily down the corridor. Yes, the warder was approaching. I rushed back and signalled the fact to my friend. I could hear the creak of his cot as he threw himself hastily upon it. I jumped for my own cot and sat upon it, my head in my hands, the picture of dejection. Through my fingers I could see the warden pause for a moment at the door of the cell. Then he passed onto the cell next door. I was off my own cot in an instant, listening at the barred door. I heard the key grate in the lock, the self-sufficient grunt of the keeper as he placed the water-cup upon the shelf, his momentary pause as he surveyed the reclining form of the prisoner, the creak of the door as he opened it again to go out, and then—Panzer was up and on him like a flash, bearing him with a dull thud to the ground, his left hand on his throat, his right reaching for the pistol that protruded ominously from the warden's pocket. I knew these things as by instinct as I raged in anticipation about my cell, panting, listening for the dread cry that might bring the other keepers. But it came not, that cry. Panzer had taken the pistol and with blow after blow of its butt end had driven back the utterance that might have foiled our plan. The keys, I heard them jingle as they came away from the keeper's belt. I heard the cell door flung clang as Panzer ran out, his cry of exultation as he rushed to my door. I waited an age, anathematizing his bungling fingers while he hunted for the key that would open my door. Any moment and a keeper might find business in that corridor. But at last—at last the door swung open and I was free—free! No, we must first get out of the jail. But that, too, we had planned.

"Tracy next," said Panzer, hoarsely.

We rushed to a cell near by.

"Thank Heaven! Free at last!" exclaimed Tracy, in a stage whisper, as he stepped from his cell.

"This way, boys; follow me!" exclaimed Panzer, With determined faces we ran along the corridor and out of a door leading to the roof, and as we rushed out, stripped suits and all, into the bright light of day, there fell upon us a roar of wild applause, the sound of multitudinous hand-clapping.

"Hurrah!" "Bravo!" "Do it again!"

"Very good!" "Hey there, stripes, yer the real thing all right! You look the part!"

"Where are you going to show that?" "Is that gun loaded?" etc.

In fact we were standing in the middle of the strangest arena ever contrived by man. We were standing upon the roof of the office building. The voices we heard came from its hundreds of back windows, which were crowded with an army of typewriters and office clerks who had been enjoying their luncheon-hour with a view of the hair-raising melodrama, The Convicts Escape, which in the manner just described, was having its first scene enacted on the roof-top in the heart of a business district.

In the streets below the tide of prosaic business ebbed and flowed, all unconscious of the proximity of romance. Only those fortunate souls with box-seats in the proscenium were aware of the sights and sounds which the theatre-going public for the most part imagine takes place far from the madding crowd.

Sights and sounds! Yes. The public taste in moving pictures (which has been sated with scenes of foreign travel and now demands 'stories,' i.e., connected series of melodramatic incidents, comic or tragic) is so exacting in the matter of realism that, in order to make the pantomimes as lifelike as possible, the performers are required to talk as well as to act their parts.

And that is why the progress of the fight between the convict and the warder in the one cell was perfectly apparent to me in the next—I could hear every word; that is why Panzer cried hoarsely, "Tracy next!"—to enable the picture machine to convey the exact expression of a man keen to release a fellow prisoner from his cell; that is why our faces were 'determined' as we ran along the corridor and out on the roof, where we met the applause of the people in the windows.

Our business on the roof was not yet completed. But in the meantime, the cells below had to undergo a transformation in readiness for the succeeding scene, which was to represent the yard of the prison. This became evident when the stage-manager said "Now, then, carpenter, tear away the partition and make an exterior of the flat; put numbers on the cell doors and hang a bell-rope down the wall for the keepers to give the alarm, while we are getting these boys out of jail. This way, convicts."

He led us round towards a half-open scuttle in the roof and told us to climb into it. The picture-machine was placed just behind the scuttle.

"Now," said the stage-manager, "as soon as I close this scuttle we will start the machine. Then you fellows push up the scuttle as though you had found your way out of the roof of the jail. Climb out and run crouching to the edge of the roof and peer over. We will have another machine down below to get you as you go down the wall."

Slowly, stealthily, as convicts might, we raised the iron cover, and with the machine recording every movement, every expression, we crept along the roof and peered over the edge. Ten feet below was a yard. An iron ladder led down to it, but at the foot of the ladder walked a sentry, an actor in jail-warder's uniform, armed with a rifle. Another camera had been recording his slow pacing to and fro, and now, of course, it began to show our heads looming menacingly above him. Farther along the stage-manager, all excitement, but out of range of the camera, was shouting directions.

"That's right, you fellows, keep on dodging back as he paces up and down. Now, when he turns his back on you, you, Panzer, run down the ladder and jump on him. That's it; come quick now!"

Panzer slid over the edge like a cat and dropped swiftly to the end. Tracy went next, and I followed. By the time I had reached the foot of the ladder the fight had begun. Panzer had the guard on his back, choking and beating him into feigned insensibility. Tracy got the rifle which had dropped from the guard's hands, and I got his revolver from his hip-pocket. Leaving him where he had fallen, we all three men ran exultingly toward and past the camera.

"Now, then, for the alarm," said the stage-manager.

We went back to the cells, what a transformation! The partition had been torn away. Numbers had been placed on cell doors, and down the face of the wall dangled a rope. Apparently it had hung from a bell for back of it was a placard with the following legend:

    1 Bell........Fire.

    2 Bells........An escape.

    3 Bells........General Alarm.

The camera was already in motion, pointing to the door of the cells. A call from the stage-manager, and out of the door of one of the cells crawled painfully the guard who had been first struck down by Panzer. Painted blood streamed down his forehead, but the rest of his face had all the pallor that grease-paint could give it. His movements were painful in the extreme, but his determination was apparent enough. He meant to reach that rope or die melodramatically in the attempt. Just before he reached the dangling cord, he managed to get upon his feet, so that the audience might be sure of his intention. Then with one wild clutch of the bell-cord he fell apparently lifeless to the floor. Instantly from all direction swarmed other warders who gazed horror-struck at their comrade on the floor.

The gesticulations were violent, their language not less so, as they told one another of the horrible thing that had happened. Yes, there could be no doubt of it; the prisoners had escaped, the cells were empty. So their leader, Denny Mullen, a character of some note, reached for the bell-cord and gave it three tremendously obvious pulls. Then they all ran off the stage. Whereupon the senseless warden, for the sake of a last human touch, stirred uneasily, got upon his feet again, reached for the cord, and fell stone-dead, to the sad music of a street-piano down in the roadway.

"Having an audience, isn't so bad as long as you can keep it at a distance," remarked the stage-manager, while the property-man struck the scene. "If you will notice any series of pictures, even those of crowded city streets, you will seldom see a person on the screen who does not belong to the scene. Now, the absence of people not required does not mean that the negative has been retouched. Retouching our negatives at least a shilling a foot, and as a good series is often one thousand feet long, the expense of retouching becomes prohibitory. No we find it better to bribe, or coax, or even to fool the crowd to move out of range. We have even gone to the trouble of using two picture-machines, one without a film in it to engage the crowd at one point, while we took another real picture at another. Again we have been interfered with by persons, who, honestly enough, thought we were perpetrating a crime."

The next scene took place in the open country. We donned our stripes again and submitted to being chased by the warders. We ran up hill and down dale, firing back as we ran, and just as soon as we had passed the picture-machine the warders would always break out of the bushes and race after us, firing as they ran. None of the warders managed to hit us during these pursuits, but, because the sympathy of an audience is always paradoxically on the side of the fleeing prisoner, we would occasionally wing a warder. That is, on of the smooth-faced pursuers would throw up his hands and do a slow, twisting fall, well out of the way of his jumping comrades. This did not deprive the picture-machine of his services, however, for disguised by a false moustache, he would be back in the next picture chasing us as hard as ever. I intimated that if we kept it up long enough all the warders would have full beards, but the joke apparently fell upon barren soil.

"You fellows have got to eat." We will have the interrupted picnic-party now," said the stage-manager. We were in truth hungry enough, but the stage-manager had reference to a stage picnic. Two actors and an actress had been engaged to depict a party of three lunching under the trees. They were already in position waiting for the picture-machine to start. so that they could give a realistic imitation of how actors eat. But the food was real enough.

"Now," said the stage-manager, "you three are eating your luncheon. The convicts will break out of those bushes over there. they will run down upon you and hold you up. The two girls will run out of the picture, leaving the young man in the hands of the convicts. Panzer, you back him up against the tree while the other two convicts grab the food. Threaten to shoot him if he does not direct the keepers the wrong way, and then all three convicts hide behind these bushes near by while the warders run into the picture. The youth will direct them the wrong way. Then the convicts will run in the opposite direction, whereupon you girls will run in and rate him for his cowardice, and when the warders return direct them the right way."

We came up the path yelling so fiercely that the girls were almost scared, and the youth quivered under the point of Panzer's pistol as though it were loaded with ball instead of blank cartridges. We 'scooped' the food artistically and waited behind a bush for the warders to run in, which they did as soon as directed. The young man sent them wrong, and then we scurried off in the opposite direction. Back came the girls, who proceeded to express their opinion of the mere man who still shivered against the tree trunk. Enter Denny Mullen heading the warders, down centre. "Halloa, Bright Eyes!" quoth Denny. "What's the trouble?"

"Oh sir, the horrid convicts! You have been deceived. They have gone off with our dinner!"

"Confound them! This way, boys!"

Exit left, and quick curtain for the lens.

But real excitement prevailed when we held up an automobile. How natural for your twentieth-century jail- breaker, after scurrying across country to the main high-way, to come across an imported motor-car all ready to carry him home to wife and children dear! We got it by pre-arrangement just after we 'broke cover' on the side of a hill, very much to the consternation of some employes who were raking hay in a field near by. They had not noticed the picture-machine, and when they saw three desperately-striped villains run up to the car and, calmly shooting its occupants, forge ahead, they were much amazed and somewhat indignant. We would have reassured them then and there, but the eye of the camera was wide open, and the oncoming warders were already requisitioning another car further back, preparatory to giving us the chase of our lives.

"What is this all about?" asked someone who was standing close at hand.

"Taking moving pictures," said the man in charge. "We have the necessary permit from the authorities."

Of course there came a time when our car gave out and broke down by the side of the road, just where there was the finest background for a hand-to-hand fight that could possibly be selected. With the picture-machine grinding rapidly, we used the tonneau as a breast-work, over which we killed some warders. The latter had taken up a position behind some wagon-trucks,

"With the machine recording every movement, we crept along."

the drivers of which had worked for us their employers by hanging around our preparations with expectant grins. But when we turned our guns their way and began to shoot, there was a sudden and valiant return to their usual occupation of driving wagons that was refreshing indeed. The warders beat us, of course. After wasting more cartridges than we could ever have carried away from the jail with us, we turned and fled down a steep bank, where we dropped flat in the grass in order to give our pursuers a chance to fire over our heads, and to do some of those slow, twisting falls in the very eye of the camera.

Now, it must not be inferred from all of this that we were aimlessly drifting about the country for the sake of being shot at by relentless warders. We had been aiming all the while to reach the cottage where Panzer's stage wife, accompanied by two 'pathetically pretty' children, was awaiting our coming. Of course, she did not know she was awaiting our coming, for the stage-manager had not yet told her about it, but we knew she would be waiting and we counted much upon her assistance. The house was a typical country cottage, with roses climbing up the sides, and a large dog chained in the wood-shed. Panzer meant to pat the dog lovingly on the head, and the dog was to fawn upon him just to prove to the audience that animal instinct always recognises an honest convict when it sees one. But the dog absolutely refused to rehearse the part, and the head convict refused to take a chance in the real scene unless the animal rehearsed first. So we passed the dog and ran to the back door, where Tracy and I waited for Panzer to break the news to his wife and tell her that we were outside. Of course the camera implied that she welcomed us for the sake of her husband, poor woman, for after a while, Tracy came outside again to keep watch, and that is where the mean guards began to get the best of us, for one of them sneaked up while he was not looking and shot Tracy in the back. He staggered into the house to warn us, and we—but the picture-machine stopped running at that moment because the rest of the scene was to be shown as an interior which we were to enact on the office roof.

We found our audience waiting for us to enact the last of our melodrama on the roof of the office building. The property-man had done wonders with hammer and brush during our absence. He had erected a cottage interior, a squalid room with plaster breaking from the walls, rickety furniture, and a general air of such dilapidation, such as the theatre-going public would naturally expect to see in the home of a convict. The convict's wife was there, too, a well-dressed actress who, when she heard of her new lot in life, promptly laid her finery aside and donned other clothes for the occasion. The children, too, a boy and a girl, looked more of the Fauntleroy that of the jail-brat class, and they, too, had to be 'undressed' for the part.

When the last scene opened the convict's wife was discovered seating with boy in her lap. She was putting on his new pair of stockings and telling him a story of the cruel enemies who had told lies about his father, who, in consequence, had been compelled to 'go away,' but who would come back soon to his darlings and take them to a happier, brighter, home. The little girl was 'helping mother' clean house, with a broom as twice as big as herself.

"And when is papa coming back, mamma? Will he be here tonight?"

"Hush, darling! Not tonight; but be a good boy, and—"

Hark! What was that. The child slipped from her arms. She stood up, impelled by a nameless dread. There it was again! That voice! That step upon the threshold! Ah! Yes. It was! It was! My husband! The swift, exciting music of the omnipresent piano down in the street took the place of a regular orchestra.

"My husband, you here!"

"Yes!" (Embracing her and the children hurriedly.) "But there is no time for words! They are after us, those fiends of warders!"

"Us?"

"Ah, I forget! My friends are outside! I will bring them in!"

Panzer ran outside and brought us in, just as he had done in the exterior view of the house. We were introduced and held the necessary confab, after which Tracy ran out again so that the warder could sneak up and shoot him. While he was doing this I was anxiously peering through the ground-glass window—ground-glass because when we broke it later the cracks would show plainly in the camera.

What was that? A shot!

Tracy reeled into the room and fell dead, well up the stage. I jumped for the open door and barred it ostentatiously. Panzer grabbed Tracy's gun and, thrusting it right through the lower panes of ground-glass, began blasting away at the outside world. I—Heaven help me!—looked at the wall. There on the hooks hung an old grandfather's gun. Thrusting its muzzle crashing through the upper panes of ground-glass, I, too, blazed away at our enemies. The children stood apart, motionless, with a fear that was almost real. The wife wrung her hands and ready for a splendid display of fortitude. The street-piano struck up faster than ever. Panzer and I pumped lead. The keepers outside got busy with their revolvers and the window glass began to break into the room.

Heavens! What was it—wha—In my excitement I had exposed my form across the window and an imaginary bullet took me squarely between the eyes. The fierceness froze upon my face; the muscles of my legs began to relax; the gun dropped from my hand and with the directions of the stage-manager ringing dimly in my ears I lurched off the washstand upon which I had climbed and fell dead upon the body of Tracy. Tracy grunted horribly.

For a moment Panzer was nonplussed. But his wife grabbed my gun and loaded it for him, and he went on shooting. Out of the tail of my half-closed eye I could see them working furiously to stem the assault. The children were running backwards and forwards, and I felt in my dead bones that something would happen to them if they did not look out. And the something did happen. The little girl was crossing the room when suddenly she threw up her hands and fell down, centre. Neither the convict nor his wife noticed it, but the other child did.

"Oh, mamma," he cried, "Sissy has fallen down!"

With a shriek the poor mother turned to her dying child. Panzer also turned, realised the sad truth, and gave up the fight. He had not a blank cartridge left, poor fellow. With a despairing cry he gathered his family into his arms. Let the warders come now, if they wanted to. What was a prison cell in the face of this? Aye, what was death itself? Down in the street the music of the hurdy-gurdy had turned soft and plaintive.

Into the house surged the keeper, more black-moustached than ever. The leader took in the situation at a glance, of course, and in the presence of such grief waved his men back. They took off their hats and solemnly 'dressed the stage'. Then their leader very gently laid his hand upon Panzer's shoulder.

The heartbroken man arose and without a word, started for the door. His wife, as directed, held him tightly by the hand, reluctant to let him go. But at last, at last, he wrenched it away an went slowly out, leaving his poor wife with a live child on one arm, a dead one on the other.

"Hey, Tracy!" said Denny Mullen, as we stood up. "You're all covered with white. What is it?"

"Oh!" answered the other. "Talcum powder! We were not allowed to shoot off guns on the roof. So every time those fellows took an imaginary shot out of the window the stage-manager threw in a handful of talcum powder to make smoke."

"The oncoming warders were giving us the chase of our lives."

9 The Fairground Bioscope

by Vanessa Toulmin

> At the end of the row of exhibitions are two Cinematograph shows. The quickness with which the invention has been utilised for exhibition purposes speaks well for the enterprise of our showmen.[1]

SO WROTE THE REPORTER FOR *THE Era* in 1898 when he visited the annual World's Fair Exhibition at the Agricultural Hall, Islington in London. The enterprising exhibitors who were presenting moving pictures at the Christmas show were Randall Williams and the Chittock family, with both showmen converting their former attractions to incorporate the latest novelty of the age—animated pictures. The exhibiting of living pictures by two such established showmen, was the culmination of a year which had seen the cinematograph find a new but temporary home on the fairground. From 1897, to the onset of the First World War, the fairground bioscope shows, as they became known, were the principal means by which a large proportion of the population was introduced to moving pictures. Although the arrival of Randall Williams converted ghost-show at the 1896 World's Fair received scant notice in a London press accustomed to ten months of such attractions. It would prove a sensation at the annual Charter fair in King's Lynn on 15 February 1897:

> About the best and most up to date of the entertainments is that of Mr. Randall Williams, who in a tent splendidly lit up by an electric arc lamp, exhibits some excellent 'living pictures' by means of a cinematograph apparatus, the collection including a serpentine dance, The Czar in Paris, a Paris boulevard and march past of the Royal Blues.[2]

The adaptation, on the part of the fairground exhibitors to moving picture, may have appeared enterprising to the correspondent for *The Era* newspaper, but to the showmen who travelled the country attending fairs and fetes, the arrival of the cinematograph show appeared at an optimum time. It equipped them with a novelty which would challenge the growing supremacy of the steam powered roundabouts. Although, the shows and exhibitions were an integral part of the late Victorian fair, the arrival of the steam powered riding machines from the 1870s had challenged their previous dominance. The merry-go-rounds with their galloping horses and exotic creatures were the modern wonder of the fairground and the waxworks, illusion and menagerie shows, appeared old fashioned and reminiscent of another era to the fairgoing public. However, in December 1896, all this was to change when Randall Williams surprised the visitors to the Agricultural Hall with his latest novelty, the cinematograph show:

> Randall Williams ghost show is again located here, but this year they have abandoned the spectral business and are giving an exhibition of moving pictures, an alteration that appears to meet with approval.[3]

Showmen throughout the country were quick to follow the example set by Randall Williams. In Scotland, George Green, a prominent roundabout proprietor from the North of England who was based in Glasgow, also displayed living pictures at the annual Christmas show held at the Carnival building in Glasgow. These early shows ranged in size and capacity and were largely dependent on the previous function of the booth. Colonel Clark and the Biddall family, like Randall Williams, displayed moving pictures in their former ghost shows, which were elaborate structures with large stages for parading and reputedly capable of accommodating a thousand people. Other show-men were not so fortunate, and the earliest type of bioscope entertainment was to be found in the ground booth shows, with their low stage fronts and a limited holding capacity of between three to five hundred people.

As the shows become increasingly more popular and attracted greater revenue, the proprietors began to adapt and improve their exhibition booths to keep one step ahead of their rivals, and more importantly to increase the earning capacity of their attraction. From 1904, the bioscope shows became increasingly lavish and ornate and ulti-mately they were capable of catering for larger audiences, with many of the shows claiming upwards of a thousand people (inclusive of seating for four hundred or more). The arrival of the mammoth organs from makers such as Gavioli and Marenghi heralded the start of a new era, the organ-fronted shows which would later be known as the 'Great Shows'. Although the most lavish of these new exhibition booths were custom built by Orton and Spooners, a firm of engineers who catered for the fairground showmen, they also adapted former waxworks and illusion booths and incorporated the mammoth organs from Europe into the new frontage of the shows. The shows and the parades, which were an essential part of the entertainment, became larger in capacity and more sophisticated in the range of entertainments offered. Where once the audience would have thrilled purely to the novelty of seeing moving pic-tures, the fairgoers in the early 1900s could find such entertainment in a variety of venues. The showmen had to go one better than their static rivals and the spectacle of the parade and the free entertainment it represented, was the key to their continual success. The latest innovations were incorporated into the presentation and from 1906 Tom Tuby was just one of the many proprietors who was utilising the Gaumont Chronophone to present talking pictures. Paraders such as the Shu-fflebottom family became so prolific on the bio-scope front with their wild west show, that William 'Texas Bill' Shufflebottom eventually acquired a cinematograph show of his own.

These 'Great Shows' with their mammoth

organs, ornate frontages and additional equipment for transportation, reputedly cost in the regions of three to thousand pounds. However, the showmen of the day considered them a worthwhile invest-ment and continued to constantly expand and update their shows until the start of the First World War. The apogee of these elaborate exhibi-tions on the fairground were found at the great Charter fairs such as Hull and Nottingham when upwards of seven cinematograph displays domi-nated the fairs in 1907 and 1908. Although Randall Williams was arguably the first showmen to exhibit this attraction on the fairground, after his death in 1898, his famous show was soon superseded in size and ornamentation by the presentations displayed by his contemporaries. In Lancashire, President Kemp travelled the famous Dreamland and The Theatre Unique. The Holland family in Notting-ham presented their film displays in the Palace of Light. The fairs of the West Country were domi-nated by Hancock's Palace of Variety and Living Pictures and the Cambridge Fair was incomplete without William Taylor and his Cinema De Luxe standing side by side with Charles Thurston's Great Show.[4] At the pinnacle of their popularity over one hundred and twenty cinematograph booths were exhibited on fairgrounds throughout the United Kingdom. These were the golden years of the fair-ground shows and the ground capacity for these exhibitions was usually fifty feet in frontage and eighty feet in length. The size of the show could be lengthened or shortened depending on the amount of ground available and at Boston May Fair in 1914, Aspland's bioscope show occupied an area in excess of eighty feet.

The range of film presented in the fairground booths were similar to those found in music-halls and cinemas throughout the country, and would consist of actualities, comic events and the latest dramatic plays. The showmen would also film a local scene in the town they were exhibiting and advertise it as part of their performance the follow-ing night. William Haggar, a showman from Wales went on to successfully produce his own films which were distributed by Gaumont, including the famous *Life of Charles Peace* (1905) and *The Maid of Cefn Ydfa* (1914).[5]

The introduction of the Cinematograph Act in

1909 did not adversely affect the fairground exhibitors because the Reverend Thomas Horne, the Secretary of the Showmen's Guild of Great Britain, had campaigned for various concessions for the travelling tenting exhibitors.[6] However, this did not safeguard showmen from prosecution if they were found to be flouting the regulations laid out in the new Act. W. H. Marshall, a prominent showmen from Yorkshire, was fined £3 for erecting his structure within thirty feet of any other building.[7] Although the 1909 Act did not pose a threat to the continued existence of the travelling exhibition, the increase in the number of picture houses opening throughout the country would effectively result in the demise of the fairground cinematograph shows.

From 1912 onwards, showmen could be found opening static cinemas. William Taylor, for instance, retired from travelling and concentrated on running a chain of cinemas in Wiltshire. Other exhibitors soon followed his example and showpeople who opened permanent cinemas included the Holland family at Meacham and John Proctor in Wombwell. Perhaps the most successful transition to static cinema presentations was made by George Green, who founded the firm of Greens of Glasgow. At the time of his death in 1915, George Green was the proprietor of thirteen cinemas in Scotland and had continued to travel his cinemato-

graph shows until the onset of the First World War. During the First World War, severe restrictions were imposed on travelling fairs and many of the prominent families settled in an area and opened their exhibitions on a permanent basis. However, this was not always a successful move and at the end of the war, when the restriction were lifted, many of the showmen disposed of their shows and returned to the travelling life.

By 1914, the days of the fairground cinematograph shows had ended and the organs and frontages of these once elaborate exhibitions were cut down and incorporated into the latest fairground attractions. However, the contribution made by the fairground exhibitors in those pioneering days has never been forgotten. Edwin Lawrence of Lawrence's Marionettes and Animated Pictures Exhibition wrote in *The World's Fair* in 1939:

> He nursed the infant cinema. Saw it through all its early trials and troubles. Mothered it or fathered it through many illnesses until it became a strong sturdy robust youth. Then like the good natured unbusinesslike creature he was he handed it over to the local coal dealer, grocer, chimney sweep and the thousand and over petty tradesman of the small towns and villages who with no showmanship but with more business acumen in their little fingers than the showman had in his own body, cashed in on all the donkey work he had done.[8]

1. *The Era*, 29 January 1898, p. 20.
2. *Lynn Advertiser*, 15 February 1897.
3. *The Era*, 26 December 1896, p. 18.
4. See Appendix 3 for further details of these exhibitors.
5. Dave Berry, *Wales and Cinema: The First Hundred Years* (Cardiff: University of Wales Press, 1994), pp. 48–56.
6. Cinematograph Act 1909, Application of Act to Special Premises, Clause 7 Para 3. See also Bioscope, 6 January 1910, for a report on the formation of the Cinematograph Defence League.
7. *The World's Fair*, 11 February 1911.
8. Edwin Lawrence, 'The Infant Cinema: A Short History of the Moving Pictures. Part Three', *The World's Fair*, 17 June 1939, p. 44.

Hull Daily Mail
12 October 1897

HULL FAIR

**From the Royal Agricultural Hall
And Victorian Era Exhibition,
Earl's Court, London.**

**Randall Williams
The King of Showmen will
Visit Hull
During the Fair**

**With His Famous
Cinematographe,
of Animated Photographs
Bang up to Date and Worked by a Most Powerful
Electric Light**

**Driven by an
Engine and Dynamo Costing Over £1,000**

Below are a few of the animated pictures shown—

The Village Blacksmith; Mme Louis Fuller in a most beautiful Serpentine dance; the teetotaller that got drunk roars with laughter; the old gardener watering the plants, very humorous; the express train coming into a station, people coming in and out of the train very realistic; the sea waves; prize fight between Fitzsimmons and Corbett, a young woman taking a morning bath, wrestling match for the Championship of the World; Grand March past of the Royal Blues; the unfaithful wife; the good wife; on the beaches in the parz; bathing at Blackpool; a snow storm; and last but not least, the

Queen's Diamond Jubilee Procession

The Queen's carriage near St. Paul's, Prince of Wales, Duke of Cambridge, Foreign Prince, Colonial Premiers & Co.

The Era
29 January 1898

THE WORLD'S FAIR
(Second Notice)

ANOTHER VISIT to the Agricultural Hall has enabled us to examine more in detail the various shows which collectively, have constituted the attraction of the World's Fair . . .

At the end of the row of exhibitions are two Cinematograph shows. The quickness with which the invention has been utilised for exhibition purposes speaks well for the enterprise of our showmen.

Chittock advertises that no indecent pictures are exhibited at his establishment, to which, he avers, parents may safely take their children. He combines with the attractions of the Jubilee procession and other views the performances of some very well-trained dogs and monkeys.

Randall Williams's Cinematograph Show contains some views of a snowballing match, and of the funeral of the late William Terrias, in which many faces well known in the theatrical profession may be recognised. There is also a representation of a young lady taking a bath. The usual Jubilee procession concludes the entertainment.

WORLD'S FAIR AT ISLINGTON

THOUGH CHRISTMASTIDE IS PAST, the popularity of the World's Fair at the Agricultural Hall continues. Our opening visit to the great conglomeration of shows was paid when each booth was bubbling over with its eager patrons, when one could scarcely breathe amidst the crowd, and when the side shows were almost inaccessible. A calmer inspection reveals new beauties and discloses fresh wonders to our widely opening eyes . . .

Randall Williams's Cinematograph contains a most interesting series of views, including those representing the Diamond Jubilee Procession, A Spanish Bull Fight, and the turn-out of the fire brigade to the City of London fire. There are also in this show many other artistic and 'up-to-date' pictures. It is a very spirited and attractive exhibition.

Chittock's dogs and monkeys, admirably trained and very docile, active and obedient, add their performance to the main attraction to Chittock's tent—the excellent cinematograph which the proprietor makes the strong point of his exhibition. A striking animated picture shown here is one representing the Charge of the 21st Lancers at Omdurman. Chittock's show is as popular as ever.

THE WORLD'S FAIR

MESSRS. READ AND BAILEY'S great gathering of shows at the Agricultural Hall this year is as attractive as ever and the old familiar names again glitter in letters of gold above the elaborately adorned booths which are arrayed around the vast area of the Agricultural Hall. The exhibitions of all kinds are now in full swing, and enjoying steady prosperity . . .

Chittock's cinematograph is certainly a marvellous pennyworth, placing the results of one of the most startling inventions of modern times within the reach of the 'very humblest'. We can easily understand how eagerly, in some of the primitive agricultural districts visited by this fine show, the local population have united in admiration of the views which the ingenuity of man has endowed with movement and apparent life. Chittock's films are well chosen; and the subjects are such as are certain to entertain, instruct, and amuse the masses . . .

Randall Williams's Cinematograph appeals to the patriotic by depictions of the everywhere popular Lord Roberts, and to the merry and humorous by its scenes of broad fun, which evoke roars of laughter. A good selection of films and a smart and genial Cicerone insure for Randall Williams's show, the popularity it so well deserves.

Above: **The Era**, 21 January 1899
Below: **The Era**, 12 January 1901

Handbill for Randall Williams's Bioscope, 1897–98.
Celine Williams.

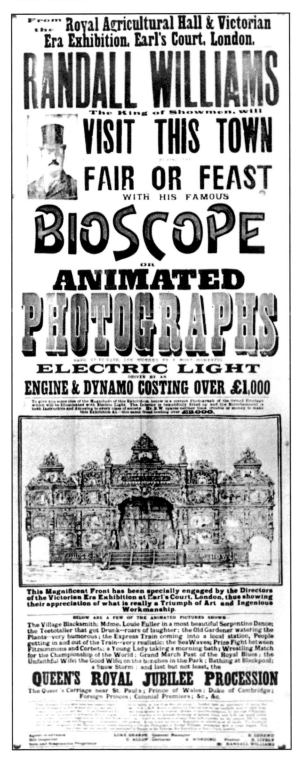

Randall Williams's No. 2 Show, Settle 1905. *Vanessa Toulmin, National Fairground Archive.*

George Green: first bioscope show, 1898. *National Fairground Archive.*

THE CINNY THAT SINNED

And the Audience that Wanted Their Money Back

The World's Fair
28 April 1906

JUDGE, JURY AND EVERYBODY in court roared again in the Salford Court of Record during the hearing before Judge Shee of the story of how the cinematograph failed to work. William Fenton Cross, St. George's Road, Bolton, a well known gentleman in the entertaining world, was claiming damages against James Morris, optician, Knowsley Street, Bolton.

The plaintiff, said Mr. Gibbons, had arranged with the defendant to work a cinematograph at Bolton, for three days in the New Year. "But," said the barrister, sadly, "it turned out worse than a broken down motor-car. The machine would not work. The band kept on playing, but the pictures were a gross and ghastly failure. There was a general uproar, the audience shouting out at the plaintiff when he tried to explain.

"When the pictures were thrown on the screen the man who had to explain them was unable to do so because the could not tell what the views represented. (Loud laughter.) The performance ended unduly early. (Renewed laughter.) The evening show was no better. The band did its duty nobly, but the pictures would not work, and the audience, which was a large one at the second show, made things lively."

William Fenton Cross said he engaged the defendant on a contract agreeing to pay £10, and Morris undertook to bring a new machine and show the latest pictures. He had to give two shows a day for three days.

Telling the Tale

What did you do when the pictures, would not work?—

I kept going on the platform and telling them the tale till they hooted me off.

And what happened then?—It got so serious that I locked myself in the dressing room. (Laughter.)

Why?—Well the folks wanted their money back, and I could not do that, because those who had paid threepence would have been asking for a shilling. (Renewed laughter.) Folks tried out the door when they were going out. (Much laughter.)

I saw the defendant after the afternoon show, and he said that the new machine was at Park Street; he said that he had forgotten that he had promised it to me.

Did you do better at the evening show?—No I was afraid to go on the platform, and I left the orchestra to fight it out. (Laughter.)

The Spice of Life

Mr. Jordan (who defended): Why did you advertise yourself as the South Australia Company, and that your pictures included the whale hunt in the Arctic region?—To give a little variety.

The plaintiff said he had to get someone else to produce the pictures for the remaining two days.

Mrs. Cross said that in previous years they had made from £40 to £70.

Several witnesses described the character of the performance. One, Mr. Sutton, said that pictures appeared on the screen with the heads at the bottom and legs at the top. (Laughter.) "Two or three friends in our street," he added, "have never spoken to me since."

Mr. Gibbons: Why?—Because I had sold them tickets. (Loud laughter.)

A witness for the defence said he played the flute in the band. There was no disturbance in the evening.

Mr. Gibbons: Wasn't there a meeting of the band on Monday night, when it became a question of whether they should refuse to play on the following day?—No.

Didn't someone throw a missile at the 'cello player?—I don't know.

Mr. Gibbons: I suppose you were hiding behind your flute? (Laughter.)

A verdict was given for the plaintiff, damages £35.

The World's Fair
5 June 1909

THE MODERN FAIR AS SEEN BY THE PRESTON DAILY POST
Cost of the Travelling Shows

Over £70,000 Worth at Preston

"AT A ROUGH ESTIMATE, I should value the portable property on Preston Pleasure Fair at between £70,000 and £80,000." This was the answer to a query put to one of the oldest and experienced showmen now in the town, writes a correspondent to the *Preston Daily Post*.

These figures seem rather startling, but on analysis are quite borne out. The unsuccessful proprietor of a travelling cinematograph or roundabout has not to be sparing in his expenditure if he is to succeed in securing patronage, and one only has to remember the vast quantities of carved and gilded work with which the modern attraction is decorated to realise that the initial expense on such things must be very great. An up-to-date cinematograph show, for instance, with its handsome exterior, an organ manufactured in Paris, and an engine for haulage and other purposes cannot be put on the road under £3,000 to £4,000. The value of this class of property now on Preston Fairground must total at least £20,000 . . .

The upkeep of a big show is also an important item, and the cost of maintaining the gilding and painting fresh, cannot be less than £200 to £300 a year, according to the size and style adopted. The staff required for a cinematograph show or roundabout, is about a dozen men, including the important individuals who invite the public to 'walk up' . . . .

The greatest changes have taken place within the last twenty-five years. Coming nearer the present day, everyone will remember how effectively the old fashioned 'ghost show' has been superseded by 'living pictures' which came into vogue at a time when the showman was at a standstill for novelties.

Interior of G. T. Tuby's Coliseum Show, South Yorkshire, 1907. *National Fairground Archive.*

Charles Thurston's Palace Show, Woodbridge, Suffolk, 1915. *National Fairground Archive.*

HOW MANY OF US REMEMBER THE TIME, which, after all, is but a few years since, when it was the custom, not only with a large section of the public, but even with those actively engaged in some department of the Cinematograph or entertainment business, to imagine that this fascinating form of amusement was of an ephemeral nature, and would very quickly live out its little life, and pass into the realms, if not of oblivion, at all events, of extreme minor importance. Certainly, few would have dared to prophesy that the Living Pictures business would have grown to its present gigantic proportions, or would have succeeded in occupying so much public attention and time. True, there has always been certain number of enthusiasts who had faith in the Art and believed it had come to stay, but seeing how few had sufficiently the courage of their convictions to invest any substantial amount of capital in the business in its early days, it becomes an exceedingly interesting retrospect to look back on the past few years and realise what an immense influence the present day Bioscope show has in all regions of entertainment.

Seeing how fitful the business was in its commercial aspect in the earlier days, it is not surprising that even those particular pioneers who went wholeheartedly into the business, particularly from its manufacturing end, should have had, from time to time, good cause to carefully, and at times anxiously scrutinise the development of the business.

The writer remembers well when, at the end of a good year, the trade generally catechised itself as to whether it would last, whether it would be safe to spend more money in further productions, and when for a time business became slack, there were many who wisely shook their heads and said 'it is finished'. But revivals came, always well on the upgrade, and the Living Pictures,

A. C. Bromhead,
of the Gaumont Company
'A Review of the
Cinematograph Business'
The World's Fair
2 May 1908

when properly shown, either as a music hall turn or as a more ambitious complete entertainment, now have a popularity and a hold on the public world-wide in its scope which no other form of entertainment has ever previously enjoyed. In the music-halls there was at one time considerable opposition, active or passive, to the Cinematograph, owing its origin largely to music-hall actors, who imagined that the mechanical form of entertainment was depriving some brother artiste of a living, and, on the other hand, from certain of the less intelligent music-hall managers, who shared the opinion, and apparently believed that the popularity for the moving pictures could be stemmed by using them as a sort of 'fill in' or 'turn out' turn. Without referring further to this kind of opposition which is now practically forgotten, I would like the reader to recall the Fairground of an earlier day, when the Living Pictures were first appearing. We can all remember the class of penny booth show which the Cinematograph so largely dispossessed. Many of the present prosperous showmen of the Cinematograph, travelling with immense portable theatres, huge and costly organs, traction engines and immense illuminated fronts, were earning much more modest livelihoods in some such show of the type we refer to. Some of these showmen with characteristic enterprise invested in the new form of entertainment; their success was instantaneous, almost overwhelming, even though the only pictures shown were two or three short lengths of a broken and disjointed film thrown from a machine of the rattle-trap and baked-potato-can type onto a dirty piece of cloth. Developments on the fairground were very rapid, the showmen made good money, and did not hesitate to spend it for new films or to improve his show, and it is, after all, only five or six years ago when there was a actually a real shortage in film subjects, almost any kind of film being snapped up as though it were worth its weight in gold.

There is no need for me to draw a comparison with the present day, which all readers of *The*

Staff in front of Pat Collins's Wonderland no. 2 Show, 1908.
Kevin Scrivens, National Fairground Archive.

World's Fair are well acquainted with, but I well remember the first short film put upon the market which emanated from my own firm, and which, being close upon 300 feet in length, was regarded as an act of great daring and unmixed with folly. Events, however proved the need for such films, and it was followed by a series of others not only from the same firm, but from other quarters as well.

I have recently had the experience of travelling through America and Canada, and noting the progress which has been made in this same business on that side of the Atlantic, as also it has been my privilege on many previous occasions to study the conditions on the Continent of Europe, and I would like to draw attention to the curious difference which exists between the development of the business in those countries and in this, for while it is pleasing to reflect that England has been in the forefront of the Cinematograph trade since its inception, it is curious to note that particularly in respect to the exhibitors development in this country, it has been on altogether different lines to those existing elsewhere, and, to my mind we are at the present moment actually behind our foreign neighbours in this one respect.

In America the travelling showman has practically ceased to exist; he is represented only by some half a dozen lecturers who employ the Cinematograph to illustrate their travels, including at the same time, a few comic films to relieve the monotony. The class of show in America, in Canada, and on the Continent of Europe which has made money, and which is still making money, and which, in my opinion, will still make more money in the future, is that type of miniature theatre which in the United States is called the 'Nicklodeon', and of which we already have a few, but only a very few in this country. It consists of a good-sized shop or similar building or small hall, capable of seating from one hundred to five hundred people, suitably decorated, very often sumptuously appointed, and on the exterior usually lavishly illuminated. This Bijou Theatre, as we call it, may be situated on a main street or elsewhere, according to the type of business it is catering for. If on a busy street, a quick show, lasting from twenty minutes to half an hour, is running practically continuously, that is, over and over again from eleven or twelve o'clock in the morning until eleven or twelve o'clock at night, and the success of this class of show may be gathered from the fact that in the City of New York alone there are over six hundred such exhibitions, while in one street in Chicago there are twenty six, and some two hundred in the whole of the City. Every respectable sized township has one, and sometimes two, while the larger towns are proportionately as well provided for as New York and Chicago for instance, in Philadelphia I was struck with seeing four such all close together, two each on either side of the street, and I watched with great interest and noted that practically eight of every ten people who went into one show then went into the one next door, and then across the street to visit the other two, all the programmes being different.

The same class of business obtains all over the Continent of Europe, and even in little out of the way towns in Spain, in Russia, and in the Balkan States, while I myself counted fifteen such places over twelve months since in the town of Naples. Yet, for some unknown reason, this type of business, which I feel convinced is the permanent institution of the future, has not caught on to any extent in this country, although I must confess I see signs of a coming boom in that direction, and I only hope that our English showmen will be into this good thing before the foreigner.

Doormen for Aspland & Howden's Bioscope show, Boston 1910–11.
Ralph Aspland Howden

I have at different times endeavoured to persuade many individual customers to consider the question, but either they have been doing too well, as they were, to bother about it, or could not see the way for some reason or other to take it up. At the present time, there are, to my knowledge, several American and Canadian syndicates, as well as a big French concern, contemplating the conquest of the country on these lines.

Now, I would like to warn the travelling showmen that, in my opinion, this class of exhibition must inevitably come, and come soon, and I believe that when it does come it will have the same effect on the fairground shows in this country, as it has had to a considerable extent on the Continent, and very signally in America, namely serious interference with the business of the travelling or Fairground showmen. There are many very strong reasons apart from observation and experience which I could urge in support of this contention but which an article of this nature can hardly deal with.

There is, however, one point which should like to touch, and it should probably come home to many of the showmen who read this paper, and that is, as a rule in this country, the average travelling showman buys his films outright, whereas the proprietor of a 'Nicklodeon' shows of

Paraders from Aspland's show, 1910–11.
Ralph Aspland Howden

the same class described invariably hires or rents, getting all the latest subjects practically as they appear. He becomes well known to his local clientele, who are aware that they can always see the latest films as stated hours at his establishment, and he is consequently in a far better position to compete for the local patronage and favour for any travelling showman who may happen into the Market Square.

It was in anticipation of this class of business that I was at considerable pains on my recent trip to America, to study the methods of the American renting concerns, and I found, with some satisfaction, that at all events, in this respect we had very little to learn, for the firm I have the honour to represent has for a year or two past been running a film-hiring or rental department on lines which are even better than any I saw in America, and which is fully equal to any demand the business may make upon it even if the new class of show which I have described springs up all over the country with the success I anticipate. A few such shows exist already in London, and a sprinkling in some other of the large towns, beyond this the field is at the present moment practically vacant.

As most of us are aware, new Legislation is on the board for the purpose of dealing with Cinematograph entertainments of all kinds, and probably to license them. This Legislation should, in my opinion, assist in giving the business its proper status, as well as reducing it to a sure commercial level, but it ought also to serve as an incentive, if not a warning, to wide-awake showmen to be sure that they apply for their licenses in good time, above all, if sooner or later they intend to embark on the class of entertainment described, which I have no hesitation in prophesying will shortly come; let them beware that they do not leave it until the foreigner will have secured all the available licenses for the best districts.

Aspland's show, Boston Mayfair, 1913–14. *Ralph Aspland Howden.*

Aspland's show, Hull Fair, 1907–08. *National Fairground Archive.*

The World's Fair
11 February 1911

THE CINEMATOGRAPH ACT
A Penistone Case

THE FIRST PROSECUTION of its kind in the Barnsley West Riding Court took place on Wednesday, when William Henry Marshall, a travelling showman, of Bradford, was summoned for a breach of the Cinematograph Act, at Penistone.

Defendant came to Penistone with a cinematograph show on January 6th, and erected it within five feet of the Rose and Crown stables, notwithstanding that he had been warned that he must not erect his structure within 30 feet of any other building. Defendant allowed the show to remain in that position until the 16th.

Supt. McDonald said this case was brought with a view to putting the facts before the public.

The Chairman (Mr. H. A. Allport) told the defendant that he was liable to a £20 fine for the first day and £5 for each day afterwards. The Bench had, however, decided to deal leniently with him and we would be fined £3 and costs.

The World's Fair
3 August 1907

PATHÉ FRÈRES LONDON
The Largest Film Manufacturers in the World.
31–33, Charing Cross Road, W.C.

Pioneers of the 4d. per foot nett.

The Maniac Juggler   Code Word—*Colonel*

A clown slightly off his head, does the most amusing and curious things with his hat, stick, boots, etc, etc. Going into a restaurant he proceeds in like manner with the knives, forks, and would very much like to take up the waiters and other people, but this being not possible, he picks up a small baby and throws it about, much to the delight and alarm of the onlookers.

    577ft.   The Subject, £9 12s. 4d.

The Nurses Strike.   Code Word—*Compere*

An enormous meeting of excited nurses — The police called out — Babies are abandoned — Strings of people carrying banners, etc. Very wild and fascinating scenes.

    626ft.   The Subject, £10 8s 8d.

Chrysanthemums   Code Word—*Crime*

Great clusters of gorgeous chrysanthemums, with here and there, little Chinese lanterns. Groups of masked people and laughing-eyed mousmes file in long processions, making a delightful set of pictures of a truly Japanese character. Magnificently coloured throughout.

    230ft.   The Subject, £3 16s 8d.; Colouring, £2 15s 0d.

Modern Painters   Code Word—*Coke*

Two untidy looking 'daubers' with long hair and eccentric manners, step out of their portfolios and begin to work. The rate at which they produce the most lovely pictures, one after another, is really surprising. Charming films.

    445ft   The Subject, £7 8s 4d.; Colouring, £2.

Spanish Views.   Code Word—*Colcotar*

Splendid views of Spain and Spanish life on postcards. Very fascinating.

    460ft.   The Subject, £7 13s 4d.; Colouring, 4s.

Our Output of Films amounts to 70,000.
All Our Films are Absolutely Steady.
The Superiority of Pathé's Films is Universally Recognised.

WE ARE SEVEN

The World's Fair
19 October 1907

Of all the sights I ever saw,
I mean that's worth recalling,
Was seven Cinnys all in a row,
And all the Showmen bawling,
At Hull's Great Fair,
The Cinnys there,
          Numbered seven.

To the last in the row
I made my very best bow,
How's business, I said, Mr. Relph?
Who replied, Just look for yourself,
To scoop in the money,
Like bees after honey,
          We are seven.

To Aspland's next I hied,
And to that Gent, I cried
Your show is simply grand, Sir;
And being in a crowd
Of course I spoke quite loud.
In a whisper came the answer-
          We are seven.

Here side by side,
In pomp and pride,
Are Farrar's old and new Shows
When shall we cease to speculate?
Who will call a halt before too late?
Goodness only knows
          Which of the seven.

Whilst his organ played the Messiah,
I'd a word with Enoch Farrar,
Whose shows are just a little glimpse of
    Heaven.
He said you're very kind,
But please to bear in mind,
We're not the only pebble on the beach-
    We are seven.

President Kemp is the next
To afford me a text,
Whose show is resplendent with gold.
I wished him good cheer;
He replied, Have no fear,
I'll beat them again, as I've oft done of old-
    All the seven.

Captain Tom Payne
Was here once again
And long may he continue to Reign,
For he's always the same,
And it's a very long lane,
That will see the end of his game
          With those seven.

The very first to lead the way
To most of those who are here to-day
Was little Monty, blyth and gay;
And like a little terrier,
He cried, The more the Merrier,
When I reminded him his neighbours say-
          We are seven.
          Walk Up.

Mr and Mrs George Aspland, Lincolnshire, 1890s.
Ralph Aspland Howden

The World's Fair
25 September 1909

SHOWMEN AND THE CINEMATOGRAPH BILL

DEAR SIR, IN A RECENT EDITION of *The World's Fair* I see that it is not the intention of the Showmen's Guild to oppose the Cinematograph Bill, in the event of Travelling Shows being exempt. But I hope you will pardon my saying, that in the interest of Showmen generally, the Bill should be opposed, whether travelling showmen are to be exempt or not. Otherwise, the bioscope business in Halls, being practically extinct, as it would be, could only bring about one result, viz: a wholesome rush into the travelling showbusiness by exhibitors who are now showing in halls, meaning increased competition to travelling showmen. In my opinion the Act arises from the agitation of large Bioscope firms who wish to create a trade monopoly, and from no other cause whatsoever.

I believe their object is the extinction of small firms, private contractors, and exhibitors who work independently of the monopolies. Now, to the best of my belief, the only exhibitions that have resulted in fire, panic, loss of life in this country, have been given by large firms, not travelling showmen or private exhibitors. It seems to be a case of first making the thing that the public have to be protected against, and then agitating for legislation against it. The Act seems entirely to overlook the fact that there is a sufficient and sensible set of regulations already in existence.

. . . I have been exhibiting and operating for the past five and a half years, and have never had a fire. During the year I show in about thirty different halls, in each of which I meet the Insurance Regulations . . . It is significant that the Insurance Companies, who in the case of fire are the losers, are the only people who have framed a set of regulations based upon common sense, understanding of their subject, and a knowledge acquired by experience of which is necessary for safety. I believe the Showmen's Guild and the Insurance Companies combined could prevent the Cinematograph Act from passing. The Act should not be allowed to pass. The effect of it would be to close scores or Machine Shops, Celluloid Castories, Printers and Bill Posters, Warehouses, Halls and kindred trades; increase enormously the competition to travelling showmen; force out of existence all the private contractors and exhibitors, and create an absolute monopoly, a ring of corner controlled by a few firms.

They have legislation in America about bioscopes, and yet they have serious fires and loss of life, upon a scale of which we unfortunately have no experience.

Yours faithfully

Fred T. Walker

Chambers's Journal
30 March 1912

A TRAVELLING KINEMATOGRAPH HALL

SEEING THAT MOVING PICTURES at the present moment are such a rage, the experiment adopted by an enterprising French showman might be emulated very advantageously in these islands. Certainly it would enable the few inhabitants in the many scattered villages to be introduced to the latest marvel of science. This Gallic showmen has acquired two motor-omnibuses from the firm De Dion Bouton. Externally they resemble the vehicles common to the streets of our cities. When a village is reached the tent is run up on the lines of our travelling circuses and the engines of the omnibus vehicles are pressed into service to drive the electric lighting equipment for the interior and facade of the canvas hall, as well as for the projector. This showman wanders up and down the country delighting thousands of villagers, and, being without that severe competition which is now rife in the towns and cities among the picture palaces, profits accordingly. Thus he introduces animated photography to delighted crowds of rural folks far removed from the towns, who otherwise might be denied a taste of this most modern form of amusement. Travelling Kinematograph shows have been attempted in this country, but have met with indifferent success, for the simple reason that the effort has been made upon antiquated lines. This ingenious Frenchman is able to provide his patrons with a picture as large and steady as, and in fact equal in every respect to, those seen in substantial buildings in town.

10 From Penny Gaff to Picture Palace

THE DECADE LEADING UP TO THE outbreak of the First World War was a period of transition for the British film industry. Cinema had evolved from being merely a novel form of entertainment into a commercially important industry. Films had become more sophisticated, incorporating longer and more complex narratives, and the notion that films could also be an art form was beginning to gain some acceptance. Cinema was becoming a major source of entertainment and information. Its growing importance could no longer be ignored by the Government and its status was officially recognised by the passing of special legislation. Of all aspects of the film industry it was, perhaps, in the area of exhibition that the effects of these great changes were to be most clearly seen.

At the turn of the century, moving pictures were still looking for a home that they could call their own. Guests in other people's houses, films were shown as part of the bill in music halls or in travelling fairground bioscope shows. By 1914, however, a transformation had taken place. Purpose-built cinemas had appeared all over the country, the result of a wave of investment that had drawn millions of pounds into film exhibition. As *The Sphere* observed in April 1913:

> The rise of the "picture palace" is one of the most astonishing features of modern life. A year or two ago and the thing was not. Now every little town has its whitewashed frontage with Empire decorations lit with a couple of assertive arc lights. The bigger towns and cities have more pretentious halls, and London itself is being provided with cinema 'palaces' which are really well-appointed theatres adapted to their special use.

The first purpose-built cinemas did not appear until films had proven that they were a lasting attraction and not just a passing novelty. A common early practice was to rent empty shop accommodation for short periods and to use these as temporary cinemas. These shop-shows were known as 'penny gaffs' because of their low admission prices. The use of shops as temporary places of entertainment was not a new idea. Henry Mayhew mentions 'penny gaffs' in his study of London's poor, written in the 1840s. Film exhibitors merely carried on the tradition. Profit, rather than customer satisfaction, was the overriding consideration for these operators and 'penny gaffs' soon gained an unenviable reputation. In her book, *Gone to the Pictures*, published in 1946, Hilda Lewis decribes a visit to a 'penny gaff' show:

> Here was another of those blacked-in shops . . . The window was pasted all over with bills; but they were so dirty and dilapidated, it was impossible to read what they said. A dark and dirty boy was standing and yelling, All the latest . . . all the latest! Every time he bawled 'late' he gave the open door of the shop a thwack with his stick . . . We walked in. It was very dark inside the shop and the smell was horrid . . . In front of us, against the blacked-in window, hung a small greyish sheet on rollers, like a blank and crumpled map.

Penny gaffs did little to enhance the reputation of moving pictures, already tainted by their association with the music hall. Cinema remained primarily a proletarian form of entertainment with a disreputable image. If it was ever to appeal to a broader cross section of society, then this stigma needed to be removed. If going to see films was to become as socially acceptable as a visit to the Theatre, exhibitors would have to leave the fairgrounds and the backstreet 'gaffs' and provide audiences with more comfortable and refined surroundings. The first buildings devoted solely to film exhibition began to appear in Britain in about 1907.

In 1906, a British franchise for Hale's Tours of the World had opened in London's Oxford Street. However, with its small auditoria, designed to resemble railway carriages, this was a diversion from mainstream cinema exhibition. It was to be the provinces rather than London that took the lead in cinema construction. One of the very first, the Central Hall in Colne, Lancashire, opened in February, 1907. Others soon followed. These first cinemas were simple structures, usually designed to seat three or four hundred people, although some were much larger. At first, most had flat floors and stuck to the theatrical tradition of charging more to sit right at the front of the stalls than at the back. Films were often projected on to a white-painted square on the end wall. These early, simple, halls soon gave way to more elaborate structures where increasing ornamentation and luxury were used to attract an increasingly better class of audience. To distinguish them from their humble predecessors they were known as 'picture palaces'.

In 1908, *The Stage Year Book* was one of the first to use the term when it identified what was soon to become a boom in cinema construction: "There are now indications that before long these picture 'palaces' will be a feature of London and the larger provincial towns". It was a soubriquet that developers tried hard to live up to. In 1905 the Egyptian Hall in Piccadilly, where Robert Paul had exhibited his Theatrograph in March, 1896, was demolished. In 1907 it was replaced by a building named Egyptian House. This new building contained a small cinema called, logically enough, The New Egyptian Hall. Here, patrons, as well as watching films, could enjoy refreshments in a tea room furnished in the style of a Japanese tea garden, complete with waitresses dressed in kimonos. The Theatre de Luxe which opened in the Strand one year later boasted an auditorium with oak panelling on the walls and an oak-beamed ceiling. The floor was thickly carpeted and there were 170 red plush tip-up seats. There was even a separate 'writing room' with free envelopes and notepaper for the use of patrons. Of course, not all cinemas were quite so grand. All, however, were aware of

the need to present an image of comfort, elegance and good taste.

The Cinematograph Act, which became law in January, 1910, effectively killed the 'penny gaff'. Premises now had to conform to exacting safety standards and many cinemas were compelled either to make expensive structural alterations or to close. The days of the hastily converted chapel or skating rink were at an end. Cinemas now had to be purpose-built and, for the first time, architects had to put their minds to designing buildings specifically for film exhibition. From about 1910 onwards the pages of specialist trade journals such as *Building News* begin to contain increasing numbers of references to cinema design and construction. The period from the passing of the Cinematograph Act in 1909 to the outbreak of the First World War witnessed a rapid expansion in the number of cinemas. Hundreds of new companies were floated and financial speculation was rife. Capital poured into the industry to such an extent that there were fears of widespread financial collapse. *The Times* advised its readership in May 1913:

> Although we are satisfied that most of the limited liability ventures are brought out in good faith, however mistaken in the calculations, there are some that are less honestly conceived—that are, to put it in plain English, swindles. Our object, however, is not to single out particular companies for attack, but once more to impress upon the people with a little spare money to invest the advisability of avoiding this kind of enterprise altogether, because in the present congested state of the business the probabilities of success are almost infinitesimal.

Such warnings, however, fell largely on deaf ears. In 1908 there were just three companies involved in film exhibition. By 1910 the number had risen to nearly three hundred and, three years later, there were about five hundred and fifty, with an estimated capital of £15 million. Most companies were very small, often running just one cinema. Others gradually built up circuits of theatres. By 1914 there were over one hundred circuits, accounting for about one in five cinemas. The largest in terms of capital was Provincial Cinematograph Theatres Ltd. Founded in 1909, by 1914 it had expanded rapidly, to the point where it owned eighteen large cinemas in the provinces and had the distinction of being the only picture theatre company to be quoted on the Stock Market.

Estimates as to the total number of cinemas in Britain before the First World War vary considerably. Frederick Talbot, writing in 1912, puts it at about 4,000 and this figure seems to tally roughly with the 1915 *Kinematograph Year Book* directory which lists about 3,500. Cinemas grew in average seating capacity throughout the 1920s and 1930s but this total number of about 4,000 was to remain remarkably constant right through to the 1960s. The pattern of distribution of picture palaces was, however, very uneven. Cinemas were concentrated in the larger industrial towns and cities. By 1914, for example, Manchester had 111 cinemas compared to Oxford's six. Bradford had 31, whilst Leicester, with almost exactly the same size of population, had just fourteen.

Slowly but surely the cinema was coming of age. It had begun to cast off the associations of its shady youth and gain a degree of social acceptance. The reign of the gilded bioscope show and the disreputable penny gaff was now over, replaced by the emergence of thousands of High Street Bijous and Majestics. Whilst the cinema was still predominantly a working-class form of entertainment, picture palaces were beginning to attract a much broader clientele. A visit to the local cinema was becoming a common and regular pastime for a large section of the population.

The Photographic Dealer
August 1897

HOW DEALERS MAKE MONEY OUT OF KINEMATOGRAPHS

THE PHOTOGRAPHIC AND LANTERN DEALER who gives but scanty attention to the boom in animated photography, is missing the chance of making an appreciable addition to his profit for the year. There have been few inventions introduced to the photographic world of recent years, possessing such money making possibilities as the Kinematograph, but so far most of the harvest has been reaped by the professional entertainer rather than by the dealer in apparatus. The manufacturers of course have also done very well, but it is quite open for the enterprising retailer to get a good share in the business being done if he sets about it in the right way. The various openings for profit making by animated photography may be set down as follows:

1. By the sale of machines, negative and positive films and accessories.
2. By the hire of ditto to amateurs.
3. By undertaking entertainments at local institutions, schools, parties, &c.
4. By the loan or sale of outfits to local stores and enterprising shopkeepers for advertising purposes.

To cultivate the sale of Kinematographs the first thing for the dealer to do is to make himself thoroughly acquainted with the prices and distinguishing features of the various machines now on the market. The easiest way of doing this is to look carefully through the description and advertisements in the present issue of this journal, and to obtain from each of the makers mentioned, their catalogues and best trade terms. It is particularly necessary that the dealer should have by him the complete lists of all the positive films now to be obtained, for half the battle in giving a successful show, or in making a satisfactory sale, is to be able to offer the newest and most attractive pictures. The prices of the machines now in the market vary considerably, but it may be taken as a general rule that whatever may be the price, corresponding value is given. Now, it is essential that the dealer should have at least one machine in his shop, to show prospective customers, and it depends largely on the class of trade he does, whether he selects for stock a high or low priced machine. If he intends catering for a hiring trade he should get a first rate machine and keep it especially for this work. Kinematographs of any description are comparatively costly articles, and it is not every dealer who can hold stock of several different patterns. But though the prices run high, the profits are in proportion, and the sale of one kinematograph outfit will probably bring as good a return as the sale of a dozen ordinary cameras.

Having decided to stock one or more machines, the next step is to inform the neighbourhood of this fact, and this may best be done by the use of window placards, by advertising in the local papers, and by the judicious distribution of brightly written circulars. One excellent means of giving publicity to the kinematograph department, if it may be so termed, would be to give a free display of animated photographs before the local photographic Society, and arrange that the members should be asked to bring their friends. On this occasion the reporters on the local press should have special invitations so that the attractions and success of the machine sold by Mr. _____ of _____ Street, would be heralded far and wide.

With regard to the business to be done in hiring and entertaining, the opportunities for this should be particularly brisk during the festive seasons at Xmas and New Year, but the cute dealer will not neglect to offer his services, on reasonable terms of course, to the committees of local bazaars, school entertainments, and the like. For private houses it will probably often happen that the dealer need only supply the apparatus and films and some member or friend of the family giving the party will do the rest. In the case of positive film there is a particularly good scope for a hiring trade, for these articles are rather expensive things for the amateur lanternist to buy. When any local events or more than usual interest, such as processions, fairs or sports, take place, the dealer should be on the spot with his kinematograph and take animated photographs of the same. The films thus secured will form very profitable items of stock for future use or hire. Such occasions as the coming-of-age of a local magnate's son, or the visit of royalty to the town, or the return of a prominent townsman after a long absence from his native place, all offer scenes and situations worthy of recording on a film.

In London last winter several big drapery houses and stores gave kinematograph displays daily, to attract customers to their premises, and the idea is one which many a provincial house might be willing to adopt, if it was suitably put before them. It is for the dealer to approach them on this point, and to endeavour to secure the order for an outfit.

In penning these few notes on the commercial side of Kinematography, it is not intended to convey the idea that kinematographs can be sold by the dozen, nor yet that it is only necessary for the dealer to make it known that he stocks these machines, for his shop to be besieged by an eager throng of customers. But it is a fact that there is a good and increasing demand for all apparatus connected with animated photography, and as it is a branch of photographic trade which can show a good margin of profit it should be assiduously cultivated by every retailer who is anxious to see his yearly balance sheet come out with an upward movement on the credit side. He should remember that every kinematograph he sells will bring him continual custom for the sale and hire of films; and for cylinders of gas, and other limelight necessaries. If he only sells three or four machines in the course of the winter he will have good reason to be satisfied, especially if he has also made the additional profit which it is possible to make out of the hiring department. In London and other big cities kinematograph shows are patronised as well as ever, and the audiences are just as enthusiastic as those of 12 months ago, in spite of the number of entertainments of this kind which are now in full swing. In smaller towns and country districts where the machines have not yet penetrated the dealer has the whole field to himself, and the one who introduces the novelty will get the best of the trade. It is a matter well worthy of consideration and of promptitude in action, and the kinematograph should be a regular boon to the photographic dealer who wants to stimulate his trade during the winter months.

Projectionist with the 1897 model of the Urban Bioscope. *National Museum of Photography, Film & Television.*

"The Upstart",
'Experiences in
Animated Photography'
The Showman
3 January 1902

MY FIRST KNOWLEDGE of photography occurred as when, as a lad, I was the handy boy and general factotum of a waxwork establishment, away in the Midlands. Not a very promising outlook, you will say. I used to pick up a few pence for doing odd jobs, and one day, being 'on the spot' I was of service to a swell, and reaped a fitting reward. I can't tell you about it now; perhaps I may be able to do so on another occasion. It helped to swell my small savings and enabled me to purchase a modest photographic outfit. I had for a long while envied the possession of such, and at last, having attained my wish, entered upon its use most enthusiastically. In my spare time, sometimes in time that should have been devoted to duties of another nature, I often experimented. To cut a long story short, I not only became proficient, but let my neighbours know it; so that when cinematography became popular, I cast about in my own mind as to what steps I should take to better my position.

Hearing in mind from a friend that the operator of an animated picture show had failed in some manner to give his employer (a showman in a good way) the necessary satisfaction, I applied for the job; and although I could not pretend to be proficient in the use and working of the instrument. I devoted some hours to its study under my employer and essayed my first performance—in private.

We were using limelight, and as it was quite new to me, the 'boss' himself put it all in order and kept and eye on it during the performance, allowing me to gradually get into its working until I was proficient.

One day I was getting all in readiness, and, as you know, there are a lot of things to attend to: I omitted to sufficiently warm the lime cylinder before turning on the gases. In a short while I found my lime had cracked, but fortunately remained on the pin, and as we were short of limes, I was quaking all the time, fearing that the lime would tumble off and I should have to stop the performance, and have a necessary interlude while I got a new lime ready. However, my luck was in, and everything went all right on that occasion.

The travelling show was a success in every way, so the proprietor one day invested in a camera, in order to be able to secure his own local subjects. I was selected to make use of it, and as we had pitched in a large manufacturing town, it was thought that a picture of the men leaving work would provide a certain draw. Accordingly the day arrived, and as it happened, a fine one. Knowing the importance of this, I was in good spirits and intended to do my utmost to secure a good result. I had carefully gone over my outfit previously, and had made a list, like a careful man, to be sure to leave nothing behind. Having arrived at the position, near the gates, I proceeded to fix up and soon had all ready and focused on the factory gates. I must mention that I have a revolving table, operated by turning a handle.

The horn sounded, the gates opened, and out trooped the men. All went well until I saw that a passing tram, if included in the view, would add interest in the scene, so turned my table; but quickly found I was pointing the camera away from the object, and did not manage to get it included in time.

'*Experientia docit*', as we are taught at school, and a few mistakes soon put one on the right road.

We did not attempt the photographic developing, etc., sending all films to be developed and printed by those who make a speciality of this work.

The narrowest shave of an accident I had was one day when I boarded the electric tram and arranged with the driver to fix my apparatus. The road was clear, and before I was quite ready off we dashed, with the result that over went my camera—not quite to the ground, however, as I managed to break its fall. I made another start, and secured my picture, which was of an exciting nature, as besides the ordinary street traffic, the tram had a desperate shave of running down a butcher's cart! That part of the film is always applauded, as the tram apparently is bound to collide with the cart.

To tell of disappointments—such as dark and gloomy weather when an interesting event is happening; of waiting among the crowd, and in one case being waited for by the crowd, etc— would take up too much space; perhaps at a future time I may be able to describe a few of them.

J. & R. Ellis, Lanternists and
Cinematographers, c. 1904.
*National Museum of
Photography, Film & Television.*

YOUR OPPORTUNITY

GRASP IT

L.C.C.

**London Cinematograph College and Situations Bureau
(F. Hate, Proprietor, Film Cleaning Co.)
6, Ingestre Place
Wardour Street, London, W.**

Phone: 9768 GERRARD

Recruitment
advertisement
May 1910

DO YOU REALISE what a hold the moving picture has obtained on the public? Have you calculated what an enormous amount of capital is invested in the business? Has it ever occurred to you that there is much more money to be made out of picture shows than at ordinary humdrum existence which millions of men have to lead?

Will you investigate the proposition which we put before you?

Consider!

Out of a hundred working-men in England at the present time fifty are earning less than 30s. per week, twenty-five are earning between 30s. and 40s; fifteen between 40s. and 50s; and only ten rise above that amount.

Consider Again!

By making yourself proficient in the moving picture business you can earn £2, £3 or £4 per week as an operator, up to £10 a week as a manager, and £10,000 a year as the proprietor of a show.

Now the first and most important thing for a would-be-showman to learn is "operating"—that is, to work and manage a cinematograph projector so as to obtain a perfect picture upon the screen. These three words "a perfect picture," are the kernel of the whole situation, and a man cannot get a perfect picture unless he has been systematically trained by some other man who is himself an efficient operator.

In order to meet the enormous demand which exists for thoroughly competent cinematograph operators,

London Cinematograph College and Situations Bureau

has been formed, expert instructors have been engage, and a complete cinematograph installation has been provided at very great expense.

The object of the College is to teach young men—or middle-aged ones for that matter—the whole art and profession of cinematograph operating, so that they can go out into the world with every prospect of a successful career in an entirely new walk of life.

Our system of teaching, which is the result of long and careful study of the business, is to follow the course of the subject from beginning to end. Electric lights forms a very important part of the instruction, as also does the method of operating with limelight as an illuminant. The optics of the lens and the condensers, the care and working of the machine, and the principles of animated photography are exhaustively treated upon, and a considerable amount of time is spent in the practice of operating under actual working conditions in a hall, in which pictures are regularly exhibited before the public. The students thus have a unique opportunity of gaining confidence in themselves by operating in a show in which the audience is seated.

No other school or college in the world can offer such an advantage. The course is divided into two parts—viz., lectures in the theory of all branches of the profession, and practical work with all the latest and most improved types of apparatus.

A very important point is, that in all probability the Government will compel all operators in charge of a picture show to be licensed, and that mere "handle-turner," who have picked up their knowledge anyhow, will not be able to pass the requisite tests.

The film drying room at Kinemacolor House, 1912.
National Museum of Photography, Film & Television.

But We Guarantee

that every student who completes a course of instruction at the London Cinematograph College will be able easily to pass any examination which the Government may impose.

Now in return for teaching you a new profession—one which has marvellous possibilities—we only charge the extremely moderate sum of

£4 4s. 0d.,

which may be paid at the rate of £1 1s. per week if desired. Surely in all the world it is not possible to learn another profession so cheaply, nor in such short time, which reminds us of a point which we had nearly forgotten—viz., that to complete the course will only occupy two hours of your time per day for a month. Consequently you can learn this new profession in your spare time, if you are at present in a situation.

Just a Few More Words

We find situations for all students who complete the course, and we undertake to assist them from time to time as they require.

We can and will lift you right out of the rut; we will place you firmly upon the first rung of the ladder which leads to success.

Please call and see the Principal and the Chief Instructor, and let them conduct you over the College. By doing so you will be placed under no obligation whatever.

Special Notice

Assistants, Operators, Ticket Collectors, Money Takers, and Managers for the Show or Office supplied on the shortest notice. (Fee. 1s.) Any operator wishing to make inquiries with reference to us may write to Messrs. Pathé Frères, 31-33, Charing Cross Road, W.C. Intending students living in this country can be provided with comfortable apartments at a low inclusive fee.

Kinemacolor House, 80–82 Wardour Street, London, August 1912.

The Stage Year Book
L. Carson, ed. (London:
Carson & Comerford)
1908, pp. 47–49

THE TRIUMPH OF THE ANIMATED PICTURE

WHEN THE HISTORY OF the present century comes to be written kinematography, or the act of animated photography, will figure largely in its records, for its rapid development had been most marked. Compare the flickering monstrosities which at one time were thrown on the screen with rock-steady representations of the present day. The magic lantern, interesting and ingenious enough in its way, died a natural death when kinematography was invented, for its process proved to be tedious, slow and mechanical. Kinematography now takes it place as a history maker, for few events of any importance in the world's progress are allowed to pass without an indelible record being made of them.

Perhaps it will be well here to record briefly the origins and development of the kinematograph. The old zoetrope, or wheel of life, was the fountain from which originally sprang the idea of living pictures. The idea is generally credited to Edison, but to Mr. Charles Urban as its real pioneer all the real credit is due. In 1896, six years after Edison's invention, the Lumiere Brothers (of colour photography fame) gave an exhibition of the kinematograph in London. Since then during the intervening twelve years there has been such a wonderful activity in this branch of science that to-day there is scarcely a town or village in England, America, or the Continent generally that has not made the acquaintance of animated photographs. Kinematography, apart from its value as an amusement factor, is also being largely used as an aid to education. Its full use in this direction has not yet been taken advantage of, but there is little doubt that in the near future the kinematograph will be a prominent feature in most schools.

Punch, 26 July 1911.

IF YOU SHOULD SEE ANY LITTLE THING YOU WANT IN THAT PET OLD CURIOSITY SHOP OF YOURS, BUY IT NOW.

TO-MORROW MAY BE TOO LATE. NEIGHBOURHOODS CHANGE SO QUICKLY NOWADAYS.

Pictures While You Wait

In naval and military matters it has already been adopted to facilitate the teaching of manoeuvres and tactics. In medicine, clever and delicate and complicated operations have been successfully shown, and even mental diseases and their effects upon humanity have been portrayed in a manner that is impossible by any other means.

To revert once more to the taking of topical pictures—the history makers already mentioned—perhaps a definitive example will best serve to show the rapidity with which these photographs are taken and developed. Six different kinematograph machines were at work in different parts of the field on the day of the Grand National Race, 1907. The instant the race was over the train bearing the operators with their machines started for London. During the journey, while running full speed, the operators were hard at work developing; indeed, not only developing, but washing and drying by special process. On arrival the films were quickly conveyed to the printing depot, where prints were quickly made; and that same evening the Alhambra, Empire and Oxford Music Halls were showing pictures of the race to delighted and astonished spectators. And so with the great events as they come along. The Kaiser and Kaiserin landing at Portsmouth, the Final Cup tie at the Crystal Palace, even the Royal Bourbon wedding at Wood Norton, all were recorded and shown the same evening at the different music halls.

Actors and Picture Making

But animated pictures, as an medium of amusement, have proved most far-reaching. In England today there is scarcely a music hall without this item on the programme. The subjects which would seem most to appeal are those of the comic order, for the public seem most responsive to humour that is put before them in a fairly obvious manner. Second in popularity would seem to be the dramatic subjects, in which the hero, heroine and villain all play their parts. In the making of these pictures, or course, the services of actors and actresses are constantly enlisted. The modern kinematograph dramatic or comic picture requires its complement of actors, actresses, scenes and stage properties. The acting has to be as forceful and natural as on the legitimate stage. The stage manager has to be a man of infinite patience and ingenuity, and, indeed, repeated rehearsals have to be called before a picture can be considered worthy of being taken. Many an actor, who in the ordinary way would be 'resting' has filled in with engagements for the kinematograph camera.

Development Abroad

Great as is the appreciation for moving pictures in this country, it is trifling in comparison with that shown abroad. With the the exception of the music halls and showmen's booths here in England, and one or two entertainments, such as West's Navy and Hale's Tours at the polytechnic, we have no organised centres for the display of the art. In Paris, Berlin and other large continental cities, however, within a few paces one of the other, are to be found kinematograph shows attracting through the day and late into the night, a steady stream of people eager to see the latest novelties the camera has caught. For a very moderate sum a twenty minutes' entertainment is procured, and the programme is entirely varied.

In America the craze has caught on even more completely, and in every important city of the States there are now to be found animated pictures 'palaces'. Although America has its complement of manufacturers producing films, the demand for films has been so great that England has been called upon to supplement the output to a considerable extent. There are now indications that before long these picture 'palaces' will be a feature of London and the large provincial towns; but England is a conservative country, and does not lend itself easily to innovations.

Leading Firms

Appended is a list of the various kinematograph firms established in England, with a few particulars about each:

Robert W. Paul: Showrooms, 68 High Holborn; film works, Sidney Road, New Southgate. One of the pioneers who first started manufacturing in 1894. First public exhibition of Paul's Animatograph in 1895. Manufacturer also machines, lamps, resistance, jets, and accessories. A new building has been erected, with suction gas plant and dynamo capable of supplying forty arc lamps during the year. Film works are now twice their previous capacity. Thirty-five new subjects of a varied nature were issued during the past year.

Charles Urban Trading Co., Limited: Address, 48 Rupert Street. Established five years. Manufacturers of machines of a special type, printers, perforators, arc lamps, lime light outfits and optical systems. Over 300 subjects have been produced in 1907. *Victoria Falls* (travel), *The Short-sighted Cyclist* (comedy), *Torpedo Attack on the Dreadnought* (topical), scientific, medical, and surgical series comprise a little of their work this year. Hold official position of Kinematographers to the King, the Admiralty, the L. and N.W., the L. and S.W., Canadian Pacific, Caledonian and Highland and Irish Railways, the White Star Line, North German Lloyd, etc. New and more important premises will shortly be built.

"Picture Personalities: Mr. G. E. Turner.
The subject of this week's 'personality' is one of the directors of the Walturdaw Company, Limited. An excellent man of business, Mr. Turner is an enthusiast on the merits of the 'Power's Cameragraph'."
The Bioscope, c. 1912.

The Walturdaw Co., Limited: Address, 3 Dane Street, High Holborn. Directors: Messrs. E. C. Turner, J. D. Walker, J. H. J. Dawson and Ernest Howard. Established twelve year ago. Manufacturers of the kinematophone, or singing picture machine, also the Walturdaw Bioscope, Nos. 1, 2, and 3. They possess a large machine depot, from whence over fifty machines can be supplied at any time. This year they have perfected an appliance for preventing film catching fire. A very large department devoted to hiring is a feature.

The Warwick Trading Co., Limited: Established in 1895 by Messrs Maguire and Baucus. Managing Director, Mr. William G. Barker. Address, 113-117 Charing Cross Road, W.C. Specialists on topical subjects. One of the successes of the year was the arrival of the Emperor and Empress of Germany at Portsmouth. On their premises there is a fully equipped theatre, besides dark rooms, developing rooms, printing, drying and cleaning rooms, wholly lit by electric light. Machine department and hiring departments a feature as well. Branches in Paris, Berlin, New York, Madrid, St. Petersburg, Milan, Melbourne, Montreal, etc.

The Gaumont Co. (formerly trading as L. Gaumont and Co.): Address, Chrono House, Sherwood Street, and Denman Street, Piccadilly. Head offices, Establishment Gaumont, Rue St. Roche, Paris. Branches in Berlin, Barcelona, Moscow, Milan, Cleveland (U.S.A.), Melbourne, and Sydney. First established in Paris, 1892; in London 1898, by A. C. Bromhead. London factories and laboratories, St. James' Street, S.W. Have a staff of about 500. Manufacturers of the Chronophone, Chronomegaphone, hand Chronophone, and singing picture machines. Have had a year's success at London Hippodrome with Chronophone. Highest awards at Paris, 1900, Grand Prix; St. Louis Exhibition, highest award, 1904; Liege Exhibition, 1905; and Milan 1906. Chronophone appeared by Royal Command at Buckingham Palace, April 4, 1907.

The Hepworth Manufacturing Co., Limited: Directors: Mr. Cecil Hepworth, Mr. S. Baker, and Mr. E. J. Humphery. Address, 15-17, Cecil Court, Charing Cross Road, London. Established in 1899 by Mr. Cecil Hepworth. Manufacturers of the Hepworth Arc Lamp, Hepworth Printing and Developing Machine, etc. Special trade mark 'Hepwix'. Most popular film of the year, *Dumb Sagacity*. *That Fatal Sneeze* has also a good run.

Messrs. Cricks and Sharp: Address, formerly 7 Great Queen Street, W.C. Established four years. Works and offices at Mitcham, amidst rural surroundings, on estate of about twenty-five acres. Mr. G. H. Cricks, formerly secretary to G. Harrison and Co. and manager to Mr. R. W. Paul. Specialise on the Lion Brand films. *Saved from a Burning Wreck; or, Ten Days on a Raft*, is one of the firm's greatest successes of the year.

The Clarendon Film Co. (Messrs. H. V. Lawley and P. E. Stow): Address, Clarendon Road, Croydon. Best production of the year, *The Pied Piper of Hamelin* and *Water Babies*.

Messrs Williamson and Co. (Mr. J. Williamson, head of firm): Established ten years. Address, Brighton and Cecil Court, London. Started in Brighton first as chemist. Studio factory started in Brighton six years ago. London office opened this year. Film manufacturers only. Best subjects of the year, *Just in Time* (dramatic) and *Bobby's Birthday* (comic).

The Vitagraph Co. (of America): Address, 10 Cecil Court, Charing Cross Road, London. Partners: Mr. W. T. Rock, Mr. Albert E. Smith, and Mr. J. Stuart Blackton. Established ten years in the States and more recently in London. Do not trade in machines in this country, only films. Success of the year, *Liquid Electricity.*

Pathe Freres: Address, 31–33 Charing Cross Road, London, W.C. One of the leading French manufacturers. Established in London at above address some years. Films and machines. Trick pictures and tinting effects a speciality.

Sheffield Photo Co.: Address, 95 Norfolk Street, Sheffield. Established ten years, and manufactured kinmematograph films for six. Films known as S.P.C. films. Specialise on a bioscope costing £15. Best film of the year, *Willie's Dream.*

The Cinematograph Syndicate (Controller, Mr. H. W. Hough): Address, 23 Cecil Court, Charing Cross Road, London, W.C. Manufacturers of films, and supply all other makers films to showmen. Best picture of the year, *The Gamekeeper's Dog, Tommy's Box of Tools.*

The New Bioscope Trading Co: Address 3 and 5, Cecil Court. Established three and a half years. Hirers of films and exhibitors. Makers of films. Manufacturers of the 'Dreadnought' Bioscope.

The Nordisk Co: A Danish firm now established with an office in London at Cecil Court. Best recent subject, The Lion Hunt.

The Graphic Cinematograph Co. (Proprietor, Mr. W. Cecil Jeapes): Address, 154 Charing Cross Road, W.C. Established eight years ago. Patentee of the Animated Graphic, one of the steadiest projectors yet devised, make a speciality of trick and jumping films. Most successful films of the year, *A Woodland Tragedy* and *The Showman's Treasure.*

Many of the manufacturers of films recently, with the object of protecting their mutual interests, formed an association, known as the Kinematograph Manufacturers Association, and though little over a year old, this Association had done appreciable work. The first annual dinner of the Association was held on October 31, at the Holborn Restaurant, with Mr. R. W. Paul in the chair. Proceeding the dinner, an address on 'Copyright in Kinematograph Films' was delivered by Mr. William Jago, F.I.C, F.C.S., barristerat-law.

The offices of the Warwick Trading Co. Ltd, 1 Warwick Court, High Holborn, London, 1896. *National Museum of Photography, Film & Television.*

**Prospectus for
Electric Theatres Ltd.**
issued 1908

PARTICULARS AND FUTURE PROSPECTS
of Electric Theatres (1908) Ltd.

CAPITAL £50,000
In 100,000 shares of 10/- each.

Directors:	ROWLAND HILL of 20, Mount Park Road, Ealing, W. (Chairman)
	SYDNEY GEORGE VERNHAM, of 'Lyncourt', Surbiton
	JOSEPH JAY BAMBERGER, of 30 Rosary Gardens, Kensington, W.
Bankers:	PARR'S BANK LIMITED
	LONDON & COUNTY BANKING CO. LIMITED
	LONDON & SOUTH WESTERN BANK, LIMITED
Solicitors:	BRANDON AND NICHOLSON, 5 Suffolk Place, Pall Mall, S.W.
Auditor:	WALTER F. MAPLESON, F.C.A., Moorgate Station Chambers, E.C.

Secretary and Offices: W. M. BORRADAILE, 21 Bedford Street, Strand, W.C.

History: The above Company is the outcome of a small Company of the same name, which was formed in 1907, with a capital of £10,000 to acquire, construct and open Cinematograph Theatres, which provide a cheap, elevating and popular entertainment for the masses. The first theatre which only had a seating capacity of 180 people, was opened at Shepherd's Bush on Boxing Day, 26th December, 1907, and proved to be an immediate success, so much so that the Directors decided at once to double the seating capacity. The second Theatre, Walworth Road, which was opened in February of this year, accommodates 600 people, and the profits in this case also proved to be excellent. That the weekly takings are steadily increasing is proved by the appended return showing a present net profit of over £80 per week. A third Theatre has just opened at Deptford, and a fourth at Hammersmith will be ready to open about 5th October. Several other sites have also been arranged for in populous localities, and negotiations are in progress for additional sites at Islington, Greenwich, Woolwich, Brixton, Edgware Road, Lewisham, Clapham Junction, and other suitable districts in and about London.

Particulars: This novel form of entertainment, for the people, was first started in America, where it has become so increasingly popular since its commencement (over five years ago), that to-day these little theatres are to be found in every big town in the United States, and there are now over 600 in the City of New York alone. The American Companies owning these theatres have proved an enormous financial success, and have returned large profits to their fortunate owners: dividends of over 100% have been regularly paid, and the shares are regarded by the general public there as one of the best industrial investments.

The General Manger is a technical expert, having been Manager of the Electric Theatres Co. in New York; from his experience he is positive that the field for this class of cheap amusement is far greater here than in New York. The profits are greater, as here the admission charge is 3d. as against 2½d. (five cents), while the wages of operators, attendants and staff are only half of what they are paid in New York.

Entertainment: The principal features of the entertainment provided by the Company are as follows:

(1) The low price of admission, which is fixed at 3d. per adult and 2d. for children. In some cases as at Walworth Road, where there is a balcony, 4d. is charged for these better seats.

(2) The length of the programme, considering the low cost of admission, as the series of pictures play from an hour to seventy-five minutes.

(3) The variety of the programme. The Bill is changed twice weekly, on Mondays and Thursdays, and the pictures are carefully chosen so as to display a constant change of subject, including those that are amusing, pathetic, dramatic and instructive.

(4) The harmless nature of the programme, which makes it suitable for families and children, who, once interested in the entertainment, come again and again to see the different pictures presented as the bills are changed.

(5) The programme is continuous. The Theatre opening at 1 p.m. and closing at 10.45 p.m. People can therefore drop in at any time of the afternoon to be entertained from a few minutes up to an hour or so in the midst of their shopping or other engagements.

(6) The steady stream of patrons throughout the day makes the earning power of the Company compare favourably with tramway and omnibus enterprises which are dependant in the same way, on a continuous flow of pence for their large aggregate of income.

(7) It is worthy to mention that no expenses in advertisements are incurred, the Theatre simply being opened to the public when ready, and allowed to gain their own patronage by the merit of the entertainment.

Present Position: These theatres appeal directly to the masses as a cheap, amusing and wholesome form of entertainment, and are as essential, in the way of recreation, to their comfort and necessities as the successful tea shops and cheaper catering establishments have proved to be. In view of the great success of the first theatres here, and having regard to the enormous field for operation in London and the United Kingdom generally, it was decided to re-organise the capital, and a new Company has been formed called "Electric Theatres (1908), Limited", with a capital of £50,000, in 100,000 shares of 10/– each, which absorbs the old Company (with its theatres, assets and undertaking) for £15,000 in fully paid shares, thus leaving the new Company with £35,000 working capital with which to open a large number of these popular places of amusement. The directors find, from actual experience, that it costs under £750 to adapt and equip suitable premises as a theatre—for instance, the cost of the Deptford theatre, just opened, was only £200 and the Hammersmith Theatre will be about £600. To be conservative it may therefore be taken as an accepted fact that on each capital outlay of £1,000 (for each theatre) a net profit of £1,000 per annum can be made as long as lease exists—the leases being taken, as a rule for a period of 7, 14 or 21 years.

It is very evident that this Company originating the enterprise in London, by opening two of these Theatres, one at Shepherd's Bush and one in Walworth Road, didn't happen on the only two localities in this City where such a Theatre can make a net profit of over £1,000 a year. The people resident in these two districts being of a different class is evidence that in any populous locality a Theatre of this kind would be just as profitable.

Financial Prospects: From the foregoing facts and figures it is seen that enormous profits can be earned by this new Company, as is the policy of the Board to continue opening theatres as good sites are obtained. Within a year there might easily be 35 of these Electric Theatres open and running in London and the Provinces, which should be bringing in a profit of at least £35,000 per annum, but probably nearer £50,000, or sufficient (after setting aside a very substantial sum yearly for the opening of still further theatres), to easily pay quarterly dividends a the rate of 50% per annum. It is therefore reasonable to predict that the 10/– shares will be standing between £2 10s. 0d. and £3 each within a year's time as such profits will undoubtedly cause an active enquiry for the shares.

"Picture Personalities: Mr. G. A. S. Porter.
Mr. G. A. S. Porter is the general manager of Electric Pavilions, Limited, and, as one of the first labourers in planting picture theatres, his knowledge is quite unique."
The Bioscope, 1912.

The World's Fair
27 November 1909

LONDON'S PICTURE PALACES
Their Large Profits and Quick Returns
Money Pouring In
Little Palaces of Entertainment Said to be Making £100 Weekly

NOT A VERY LONG TIME AGO—it seems only like the day before yesterday—cinematograph theatres were almost unknown in this country. Today Londoners see them popping up here, there and everywhere.

Their generously lighted portals are among the most dazzling sights of the street. They have scattered themselves with astonishing rapidity in the suburbs. Already they are enormously popular—fathers, mothers and children regard a weekly visit to the picture palace as indispensable to happy life.

They are opening by scores in the provinces. Altogether the United Kingdom has something between six hundred and a thousand of them. Yet these are only the pioneers, and entertainment experts tell us that they will multiply here on the same liberal scale as in the United States.

There, eleven thousand were licensed last year. Chicago alone has 900, New York more than 600. Americans say they are as gladly welcomed as tea shops, nearly as numerous, and "sure money getters".

The cinematograph theatre seems to have had a hesitant start here in musty vacant shops, and small halls perched at the top of narrow staircases. These were, of course, apart from the really first-class touring shows organised by the most enterprising cinematograph firms.

£150 Weekly Profits

Then pioneers of entertainments saw that the public so far from tiring of moving pictures were increasingly fascinated by them, and appreciated every improvement, both in their subjects and the way they were presented.

Capital was easily found for the establishment of the neat little theatres we have now, brightly furnished, with well upholstered seats, at low prices, safeguarded from fires, and offering ingeniously mixed exhibitions of comedy, sentiment and news in pictures.

A representative was told that two cinematograph theatres in London have a weekly profit of over £150 each, and that a cosy one holding but a fifth of that number of people that can get into an ordinary dramatic theatre brings a steady profit of nearly £100 a week.

One in South London holds from 800 to 1,000 people, and is filled every evening. It has the children's Saturday matinees, that regular feature of the cinematograph theatres, and about a thousand children attending between 2 and 5 o'clock. About two thousand people pay on Saturday evenings.

Over £500 has just been spent in altering and decorating the place, and four fans have been installed to keep out the fogs of winter and to cool the air in summer. The programme is changed twice a week. Hot on the heels of newspaper reports of important events, photographs of them are shown on the screen.

Penny Matinees

Another, with accommodation for 355, has an interior of dark oak, with crimson panels, smoking is permitted the show is continuous from two to eleven on weekdays and three to half past ten on Sundays. These are a typical pair.

At some of the theatres there are penny seats—these for the children at matinees—and at nearly all the workman and his wife can have their two children for sixpence.

In the provinces the cinematograph theatres are developing amazingly. One who is intimately concerned in Provincial Palaces, Limited, a parent company with local offshoots all over the country, said to *The Evening News* representative:

"The British cinematograph theatres are only in their infant stage. We are a long way behind America and the Continent yet. But we shall catch up—and then our shows will be marvels of organisation.

"In Manchester £20,000 of local money has been subscribed to open fifteen or twenty theatres, in Glasgow £1,000 for six or eight, and there will be shortly no town of any considerable size which has not a cinematograph theatre or more, with the same expensive films that are shown in London.

Sport by Pictures

"As an example, we shall be able to put on pictures of the race for the Derby, on the same day that it has been run, in every place within four hours train journey of London. We have contracts with the film makers guaranteeing us 300 copies of any picture within three hours of their receipt of the order.

"The manager of a big London music-hall which gets pictures of such an event as the Grand Prix motor race at Dieppe has to pay two or three hundred pounds for them. In a few days they are stale and must be taken off.

"The provincial cinematograph theatre with small capital could not afford to produce such costly films by itself. But, by combining, these theatres can each have copies for 25s. each.

"The film is generally 400 feet long, and the theatre shows 4,000 feet in its complete show. The cost would be just £100 a week for films to a single theatre. But on the multiple system we can send round the copies at less than £10 for the 4,000 feet and give new subjects every week.

Advertisement from *The Handbook of Kinematography* by Colin N. Bennett, 1913.

"Obviously the profits are bound to be relatively great. There is a continuous show, for say, nine hours a day. The spectators have not to wait. They can go in at any moment, stay up as long as they like, and have tip-up plush seats for threepence.

Coining Money

"They 'drop in' without fuss—without talking over the matter with the formality that a visit to an ordinary theatre appears to demand. They can see the whole show in an hour, though they may stay and see it twice or ten times for the same money if they please.

"The result of this free-and-easy access is that the theatres are full most of the evening.

"What, on the other side, is the cost? Under ten pounds for the films, the wages of the operator for the machine, a pianist, a girl to sell tickets, and two attendants. You will not be surprised to hear that all the theatres are coining money.

Realism

"We are showing pictures in colours, and they are improving all the time. We shall be able to offer, say, 150 guineas to star actors to play in cinematograph sketches for us. We shall push the educative pictures for children's entertainments. We shall send our photographers out as correspondents are despatched from newspapers.

"Then we have a German invention—a synchroniser—which works the cinematograph and the gramophone in combination, so that we shall be able to give you the actor's gestures in perfect correspondence with his words.

"We are training our accompanists to have the skill at effects that Americans have; for instance, the slamming of doors, the wash of the sea on the shore, and the rumble and rattle of trains. For these things we have special apparatus, sand swishing over a rough surface for the sea, and so on.

"We are persevering with every detail, because we believe that the cinematograph theatre has come for ever."

The World's Fair
12 March 1910

TROUBLE AT A PICTURE SHOW
Dissatisfied Spectator Interrupts the Performance

A NOVEL DIVERSION IN A CINEMATOGRAPH SHOW was provided at the new Gaiety Picture Palace, Tottenham Court Road, on Monday evening, by a woman.

At Marlborough Street Police Court, on Tuesday, the offender, Mary Daly, thirty-five, well dressed, living in Great James Street, WC., was charged with behaving in a disorderly manner.

Stephen Baker, an attendant at the Palace, said that about 8.30 on Monday evening, the prisoner came to the theatre and paid 3d. for admission. As he had had occasion to speak to her on a previous occasion, he followed her in, and saw that she had a good threepenny seat. He then saw her speak to a lady and gentleman, and change from one seat to another, the charge for which was sixpence. He told her that she was in the sixpenny seat, and suggested that if she wished to remain there she could pay the extra threepence. Upon that she stood up and said:

"You are a lot of swindlers. I have been asking all the people how much they paid, and you have no barrier to make a distinction between the seats, I shall sit where I like, and do what I like, and I mean to ask the people how much they pay for admission."

The Prisoner: I didn't say anything of the kind.

The attendant went on to say that Miss Daly spoke in a loud voice, causing considerable disturbance. He asked her to return to the threepenny seats, but she refused to do so, and continued to make a disturbance and annoy the audience. He then told her that she would be ejected, and turned out without using any unnecessary force. She went out by one door, but returning by another, exclaimed "I will stop here all night and cause annoyance." Police-officers came up, and a crowd gathered and blocked the footway. As she could not be induced to go away she was taken into custody. He wished to add that she had only forbidden to enter the theatre because she smoked cigarettes there. When he spoke to her about it she said that a notice ought to be put up stating that ladies were not permitted to smoke. She added, "My brother is a K.C. at the Temple, and I know the law".

Thought She was a Lady

Miss Daly: I want to know, if I was forbidden the theatre, why they gave me a ticket last night?

Witness: I thought that as you were a lady you would behave yourself.

Miss Daly: It is all a tissue of lies.

Police-constables Broomfield and Tilley deposed to arresting Miss Daly, who they said, was creating a great disturbance outside the theatre, surrounded by a crowd of people.

In her defence, Miss Daly said she could bring forward "endless numberless witnesses" to prove that the seats in which she sat were charged at threepence. She took a threepenny ticket, but as she was unable to see properly from the one she was shown to she moved to another, after asking several ladies and gentlemen who were sitting close by what they had paid. They all replied "Threepence". Then the attendant came up and said she was in a sixpenny seat. The attendant told the inspector at the police-station that there was no barrier between the different priced seats. She denied saying that her brother was a K.C. Mr. Dominic Daly, of the Inner Temple, now dead, was her father.

Mr. Denman said this was a case in which he was quite prepared to accept prisoner's statement, as being uncontradicted as to the facts. She had, however, put herself in the wrong by arguing the matter out at the theatre, her remedy lying in a civil court, if there really had been a breach of contract on the part of the theatre authorities. He ordered her to be bound over in £5 to be of good behaviour for six months.

" 'Ere we are, Bill! Let's 'ave 'arf-an-hour's lux!"
***Punch*, 26 March 1913.**

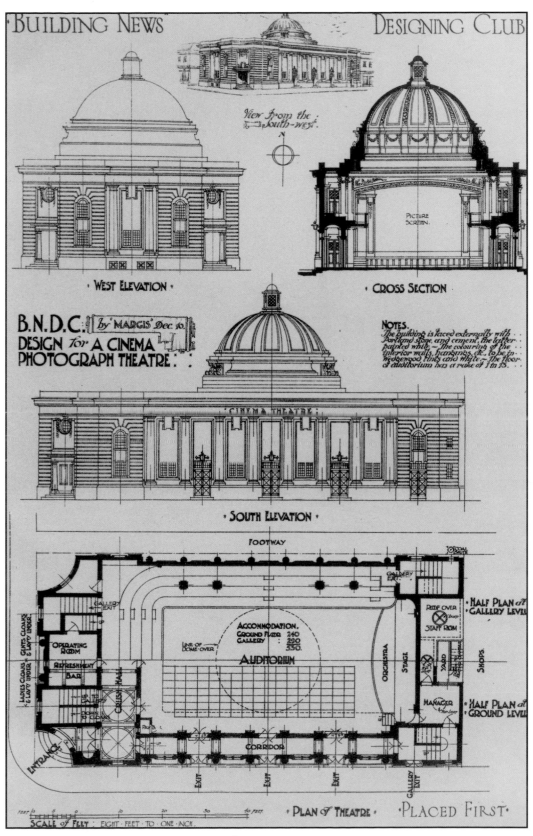

Early cinema design. *The Building News,* 3 February 1911.

[Anonymous author]
How to Run a Picture Theatre: A Handbook for Proprietors, Managers and Exhibitors
1912, pp. 11–20

THE BUILDING AND ITS FITTINGS

HAVING SATISFIED YOURSELF upon the selection of a site, the next consideration is the building.

If your venture is to be a 'converted' building, either shop premises, a public hall, or a chapel, make certain that the alterations planned are practicable before you sign a lease. But whatever you decide upon, be sure you place the conduct of affairs in the hands of a competent architect, a man with experience in the building of electric theatres and who understands what such places should be like.

In the early days of the picture theatre, the mistake was frequently made by those who should have known better, of thinking that anything was good enough for such a place, with the result that ofttimes endless expense had to be incurred after it was opened, to the dislocation of business and irreparable financial loss to the proprietors.

Strange to say, from the very start a certain type of construction has been adopted and has been followed by nearly everyone; a white exterior, a long hall with very little light, bad ventilation and no gallery, a waste of space for a lobby, open to the winds and decorated with a profusion of plaster reliefs and white and gold paints.

The 'converted' theatre is now almost a thing of the past. The successful picture theatre of to-day must not only be especially arranged for the purposes, but it must present as pleasing an architectural and decorative aspect as it is possible to make. Such a house must naturally represent a considerable investment of capital, and yet with carefully thought-out pre-arrangement, the avoidance of waste, and the knowledge of obtaining the best return for small outlay, many excellent theatres have been erected and started on quite a moderate expenditure.

One is apt to confound elegance with size, and so it is not infrequently thought that a theatre to be imposing, must needs present a front forty feet or more in width. Yet some of the most imposing and at the same time cosy and comfortable theatres occupy not much more than half that frontage.

The Lobby or Entrance Hall

Starting at the entrance, the first consideration is the lobby, which has to be depended upon to create the first impression in the minds of the patrons. A dingy lobby betokens in the minds of many a poor entertainment. How often the mistake is made that all the public expect for outside appearances is a blaze of light.

Nothing short of 18ft. should be devoted to the lobby. Nor is this waste space, for it enables an advertising display to be made to advantage, and the passers-by who stop to read the program boards or day bill are well against the pay box before they realise that their curiosity has already got them almost inside the theatre.

The flooring should be of tiles and cement. A board flooring is an abomination suggestive of hasty construction and a fleeting stay. The cement floor is not as attractive, though more durable, and is to be advocated only when tiles are too expensive. Even then the name of the theatre may be sunk in the flooring, breaking the grey expanse of the cement.

Greater variety of material is permitted in walls and ceiling. As a general thing, plaster casting is to be preferred to imitation marble. The last may be sparingly used in the large lobbies, but is almost too heavy to be in keeping with the style of performance. A plaster casting lobby, if tastefully done, finished in white and gold, and kept always fresh by the use of paint and gold leaf is much to be preferred.

White and gold is advocated as a general colour scheme; any combination of light tints is pleasing, though not as brilliant as the gleaming white. In the larger towns and cities, where the atmosphere is more vitiated, darker tones are preferable, as they do not entail so frequent an outlay on re-decoration.

Wood may be employed, but its use is not so effective. Most of the newer houses contain provision for built-in lobby display, frames for the showing of pictures of the stock companies, or the hanging of the posters.

These frames should be provided with swinging doors, covered with a good quantity of glass and with a lock and key to prevent depredations. They should not be so numerous as to seem to crowd the space, but they should be used wherever possible, for they form valuable advertisements.

Where frames are not set into the walls, or where an additional display is desired, brass frames and easels are to be had very cheaply, or these may be made of white wood. In either case, the glass is essential, and those frames exposed to the elements should be made water-tight to prevent damage to photographs or posters by a sudden shower.

When the easel frames are used, care must be exercised that they are properly disposed, and in any event, they should not be so numerous as to crowd the lobby. A lobby is a place for people, not for the display of advertisements to the exclusion of the people.

There are arguments for and against the isolated box office, as distinguished from the pay window built into the house. If the tickets are sold close to the entrance, the man who wants to look at the pictures on both walls finds the ticket seller handy, but, on the other hand, only a lobby that is both wide and deep will afford room for the ticket window in the centre. Where the lobby is unusually spacious, the ornamental box office becomes an additional attraction.

In such a case, it is as well to have the box glass walled, that the ticket seller may keep an eye on the lobby, as well as that the glass may not obstruct the view as more solid material would.

It is better to keep the lobby clear unless it is large enough to furnish permanent house room to the ticket office.

The Waiting Room or Lobby Adjunct

A waiting room offers advantages frequently overlooked. For instance: in too many of the theatres the spectators are treated to currents of cold air falling on their shoulders and making them so uncomfortable as to discourage them from ever returning. A waiting room or ante-room, if you wish to call it so, would obviate this. It can also be used as a cloak room and thus another source of income is added.

A waiting room has another advantage which should be seriously considered by the exhibitor. With the present system of continuous performance and of allowing anyone to enter or leave the auditorium while a picture is on the screen, you may discourage many devotees of motion pictures who, deeply interested in a scene, have either to move or allow someone to pass in front of them, or to have some newcomer masking the view while looking for a seat, or a lady removing her hat as slowly as possible, and this at the most pathetic moment. More than one spectator has expressed his disgust when reading a sub-title, to have someone pass in front of him and shut off the view, and the moment he cannot read the sub-title on the screen, he loses the thread of the story and becomes dissatisfied with the show.

A waiting or ante-room would be a genuine remedy to this draw-back, or the ushers would allow no one to either enter or leave the auditorium while a picture is on the screen. Many exhibitors have lost money by the lack of a proper waiting room. Such an ante-room does not need to be very high pitched, and could be built under the gallery, so that every inch of the floor space would be used to the best advantage. It could also be made remunerative by installing a few automatic machines for the benefit of patrons. In this waiting room posters and notices of the coming shows could neatly be framed and displayed on the walls; they would certainly tempt many of the visitors to return the next day or next week. The ante-room would decrease the length of the auditorium proper and give a shorter and better throw for the pictures.

The Auditorium

The good impression created by the outside appearance and the entrance lobby is of no avail if it is not sustained by the auditorium.

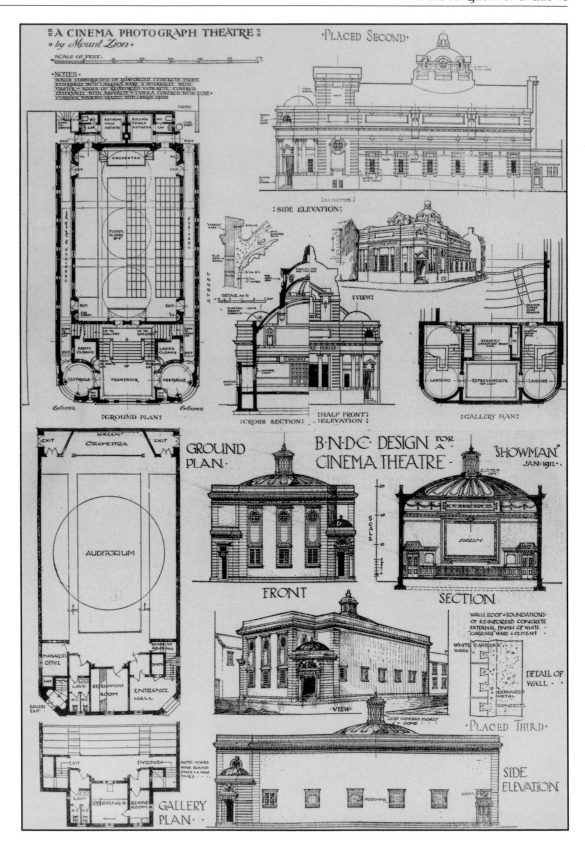

Early cinema design. *The Building News,* 3 February 1911.

The prosperity of the picture theatre depends upon its attracting a regular patronage. The evanescent visitor is of but little use to the exhibitor, except as a walking advertisement spreading the fame of the show and thus attracting the other patrons.

It has been said that the way to an Englishman's heart is through his stomach. Be that as it may, the only way in which to secure a regular throw of patronage is to make people comfortable when they are in the theatre.

For floor covering, it is becoming increasingly universal to use good carpeting instead of linoleum. There is something in the feel of a velvet pile that sub-consciously suggests and conveys the impression of luxury. It is hard to keep clean on muddy days, but it is worth the care and if you can afford it will pay. Besides, a vacuum cleaner does a lot of work in a little time, and at a comparatively cheap cost. If carpet is too expensive for the character of the house, use linoleum in solid colours for the aisles and have a hardwood floor well waxed, but not to the point of slipperiness, and keeping the floor clean will be a far easier matter. The aisles can, of course, have a crumb cloth covering over the lino or carpet, which can be taken up and washed as occasion demands, and thus always presents a clean appearance.

On no account omit to have a few mirrors at convenient points—this is a kindly consideration which always pleases the ladies and enables them to adjust their headgear correctly.

Precautions from Fire and Disinfection

It is well to install means for the speedy extinction of an outbreak of fire. Forewarned if forearmed, and every well-equipped building should contain a plenitude of automatic sprinklers, hand grenades and the like. It should also be well provided with fire hydrants, and it is well to give the staff a periodical turn out in order, not only that they shall be thoroughly drilled, but that the appliances themselves may be kept in an efficient state.

In a theatre will equipped with fire appliances the audience experiences are added degree of safety and the likelihood of panic is reduced to a minimum. Messrs. Merryweather and Messrs. Shand, Mason and Company supply portable fire extinguishing appliances, and as they specialise in these it is far better to place their provision in the hands of such firms as one can rest assured that an efficient equipment will be installed at a minimum of expense.

The interior of the theatre should also be well disinfected not only after each performance, but during the time the pictures are being shown. There is a multiplicity of sprayers and deodorising compounds on the market, most of which are of great service not only in warding off disease but in keeping the atmosphere pure and sweetly scented.

A glance at the trade papers or catalogues will give one an idea of the multiplicity of deodorising appliances on the market, as well as the compounds used in them, but it may be stated that the ordinary hand sprayer which an attendant uses frequently during the show, and which is of handy and light construction, is the best. As deodorisers, Pinozal, Ozone, Empire Essence are probably the most effective.

The Rake

The most important item in the auditorium is the rake. Yet, strange to say, this is the last thing considered by many proprietors and in the early days of the motion picture, if frequently happened that not until the place was ready for opening, the seats fixed, and all that was necessary was the audience, was it discovered that those at the rear were unable to see the picture. The floor must be inclined from screen to rear, a good rake being one in ten. Steps should always be avoided, as when the hall is in semi-darkness, accidents are likely to happen, with consequent actions at law, besides which, in an emergency, steps militate against a speedy emptying of the house.

Lighting the Inside

There is no need to have the auditorium at any time in absolute darkness so long as it is made impossible for any direct rays of light to fall upon the screen from any source save the projector.

Lights that are shaded so that the incandescent filament is not visible to the eye when seated interfere only in a negligible quantity with the screen. A competent electrician should be considered as to lighting, preferably an expert in matters appertaining to kinematography.

The Screen

The position of the screen has, up to the present, invariably been at the end farthest from the entrance, but it has been urged by authorities on this matter that experience has proved that it would be better to throw the picture to the opposite end. Those who argue thus say—and there is undoubtedly something in their argument—that the best seats are always farthest from the screen. Under the system at present pertaining, the majority of the audience (those occupying the cheaper seats) have to pass down the entire length of the hall to reach their seats nearest the screen, whereas if the system here was advocated were adopted, they would come right upon their seats as soon as they entered the auditorium. At any rate, the alteration here suggested seems to have many points in its favour.

It must be borne in mind that with the screen at the street end and the projection room at the rear, there is less danger in case of fire, and at all times the audience is the more easily handled.

There are numerous devices for shielding the screen, but the best appears to be a kind of shadow box resembling the protection used around the frame of a valuable painting. The depth of this may vary from 3ft. to 6ft., the sides being slanting so that occupants of the extreme end seats in the first few rows can see the entire picture without discomfort. A deep box also gives a better effect of perspective and makes the projection appear more brilliant, especially in a very light house.

There are many kinds of screens, patent and otherwise, daylight and mirror, but the best is generally said to be one of plaster built into the wall and coated with preparation. The surface must be absolutely true, and the screen must be set square with the firm.

Many writers advise frequent paintings of the screen to keep it fresh, but there are almost certain to be brush marks, and a better plan is to clean the screen with kneaded rubber, to be obtained at art stores, or with the soft crumb or bread. If properly done, it is better than painting, and there is no possibility of brush marks showing. The bread should be thrown away as soon as it begins to get dirty. The soft crumb will take off the dirt, but it will not be hard enough to scratch the plaster, if the crust of the loaf is removed with care. A daily cleaning is best. The work should be done once a week at the longest with dusting night and morning.

Seating

Tip-ups for seating cannot be beaten and care should be taken to see that they are comfortable, but remember that you do not wish your audience to remain the entire evening unless you are giving a one house a night show. The price of tip-ups varies considerably, and they are supplied new at such a moderate rate that it is well never to purchase second hand stuff. If, however, a good opportunity arises for so doing, the purchaser should be absolutely certain that the seats are in good condition before parting with his money.

It is well to have a centre, as well as two sides aisles where floor area permits. The sides can be used for entrance and the centre for exit. Give as much space as possible between the rows of seats, from 2ft. 6in. to 3ft. is a fair distance. The number of seats in a row is, of course, dependent on the width of the hall.

It is a good plan to have hat racks under the seats, as these not only conduce to the comfort of those who are considerate enough to remove their hats, but leave the hands free to hold the cup of afternoon tea, or the programme, or what not.

There are many useful devices which are fixed in a well appointed theatre to the backs of the seats, such as ash trays, umbrella and stick clips, shelves for cup and saucer, match holders and the like, but where these are employed, every precaution must be taken to see that they are not of a description likely to damage the clothing of passers-by. Make it the business of one man to go over the house every morning tightening loose screws and replacing missing parts. At least once a week, but not always on the same day, make a personal inspection to check this man's work. You don't know that the seats are right unless you see for yourself.

Decoration and Upholstery

Many of the pictures theatre are erected and decorated by local people, who may know how to build factories and dwelling houses, but who have no knowledge of exhibition hall requirements. In the construction of a moving picture theatre attention should be given to the light effects, and this is where most of the architects, builders, decorators and exhibitions are making a grave mistake, in having the interior walls and ornaments of light colours. Such colours will suit an opera house, but not a moving picture theatre. Sombre colours will undoubtedly bring out better effects from the screen.

In a light coloured theatre, the light of the machine naturally reflects on the cream coloured walls and then the screen, and many exhibitors not acquainted with this fact, blame the operator for a bad light.

An experienced operator can suggest some colour effects that will suit your particular house better than general suggestions, but avoid glaring contrasts of colours and vivid hues, and kill the man who wants to put a couple of pounds of gold leaf on the walls. Light greens, blues or pinks, with a deeper tint in the shadow, work well, as will a French grey worked up with a very little white. Two shades of the same colour are to be preferred to contrasting colours, but the great requirement for a moving picture theatre is that the paint shall be flat. It is not enough that the paint is said to be flat. If there is the slightest gloss that will cause cross reflections, have the walls sand-papered.

A light hint will economise lighting current, and an 8 c.p. lamp will be as effective as your 16 c.p. in an auditorium done in deep red or brown. In some cases tinted globes to match the colour scheme will be striking. If you are careful not to get the colours on too thick, the diminution of light will not be too excessive. You can obtain solution of almost any colour to tint the electric glass bulbs. In most cases the solution should be used far thinner than the directions indicate, since you merely wish to tint your light, not to use the lamps for direct display.

A good plan is to have the panels in a rich red colour with the border of still a darker shade, and have all the plastic ornaments painted imitation walnut or mahogany, and you will have one of the richest interiors that you can wish. When you use green colour for your panels and borders, you can have the plastic ornaments in either walnut or ebony colour. Brown coloured walls and the plastic ornament, imitation old ivory or old oxidised silver would also produce a rich and tasteful interior.

The real object is to decorate the interior of your house in rather sombre colours and avoid the prevailing idea that a light coloured interior is more cheerful to the eye. Remember that when your patrons visit your picture they do not do so to examine your walls, but to look at the pictures, and they want them good and well projected.

For upholstering, pegamoid, leather, plush, or moquette can be employed for the colour scheme, of course, being devised to harmonise with the whole interior decoration.

The World's Fair
17 December 1910

CINEMATOGRAPH TROUBLE IS LOOMING DARKLY AHEAD

Complication of Finance and Mortgages Make
Some of the Factors of a Threatening Outlook

THERE CAN BE NO DOUBT that in the course of the last two years picture palaces have been built recklessly—particularly in London. There are, indeed, still many provincial towns not yet adequately supplied; but in London the flame arcs, and the fairy lamps, and the dazzling stucco of the facade salute the wayfarer in almost every thorough-fare. Formerly any old corner shop was thought good enough for the purposes of conversion; but now large buildings are specially erected, at a cost varying from three thousand to as much as thirty, with smoking lounges, tea rooms, palmariums, and every conceivable provision of luxury. Five or six thousand pounds is quite a common sum to spend upon construction, and with the acquisition of expensive leases or freeholds, nine or ten thousand pounds in very many cases represents the sum which a single theatre has cost the shareholders in the company who owns it. The question which naturally arises is: How long will a hall capitalised, say, at £10,000 continue to pay ten or twenty per cent dividends to its proprietors?

The general opinion in the trade is that in the Metropolis we are on the edge of a 'shake-out'. It has seemed so easy to run a picture house that persons with very attenuated resources have gone gaily into the business, entirely unfortified for a bad month or two, and unable to withstand it when the period of depression has arrived. The shows organised by the speculators have been carried out in ill-adapted premises, with scanty accommodation for patrons, and the film service has been of the cheapest. We understand, on excellent authority, that places of this description are now being closed every week; so that, although the larger halls are multiplying, the competition of the smaller places is rapidly ceasing. This fact provides a certain amount of consolation for holders in the more important companies, which by running a 'circuit' of theatres, can work infinitely more cheaper than the owner of only two or three theatres, however excellent they may be in point of equipment and pictures.

If an individual theatre-owner wants to give a really excellent show he cannot work for much less than £40 per week. Film service (two changes weekly) including a fair amount of 'first release' stuff, will cost him about £12; his singing pictures will cost him, with hire of synchroniser, about £2 7s. 6d. to £2 10s.; if he has spent, say £4,000 on a freehold hall he is standing at a rental of £160 a year, say £3 5s. per week; his rates (on a moderate assessment) will amount to 12s per week; his electric light; outside flame lamps, strings of fairy lamps, flashing sky-sign, the cinema arc, and inside lights will cost him anything from £3 to £5 per week, according to the best rate he can get from his generator, if he is on an alternating current—as so many people are; his staff, consisting of manager, operator, assistant operator, programme-girls, cashier, attendants, bill-man, effects man, and so on, we may put down at £12 per week; his printing will cost him £2 per week; his billposting £1; his advertising £1 10s.; and pretty disbursements may easily be another £3 or £4 per week. These sums bring us well over £40.

With reference to receipts, everything depends upon the 'pitch'. He may cover his expenses or he may not. Forty pounds requires a good deal of taking in threepences and sixpences, and, in some cases, pennies and twopences. If his 'pitch' is well chosen, and he knows how to cater for his particular audience, he may quite possibly, at the expense of fourteen hours work a day and a mountain of anxiety, make £10 or £20 a week profit. On the other hand, a local strike or some unexpected opposition may drive his receipts down to £30, and there is always that aggravating deficiency of £10 staring him in the face when he makes up his weekly accounts. He will economise wherever he can, of course; but the last thing he dares to save money on is his film hire, which is an important item in the weekly balance-sheet. If he were on a 'circuit' of six or dozen halls he could work much cheaper. His films, travelling round from hall to hall on the circuit, would probably not average him out at more than £7, including singing pictures—an immediate saving of £7 10s.; his manager, at a fair salary, would be replaced by a kind of head clerk, accountable to the travelling manager of the circuit, and in a dozen little ways he would save money, probably until his expenses were brought down to about £25 a week.

Then there is the mortgage difficulty. In the course of an interview with a representative of *The Financial News*, a director of one of the most important of the cinematograph companies said:

"You will find that the extreme difficulty which now exists of obtaining money or mortgage of property will prove an effective barrier to further building operations by the small men in the business. Thanks to the Budget, property has now become the worst investment in the county. Private lenders absolutely decline to advance money on it, excepting on terms that suggest the cent per centum more than anything else. This applies not only to picture theatres, but to all classes of property. A friend of mine who been living quite comfortably on the margin between the mortgages on 25 houses and the rents he derived now finds the mortgages called in and himself utterly unable to replace them.

"The result is that he will lose his houses, and his present means of livelihood will be at an end. I would advise no man to begin the construction of a picture theatre unless he has money in the bank to pay for it in its entirety. Ours is a large and prosperous company but we have had serious difficulties to contend with in respect to mortgages during the past few months. I hear of picture places roof high which cannot be completed because loans have been ruthlessly called in. It is not that picture theatres are worst security than any forms of property. They usually occupy commanding sites and are easily capable of transformation into shops or business premises if the worst came to the worst. It is simply that Mr. Lloyd George has killed the building trade generally and paralysed all forms of finance associated with it."

All these considerations make up a warning or unmistakable significance to intending investors in cinematograph shares. If there is a 'shake-out' coming their money should be kept outside the radius of the trouble.

Inside a picture palace. *The Sphere*, **12 April 1913.**

The World's Fair
18 June 1910

MR. HARRY KEMP'S PICTURE PALACE AT EARLESTOWN

MR. HARRY KEMP'S CINEMATOGRAPH show is rapidly becoming an Earlestown institution. It has been visited during the course of the last two or three weeks by people who have never entered within the precincts of a travelling show before and who never dreamt that they would ever do such a thing. The reason is obvious. Mr. Kemp has laid himself open to give a good show, and one that the most fastidious person can raise no objection to, whilst comfort and order reign supreme during the time that the lantern operator is manipulating the machine that tells the picture stories. And these stories are told as dramatically as many a stage piece is acted, with like effect upon the audience, who are quite often carried away by excitement. Pathos and farce each receive their share of attention, and one has only to pay a visit or two to appreciate the reason why the name of 'Kemp' has become a household name in Earlestown. The proprietors inform us that the King's funeral pictures have created almost record interest, so much so that the film produced by another photographer has been obtained has been obtained so as to give further views of the scenes, made interesting by the fact that they are taken from different points of view to those shown before.

The World's Fair
6 July 1912

MR GEO. GREEN'S ENTERPRISE

Irvine's New Picture Palace

THE ABOVE NEW EDITION, which was opened on Thursday night, is certainly one of the outstanding buildings of the town, and provides what Irvine has so far conspicuously lacked, hall accommodation of reasonable dimension on first class modern lines. The frontage of the building has at present quite a commanding appearance, and its prominence will be emphasised when the large electric lights with which it is to be fitted are placed in position. The decorative scheme of the interior has been carried out in blue, vermilion, and white, and everything within the building is fitted up on lines that are seldom followed in halls of small provincial towns. The balcony, which is seated for 220, is fitted with plush-covered tip-up chairs, and the front of the area has exceedingly comfortable and ingeniously designed wooden tip-up chairs. The automatic tipping up of these chairs, it may be noted, is an invention of Mr. Green, and the simplicity and efficiency of the design have but to be seen to be appreciated. Seats in this section are provided for 400, while in the pit, which is behind this, and divided from it by artistic trellis work, comfortable accommodation is provided for over 250. The stage, it may be noted, stands high, and this, coupled with the slope at which the floor has been set, ensures everyone present at any of the entertainments of a full view of the performance. A dynamo driven by a gas engine will provide electric light for the entire building, and great care has been taken to render the whole structure fire proof.

Another feature of the building worthy of notice is to be found in the arrangement of the exit. Stalls, pit and balcony all have separate entrances, and over and above their separate exits. An exit can also be used in case of emergency at the back of the hall, giving in all no fewer than seven ports of entrance and exit. Conditions such as these, of course, make for speedy work in the matter of emptying the hall, which, though it holds about a thousand in all, could be cleared without inconvenience in two and a half minutes. The lantern box, which is at the end farthest from the stage, is thoroughly fireproof, and even the small aperture through which the light finds egress can be closed should occasion demand by a fireproof shutter that can be operated from either the inside or from outside the box. Mr. Green and Mr. Sam Stott, his general manager, as well as Mr. Tom Russell, the local manager, have been superintending for the past few days the completing of the building.

'LOVE AT THE CINEMA'

Punch
21 January 1914

Inert I watched the Hero sacked
For lapses clearly not his own;
The midnight murder on the cliff,
The wonted ante-nuptial tiff,
The orange-blossoms, bored me stiff.
The picture-hall was simply packed,
But I was all alone.

Alone! Two little hours could span
The gloom that bound me stark and grim
(No melancholy pierced me through
Before the 7.32
Had ravished Barbara from view),
And yet I brooked it like a man
Until I noticed HIM.

He sat extravagantly near
His Heart's Delight. To my distress,
When temporary twilight fell,
He squeezed her hand (and squeezed it well!)
Possessed her waist, and in that shell,
That damask shell she calls an ear,
Breathed words of tenderness.

The blood ran riot in my head
And still I held my madness thrall,
My lips repressed the frenzied shriek,
My straining heart was stout as teak;
But, when he kissed her mantling cheek,
I broke—and two attendants led
Me wailing from the hall.

THE NEW ELECTRIC THEATRE BOSTON

Corn Exchange Transformed

The Boston Guardian
17 December 1910

SUCH A TRANSFORMATION has taken place in the appearance of the Corn Exchange as will surprise Boston people. Mr. G. Aspland Howden has taken over the lease of the building from the Premier Rinks, Ltd., and on Thursday next, December 22nd is opening the New Electric Theatre there. The old place has been entirely changed into an up-to-date house of amusement. The stage is one of the largest in Lincolnshire, the proscenium opening being 30 feet by 19 feet high, and from the front of the stage to the back is 24 feet. The building has been re-seated throughout, and the seats are on a raised floor gradually sloping to the front of the stage. The best seats at the back are upholstered in peacock blue plush. The second seats are polished hard wood tip-up forms. Persons in every seat will get a clear view of the stage. The arrangements for admission to the building are such as to avoid any confusion. There are three classes of seats and all have separate entrances. Persons going to the threepenny seats enter by the first doors in Petticoat-lane, those entering the sixpenny seats do so by the right-hand doors at the main entrance. The back of the theatre is securely screened off to prevent draughts reaching those occupying the best seats. Over the entrance is an iron fireproof cinematograph operating-box, from which the pictures are projected onto the screen. The lighting will be electric from a 12 h.p. engine placed in the cellar below. The stage has been provided with suitable screens and the building interior richly decorated, all work having been carried out with local labour as far as possible. The principal cinematograph pictures for the first three days will be Faust a magnificent subject, 2,000 feet in length. It is intended when the theatre has made a start, to run a good-class variety entertainment as well as pictures and the New Electric Theatre which supplies a real want in Boston should prove a permanent attraction in the town.

Kinema House, Warrington. *The Building News*, 1 May 1914.

The Times
16 May 1913

CINEMATOGRAPH FINANCE
Recent Flotations and Failures

THE RATE AT WHICH THE SO-CALLED PICTURE PALACES are multiplying means, sooner or later, a serious financial collapse. Without impugning for a moment the utility or the permanency of the industry as a whole, it is impossible to ignore the fact that the promotion of picture theatres that are not wanted and that can never pay has become a business. On February 20 we gave some particulars of the capital invested in shares in cinematographs shows and uttered a warning as to the risk of making such investments so late in the day and under hazardous auspices. Since the position has become worse. Between January 1 last and April 30 161 new picture theatre companies were registered with a total nominal capital of £930,500. This, does not include companies formed for the manufacture and distribution of film or accessories. The 161 companies are formed for exhibition purposes solely, and for exhibition purposes in which the bioscope in some form or another is the central, if not the only, attraction. For the whole of 1912 the number of similar companies registered was 59, with a nominal capital of £771,475, and for the four years 1910–12 inclusive the total number of companies was 133 and the capital £1,940,825.

It does not follow, of course, that the amount of capital actually subscribed at all coincides with the amount registered. Until these companies have, in due course, made their returns to

Somerset House it is not possible to say how much money they have obtained from the public. As a rule the subscriptions are obtained by means of circulating prospectuses. The promoters are careful not to invite outside financial criticism on their rosy comments. The dividends paid by some of the pioneer companies before competition grew keen are quoted as a sample of what it is insinuated can be done by insignificant shows in little country towns. An examination of the capital conditions reveals the fact that in a large proportion of companies the ordinary shareholders who find the bulk of the capital are at the mercy of a clique of so-called founders, whose 1s. shares are vested by the articles of association with an outweighing power when measured against the £1 shares. Thus, the management, the control, the appointment of directors, the declaration of dividends, everything in fact is in the hands of the little promoting knot to whom the company owes its birth.

Efforts to Restrict Licenses

From the point of view of the investor, there is no way of arresting this portentous growth of hopeless companies. It would be a new principle to hinder competition for the protection of shareholders. In some districts, however, the magistrates have recognised that, on other and public grounds, it is possible to have too many picture palaces. That the existing proprietors and exhibitors are in sympathy with this view goes without saying. A district which is able to support one picture theatre may not be able to support two: the result is that the first experience a falling off in its receipts, and the second fails to make a living. The competition does not enrich the one and makes the other 'poor indeed'. One is not surprised, therefore, to find that at Newcastle-on-Tyne the Northern Exhibitors Association is taking action against any increase in the existing number of licenses: or that at Bristol the magistrates and exhibitors are both aiming at the same thing: or that at Liverpool and Southport the magistrates alone are exercising what powers they have to limit the numbers. The country Justices, however, are not moved by the financial inadvisability of mere picture theatres, an even the exhibitors opposition can only be regarded as a measure of self protection. Our view is that the origin of the mischief lies in the registration of so many companies doomed to failure form the outset.

Recent Failures

You can ride a willing horse to death, and you can do the same thing with the investors in a prosperous and entertaining industry. if private people chose to risk their own money in building or running picture palaces no one has a right to object: the only ground for criticism is that furnished by company promotions which, however much they may benefit the promoters, mean disaster, first or last, for the shareholders. A considerable number of picture shows have closed down since the beginning of the year and the buildings are advertised to be let, and if it be an exaggeration to talk of the bittern dwelling in the portals thereof, the desolation of the prospect is almost as evident as if it did. Electric theatre companies are coming to grief nearly every week, as a glance at the files of the London Gazette will show.

The picture palace may have come to stay but it is being overdone, the company side of it in particular. There may be, here and there, openings for new exhibitions with a chance of making money, but if so they are few and far between. Although we are satisfied that most of the limited liability ventures are brought out in good faith, however mistaken in the calculations, there are some that are less honestly conceived—that are, to put it in plain English, swindles. Our object, however, is not to single out particular companies for attack, but once more to impress upon the people with a little spare money to invest the advisability of avoiding this kind of enterprise altogether, because in the present congested state of the business the probabilities of success are almost infinitesimal. The correctness of the views set forth in our previous article has been confirmed and emphasised by recent developments, and that is why we consider it necessary to repeat the warning.

Meeting of leading European film producers in Paris, 2 February 1909.

Photograph includes:

Cecil Hepworth
(seated, third from left)

Robert W. Paul
(seated, fourth from left)

James Williamson
(seated, far right)

Georges Méliès
(standing, third from right)

Charles Pathé
(standing, far right)

National Museum of Photography, Film & Television

'DISTRESS'

"Oh give me a penny," the poor boy wailed.
As he shivering stood in the street,
A picture of misery all forlorn,
No stockings or shoes to his feet:
No cap on his head, and his coat all torn.
Whilst tears to his eyes did start:
"Oh pause for awhile, you passer-by,
Is there pity or love in your heart!"

"Pray tell me, my boy," said a lady fair,
As she stooped o'er the urchin's head.
"Does poverty dire possess thy home,
Is your father at work?" she said.
"Do your sisters and brothers and mother, too,
Cry out with hunger's pain?
Oh! tell me, my lad, what is the cause
Of your pitiful plight so plain?"

"I want a penny," the youngster sighed,
"But not to take home, as you think,
My mother and sisters have food enough,
And my father, he doesn't drink;
But I can't go home, for I haven't got time,
It's a long way after three,
And I want to go down to the picture show
To be in at the matinee."

Poem by M. Casey
The Picture Paper
11 May 1919

"'Take me to see the pictures, muvver, will yer?'
'Now ain't you just been an 'ad your 'air cut? Blow'd if you ain't always a-craving after amusement!'"
London Opinion, 2 November 1912. *Stephen Bottomore.*

Appendix 1
The British Film Copyright Archive

by Richard Brown

A SUBSTANTIAL BODY OF IMPORTANT primary material relating to the copyright of film in England between 1897 and 1912, has recently been identified and listed.[1] A considerable amount of valuable research has been done over a number of years on the much larger Library of Congress archive,[2] but although the early history of film in the United States indicates that both countries shared broadly similar legal systems and legislative structures for dealing with intellectual property infringement, there are nonetheless many important differences in the comparative treatment of film copyright. As a result of the deposit in the Library of Congress of a considerable number of complete bromide contact copies (or Paper Prints as they are usually termed) it has been possible for historians to extend their study of the development of film form. The British collection, which consists entirely of film clips of various lengths, and some frame enlargements, does not offer this opportunity, focusing attention instead on the legal and commercial aspects of copyrighting, which were the immediate concern of early cinematographers.

Copyright legislation in England developed from an ancient private body, The Worshipful Company of Stationers and Newspaper Makers, whose registers, dating from 1554, originally offered a record of ownership in books and a form of Guild protection to nascent publishers. Such a need was the direct result of the invention of printing and the rapid increase in publishing in England during the early sixteenth century. Over the centuries demand increased considerably and the scope of copyright registration also widened. In time, what had originally been a private institution, was given official status and registration at Stationers Hall as proof of ownership in intellectual property, became mandatory for anyone wishing to bring a Common Law action in the English courts. Although the Copyright Act of 1842 (5 & 6 Vict. c.45) still suggested a limited application, referring to "literary matter of lasting benefit to the world", actual practice was far less restrictive and by the end of the nineteenth century almost any kind of printed materials, including advertising ephemera, was being accepted. By this time, Stationers Hall had become a highly organised and commercial organisation, deriving a considerable income from registration fees. But late nineteenth century copyright legislation was still based on complicated and not altogether appropriate foundations, and between 1897 and 1900, a wide ranging enquiry was instituted by Parliament into current copyright practice and the way in which it might be improved and modernised.[3]

Photographic protection at this time was covered by a section in the fine Arts Copyright Act of 1862 (25 & 26 Vict. c.68) which seemed to work well and the Herschell Committee proposals for amending it, announced in 1899, were immediately opposed by both amateur and professional photographers, fearing both loss of status; as photography was no longer to be considered a 'fine Art'; and an increase in the expense of registration.[4] The old Act had been rather loosely drawn and did not insist that a photographer should register his work unless he wished to bring an action for infringement. Most professionals saved their money and simply waited to see if any of their work was copied. Only if it was, did they then bother to register. It was this liberal interpretation of the existing law that was directly responsible for determining both the extent and the somewhat fragmentary nature of the British film Copyright Archive.

Although no cinematographers were called to give

evidence before the select committee, attention was drawn at the hearings to the fact that films could be of great value and that protection ought to be extended to them. The dilemma faced by film makers was particularly noted:

> *Viscount Knutsford:* Take the Prize Fight at the Aquarium. It ought to be registered as one photograph, the whole thing?
> *Witness:* Yes, the combination. And that is necessary to avoid the difficulties that have already arisen.
> *VK:* What words do you suggest?
> *W:* The expression 'photograph' shall include a series of photographs constituting one picture, as well as the photographic negatives or positives connected therewith.[5]

There seems little doubt that film would have been recognised and protected as a separate entity in England by 1900, if the Herschell Bill had been accepted. But it was not, and filmmakers therefore continued to register single scenes as still photographs. Perhaps rather surprisingly, this system appears to have worked out quite well and *The British Journal of Photography* remarked as late as December 1905, that "No case of the infringement of the copyright in a cinematograph film has, so far as we are aware, yet come before any of the English Law Courts".[6] Responding to this, someone identifying himself only as a 'film Maker', instead of complaining about 'duping', drew attention instead to a problem which he characterised as "an open sore in the cinematograph trade" but for which there seemed no solution:

> . . . producers of cinematograph films incur great expense in preparing subjects of the story and incident class. Models have to be found, costumes made, scenery painted, and an immense amount of thought expended before everything is in readiness for the taking of the negative. Then, as soon as the film is on the market, it is not at all unusual to find another maker copying the story, incident for incident and thus robbing the originator of the first fruits of his invention. A really taking film is not an easy thing to produce. Out of a dozen which may be made, only one most likely will be acceptable for exhibition purposes. The film pirate—if I may use the term—steals the cream of one's labours and there seems no remedy for or preventative of his sharp practices.[7]

Imitation of an idea or a scenario (as distinct from actually copying or duping a film) was a practice that went back to the origins of film in England and was caused by an understandable wish to imitate proven commercial successes. A number of the films taken by Birt Acres for Robert Paul in the Spring and Summer of 1895, had obvious similarities to Edison originals, and when projected film arrived, this habit of borrowing popular themes continued.

Yet despite the apparent chaos, it would be misleading to think that early English film makers were defenceless. On the contrary, Common Law—sometimes involving the 1862 Fine Arts Act—was frequently used to provide a check against the worst excesses of commercial rivalry. These cases, dating from the very beginning of film in England, represent a rich resource of unpublished primary information, although unfortunately they have been hitherto ignored. A representative selection of Chancery cases only, and restricted to just the 1890s, gives an indication of the type of action brought and the wide range that could be covered. For a contemporary film maker, copyright protection would have been seen less in an isolated sense and more as one part of an integrated system of defence available to him.

In *A. & L. Lumière* v *The Anglo-Continental Phonograph Company and Ernest O. Kumberg* (L. 696 of April 1896) and *British Mutoscope and Biograph Ltd* v *Nicole Frères and George Barron* (B. 3422 of November 1899), the problem of 'passing-off', or falsely claiming that another's products were one's own, was dealt with. More or less the same offence, but involving the infringement of a projector movement covered by a British patent, was the subject of *J. H. Rigg* v *Simpson Brothers* (R. 1512 of September 1896), while unauthorised use of a registered trade mark was prevented in *Koopman* v *The Manchester Palace Theatre of Varieties* (K. 365 of June 1897). Cases involving the illegal use of photographs taken from a film image registered at Stationers Hall are a particularly interesting class and they occur throughout the period during which compulsory registration was required. For example, *British Mutoscope and Biograph Ltd* v *Burns and Oates* (B. 1161 of March 1899) involved the illegal use of photographs of Pope Leo XIII, taken from a film shot by W. K. L. Dickson in Rome in June 1898, which were subsequently published in a journal called

Catholicum. Similarly near the end of this period, *Barker Motion Photography* v *Edward Hulton and Company* (B. 3221 of June 1912) concerned another unauthorised use of film images taken by Barker at the 1911 Delhi Durbar.[8]

It can therefore be seen that copyright protection was always available in England to cover individual scenes in a film, if they had been registered as single photographs, but not for the combination, or sequence of photographs that constituted a film. film makers were certainly fully aware of the distinction and, when, at a slightly later period, multi-scene fictional films were being produced, several were careful to register a frame from each scene—in effect copyrighting the entire appearance (rather than the thematic development) of the subject.[9] It is probably for these reasons that no complete films (so far as is known) were submitted to Stationers Hall.

Like the English Law Courts, Stationers Hall offered more ways of protection to those involved with early film that might be thought. In addition to enabling film producers to register images, film exhibitors were also able to register their style of presentation if it had some distinctive quality. Such applications made in the 'Dramatic and Musical Representation' class, are particularly informative in regard to dates. Early entries include William Walker's show of 'Cinematograph Exhibitions, Animated Photographs, Floral Tableaux Vivants Representations and Electro-Drama Sketches' first given at Gordon Castle Fochabers, on 21st October 1896; A J. West's *Our Navy: A Patriotic Scenic Entertainment*, which made its debut at St James's Hall, Piccadilly in London on 7th November 1898; and R. W. Paul's *Army Life—or How Soldiers are Made*, first presented at the Alhambra Theatre in Leicester Square in London on 18 September 1900.[10]

It seems unlikely that 'Dramatic and Musical' protection would have extended to the film performance and was probably applicable solely to the unique aspects of the presentation—for example the titles of the films used, the running order chosen, the lecturer's commentary, the use of particular music for specific films, and perhaps the incorporation of live performers at pre-determined parts of the programme. Clearly if a rival exhibitor mounted a performance similar in every respect to the one that had been registered, then that would be infringement, but the fact that such an eventuality was extremely remote, rather limited the real effectiveness of the protection offered.

But suppose, instead of copying a film, or imitating its scenario or presentation, a film maker reconstituted a stage performance (which had been registered at Stationers Hall) and then filmed it? Suppose additionally, that instead of presenting the film himself, he sold prints to exhibitors who had taken no part in the production. Would he, or they, be liable for damages? Was it indeed infringement of a dramatic work, to film a private stage presentation, and then subsequently present it to the public in a totally different medium from that for which it had been written? Did such unauthorised film presentation of a stage play constitute infringement, as another stage presentation would certainly have done? These were the dilemmas that an English law court had to resolve in 1908. The result defined for the first time the rights of a dramatist in relation to a filmed version of his work.

In the case of *Karno* v *Pathé Frères*,[11] Karno claimed that Pathé had infringed his copyright and damaged his business by issuing a film called *At the Music Hall*, which was based, in all but minor details, on his music hall sketch 'The Mumming Birds or Twice Nightly'.[12] This sketch had first been performed at the Star music hall in Bermondsey on 14th April 1904, and Karno had subsequently protected it in the Dramatic and Musical Class on 13th January 1906. During the course of the trial held in April 1908, the Court adjourned to the Oxford music hall and Karno's sketch was performed for the Judge who then viewed the film twice. In his judgement, Mr. Justice Jelf had no hesitation in finding that the film was a copy "in all essential particulars" of the sketch, but unfortunately for Karno, he held that the sketch itself was not a 'Dramatic or Musical Performance' within the meaning of the 1833 Dramatic Copyright Act, and that consequently reproduction of it by a film—or any other method—would not constitute infringement. He said however:

> In my opinion if the Mumming Birds were within the protection of the Act, the cinematograph reproduction of it, such as I find this to be, would in fact and in law, be a representation of the plaintiff's sketch within the meaning of the Act.

And in dealing with the question of redress, he added:

> . . . even if the action were otherwise maintainable, it ought to have been brought, not against the defendants, but against the actual proprietors of the piratical performance impugned.[13]

Although there was still some doubt about the extent of culpability of the film producer, exhibitors were probably careful not to book further films of this type in view of the judge's clear indication of their liability. At least no further cases of a similar nature have been traced. For dramatists this case had established an important precedent, confirming that their work could not—if Stationers Hall registration had taken place and the dramatic piece was held to fall within the definitions of the 1833 Act—be filmed and subsequently exhibited in England without their prior consent. It is particularly interesting that this opinion was given at a time when film, as a creative work, was not yet legally recognised.

The Karno case took place against a background of growing dissatisfaction in many countries with the general state of the Copyright Law. The Berlin Convention of 1908 represented a co-ordinated international attempt to simplify procedure, agree common aims, and extend protection to newer forms of communication such as film and sound recording. Article 14 of the Convention dealt specifically with film. It recommended that full copyright should be extended and that film productions should be recognised as a literary and artistic work.[14]

The British Committee that was set up in 1909 to consider these proposed changes accepted Article 14 without amendment. Ratification was therefore embodied in the terms of the new Copyright Act 1911. Statutory registration at Stationers Hall ended for most classes, including photography, on 30th June 1912.[15] The formation of the Stationers Hall film collection began on the 18th March 1897, when Robert Paul submitted a clip of the *Bocca D'Inferno Sea-Cave near Lisbon, Portugal* for protection.[16] A realisation that 'protection' and 'preservation' could apply both to film ownership and to a film maker's reputation, is indicated by Paul's interest during 1896 and 1897, in founding a National film Archive, using a somewhat reluctant British Museum to give status to the venture.[17]

It is important to emphasise that a high proportion of titles in the British collection are previously unrecorded and that the associated images, present as positive nitrate clips, bromide contact prints, or contemporary frame enlargements, now constitute, in the vast majority of cases, the only surviving record of the subject. A wide selection of producers (some previously unknown) are represented. In addition to major companies such as Warwick Trading Company, Charles Urban, British Mutoscope and Biograph and British Gaumont, there are multiple examples of lesser known, but equally important early British film makers such as T. J. West of Southsea, John James Wood of Liverpool and William Haggar of South Wales. Because comparatively little is known of these men, examples of their work are particularly valuable and there is now a unique opportunity available to assemble and illustrate more detailed and authentic accounts of their filmmaking.

Clips include Naval and Military items, the Royal family and of course the Diamond Jubilee of June 1897. Especially noteworthy in the latter case is a long series of shots on 60mm taken by John Le Couteur. Among the less easily classified items, are four scenes from the first filmed extract of a Shakespearean play *King John* (1899) and a reconstruction of the story of *His Master's Voice* (1904) with a decidedly poor imitation of 'Nipper' in the title role! Apart from film illustrations, the entry forms that Stationers Hall required each film maker to complete at the time of registration also contain valuable data on dates, correct titles (except in the case of British Gaumont) and—perhaps most interesting of all, since the information is not normally available from any other source—the names of the cameramen who shot the films.

Because the archive was created for a specific reason, within a specific time frame and by specific film makers taking common action, it possesses a unity and integrity which is not compromised by its fragmentary nature. It represents an unusual and unexpected opportunity for researchers, writers and film archivists to increase their database of authentic early material. Perhaps the most valuable use of the new information now available, will be in identifying and correctly dating and titling currently unidentified but complete films of the period.

1. The existence of this archive, and an indication of its extent, was reported to Clyde Jeavons at the National Film and Television Archive by the author in April 1993.The original artifacts were transferred after the Second World War from Stationers Hall to the Public Record Office in Chancery Lane in London; from there to the Public Record Office at Kew, and are now stored at the J. Paul Getty Jnr. Conservation Centre at Berkhamstead. The majority of the collection is available on CD-ROM at the British Film Institute.

2. For a complete listing of the Library of Congress holdings, see Howard Lamarr Walls, *Motion Pictures 1894–1912* (Washington: Library of Congress, 1953). Surviving prints were catalogued by Kemp R. Niver in *Motion Pictures from the Library of Congress Paper Print Collection, 1894–1912* (Los Angeles and Berkeley: University of California Press, 1967). A recent overview of early American film history and the important part copyright and other legal disputes played in it, is given by Charles Musser in *The Emergence of Cinema: The American Screen to 1907* (New York: Charles Scribner, 1990). Detailed examinations of American copyright practice in relation to film include: Jeanne Thomas Allen, 'Copyright and Early Theater, Vaude-ville and Film Competition' in John L. Fell, ed., *Film Before Griffith* (Los Angeles and Berkeley: University of California Press, 1983), pp. 176–187; David Levy, 'Edison Sales Policy and the Continuous Action Film, 1904–1906' in ibid., pp. 207–222; and André Gaudreault, 'The Infringement of Copyright Laws and Its Effects (1900–1906)' in Thomas Elsaesser, ed., *Early Cinema: Space Frame Narrative* (London: British Film Institute Publishing, 1990), pp. 114–122.

3. See Copyright (Amendment) Bill, House of Lords Select Committee, with Report and Minutes of Evidence, 1897, (385) x. Copyright Bill and Copyright Amendment Bill, Select Committee of the House of Lords, with Report and Minutes of Evidence, 1898, (393) ix. Copyright Bill and Copyright (Artistic) Bill, House of Lords Select Committee and Minutes of Evidence, 1899, (362) viii. Report from the Select Committee of the House of Lords on the Copyright Bill, and Copyright (Artistic) Bill, with the Proceedings, Evidence and Appendix, 1900, (377) vi.

4. For the reaction, see 'Photographic Copyright: Special Meeting convened by the Royal Photographic Society' in *The Photographic Journal* 23 (30 June 1899): pp. 288–291. See Copyright Bill, 1899, (see note 3) for

the evidence of two photographic witnesses, Joseph J. Elliott, of Elliott and Fry (paras. 2365–2402) and John L. Mitchell of the London Stereoscopic Company (paras. 2403–2427).

5. Evidence of Herbert Bentwich, Solicitor, and 'Copyright Expert', given on 21 July 1899, in Copyright Bill, 1899, paras. 3128–3130 (see note 3); see also paras. 2419–2420 and 3125–3127. The Fitzsimmons-Corbett boxing match was the most extreme example of film length that could be cited at this time. It ran for 1½ hours and opened at the Royal Aquarium in September 1897. It was registered for English copyright protection on 27 September 1897 (PRO.COPY1.432) by Dan A. Stuart for William Kenyon Wheelock.

6. 'Copyright for Cinematograph Films', *The British Journal of Photography* 52 (8 December 1905): p. 961. Whilst film 'duping' probably existed in England before 1912, it was certainly not the high profile activity it was in the United States. In response to an enquiry, John Barnes confirmed to the author that during many years of research, he had never seen a single reference to either film piracy or to the use of trademark symbols in English Films (unpublished letter to the author dated 9 August 1995). Rachael Low has suggested that any pirated copies that might have been in circulation in England before the First World War had been imported (see Rachael Low, *The History of the British Film 1906–1914*, London: George Allen & Unwin, 1948, pp. 42 and 46). Although Gaudreault ('The Infringe-ment of Copyright Laws', p. 114—see note 2) claims in a sweeping way that film piracy was "extremely common" between 1900 and 1906 and something in "which all the major production companies partook in England . . ." He offers no evidence for this assertion.

7. 'Copyright in Cinematograph Films', *The British Journal of Photography* 52 (15 December 1905): p. 998.

8. Common Law case papers for the Supreme Court of Judicature are held at the Public Record Office at Kew. An apparently unique case of a British filmmaker—G. A. Smith of Brighton—attempting to use the Patent laws to protect a film production process, is noted by John Barnes in *Pioneers of the British Film* (London: Bishopsgate Press, 1988), p. 35 and ill. 21, pp. 36–39.

9. Done by both the Warwick Trading Company in the case of *The Smugglers*, registered 23 February 1904, and by British Gaumont for *A Railway Tragedy*, registered 16 February 1905.

10. During 1905 and 1906, British Gaumont used this class (probably in error) to register a number of individual films. Examples include *The Christmas Goose* (2 December 1905) and the *The New Woman* (2 January 1906).

11. For a detailed report of the proceedings, see 'Alleged Infringement of Copyright by Cinematograph', *The Times*, 4, 7, 10 and 30 April 1908, and 22 January 1909, (Court of Appeal Proceedings). For an informed photographic comment on the case, see 'Copyright in Cinematograph Films', *The British Journal of Photography* 55 (8 May 1908): pp. 355–56, and 'Infringement of Copyright by Cinematograph', *The British Journal of Photography* 55 (29 January 1909): pp. 77–78. It is significant that none of the precedents cited in this case—including the main one of *Tait v Fulbrook* (1 King's Bench 1908, pp. 821–35)—have any connection with cinematography, thus suggesting that no case of film piracy had been brought before this date and confirming *The British*

Journal of Photography's statement of December 1905.

12. Charles Chaplin appeared in the stage version of *The Mumming Birds* and later filmed a version of it as *A Night in the Show*, released by Essanay in November 1915.

13. *The Times*, 30 April 1908.

14. See *Report of the Committee on the Law of Copyright 1910*, Cmd. 4976, p. 27. See also 'Evidence and Appendix' [to the Report] 1910, Cmd. 5051.

15. There are a few registrations for film scenarios in the Dramatic and Musical class after 1912. For a contemporary film trade reaction and assessment of the new Act, see 'Copyright in its Relation to Cinematography', *The Bioscope*, 21 November 1912, pp. 571–72.

16. PRO.COPY 1, 429.

17. Stephen Bottomore, 'The Collection of Rubbish—Archives, Animatographs and Archives', *Film History*, vol. 7, no. 3 (Autumn 1995): pp. 291–97.

Appendix 2
Cartoons and Film: a Two-Way Street

by Stephen Bottomore

WHAM! THE BOXER'S FIST smashes into the face of an unsuspecting gentleman. Thus, in the spring of 1896, the magazine *Pick-Me-Up* portrayed the impact of the newly invented cinema on an innocent British public. The message was simple: seeing the *cinématographe* could leave one seeing stars as well.

Appearing only a month or two after the first British film shows, this is probably the first British cartoon to satirise the new medium. Appropriately it is by the Franco-Irish artist René Bull, brother of Lucien Bull who was an important pioneer of high-speed cinematography. It seems that René himself briefly took up cinematography in the early years, but his real métier was as an illustrator and cartoonist. He was but one of the many cartoonists who were to poke fun at the cinema in the years up to 1914, some of whom were major figures in their profession. In Britain they included Harry Furniss, W. Heath Robinson, H. M. Bateman, Alfred Leete and George Morrow. Among the foreign artists were Heinrich Zille, Dimitri Moor, Albert Hahn, Henriot, Storm Petersen, Hy Mayer and Rube Goldberg.

A large number of lesser-known cartoonists also tackled the film theme and clearly there was no shortage of material for them to work on, for this was a time of spectacular achievement. Within the first twenty years, much of the cinema's visual language was developed, a completely new industry of film production was born and a new social phenomenon of cinema-going entered the everyday lives of millions of people.

In an international project which I co-ordinated to locate some of these cartoons, many of the comic and satirical journals of the period have been searched page by page, along with some of the film trade press. As a result, several hundred cartoons have been found on a wide variety of film-related issues, including production, exhibition, censorship, as well as more specific themes such as westerns, melodramas, war films, faking, the relationship of cinema to theatre and the work of the film actor. The impact of the cinema on the public is also covered, in such matters as the cinema building boom, star-struck cinemagoers and picture-palace doormen.

These cartoons often reveal interesting and unexpected public attitudes to the new phenomenon of cinema in the early period, as well as indicating little-known practices such as the work of the film lecturer and the use of a round screen format for projection (presumably based on magic lantern practice).

British comic journals have been a particularly rich source for cartoons about the cinema, possibly because the British comic publishing industry was so well developed at the turn of the century. At this time there were literally dozens of cheap weekly cartoons appearing, with titles such as *Chuckles*, *Lot-o-Fun*, *Illustrated Chips* and *Comic Cuts*. There were also a number of rather more sophisticated journals (and often dearer too) aimed mainly at the middle classes, including *London Opinion*, *Judy*, *Sketchy Bits* and the best known of them all, *Punch*.

But the relationship between the older art of the printed cartoon and the newer one of cinema did not simply consist of the former satirising the latter. There were a variety of other connections which are worth exploring, which might be put under the headings of common themes, personnel and form.

The common themes: it has sometimes been suggested that the graphic techniques used in cartoons of the nineteenth century helped influence the development of film form, especially editing, at the turn of the twentieth century. Though this particular causal relationship is no longer generally accepted, it seems clear that there was an influence, but rather at the level of content, with a considerable number of plots and themes from printed cartoons being taken up by filmmakers.

One film plot that may have been inspired by printed cartoons is the 'miller and sweep' gag, made into an 1898 British film, *The Miller and the Sweep*. A cartoon with some similarities to this appeared in the comic *Varieties* on 16th May 1896. It shows a black man and a white man throwing whitewash and tar at each other consequently reversing their colours. While this is not exactly the same story as the film, no doubt a detailed search of cartoon journals before 1896 would find closer matches and I have certainly found them for shortly afterwards, in for example, 'The Sweep and the Baker' (*Funny Cuts*, September 1898).

Some film-makers in the early period have admitted that printed cartoons were an important source for film plots and the Hepworth company made direct use of the halfpenny comics according to director Hay Plumb. He recalled a slack day at the studio in 1910:

> Undismayed, the company . . . proceed to pore over the back numbers of *Chips* and *Comic Cuts*. With a gay disregard of all authors' rights they concoct between them a comedy suitable to the style of all present . . . there will be no interior photography and, therefore, the comedy must be written for exteriors only. This dictates the line of research through the comic papers. [1]

The 'script' was rapidly completed and filmed the same day as *A Wife for a Day*, much of the comedy for which involved people falling in the river—classic knockabout material which is ubiquitous both in the British comic press of this period and in many early films.

In terms of general content, there are a variety of similarities between these two media at the turn of the century. Both film comedies and printed comics frequently used the slapstick device of the catastrophic ending, in which someone is caught and punished. This was often preceded by a chase, which, in film versions from about 1903 was expanded to become a major sequence and chase films were one of the most common film genres at one time. There are similarities too between some of the stock characters in movies and cartoons, such as

the 'naughty boy' character. And indeed, the entire comic universe of anarchic, amoral fun and the challenging of authority which Noel Burch and other film historians have stressed in some of the films of this era, has much in common with the tone to be found in British (and American) printed comics.

Personnel

Another influence of printed cartoons on early film-making comes through the fact that a number of cartoonists had their work adapted for films, or themselves became filmmakers. Also, many cartoonists were filmed while drawing their own cartoons. Tom Merry was probably the first, filmed by Birt Acres in 1895, sketching *Bismark and the Kaiser*, followed in 1896 by the *New York World*'s J. Stuart Blackton (co-founder of the Vitagraph Company) who appeared on screen sketching *Thomas Edison*.

Propaganda for the First World War seems to have brought out the screen cartoonists in droves: Alec P. Ritchie, Harry Furniss and Lancelot Speed were filmed doing lightning sketches, while G. E. Studdy and Sidney Aldridge of *Punch* also produced anti-German screen cartoons.[3]

Several cartoon characters and strips were adapted for films, including the Katzenjammer Kids and Ally Sloper and a variety of cartoonists were to become involved in live-action film production, including Storm Petersen, Denmark's famous cartoonist and Jean Durand, who had been a cartoonist for the French comic Le Pêle-Mêle before becoming Gaumont's star comedy director of the early period. Cartoonist and writer Harry Furniss went to America before the First World War to write and appear in films for the Edison company and also wrote a charming book about the new world of films and filmmaking, *Our Lady Cinema* (Bristol, 1914), illustrated with his own cartoons.

Form and Metaphor

The conceptual traffic between cartoons and early film was not all one way and the printed medium took as well as gave. Cartoon strips sometimes appropriated the physical and stylistic form of the cinema. In *Ally Sloper's Half Holiday*, shown on 1 July 1899, there is a cartoon strip captioned 'Our Cinematograph' about the various guises of Mr. Coney Brain, a stage performer, drawn as five frames with perforations along the edges. By 1913 a cartoon strip drawn as a series of sprocketted frames was a well established convention in cartoons in the American comic journal *Life* and elsewhere.

As films become more complex, being made up of a series of individual scenes with intertitles to tell a story, so some cartoons also went beyond satirising merely the physical form of the film strip, to be inspired by these new multi-scene films. *Punch* in its 1913 Almanac used this format to satirise the cinema's improbable plots, publishing a ten picture western film story, in which Buckjumping Ike steals a horse after his own is laid up with rheumatism. At about the same time Chuckles was running a 24-image weekly picture strip, 'Chuckles' Coloured Cinema', which further accentuated the film reference by using a main title depicting a cinema interior and putting all captions on a 'screen' with curtains at the sides, as in a real auditorium.

Another way in which cartoons were influenced by the cinema was in a more metaphorical sense. As a cartoonist's pretext to create a cavalcade or montage of images, rather like the mixture of places and events that people were starting to see in film programmes at this time. In the *Punch* Almanac of 1901 a page entitled 'Mr. Punch's Own Cinematograph' is crammed with images to sum up recent history, showing everything from sports events to the Boer War to Queen Victoria, all watched over by Mr Punch and Father Time (see illustration on page 90). Interestingly, this idea of cinema as a medley or pot-pourri seems to have been widely felt at this time, not only amongst cartoonists, and some writers named their collections of diverse short stories or essays after words for cinema—for example, George Sims's *Biographs of Babylon* (1903), Van Hulzen's *Cinematograaf* (1903) and Paulo Barreto's *Cinematographo* (1909).[4]

1. 'Those were the days', *Picture Show Annual*, 1949.
2. Noel Burch, *Life to those Shadows* (London: British Film Institute, 1990), pp. 98–104.
3. Aldridge Speed, *The Bioscope* 5 (November 1914): pp. 497–99; *The Bioscope* 5 (17 September 1914): p. 1091. Studdy: *Kinematograph and Lantern Weekly* (24 December 1914): p. 24.
4. George Sims, *Biographs of Babylon: Life-Pictures of London's Moving Scenes* (London: Chatto and Windus, 1902). G. Van Hulzen, *Cinematograaf* (Amsterdam: L. J. Veen, 1903). Paulo Barreto, *Cinematographo* (Porto: Livreria Chardron, 1909).

Appendix 3
Bioscope Biographies
by Vanessa Toulmin

THE FOLLOWING BIOGRAPHIES are a representative sample of the life histories of the fairground exhibitors who pioneered the use of the the bioscope in the United Kingdom. Between 1897 and 1914 there were approximately one hundred and twenty exhibition booths travelling around the country. Many of these shows would have originally have been wild beast performances, waxwork displays or fine art exhibitions. The largest of these pre-cinematograph attractions were the ghost shows. The showpeople who presented the ghost illusions were adopting the idea fist exhibited by Professor G. Pepper in London in 1863. At the height of their popularity, these illusion booths could hold between six and eight hundred people, with Randall Williams claiming to house over one thousand in his show.

These stories provide only a brief outline of the careers of some of the individual show people who presented the bioscope. Further information on these individuals and the community as a whole can be found by consulting the references and the bibliography provided.

ANDERTON AND ROWLANDS

THE FIRM OF ANDERTON AND ROWLANDS was one of the first families to exhibit moving pictures on the fairground in the West Country. They presented cinematograph performances in 1897–8, a year or so later than their northern counterparts, but they were still amongst the first of their kind in the area. The founder of the firm was Albert Haslam, a former apprentice of Professor Anderson, the so-called Wizard of the North. In 1854 he left the employee of J. H. Anderson and started to perform under the stage name of Professor Anderton.

By the 1890s, Albert Haslam's illusion booth had opened with a wide variety of exhibitions including the Four Pawrs Circus and Menagerie with the Ginnett family and his own wagon fronted illusion show which travelled under the name of Anderton's Home of Mysteries. In 1895, he finally went into partnership with his son Arthur Haslam who performed his lion taming act under the stage name of Captain Rowlands. The family presented their illusion and menagerie show in a small wagon fronted exhibition booth which they had purchased new in London in 1890. According to Father Greville, writing in the 1940s, this show was of the two

wagon fronted type and elaborately decorated in blue, red and gold with the name Anderton carved and highlighted in gold leaf. A small trumpet organ stood on the platform in front of the left-hand wagon and musicians played percussion on the right. This first show was travelled until 1906 during which time it exhibited under a variety of guises including the Electric American Bioscope and from 1903 onwards the Grand Empire Palace.

In 1906, Anderton and Rowlands purchased one of the purpose built cinematographs from Orton and Spooner's to replace their old two wagon fronted booth. The large 104-key Marenghi organ became the centre piece of the exhibition which was now known as the Theatre of Varieties, with transportation and electricity provided by the Burrell traction engines. The range and type of performance presented in these new more elaborate bioscope shows is demonstrated by the number of staff that the firm employed. The performance aspect of the show was provided by Professor Anderton and his magic show, Mr Fox the ventriloquist, the Harvey sisters who with the family paraded on the showfront and the comedian Charles Bruno. The technical element comprised of a pianist, compère, stage manager, projectionist, two box office staff, an organist and finally the engine driver. After fifty five years of presenting shows on the fairground Professor Anderton was killed in a accident at Sidmouth. However, the family continued to travel the show until 1912 when it was finally discarded in favour of the latest more profitable attractions found on the fairground at that time.

The firm of Anderton and Rowland continues to operate in the West Country under the ownership of the De-Vey family who became associated with Andertons and Rowlands when Arthur Haslam's daughter Martha married George De-Vey in the 1900s. Their grandchildren still travel the family business and recently celebrated their 150th anniversary on the fairground.

REFERENCES:

Greville, Father P. 'Brief Particulars of Bioscopes Shows, Their Organs, Parades, Engines, etc: The West of England Shows', *Merry-Go-Round* 7, no. 3 (1951)
Lawrence, Edwin. 'The Infant Cinema: A Short History of the Moving Pictures'. *The World's Fair*, 3, 10 and 17 June 1939.
Middleton, P. 'Anderton and Rowland Story: Part 1', *Fairground Mercury* 12, no. 3 (1988). [Published by the Fairground Association of Great Britain.]
'Pegasus'. 'Old Time Showmen of the West', *The World's Fair*, 27 February 1932.

ASPLAND AND HOWDEN

THE FIRM OF ASPLAND AND HOWDEN was formed unofficially in 1875 when Ben Howden went to work for his brother in law George Aspland as manager of his fairground roundabouts. However, George Aspland had been appearing at the local hiring fairs with his tube shooter. This was then followed from 1872 onwards by a variety of rides manufactured by Savages of King's Lynn. In 1892, Ben Howden was taken officially into the partnership and following George's retirement in 1895, continued to run and expand the business with his son George Aspland Howden, who had been brought up by his partner. In 1906 the firm of Aspland and Howden purchased their first bioscope show from Orton and Spooner's, which incorporated the latest 110-key Gavioli organ in the showfront and a projector from Jimmy Monte of Leeds. The inherent dangers of the early projectors can be found in a report from *The World's Fair* from 1907. One night when the show was open at Shipley the nitrate film caught fire and £100 worth of film stock went up in smoke. Disaster was averted by the action of the projectionist who grasped the films in a wet blanket and threw them out.

In the winter of 1910, after a disagreement with his father, George Aspland Howden left the family business to open a permanent picture palace in Boston. He took the lease for the Corn Exchange, a building in the centre of Boston which had previously functioned as a skating ring and theatre. News of this transaction was soon appearing in the local press and by 7 January 1911, George was advertising 'Alice in Wonderland' and 'A Rake's Romance' in the *Boston Guardian*. After the success of the Electric Picture House in Boston, George decided to expand and in 1911 he built a purpose built cinema, The Picture House, in Spalding. In May 1911, George Aspland died and Ben Howden took overall control of the fairground equipment. The bioscope continued to travel until the outbreak of the first world war, when it was eventually replaced by the family. In 1933 Ben Howden Snr died leaving his business to all three sons including George Aspland Howden. Following his death, the name of Aspland and Howdens disappeared from the fairground, but the Aspland-Howden line of the family continued to present and run picture houses in Boston until very recently.

REFERENCES:

Boston Guardian, 17 December 1910; 7 January 1911.
Greville, Father. 'Famous Bioscope Shows and their Engines', *Merry-Go-Round* 7, no. 9 (1951–53).
Toulmin, Vanessa. 'Telling The Tale: the Story of the Fairground Bioscope and the Showmen Who Operated It'. *Film History* 6, no. 2 (1994): pp. 219–37.
The World's Fair, 3 and 19 August 1907; 8 August 1908.

BIDDALL FAMILY BIOSCOPES

THE BIDDALL FAMILY TRAVELLED A variety of exhibitions consisting of menagerie attractions, freak shows, ghost illusions and finally bioscopes. The family consisted of the sons of Henry Freeman a flamboyant character whose hair turned white after landing amongst cannibals and seeing his shipmates eaten. This new appearance helped him impersonate a wizard in an early walk-up show. To add to the confusion, his sons, who included Albert, William and George, all presented shows under the Biddall family name in different regions of Great Britain.

George Biddall was the youngest son of Henry Freeman who married Selina Smith, daughter of King Ohmy and travelled with a theatre booth around Scotland and the north of England. Possibly due to the influence of his father-in-law, George Biddall started to exhibit a ghost illusion show and advertised it as the main presentation. The exhibition comprised of a two-wagon fronted show, with Phantospectra Biddall's Ghostodramas in gold lettering across the top. Some of the adventures and experiences that happened to the family in the pre bioscope days are recalled in an article that appeared following his death in 1909 in *The World's Fair*. This includes an account of how the locals believing his show to be responsible for bad luck in the area were convinced that the family had the evil eye. However, despite this mishap, the show continued travelling, with his children helping with the main feature The Ghost Illusion and his son Joey performing a clowning routine. In 1898, the show was converted for the use of moving pictures and travelled extensively to the major fairs, including Newcastle for the 1899 for both the Hoppings and the Christmas festivities and Cockmouth in 1906.

Another member of the Biddall family who presented moving pictures was William Biddall, a nephew to George Biddall, who travelled around the London area. William or Billy Biddall was one of four sons of William Biddall, elder brother to George and travelled with a menagerie under the name of Biddall Brothers. Billy left the family in 1901 and it was possibly then that he started to exhibit moving pictures in one of his uncle's former shows. Biddall Brothers also continued to travelled the Menagerie. The new show was recorded open at Wormwood Scrubs at Easter 1901, whilst the Menagerie was reported open on Deptford High Street and Banbury the following year. By 1908 the two shows were appearing together at Mitcham. Biddall Brothers show travelled until at least as late as 1912. Although this show never achieved the status or size of one of the larger organ fronted parading shows it was still exhibited by the London branch of the family who travelled the show extensively until its final appearance at Wanstead flats in 1915.

Another family member who presented shows and moving pictures was Albert Biddall, yet another son of George Freeman Biddall. Albert's involvement with the cinematograph began when he purchased Randall Williams's No. 1 show, billed as 'Biddall's Electric Bioscope' and transported by the Fowler traction engine. Eventually Albert's show was updated and the old barrel organ was replaced by an 87-key Gavioli organ.

In 1914 Biddall's cinematograph show exhibited at opposite Cyril Getcliffe's New Picture House in Braintree, Essex,. Despite this, the show continued to attract packed audiences due to the presence of soldiers awaiting transfer for the hostilities in Europe and there were more than enough customers to keep both proprietors happy. George Freeman Biddall died on April 7th 1909 and after the demise of the bioscope shows, the other members of the family built up their various travelling concerns.

The Biddall connection with early cinema continued when Victor Biddall, grandson of Henry Freeman, opened permanent cinemas in south Scotland.

REFERENCES:

Brown, Frances. 'Parades and Entertainments'. *The Fairground Mercury* (December 1988). [Published by the Fairground Association of Great Britain].

The Era, 2 January 1904.

Greville, Father P. 'Brief Particulars of Bioscopes Shows, Their Organs, Parades, Engines, etc: The London Area Shows', *Merry-Go-Round*, 7, no. 1 (1951).

The World's Fair, 10, 17 and 24 April 1909; 15 December 1934.

PAT COLLINS

PAT COLLINS, LIKE HIS CONTEMPORARY George Green, was a lessee, roundabout proprietor, bioscope exhibitor and also went on to build up a chain of over thirteen cinemas. He was born on 12 May 1859 and until his death in 1943 he was the most successful showman of his generation both on and away from the fairground. However, although Pat Collins went on to travel at least five bioscope shows and open thirteen cinemas, his involvement into the cinematograph business appears to be that of a investor and proprietor. Unlike his contemporaries, amongst whom Collins was known as the 'King of Showmen', he never joined the Cinema Veteran's Association, as did for example Richard Monte and Richard Dooner.

Pat Collins's first presented moving pictures in 1899–1900 when he took over the ghost show from Wall and Hammersley. According to Ned Williams in his detailed biography, this show was first included in the advertisement for the Bloxwich Wake Fair in 1900. His second show was a two-wagon fronted show, built by Savages and may have been the one Savage's made in 1898 for the King's Lynn Novelty Company, a group of investors from Norfolk and which appeared at the 1898 fair in Hull. This show with its 87-key Gavioli and electric light engine was sold to Pat Collins in c. 1901-02. The exhibition booth had been designed to travel on rail and formed part of the Collins's Amusements attraction until 1905 it was acquired by Sagar and Scott of Otley. The third show that the firm presented was reputedly an organ fronted show with illumination provided by over fifteen hundred lights. However, no photographs of it survive to prove the authenticity of Father Greville's account in the *Merry-Go-Round* magazine.

By 1907 it appears that Pat Collins had decided that the cinematograph shows on the fairground were apparently lucrative enough to invest in what would become known as the Wonderland Shows. Both Wonderland No. 1 and the No. 2 show were built by Orton and Spooner's of Burton upon Trent and were part of the great organ fronted parading shows that would dominate the fairground landscape until 1914. The first

Wonderland was a show constructed around a 104-key Marenghi organ, with an art nouveau proscenium and made its debut on the second Saturday of Wrexham Fair in April 1907. With the introduction of the Gaumont Chronophone in 1906 sound was added to the films on show in the bioscopes and both of the later exhibitions utilised this latest innovation. The No. 1 show continued to travel until the first World War, where it was put in store. By the end of 1907 a second Orton and Spooner great show had been delivered to Pat Collins, the No. 2 Wonderland with its mammoth 112-key Marenghi organ.

The second Wonderland show made its debut at Olympia over Christmas and New Year 1907–08 and until 1914 it dominated the skyline of Nottingham Goose Fair. The distinctive decorative work of the No. 2 exhibition included a figure of Boudicea in a chariot with horses surmounting the organ facade and four enormous Corinthian columns which supported a carved top above the platform. The show was essentially a cinematograph, but from 1910 a circus act formed part of the attractions.

With the demise of the moving image on the fairground and the transition to permanent cinema, Pat Collins ceased travelling both shows by 1914 and then expanded into the cinema business. By the mid 1920s, Pat Collins claimed to own fourteen cinemas or assorted variety establishments. These included three cinemas in the Black Country of which the Grosvenor in Bloxwich is the only one still remaining, as well as the purpose-built Cinema De Luxe in Chester, the Waldorf Skating Ring in Birmingham and many others throughout the Midlands.

Other aspects of Pat Collins's illustrious career include being the longest serving President of the Showmen's Guild and councillor, Mayor and Member of Parliament for his adopted home town of Walsall in 1922. The news of his death in 1943 was reported in *The World's Fair* with the headline "Showland loses its G. O. M", with the whole of the front page given over to tributes and reports.

REFERENCES:

Allen, Freda and Ned Williams. *King of Showmen*. Wolverhampton: Uralia Press, 1991.
Greville, Father P. 'Famous Bioscope Shows and their Engines: Pat Collins's Shows'. *Merry-Go-Round,* 7, no. 6 (1953).
Lawrence, Edwin. 'A Short History of the Infant Cinema: Parts 1–3'. *The World's Fair,* 3, 10 and 17 June 1933.
Peart, Stephen. *Picture Houses in East Anglia*. Lavenham: Terrence Dalton, 1980.
The World's Fair, 11 and 18 December 1943.

GEORGE GREEN

GEORGE GREEN WAS PROBABLY ONE OF the most successful of the showmen who pioneered the cinematograph on the fairground. With Randall Williams, he was one of the original pioneers of fairground cinema, when he exhibited moving pictures at the Carnival building in December 1896. According to a letter from his son Herbert in 1946, George Green visited London with his brother John in the autumn of 1896 and purchased a theatrograph of Robert W. Paul. After many hours of practice the family exhibited films in the Carnival during the Christmas festivities but it did not appear on the fairground until 1898. George Green travelled several large shows, including the ex-Leo American Exhibition, and the most extravagant one he purchased was from President Kemp in 1913 called the Theatre Unique. This show was advertised for sale in *The World's Fair* at the beginning of August and the advertisement provides us with a detailed description of the show, its seating capacity and interior decorations.

The Theatre Unique could claim to be one of the most lavish shows ever travelled throughout the United Kingdom and part of the great shows constructed by Orton and Spooner's from 1906 onwards. It had been purchased from Orton and Spooner's in 1908 around a new 104-key Marenghi organ. The cost of the organ alone was £2,000 with the centre truck constructed to carry twenty tons costing in the region of three hundred pounds. The organ was lowered onto the truck which then opened out to form a fifty foot parading stage. The two carved and gilded staircases which were surmounted by four tall elegant columns from which arc lamps were suspended, cost a further three hundred pounds. The booth supposedly held over one thousand people and measured forty foot by seventy two foot.

George Green travelled the Theatre Unique with the ex-Leo show and replaced the original ground booth show. The decline in popularity of these shows is illustrated by the constant presence of 'For Sale' notices for these shows. In 1914, John Green, George Green's oldest son, died and George announced his retirement from the road in order to look after their increasingly successful picture houses which they had opened as early as 1904 in Scotland. By the time of his retirement as a showman in 1914, George Green had opened a circuit of numerous picture palaces in and around Glasgow, Dundee and Ayr. *The World's Fair* in 1914 lists that George Green had ten cinemas however other sources show that it was possibly thirteen. He had also opened a film hire and production company known as Greens of Glasgow and a cinema construction company.

George Green died in 1915 but his sons continued to expand the cinema business into one of the most successful in the United Kingdom, with the opening of Green's Glasgow playhouse in 1927. The Green family's dominance in the cinema business was further consolidated by opening of the marginally smaller Playhouses in Dundee and Ayr. His sons went on to expand the Movie Reel business into the 1920s with the production of various newsreels entitled Greens of London and Glasgow. They also became involved in producing propaganda films for the War Office, in particular the *Patriotic Porker* (1916).

REFERENCES:

Greville, Father P. 'Brief Particulars of Bioscope Shows, Their Organs, Parades, Engines, etc'. *Merry-Go-Round,* 7, no. 1–11 (1951–53). [Published by the Friendship Circle of Fairground Friends.]

McBain, J. *Pictures Past: Scottish Cinemas Remembered*. Edinburgh: Moorfoot Publishing, 1985.

Scottish film Archive for listing of Green's films.

Swallow, Johnnie. *Roundabout Scotland*. Privately published by Johnnie Swallow, 1989.

Toulmin, Vanessa. 'Telling The Tale: The Story of the Fairground Bioscope and the Showmen Who Operated It'. *Film History* 6, no. 2 (1994): pp. 219–237.

The World's Fair, 4 and 11 July 1914; 2 August 1913.

MRS. ANNIE HOLLAND

THE HOLLAND FAMILY WERE PERHAPS one of the most famous of the fairground bioscope proprietors with both Annie Holland, née Payne, and her brother George Payne travelling two of the largest and most lavish shows on the fairground. Annie Holland's family's entry into the fairground business arose out of necessity. Her mother had been left a widow, when her father died at the age of forty. Mrs. Payne's solution to the problem of no income was to publicly exhibit one of her children, who, according to family tradition, weighed in excess of forty stone. Arthur Holland, her great grandson, recalls how the family first began on the Brit-ish fairground:

> She had two sons, this Mrs. Payne and one daughter, my grandmother, Annie Holland and she got this forty stone son and one of these here chorus girls said, you ought to take him around the shows, show him. That was the only thing she could do because her husband died . . . What she did, she used to hire a town hall out for half a crown and she used to take him round all the town halls, where ever she could, you understand and show him. This went on until I think she eventually decided to have a little booth of her own . . . and then she used to go around the fairs, with this fat boy, her other son, he had been introduced into the fairground business through the fat boy, through him you know being forty stone and he started up then and in the olden days he was called Captain Payne.

The exterior and interior of the Holland cinematograph show were elaborately decorated. Arthur Fay in his book *Bioscope Shows and Their Engines* provides us with a firsthand description:

> In the Palace of Light there was seating accommodation for six hundred people with standing room in the gallery for another four hundred. The seating was upholstered in Italian green wgured cloth with backs to match, while the side linings were of heavy blue wgured plush trimmed and ornamented with gold tassels as also were the side door curtains.

After she became estranged from her husband, Annie Holland left London in 1901 and returned to the fairground. Her first show, the 'Palace of Light' began as a two-wagon fronted booth, built by the firm of Orton and Spooner's and included a gilded, carved proscenium which framed the screen comprising of statues of angels carved pillars and lavishly decorated masks. From 1904 onwards the show underwent dramatic renovations and after the tragedy in 1912 when the original booth was damaged in a fire on Anglesey it became an amalgamation of other shows. Mrs. Holland then bought Edwin Lawrence's show to replace it. However, it appears that only the two wagons at the front of the original exhibition sustained damage. An advertisement in *The World's Fair* in March 1912 suggests that Annie Holland bought Lawrence's show purely for the showfront and organ:

> For Sale—Wanted known that Mrs. Holland has purchased the whole of Lawrence's cinematograph show.

> For Sale—Marionette stage, wt up with truck for sale, one set of seating, standing gallery, cinebox, two Gaumont cameras and three trucks to go behind the traction engine. All lots to be sold cheap.

The Holland family presented both the 'Palace of Light' and 'Wonderland', which was travelled by Annie's son Albert. Arthur Fay, writing as 'Southdown' in *The World's Fair* in the 1930s, provides an interesting account of the type of performance the exhibitors presented. In April 1912 when the news of the sinking of the Titanic broke, a Gaumont film Company newsreel was shown of the event. To accompany the film of the disaster, the Holland family arranged a musical sketch which incorporated tunes such as 'Afloat on the Ocean Blue', 'Ship's Bell Rings', 'The Sailor's Two Step', 'Crash', 'An Iceberg', 'Excitement on Board', 'Lowering the Boats', 'Women and Children first' and finished with 'Nearer my God to Thee' and Chopin's 'Funeral March'. *The World's Fair* of February 1936 includes a description of a bill used by the Holland family and provides us with a guide to the admission charges which range from 3d up to 6d. Both shows continued to travel until the outbreak of the First World War, when the Palace of Light was settled permanently at Measham by James Holland where it continued to present moving pictures whilst the permanent cinema was constructed around it.

REFERENCES:

Fay, A. *Bioscope Shows and their Engines*. Dorset: The Oakwood Press, 1966.
Interview with Arthur Holland, June 1994.
Greville, Father P. 'Brief Particulars of Bioscope Shows, Their Organs, Parades, Engines, etc.' *The Merry-Go-Round*, 7, nos. 1–11 (1951–1953). [Published by the Friendship Circle of Fairground Friends.]
Lawrence, Edwin. 'A Short History of the Infant Cinema, Parts 1–3'. *The World's Fair*, 3, 10 and 17 June 1933.
The World's Fair, 9 March 1912; 2 and 29 February 1936; 18 March 1972.

ROBERT MACKNEY

AFTER THE DRAMATIC APPEARANCE OF Randall Williams's ghost show, exhibiting pictures at the 1897 King's Lynn Mart, many ghost show proprietors converted their shows in order to exhibit this new attraction. However, until the emergence of the picture shows, the ghost or illusion booths had been one of the main attractions on the fairground since their introduction. Robert Mackney, from Leeds, like many of his showmen, adopted the principle introduced by Professor Pepper in 1863, when he dazzled London with an entertainment advertised as Pepper's Ghost.

Mackney's cinematograph show travelled throughout the north of England. It was not until the introduction of moving pictures that Robert Mackney returned from presenting the former two-wagon fronted ghost show with its trumpet barrel organ in Scotland.

Although the Mackney ghost show was adapted to show pictures, it retained its two-wagon front and never incorporated electricity into the presentation. Lighting was supplied by naphtha lamps and the show continued to be transported by horse rather than by traction engine or rail. Although the show maintained its ghost show decor, the quality of the paraders and the presentation of the performance enabled it to hold its own when exhibiting with larger more ornate displays. The family showed moving pictures from 1898. It was still presenting the ghost show as part of the performance in 1907 when *The World's Fair* reported its appearance as a 'Ghost Illusion Show' at Dumbarton Fair. The family settled in Houghton-le-Spring and stopped travelling in 1912, when they took over the Gaiety Theatre in the town.

REFERENCES:

Greville, Father P. 'Brief Particulars of Bioscope Shows, Their Organs, Parades, Engines, etc.: The Far North and Scotland'. *The Merry-Go-Round,* 7, no. 10 (1953). [Published by the Friendship Circle of Fairground Friends.]
Sellman, Arthur. *Travelling Shows and Roundabouts.* Locomotion Papers no. 84. Blandford: Oakwood Press 1975.
The World's Fair, 31 August 1907.

JAMES MANDERS

THE MANDERS FAMILY WERE ONE OF THE most illustrious showland families of the nineteenth century, famous for both their menagerie and waxwork exhibitions. By 1900, their Royal Waxworks exhibition had started to feature Edison's Electric Animated Pictures in the two-wagon fronted booth. Although this show never evolved into the more elaborate organ-fronted kind, it was one of the most ornate of its type which exhibited on the Edwardian fairgrounds. Lighting was generated by a Gavioli trumpet organ and the presentation was similar in type to that of the Mackney family, in that moving pictures were incorporated into its more established exhibitions. Photographs dating from 1904 of the October Fair in Hull illustrate the combined nature of their performance and an article from *The World's Fair* from 1909 reports that Mander's menagerie was open at Cleaton Moor but makes no mention of moving pictures. Father Greville

places the Manders family in north Wales, but they were associated the north of England through their membership of the Lancashire Section of the Show-men's Guild of Great Britain.

In 1907 the family suffered a tragedy when James Manders was killed when crossing over a railway line in Portsmouth. However, his widow continued to travel the show and reports of the combined waxworks and moving picture exhibition continued to be published in *The World's Fair* until 1914. Mrs. Manders gradually updated the exhibition and in 1911 the Savage light engine was replaced by a Burrell traction engine which allowed the family greater transportation facilities. The family settled in north Wales during the war years and, like many of their contemporaries, resumed travelling after the War. However, they no longer presented moving pictures and the famous old exhibition booth was used once more as a menagerie or wild beast show.

REFERENCES:

Greville, Father P. 'Brief Particulars of Bioscope Shows, Their Organs, Parades, Engines, etc.' *The Merry-Go-Round,* 7, no. 5 (1953). [Published by the Friendship Circle of Fairground Friends.]
Scrivens, Kevin and Stephen Smith. *Hull Fair: An Illustrated History.* Beverley: Hutton Press, 1991.
The World's Fair, 26 January 1907; 2 February 1907; 22 March 1907; 4 December 1909.

JACOB STUDT

JACOB STUDT, SNR., WAS BORN IN 1857, son of John Studt and brother to Henry and John Studt who also travelled bioscope shows. Jacob set up on his own and eventually acquired a set of steam dobbies and later a Switchback. In 1897 he invested in his first cinematograph exhibition, which he gradually enlarged and perfected into one of the most complete and luxurious on the road. Built as a standard two-wagon fronted show, it later contained one of the massive 112-keyless Gavioli organs. Inside it was tastefully draped and equipped not only with pit seats but also with plushly covered tip-up stall chairs. In hot weather the inside of the booth was cooled with electric fans, similar to the ones in Aspland's show.

The original exhibition booth was built by Orton and Spooner's with an 87-key Gavioli and portable light engine driving a dynamo which was reputed to have been designed by Studt himself. Arc lamps provided illumination on the front of the show, whilst two projection arc lamps with coloured glasses were used during battle scenes. Jacob Studt, like other fairground showmen, would, whenever possible, exhibit their films in town and village halls. Paul Marriot in his book Early Oxford Picture Palaces reveals that Jacob Studt exhibited a colour film in 1900 at Oxford Town Hall, called The

Passion Play. He then returned in 1904 for the St Giles fair in the company of five other fairground showmen to exhibit their films at the annual Charter Fair. Initially, Studt used horses to transport his show, but in 1901a traction engine was acquired for haulage and lighting purposes.

In 1906 the showfront was extended yet again when a new 110-key Gavioli was installed between the two wagon fronts. Ever prepared to invest in the latest technology, this organ lasted only a year before being sold to Richard Dooner when its place was taken by an even larger 112-keyless Gavioli. The showfront was completely remodelled and gilded figures, carved columns each surmounted by classical Corinthian capitals, now completed the exterior decoration. With the new organ came an amazing lighting show with 2,000 incandescent lamps which changed colour creating an impressive effect at night. The show was still travelling in 1912 when it appeared at Dursley Feast. *The World's Fair* described the cinema as the largest and best appointed hitherto seen at the fair. Unlike other members of his family who made the transition into cinema, Jacob Studt remained with the fairground and with the demise of the bioscope expanded his fairground interests by investing in the latest fairground attractions.

REFERENCES:

Greville, Father P. 'Jacob Studt of Gloucester'. *Merry-Go-Round,* 9, no. 5 (1956).
Mariott, P.J. *Early Oxford Picture Palaces*. Oxford, 1978.
The World's Fair, 3 August 1912. [For account of Jacob Studt's show at Dursley Feast.]
Southdown [Arthur Sellman]. 'The 40th Anniversary of the Cinematograph'. *The World's Fair,* 29 February 1936.

WILLIAM TAYLOR

ALTHOUGH THERE APPEARS TO BE NO doubt in the minds of the early reporters in *The World's Fair* about the identity of the showman who introduced moving pictures to the fairgoing public, confusion does arise over the showmen who followed Randall Williams's example. One of those who claimed to be the second showmen to present bioscope shows was William Taylor. William Taylor was born in 1853 and was the son of the Ilkeston Giant and Mme. Reader, whose family had a glass blowing act on the fairground. The family travelled a marionette show, but William's brother died and he married his widow Louisa Proctor who was a member of another famous show-family that would eventually become cinematograph proprietors.

His first bioscope had a small barrel organ and was lit by naphtha flares. Electric lights were added at a later stage when a portable engine was acquired. In 1902 the showfront was further improved by additional carved work which replaced painted canvas banners above the waggons and entrance and a larger trumpet barrel organ added. The famous row of bioscopes at the 1904 St Giles Fair included Taylor's No 1 show which was then called The Electric Living Picture Show. Taylors and Thurstons shows dominated the skyline of St Giles's Fair with both showmen vying with each other to exhibit the largest and greatest presentation at the fair. This rivalry continued when William Taylor purchased one of the largest shows ever built by Orton and Spooner's in 1907.

With this acquisition, William Taylor purchased arguably the most lavish of all the cinematograph shows to exhibit films to the fairgoing public, the new Cinema de Luxe. The organ truck which incorporated the showfront, when opened was fifty foot in length with the gigantic 104-key Marenghi dominating the stage. In a similar style to Annie Holland's show, the opening sides of second box truck folded out to provide dummy royal boxes on either side of the screen and interior stage. A review published in *The Kettering Leader* of 1909 and reprinted in *The World's Fair* in 1932, includes a description and tribute to William Taylor's show:

> The principal attraction of Kettering Feast is Taylor's Royal Coliseum de Luxe, the largest and most costly exhibition in England. This year the entire concern has been reconstructed and everything is arranged on the most elaborate style and design it is possible to conceive. The interior of this palace on wheels is equal to any West End place of amusement and the entertainment is of the highest order and second to none.

Not to be outdone, Charles Thurston ordered the Great Show, which included an ever bigger showfront constructed around the mammoth 120-key Gavioli organ. Both William and Charles, continued to present these attractions until 1913 when they could be found side by side at Oxford and Cambridge Midsummer Fair with their latest cinematograph shows.

However, the rivalry between the two showmen was never malicious. A report in *The World's Fair* from 1928 includes describes the showmanship that operated between these two great exhibitors. Both Charles Thurston and William Taylor made it a rule that their show organs would not be playing at the same time, therefore allowing the showmen to alternate the parading and then the exhibiting of the performances inside each show. The Coliseum de Luxe travelled widely until 1913–1914, when William Taylor settled at Calne in Wiltshire to take control of the cinema he had built in 1913. *The World's Fair* in 1913 mentions, in the account of the opening of the new cinema, that although Mr. and Mrs. Taylor had retired, the travelling concerns were to be carried on as usual by the family. They may have continued to travel the bioscope show after William Taylor's retirement but there is no record of it in *The World's Fair*.

REFERENCES:

Essex, George, W. *The William Taylor Bioscope Show*. London: Traction Engine Enterprise, 1968.
Greville, Father P. 'Brief Particulars of Bioscope Shows, Their Organs, Parades, Engines, etc.' *The Merry-Go-Round,* 7, no. 1–11 (1951–53). [Published by the Friendship Circle of Showland Friends.]
Lawrence, Edwin. 'A Short History of the Infant Cinema, Parts 1–3'. *The World's Fair*, 3, 10 and 17 June 1933.
Mariott, Paul. *Early Oxford Picture Palaces*. Oxford, 1978.
Southdown [Arthur Sellman] 'The 40th Anniversary of the Cinematograph'. *The World's Fair,* 29 February 1936.
The World's Fair, 26 January 1907; 24 May 1913; 25 February 1928; 9 July 1932.

CHARLES THURSTON

THE FIRST MENTION OF THE THURSTON bioscope shows is at Oxford's St. Giles Fair where it traded under the name of Barker and Thurston's Electric Veniscope. However, by the time of the 1904 fair, the show was advertised under the name of Thurston's. Charles was the eldest son of Henry Thurston a brickmaker who found success on the fairground. His first venture, independent of his father, was his Royal Show, a two-wagon fronted bioscope which he travelled with his wife Charlotte. Between 1902 to 1907 the show was extensively adapted and refitted to keep ahead with the latest fashions. finally a long-case 89-key Marenghi organ was added and with this larger instrument the show was extended, with a larger central arch and a canopy over the organ and engine.

Around 1911, this organ was then built into a new parading fronted show, possibly using the original booth. However despite the alterations made by Charles Thurston to his show, the appearance of his arch rival William Taylor at Cambridge Midsummer Fair with the latest Orton and Spooner show, resulted in the ordering of new equipment. With the purchase of the cinematograph which became known as the Great Show from Orton and Spooner's in 1908, Thurston had two Bioscopes on the road.

However, the description of the Great Show at the St Giles's Fair in 1907 refers to the 'No. 1' show which by then had been extensively refitted. Thurston's first show is described as having shuttered walls, draped black cloth ceiling and walls adorned in gold braiding. However, this first show never achieved the extravagance of Charles's second show. The design of the Great Show was similar to Pat Collins's Wonderland exhibition as they were both built around a 120-key Marenghi organ. The exhibition was new in 1908 and its distinctive heavily gilded carved work and countless coloured incandescent lights on the showfront caused a sensation when it appeared at the 1908 Kettering Feast.

Unlike William Taylor who was often seen on the front of his show, Charles Thurston's role was more distant. He employed a manager by the name of Jim Norman to oversee the performance and manage the variety acts. A reporter writing in *The World's Fair* in 1932 recalls Thurston's show with its latest novelty in the form of Colormatography appearing at the 1910 Kettering Feast. The films on display included The Pearl Fishers and all the films were reputedly in colour. In the years leading up to the First World War, the show expanded and incorporated more variety acts which included Paulos and Mystic, an illusion act with Egyptian magicians. Like William Taylor and George Green, Charles Thurston had anticipated the decline in popularity of the fairground bioscope shows and had previously invested in static cinemas in 1911 when he opened the Electric Palace in Harwich. His cinema concerns were further consolidated in 1913, when he built the Empire Cinema in Biggleswade, a purpose built affair which seated six hundred people, and the Palace Cinema in Norwich.

By the 1920s Charles sold his cinemas and concentrated solely on his travelling concerns. After this death in 1928, the firm was continued by his sons. However the cinemas he built in 1913 still continued to be used for the presentation of movies until the 1960s when finally the Empire Cinema in Biggleswade was converted into an electronics factory.

REFERENCES:

Essex, George W. *The Famous Thurstons.* The Fairground Society, 1968.
Greville, Father P. 'Brief Particulars of Bioscope Shows, Their Organs, Parades, Engines, etc.: Eastern Counties Shows'. *The Merry-Go-Round,* 7, no. 10. (1953). [Published by the Friendship Circle of Showland Friends.]
King, Tom. 'The House of Thurston', parts 1–4. *The Tober* (1951-1953). [British Fairground Society.]
Mariott, Paul. *Early Oxford Picture Palaces.* Oxford, 1978.
Page, Ken. 'The Electric Vaudeville'. *Fairground Mercury* 17, no. 2 (1994).
Peart, Stephen. *The Picture House in East Anglia.* Lavenahm: Terrence Dalton, 1980.
Taylor, Ron A. 'All For Your Joy'. *Fairground Mercury* 10, no. 3 (1987).
The World's Fair, 9 December 1911; 12 September 1912; 12 October 1912; 7 December 1912; 25 February 1928; 3 March 1928; 9 July 1932.

GEORGE THOMAS TUBY

GEORGE THOMAS TUBY MADE THE transition from roundabout proprietor to showman exhibitor at a far later stage than his contemporaries. His first bioscope show was first shown in 1905 and was one of the great shows built by Orton and Spooner. This was constructed around a long-case 89-key Gavioli organ. In 1907 they introduced sound to accompany films using Chronomegaphone Singing Pictures which were then presented that season with some of the bigger shows. George Tuby travelled with this show for only a short time and appeared at Sheffield Christmas Fair in 1907, where it was advertised as Tuby and Son's Electric Coliseum.

The variety of problems faced by the early cinematograph proprietors are illustrated by an account in *The World's Fair* from December 1907. During the annual winter fair in York, a complaint was made against G. T. Tuby regarding the types of films exhibited in his show, in particular *The Thaw Picture*. This film had achieved a certain notoriety for a drugging scene involving a young girl. In a letter to *The Yorkshire Herald*, G. T. Tuby explained that the variation of the film that he was exhibiting was not the immoral version, but one that was a sight fit for women and children. The matter was dropped after an inspection by both the chairman of the Markets Committee and the Chief Constable of York, with the added notoriety of the presentation resulting in a great rush of visitors to the shows. This show was sold at the end of 1907 to Joseph Wingate and replaced with the Palace of Ceylon.

The Wingate family travelled the ex-Tuby bioscope until a disastrous accident occured in 1910. When travelling from Alloa to Kirkintilloch, the loads caught fire destroying the organ truck. Unfortunately for the Wingates, the show was not fully covered by insurance and the £1,000 loss was a considerable setback.

The second and final cinematograph show travelled by George Tuby was the Coliseum show or alternatively known as the Palace of Ceylon. It was exhibited for the first time at the King's Lynn Mart in February 1908. The reporter for *The World's Fair* described the show as the latest creation in travelling cinematograph pictures. Constructed around a huge 112-keyless Gavioli organ by Orton and Spooner, at a cost of a £1,000, this exhibition soon became a major attraction on the Yorkshire fairs.

A famous shot of the Coliseum being transported was taken by the Welsh Brothers and captures the traction engine, The Leader, driving past Retford Town Hall with five loads. These consisted of the organ truck, the packing truck, two rail trucks and Mr Tuby's Orton living wagon. The Tuby family employed Jim Watson to manage the show and a range variety acts including comedians, illusionists and dancers. Other staff employed for the exhibition included an electrician, a projectionist and the engine driver. The size of this great show can be gauged by an account in the *Showmen's Year Book* which describes an occasion in the Palace or Ceylon when the chaplain of the Showman's Guild, the Reverend Thomas Horne, reputedly conducted a service for an audience of fifteen hundred people. A further claim is made by *The World's Fair* in April which reports that on 28 Sunday March 1908, a church service was conducted in the Palace of Ceylon by the Reverend J. T. Munford which was attended by a congregation of two thousand people.

Despite their other fairground concerns the Tuby family all helped to run the show. Tom Tuby, Jnr., was manager and Mrs. Tuby, Snr., was manageress. Miss Tuby was assistant and Miss Gladys Tuby was Auxiliary. The Sole Manager was, of course, G. T. Tuby, whose portrait was in the centre of the stage curtain, accompanied by the smaller portraits of Arthur, Harry, Tom and George in the four corners.

REFERENCES:

Horne, Thomas. *Showmen's Year Book.* London: *The Era*, 1909.
Wilkes, Peter. *Whilst I Live I'll Crow: An Illustrated History of the Tuby Family Doncaster's Showmen Supreme.* Burton upon Trent: Trent Valley Publications, 1990.
The World's Fair, 5 January 1907; 7 December 1907; 29 February 1908; 4 April 1908.

RANDALL WILLIAMS

RANDALL WILLIAMS, THE 'KING OF Showmen', is generally acknowledged to be the first showman to introduce moving pictures to the fairgoing public. When his already famous Grand Phantascopical Exhibition opened on Valentine's Day in King's Lynn, to the surprise of showmen and fairgoers alike, it was advertising a new attraction, namely moving pictures. However, he had already anticipated the popularity of this new phenomenon on the fairground. At *The World's Fair* Exhibition in December 1896 he had converted his elaborate ghost show for the exhibiting of this latest novelty. The early films shown in this exhibition booth included Louis Fuller and the Serpentine dance, the Czar in Russia and a selection of Lumière films.

As early as 1890, Williams was travelling his Phantascopical Exhibition advertising it as the greatest ghost show in the world. There may be an element of truth in the advertisements and hand bills which further advertised the fact that 1,000 people could be comfortably accommodated. As well as the illusions, Williams gave variety acts in the show and incorporated the tricks he had learnt from his first conjuring act that he had originally presented on the fairgrounds. Until his death in 1898, Randall Williams kept one step ahead of his fellow showmen and the ex-ghost show could be found exhibiting at the October Fair in Hull and the Sheffield Christmas Fair in 1897. When Randall Williams died, while at Grimsby Status, the 1899 Hull newspapers carried a tribute to his shows which had always been the major attraction at the annual October fair. His funeral in Manchester in 1898 was attended not only by the notable people of showland but also by hundreds of local people who had patronised his shows, from his first conjuring booth to its final presentation in the form of moving pictures.

During his lifetime he was perhaps the most famous showman of his day and instrumental in the founding of the United Kingdom Van Dwellings Protection Association in 1889, the forerunner of today's Showmen's Guild. After his death his show continued to be presented by his son in law, Richard Monte and his brother James Monte. Realising the reputation of the name Randall Williams, the two brothers travelled under the Williams name, with Richard Monte in later years often being mistaken for the original showmen. The name continued to be displayed on the variety of bioscope shows that the brother travelled. The shows were constantly adapted and converted to keep the Williams name ahead of the latest innovations on the fairground.

In 1906 Richard Monte and James Monte Williams acquired a larger show built around a 110-key Gavioli organ. The facade featured automatic coloured light changes, as well as a simulated second organ mounted above the 110-key instrument. It was claimed at the time to be the largest and most powerful organ in the world. In 1907 the show incorporated the Gaumont Chronophone and advertised this latest novelty as singing and talking pictures at Hull Fair in October. The famous name of Randall Williams disappeared from the front of the cinematograph show he had originally pioneered in 1913, when a disastrous fire destroyed the whole show on 24 January 1913 when the show was at Thirsk Market Place. Richard Monte continued to travel on the fairs until finally settling down in Canvey Island and opening a chain of cinemas.

However the firm of Randall Williams never achieved the success and notoriety that it had held in the nineteenth century, during which, for thirty years or more, Randall Williams's shows had dominated the skyline of the every major fair in the country.

REFERENCES:

The Era, 1 and 29 January 1898.

The Era, 19 and 26 November 1898.

Greville, Father P. 'Brief Particulars of Bioscope Shows, Their Organs, Parades, Engines, etc, The Far North and Scotland'. *The Merry-Go-Round,* 7, no. 10 (1953). [Published by the Friendship Circle of Fairground Friends.]

Heard, Mervyn. 'Giving Up the Ghost'. Paper presented at the 'film before 1920: an International Conference', 1995.

Norman, Tom (with contibutions by his son George Norman). *The Penny Showman: Memoirs of Tom Norman "Silver King".* Privately published, 1985.

Toulmin, Vanessa. 'Telling the Tale: The Story of the Fairground Bioscope and the Showmen Who Exhibited Them'. *Film History* 6, no. 2 (1994).

The World's Fair, 2 March 1912; 29 February 1936; 19 June 1954.

✵

WADBROOK AND SCARD

WADBROOK'S ROYAL ELECTROGRAPH and Palace of Light was originally a ghost show, but the two-wagon fronted show turned to moving pictures in 1897. It has been suggested that this was only the second show to travel in this country and certainly it was well-known after the family had shown films to Queen Victoria at Balmoral Castle. The show incorporated an electric light engine for suppling power and the small trumpet barrel organ was replaced in 1901 by an 87-key Gavioli. A Burrell engine (2631) 'King Edward VII' was supplied in 1903. This was highly decorated with scrollwork covering almost every inch of space on the boiler, motion cover, belle tanks and tender. Its canopy was inscribed "Wadbrook's Palace of Light".

Henry James Scard began his travelling life as a stud groom for Messrs. Bostock and Wombwell. He was married to Polly Wadbrook and, after the proprietor's death, they brought up his surviving family. Scard shot his own films—one showed scenes of Stratford Mop in 1909 and he had sole rights to photograph international football matches played in Wales. In 1908–09 the show was substantially rebuilt, placing the organ in the centre and moving the two living wagons further apart. To manage the extra loads, they acquired a second Burrell (3072) 'Shakespeare'.

The show travelled until 1913 when the family settled at Milford Haven. It was used as a permanent show on the Market Square until destroyed by fire in 1917, when it was replaced by a permanent cinema, the Astoria. For some years the original projctor used at Balmoral was on display in the cinema. Carved work from the showfront was used on the figure Eight at Porthcawl and parts of it are now at Wookey Hole Museum. The engines were sold to Henry O'Brien and John Hoadley. After Henry's retirement to Stratford upon Avon, his son Harry continued in the cinema business by opening pernamemt cinemas in Milford. After the construction of the Astoria Cinema on the site of the old market, Harry went on to open the Palace Theatre and the Plaza Cinema in Neyland.

REFERENCES:

The World's Fair, 6 October 1923 [Interview with Harry Scard]; 28 May 1966 [item on the death of Mrs. Harry Scard].

THE BIOSCOPES AND OTHER SHOWS: FURTHER READING

Beaver, Paul. *The Spice of Life: Pleasures of the Victorian Age.* London: Hamish Hamilton, 1979.

Colonel Bromhead, 'Reminiscences of the British film Trade'. *Proceedings of the British Kinematograph Society,* no. 21, 1933.

Edwin Corrigan, *Ups and Downs and Roundabouts.* Driffield: Ridings Publishing Company, 1972.

Fay, Arthur. *Bioscope Shows and their Engines.* Lingfield: The Oakwood Press, 1966.

Haggar, Walter. 'My Life'. MSS held at the British film Institute and the National Fairground Archive, University of Sheffield.

Heard, Mervyn. 'Wild Beasts and Living Pictures'. Orchard Theatre Company, 1985.

Horne, Reverend Thomas. 'British Shows and Showmen'. In T. Horne, ed., *Showmen's Year Book,* London: The Era, 1906.

Ling, John. *Memories of a Travelling Life.* Edited by Stephen Smith. Newcastle under Lyme: Fairground Association of Great Britain, 1992.

Lynton, John. 'Old-time Picture Shows'. *The World's Fair,* 27 November 1954.

Marriott, Paul J. *Early Oxford Picture Palaces.* Oxford, 1978.

Peart, Stephen. *The Picture House in East Anglia.* Lavenham: Terrence Dalton, 1980.

Priest Reader. 'Famous Bioscope Shows'. *The World's Fair,* 22 December 1934.

Rendell, J. 'Fairground Pioneers'. *Western Daily Press* 26 July 1973.

Scott, Leo. 'Old Time Cinema Shows'. *The World's Fair,* 14 March 1936.

Southdown [Arthur Sellman]. 'The Evolution of the Cinema'. *The World's Fair,* June 1954.

Williams, Ned. *Fairs and Circuses of the Black Country.* Wolverhampton: Uralia Press, 1991.

Woods, Lesley. *Miracle of the Movies.* London: Burke Publishing Company, 1948.

A Select Bibliography and Guide to Resources

ARTICLES

Barry Anthony. 'Shadows of Early Films'. *Sight and Sound* (summer 1990).
Barker, W.G., R. W. Paul and Cecil Hepworth. 'Before 1910: Kinematograph Experiences'. *Proceedings of the BKS*, no. 38 (1936).
Bottomore, Stephen. 'Joseph Rosenthal: The Most Glorious Profession'. *Sight and Sound*, (autumn 1983).
———. 'Frederic Villiers—War Correspondent'. *Sight and Sound* (autumn 1980).
———. 'In Time of War'. *Sight and Sound* (September 1993).
———. 'The Coming of the Cinema'. *History Today* (March 1996).
Bowen, Harold G. 'Thomas Alva Edison's Early Motion Picture Experiments'. *SMPTE Journal* (September 1955).
Bromhead, A.C. 'Reminiscences of the Film Trade'. *Proceedings of the BKS*, no. 21 (1933).
Brown, Richard. 'England's First Cinema'. *The British Journal of Photography* (24 June 1977).
———. 'England's First Film Shows'. *The British Journal of Photography* (31 March 1978 and 7 April 1978).
Brownlow, Kevin. 'Silent Films—What was the right speed?'. *Sight and Sound* (summer 1980).
Carrol, Kevin. 'The Cinematograph in the London Music Hall'. *Cinema Studies* (June 1964).
Coe, Brian. 'Wordsworth Donisthorpe'. *Cinema Studies* (August 1961).
———. 'William Friese-Greene and the Origins of Kinematography'. *The Photographic Journal* (March/April 1962).
Dickson, W. K. L. 'A Brief History of the Kinetograph, the Kinetoscope and the Kineto-Phonograph'. *SMPE Journal* (December 1933).
Gunning, Tom. 'The Cinema of Attraction: Early Film, Its Spectator and the Avant-Garde'. *Wide Angle*, vol. 8, nos. 3 & 4 (1986).
Lumière, Louis. 'The Lumière Cinématographe'. *SMPE Journal* (December 1936).
Paul, Robert W. 'Kinematographic Experiences'. *SMPE Journal* (November 1936).
Salt, Barry. 'Film Form 1900–1906'. *Sight and Sound* (summer 1978).
Strebel, Elizabeth Grottle. 'Primitive Propaganda: The Boer War Films'. *Sight and Sound* (winter 1976/77).

BOOKS

How To Run A Picture Theatre. London: *The Kinematograph Weekly*, c. 1911.
Abel, Richard. *The Ciné Goes to Town: French Cinema 1896–1914*. Berkeley and Los Angeles: University of California Press, 1994
Adair, Gibert. *Flickers: An Illustrated Celebration of 100 Years of Cinema*. London: Faber & Faber, 1995.
Allister, Ray. *Friese-Greene, Close-up of an Inventor*. London: Marsland, 1951.
Atwell, David. *Cathedrals of the Movies*. London: The Architectural Press, 1980.
Barnes, John. *The Beginnings of the Cinema in England*. London: David & Charles, 1976.
———. *The Rise of the Cinema in Great Britain*. London: Bishopsgate Press, 1983.
———. *Pioneers of the British Film*. London: Bishopsgate Press, 1983.
———. *Filming the Boer War*. London: Bishopsgate Press, 1992.
———. *Dr Paris's Thaumatrope or Wonder-Turner*. London: The Projection Box, 1995.
Barnouw, Erik. *Documentary, A History of the Non-fiction Film*. Oxford: Oxford University Press, 1974.
———. *The Magician and the Cinema*. Oxford: Oxford University Press, 1981.

Bennett, Colin. *The Handbook of Kinematography*. London: *The Kinematograph Weekly*, 1913.

———. *The Guide to Kinematography*. London: E. T. Heron, 1917.

Berry, David. *Wales and Cinema: The First Hundred Years*. Cardiff: University of Wales Press, 1994.

Bitzer, Gottfried Wilhelm. *Billy Bitzer: His Story*. New York: Farrar, Straus & Giroux, 1973.

Bottomore, Stephen. *I want to see this Annie Mattygraph: a Cartoon History of the Coming of the Movies*. Pordenone: Giorante del Cinema Muto, 1995.

Bowser, Eileen. *The Transformation of Cinema, 1907–1915*. New York: Charles Scribner's Sons, 1990.

Braun, Marta. *Picturing Time. The Work of Etienne Jules Marey, 1830–1904*. Chicago and London: University of Chicago Press, 1992.

Brown, Richard and Barry Anthony. *The History of the British Mutoscope and Biograph Company*. Trowbridge: Flicks Books, 1996.

Brownlow, Kevin. *The Parade's Gone By*. London: Paladin, 1968.

———. *Hollywood: The Pioneers*. London: Collins, 1979.

———. *The War, the West and the Wilderness*. London: Secker & Warburg, 1978.

Buckle, G. R., ed. *The Letters of Queen Victoria*. 3rd Series. 3 vols. London: John Murray, 1932.

Buñuel, Luis. *My Last Breath*. London: Jonathan Cape, 1984.

Burch, Noel. *Life to those Shadows*. London: BFI Publishing, 1990.

Ceram, C. W. *Archaeology of the Cinema*. London: Thames & Hudson, 1965.

Chanan, Michael. *The Dream that Kicks*. London: Routledge & Kegan Paul, 1980.

Christie, Ian. *The Last Machine*. London: BFI Publishing, 1995.

Coe, Brian. *The History of Movie Photography*. London: Ash & Grant, 1981.

———. *Muybridge and the Chronophotographers*. London: BFI Publishing, 1992.

Cook, Olive. *Movement in Two Dimensions*. London: Hutchinson, 1963.

Cosandey, Roland, André Gaudreault and Tom Gunning, eds. *An Invention of the Devil? Religion and Early Cinema*. Montreal and Lausanne, 1992.

Crafton, Donald and Emile Cohl. *Caricature and Film*. Princeton: Princeton University Press, 1990.

Dickson, W. K. L. *The Biograph in Battle*. Trowbridge: Flicks Books, 1995.

Edgar, George, ed. *Careers For Men, Women and Children*. X vols. London: Caxton Publishing Co., 1911.

Elsaesser, Thomas. ed. *Early Cinema: Space, Frame Narrative*. London: BFI Publishing, 1990.

Eyles, Allen and Keith Skone. *London's West End Cinemas*. London: Keytone Publications, 1991.

Fell, John L. *Film Before Griffith*. Berkeley and Los Angeles: University of California Press, 1983.

Field, Audrey. *Picture Palace, A Social History of the Cinema*. London: Gentry Books, 1974.

Fielding, Raymond, ed. *A Technological History of Motion Pictures and Television*. Berkeley and Los Angeles: University of California Press, 1967.

Gifford, Denis. *The British Film Catalogue 1895–1985*. London: David & Charles, 1986.

Grafton, Donald. *Before Mickey - The Animated Film, 1892–1928*. Cambridge: MIT Press, 1982.

Gunning, Tom. *D. W. Griffith and the Origins of American Narrative Film*. Champaign: University of Illinois Press, 1990.

Harding, Colin, Stephen Herbert and Simon Popple. *Victorian Film Catalogues*. London: The Projection Box, 1996.

Hecht, Hermann. *Pre-Cinema History: An Encyclopaedia and Annotated Bibliography of the Moving Image Before 1896*. London: Bowker-Saur, 1993.

Hendricks, Gordon. *The Edison Motion Picture Myth*. Berkeley and Los Angeles: University of California Press, 1961.

———. *Eadweard Muybridge. The Father of the Motion Picture*. London: Secker & Warburg, 1975.

Hepworth, Cecil. *Animated Photography: The ABC of the Cinematograph*. London: Hazell, Watson & Viney, 1897.

———. *Came the Dawn: Memoirs of a Film Pioneer*. London: Phoenix House, 1951.

Herbert, Stephen. *When The Movies Began. A Chronology of the World's Film Productions and Film Shows before May, 1896*. London: The Projection Box, 1994.

Herbert, Stephen and Luke McKernan. *Who's Who of Victorian Cinema*. London: BFI Publishing, 1996.

Hofman, Charles. *Sounds for Silents*. New York: Drama Book Specialists, 1970.

Holman, Roger, ed. *Cinema 1900–1906*. FIAF, 1982.

Hopwood, Henry. *Living Pictures*. London: Hazell, Watson & Viney, Ltd., 1899.

Hunnings, Neville March. *Film Censors and the Law*. London: Allen & Unwin, 1967.

Hutinet, Jacques Rittaud. *Le Cinéma des Origines: Les Frères Lumière et Leurs Opérateurs.* Editions du Champ Valon, 1985.

Institut Lumière. *Lumière: Le Cinéma.* Catalogue to an exhibition at the Institut Lumière, Lyon, 1992.

Jones, Bernard E., ed. *The Cinematograph Book: A Complete Practical Guide to the Taking and Projecting of Cinematograph Pictures.* London: Cassell & Co. Ltd., 1915.

Josephson, Matthew. *Edison.* London: Eyre & Spottiswoode, 1961.

Koszarski, Richard. *An Evening's Entertainment: The Age of the Silent Feature Picture, 1915–1928.* Berkeley and Los Angeles: University of California Press, 1994.

Leyda, Jay and Charles Musser, eds. *Before Hollywood.* Hamilton Hill: American Federation of the Arts, 1987.

Liesegang, Franz Paul. *Dates and Sources: A Contribution to the History of the Art of Projection and the Cinematograph.* Edited by Hermann Hecht. London: Magic Lantern Society, 1986.

Low, Rachael. *The History of the British Film: 1906–1914.* London: Allen & Unwin, 1949.

——— and Roger Manvell. *The History of the British Film: 1896–1906.* London: Allen & Unwin, 1948.

Mathews, Tom Dewe. *Censored.* London: Chatto & Windus, 1994.

McKernan, Luke. *Topical Budget: The Great British News Film.* London: BFI Publishing, 1992.

Mellor, Geoff. *Movie Makers and Picture Palaces: A Century of Cinema in West Yorkshire.* Bradford: Bradford Libraries, 1996.

———. *Picture Pioneers, The Story of the Northern Cinema 1896–1971.* Newcastle upon Tyne: Frank Graham, 1971.

Mesguich, Felix. *Tours de Manivelle: Souvenirs d'un Chasseur d'Images.* Bernard Grasset, 1933.

Modern Bioscope Operator, The. London: Ganes Ltd., 1911.

Musser, Charles. *Before the Nickelodeon: Edwin S Porter and the Edison Manufacturing Company.* Berkeley and Los Angeles: University of California Press, 1991.

Musser, Charles. *The Emergence of Cinema: the American Screen to 1907.* New York: Charles Scribner's Sons, 1990.

———. *Thomas Edison Papers: A Guide to Motion Picture Catalogues by American Producers and Distributors, 1894–1980.* Bethesda: University Publications of America, 1985.

Muybridge, Eadweard. *Animal and Human Locomotion.* 3 vols. Reprint (3 vols. in 1), New York: Dover Publications, 1979.

Pearson, George. *Flashback: The Autobiography of a British Film Maker.* London: Allen & Unwin, 1957.

Phillips, Ray. *Edison's Kinetoscope and its Films: A History to 1896.* Trowbridge: Flicks Books, 1995.

Ponting, Herbert. *The Great White South: or With Scott in the Antarctic.* London: Duckworth, 1950.

Pritchard, Michael. *Sir Hubert Von Herkomer: Film Pioneer and Artist.* Bushey: ALLM Books, 1987.

Ramsaye, Terry. *A Million and One Nights.* New York: Simon & Schuster, 1926.

Rawlence, Christopher. *The Missing Reel.* London: Collins, 1990.

Renoir, Jean. *My Life and My Films.* London: Collins, 1974.

Rittaud-Hutinet, Jaques, ed. *Auguste and Louis Lumière Letters.* London: Faber & Faber, 1995.

Robertson, James C. *The British Board of Film Censors: Film Censorship in Britain, 1896–1950.* London: Croom Helm, 1985.

Robinson, David. *George Melies: Father of Film Fantasy.* London: BFI Publishing, 1993.

———. *The Lantern Image. Iconography of the Magic Lantern 1420–1880.* London: Magic Lantern Society, 1993.

Salt, Barry. *Film Style and Technology: History and Analysis.* London: Starword, 1983.

Sharp, Denis. *The Picture Palace.* London: H. Evelyn, 1969.

Smith, Albert. *Two Reels and a Crank.* New York: Doubleday Press, 1952.

Steer, Valentia. *The Romance of the Cinema.* London: Arthur Pearson, 1913.

Talbot, Frederick A. *Moving Pictures: How They are Made and Worked.* London: Heinemann, 1912.

———. *Practical Cinematography.* London: Heinemann, 1913.

Taylor, Richard and Ian Christie, eds. *The Film Factory: Russian and Soviet Cinema in Documents 1896–1939.* London: Routledge & Kegan Paul, 1988.

Thomas, D. B. *The Origins of the Motion Picture.* London: HMSO, 1964.

———. *The First Colour Motion Pictures.* London: HMSO, 1969.

Thompson, Kristen. *Exporting Entertainment: America in the World Film Market, 1907–1934.* London: BFI Publishing, 1985.

Toulet, Emanuelle. *Cinema is 100 Hundred Years Old.* London: Thames & Hudson, 1995.

Tsivian, Yuri. *Early Cinema in Russia and its Cultural Reception*. London: Routledge, 1994.

———. *Silent Witnesses: Russian Films, 1908–1919*. London: BFI Publishing, 1990.

Tyacke, George W. *Playing to Pictures*. London: E. T. Heron, 1914.

Usai, Paolo Cherchi. *Burning Passions : An Introduction to the Study of Silent Cinema*. London: BFI Publishing, 1994.

Vardac, Nicholas. *From Stage to Screen*. Cambridge: Harvard University Press, 1949.

Villiers, Frederic. *Villiers: His Five Decades of Adventure*. London: Hutchinson, 1921.

Wendon, D. J. *The Birth of the Movies*. London: Macdonald, 1975.

Williams, Christopher, ed. *Cinema: The Beginnings and the Future*. London: University of Westminster Press, 1996.

FURTHER READING

Briggs, Asa. *Victorian Things.* London: Batsford, 1900.

Beckett, Jane and Deborah Cherry, eds. *The Edwardian Era*. Oxford: Phaidon, 1987.

Dimond, Frances and Roger Taylor. *Crown and Camera. The Royal Family and Photography, 1842-1910*. London: Viking, 1987.

Glasstone, Victor. *Victorian and Edwardian Theatres*. London: Thames & Hudson, 1975.

Johnson, Peter. *Front Line Artists*. London: Cassell, 1978.

Knightley, Phillip. *The First Casualty: The War Correspondent as Hero, Propagandist and Myth-Maker*. London: André Deutsch, 1975.

Lee, Emanoel. *To the Bitter End: A Photographic History of the Boer War 1899-1902*. London: Viking, 1985.

Mander, Raymond and Joe Mirchenson. *British Music Hall*. London: Gentry Books, 1974.

———. *Victorian and Edwardian Entertainment from Old Photographs*. London: Batsford, 1978.

Marcus, Steven. *The Other Victorians*. London: Weidenfeld & Nicolson, 1966.

Pakenham, Thomas. *The Boer War*. London. Weidenfeld & Nicolson, 1979.

Pearsall, Ronald. *Tell Me, Pretty Maiden: The Victorian and Edwardian Nude*. Exeter; Webb & Bower, 1981.

Priestley, J. B. *The Edwardians*. London: Heinemann, 1970.

Thompson, Paul. *The Edwardians*. London: Weidenfeld & Nicolson, 1975.

Villiers, Frederic. *Villiers—His Five Decades of Adventure*. London, 1921.

Wilkinson-Latham, Robert. *From Our Special Correspondent: Victorian War Correspondents and their Campaigns*. London: Hodder & Stoughton, 1979.

PERIODICALS

The periodicals listed below were published during all or part of the period represented by this book and will contain material of interest to anyone researching early cinema.

The Athenaeum
The Bioscope
Black and White
The British Journal of Photography
Chambers's Journal
Daily Telegraph
The Era
The Graphic
The Harmsworth Magazine
The Illustrated London News
Kinematograph Weekly
The London Magazine

The Optical Magic Lantern Journal
The Pathé Movie Gazette
Pearson's
The Photographic News
Photography
Punch
Review of Reviews
Royalty
The Showman
The Sketch
The Sphere

St Paul's Magazine
The Stage
The Strand
The Talking Machine News
The Tatler
The Times
Titbits
The Windsor Magazine
The World's Fair
The World's Work

ARCHIVAL SOURCES AND COLLECTIONS

MUSEUMS

The Museum of the Moving Image
South Bank
Waterloo
London
SE1 8XT

The National Museum of Photography,
    Film & Television
Pictureville
Bradford
West Yorkshire
BD1 1NQ

The Science Museum
Exhibition Road
South Kensington
London
SW7 2DD

ARCHIVES

The Bill Douglas Centre for the History of
    Cinema and Popular Culture
The Old Library Building
The University of Exeter
Prince of Wales Road
Exeter
EX4 4QJ   *(Due to open late 1996)*

East Anglian Film Archive
Centre of East Anglian Studies
University of East Anglia
Norwich
NR4 7TJ

Imperial War Museum Film Archive
Lambeth Road
London
SE1 6HZ

London Film Archive
C/o 78 Mildmay Park
Newington Green
London
N1 4PR

National Fairground Archive
The Main Library
University of Sheffield
Western Bank
Sheffield
S10 2TN

National Film and Television Archive
The British Film Institute
21 Stephen Street
London
W1P 2LN

North West Film Archive
The Manchester Metropolitan University
Minshull House
47–49 Chorlton Street
Manchester
M1 3EU

Northern Film and Television Archive
36 Bottle Bank
Gateshead
Tyne and Wear
NE8 2AR

Scottish Film Archive
Dowanhill
74 Victoria Crescent Road
Glasgow
G12 9JN

Wales Film and Television Archive
Unit 1, Aberystwyth Science Park
Cefn Llan
Aberystwyth
Dyfed
SY23 3AH

Wessex Film and Sound Archive
Hampshire Record Office
Sussex Street
Winchester
SO23 8TH

Yorkshire Film Archive
Ripon College
College Road
Ripon
HG4 2QX

ORGANISATIONS AND SOCIETIES

Cinema Theatre Association
44 Harrowdene Gardens
Teddington
Middlesex
TW11 0DJ

An organisation dedicated to the preservation and recording of cinemas and cinema architecture.

Domitor
English Membership
C/o Stephen Bottomore
27 Roderick Road
London
NW3 2NN

The international organisation of early cinema historians.

The Magic Lantern Society
The Secretary
South Park
Galphay Road
Kirkby Malzeard
Ripon
HG4 3RX

A society dedicated to the history of the magic lantern and pre-cinema technologies.

The Projected Picture Trust
Ernest Lindgren House
Kingshill Way
Berkhamstead
HP4 3TP

The trust is dedicated to the collection and conservation of cinema equipment.

Index of Films

Index of Names